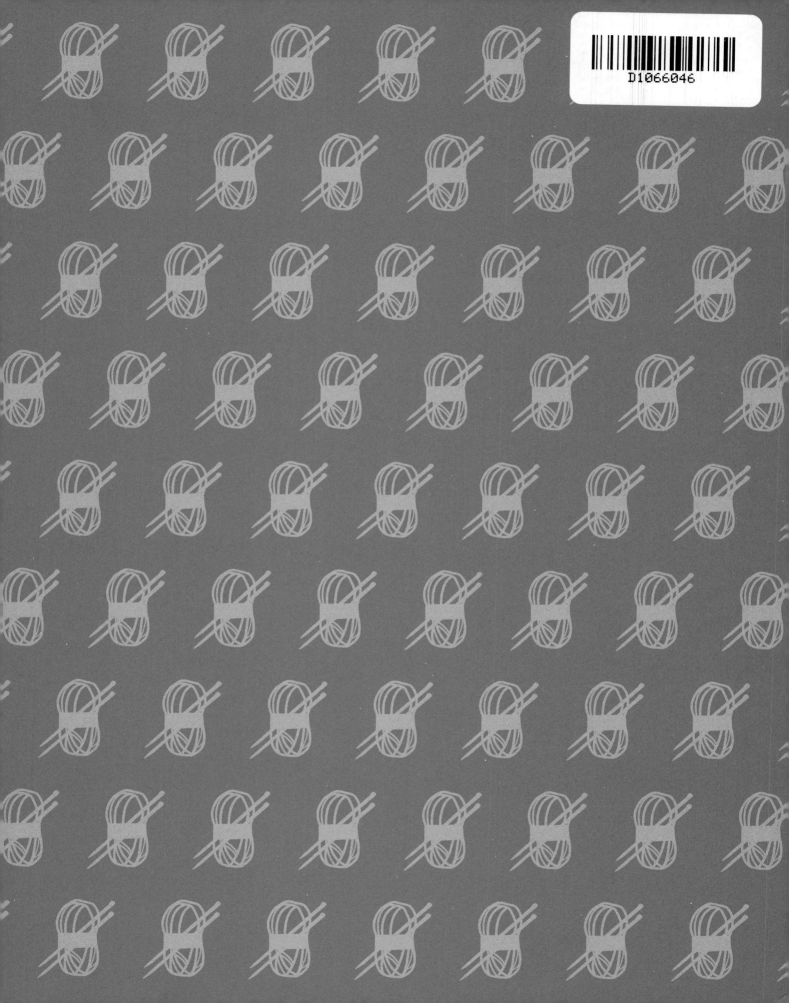

750 Knitting Stitches

750 KNITTING STITCHES

For information, address St. Martin's Press,
175 Fifth Avenue, New York, N.Y. 10010.
www.stmartins.com

Library of Congress Cataloging-in-Publication Data
Available Upon Request

ISBN 978-1-250-06718-0

First U.S. Edition: August 2015

10 9 8 7 6 5

750 Knitting Stitches

The Ultimate Knit Stitch Bible

ST. MARTIN'S GRIFFIN
NEW YORK

contents

Introduction

Whether you're a knitting novice who is picking up a pair of needles for the first time, or a seasoned professional with years of experience, you will find inspiration and technical know-how within these pages. There is always something to learn and to pass on.

This book is divided into five sections. The first one introduces basic combinations of knit and purl. These two stitches can be configured into patterns and constructed into all kinds of fabrics. Texture is the main inspiration for this section.

The second section features cable and Aran stiches. These patterns are traditionally romantic, rugged, and instantly recognizable; they create wonderful surface interest and give scale to any knitted fabric. You can apply these patterns to Aran sweaters, which are characterized by a large central panel bordered by varying numbers of side panels on a textural background. Usually symmetrical, these side panels are knitted in simpler stitch patterns—a useful device for scaling up larger sizes. Even the welts, cuffs, and neckbands can be worked with complex stitches to create highly decorative and unique textiles.

Lace and eyelets are the focus of the third section. These intricate stitches are intriguing and absorbing, and they offer endless possibilities for experimentation. For the beginner knitter, lace knitting may seem daunting because it requires a little more technique—wrapping the yarn over the needle a few times, dropping a stitch or two, or (intentionally) slipping unknitted stitches over a knitted one, for example. However, the sense of accomplishment when creating a simple eyelet will encourage you to attempt and experiment with the more challenging effects.

The fourth section focuses on colorwork, with most of the designs drawing inspiration from traditional Scottish and Scandinavian patterns knitted using the Fair Isle technqiue. Fair Isle knitting uses design repeats and motifs in horizontal and vertical bands, and in small and large panels. Typically, these patterns feature diagonal lines, which means that the color-change positions are offset, creating an elastic fabric. No more than two colors are used in any row, with one color being "stranded" across the back of the other. There is also a symmetry to the patterns that means they can be easily memorized. Intarsia knitting is a similar technique, although the yarn is usually not stranded across the back of the work and patterns often involve larger blocks of color and picture motifs.

The final section concentrates on edgings and trims. From simple yet decorative ribbing to intricate lace borders, there is an almost endless variety of edgings. They offer a quick way to turn a plain knit garment into something supremely stylish. Often you will be able to simply add the edging to an existing pattern, but if you need to make some calculations to make a new trim fit an old pattern, you will find advice on page 23. It is usually possible to combine an existing pattern with a fresh edging. As most edgings are worked over just a few stitches, it is easy to knit up a few inches to see how a pattern might suit your project.

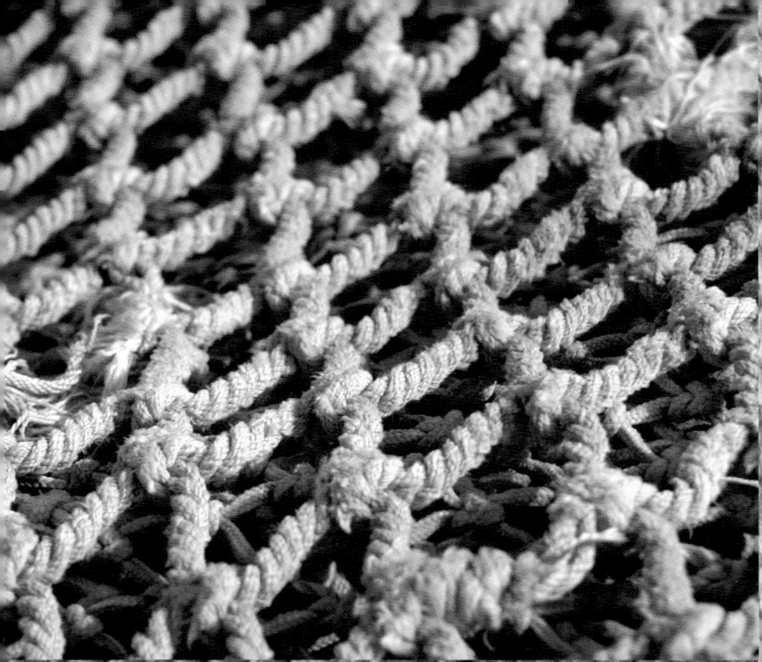
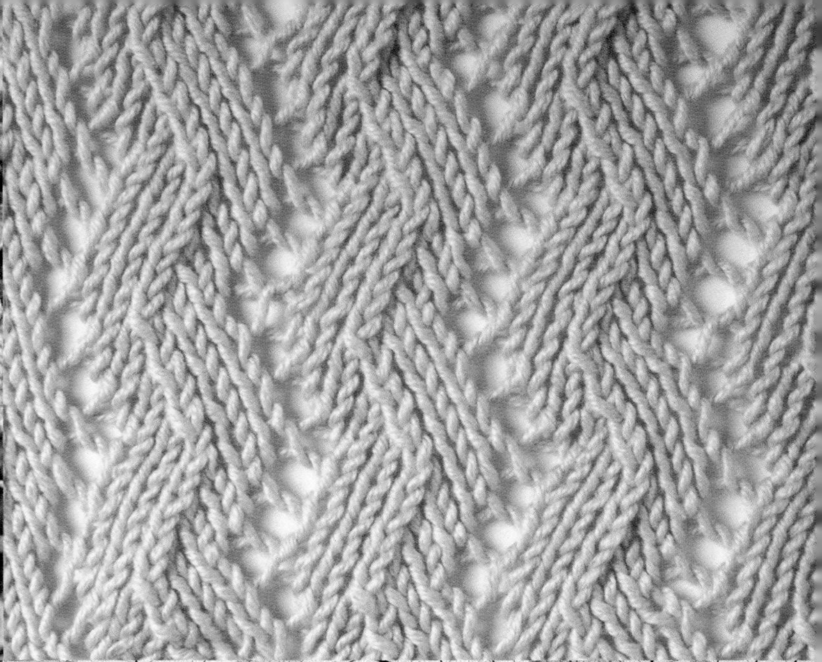
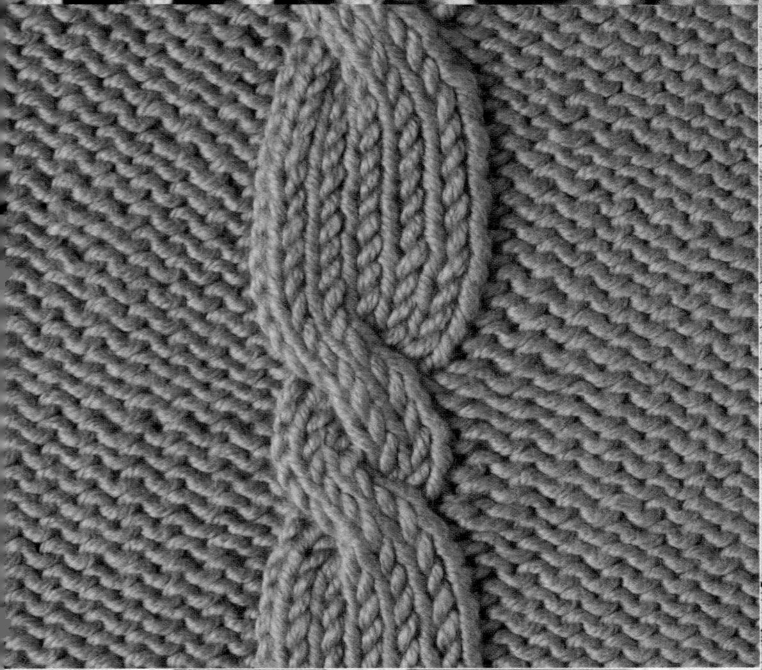
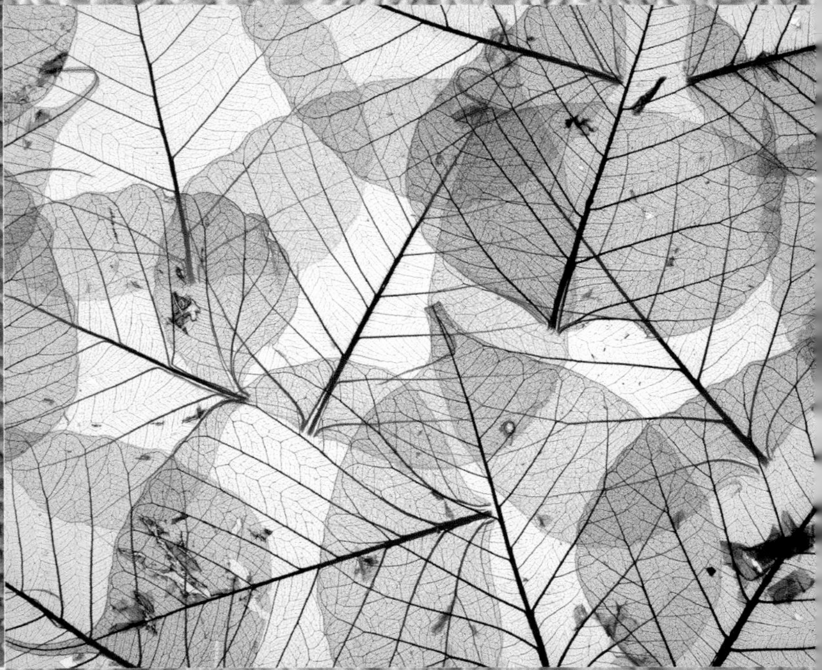
 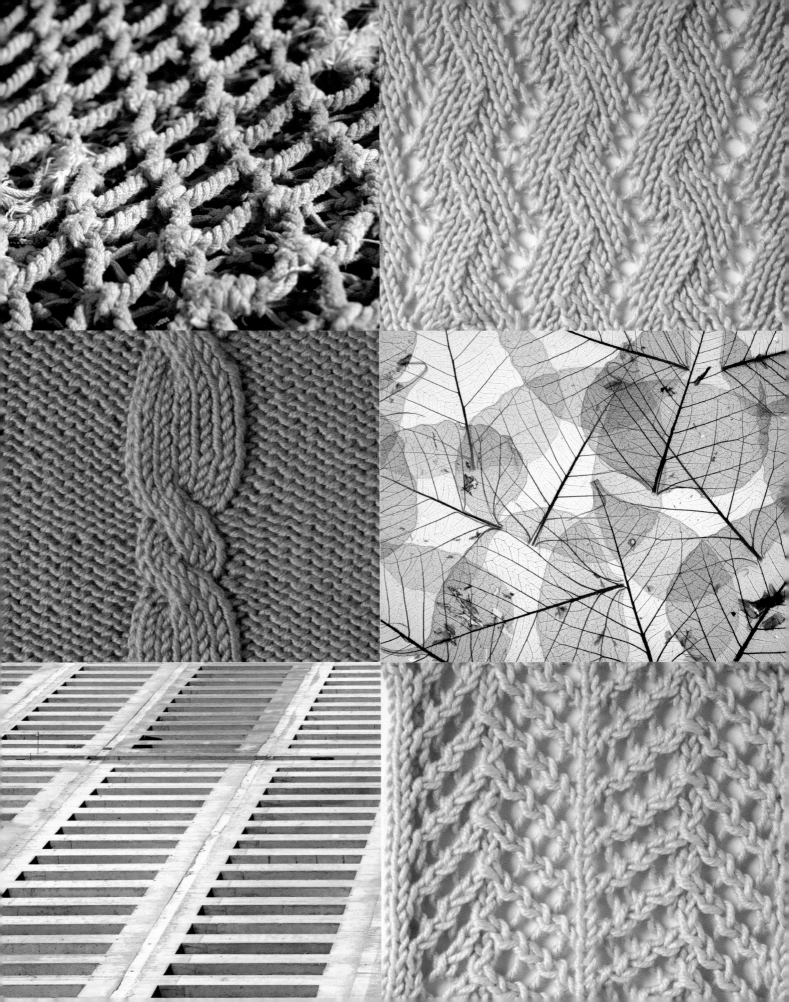
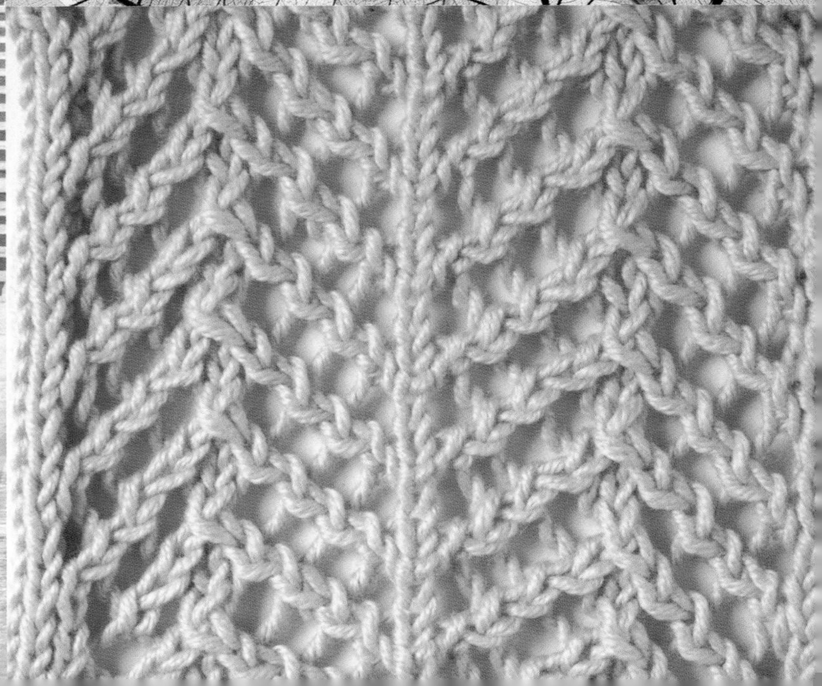

Tools and equipment

To master any skill, it is imperative to have a solid foundation in the techniques. This section provides useful information for knitting.

Knitting needles

Knitting needles are used in pairs to produce a flat knitted fabric. They are pointed at one end to form the stitches, and have a knob at the other to retain the stitches. They may be made from plastic, wood, steel, or alloy, and they come in a wide range of standardized sizes or thicknesses. Needles are also made in different lengths that will comfortably hold the number of stitches required for each project. It is useful to have a range of needle sizes so that gauge swatches can be knitted up and compared. Discard any needles that become bent. Points should be fairly sharp, as blunt needles reduce the speed and ease of working.

Circular and double-pointed needles are used to produce a tubular fabric or flat rounds. Many traditional fishermen's sweaters are knitted in the round. Double-pointed needles are sold in sets of four or five. Circular needles consist of two needle points joined by a flexible length of plastic. The plastic varies in length. You can use the shorter lengths for knitting sleeves and neckbands, and the longer lengths for larger pieces such as the bodies of sweaters.

Cable needles are short double-pointed needles, sometimes with a kink in them, that are used to hold the stitches of a cable to the back or front of the main body of knitting.

Other useful equipment

Needle gauges are punched with holes corresponding to the needle sizes. They are usually marked with both US and metric sizing, so you can easily check the size of any needle.

Stitch holders resemble large safety pins and are used to hold stitches while they are not being worked—for example, around a neckline when the neckband stitches will be picked up and worked after the back and front have been joined. As an alternative, thread a blunt-pointed sewing needle with a generous length of contrast-colored yarn, thread it through the stitches to be held while they are still on the needle, then slip the stitches off the needle and knot both ends of the contrast yarn to secure them.

Yarn sewing needles or tapestry needles are used to sew completed pieces of knitting together. They are large, with a broad eye for easy threading and a blunt point that will slip between the knitted stitches without splitting and fraying the yarn. Do not use sharp-pointed sewing needles to sew up knitting.

A row counter is a cylinder with a numbered dial that is used to count the number of rows that have been knitted. Push it onto the needle and turn the dial at the end of each row.

A tape measure is essential for checking gauge swatches and for measuring the length and width of completed knitting. For an accurate result, always smooth the knitting (without stretching) on a firm, flat surface before measuring it.

A crochet hook is useful for picking up dropped stitches.

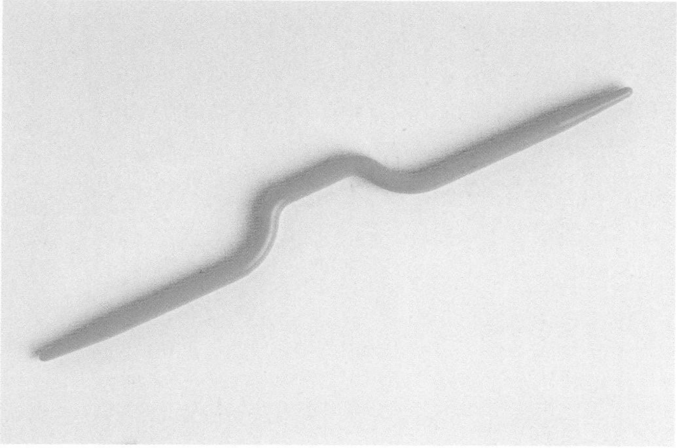

Cable needle

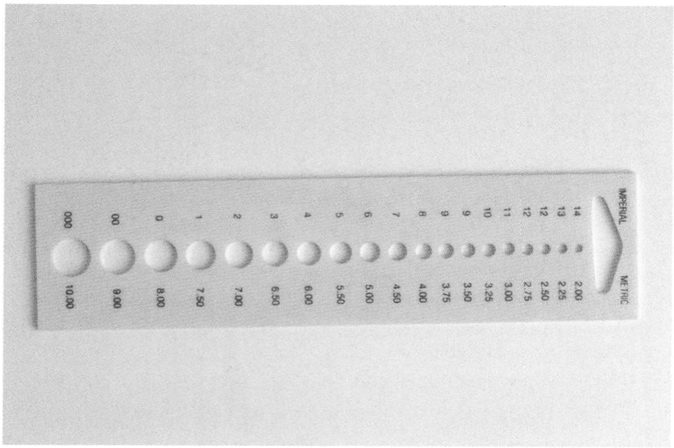

Needle gauge

Knitting yarn

Yarn is the term used for strands of spun fiber that are twisted together into a continuous length of the required thickness. Yarn can be of animal origin (wool, angora, mohair, silk, alpaca), of vegetable origin (cotton, linen), or man-made (nylon, acrylic, rayon). Knitting yarn may be made up from a combination of different fibers.

Each single strand of yarn is known as a ply. A number of plies are twisted together to form the yarn. The texture and characteristics of the yarn may be varied by the combination of fibers and by the way in which the yarn is spun. Wool and other natural fibers are often combined with man-made fibers to make a yarn that is more economical and hard-wearing. Wool can also be treated to make it machine-washable. The twist of the yarn is firm and smooth, and it knits up into a hard-wearing fabric. Loosely twisted yarn has a softer finish when knitted.

Buying yarn

Yarn is most commonly sold wound into balls of specific weight, measured in ounces or grams. Some yarn, particularly very thick yarn, is sold in a coiled hank or skein that must be wound into a ball before you can begin knitting.

Yarn manufacturers wrap each ball with a paper band on which is printed information, such as the weight of the yarn and its composition. It will give instructions for washing and ironing, and will state the ideal range of needle sizes to be used with the yarn. The ball band also carries the shade number and dye lot number. It is important that you use yarn of the same dye lot for an entire project. Different dye lots vary subtly in shading. This may not be apparent when you are holding the two balls, but it will show as a variation in shade on the finished piece of knitting.

Always keep the ball band as a reference. The best way is to pin it to the gauge swatch and keep them together with any leftover yarn and spare buttons or other trims. That way, you can always check the washing instructions and also have materials for repairs.

Starting off

Once you have mastered the basics of knitting, you can go on to develop your skills and start making more challenging projects.

Casting on

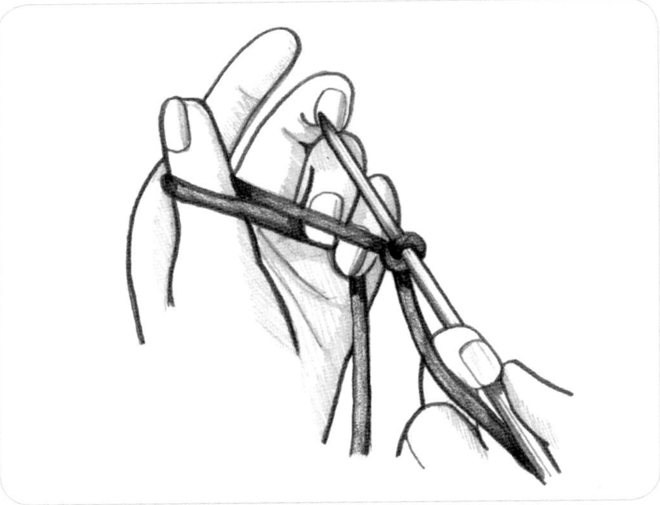

1 Make a slip knot 39 in. (1 m) from the end of the yarn. Hold the needle in your right hand, with the ball end of the yarn over your index finger. Wind the loose end of the yarn around your left thumb from front to back.

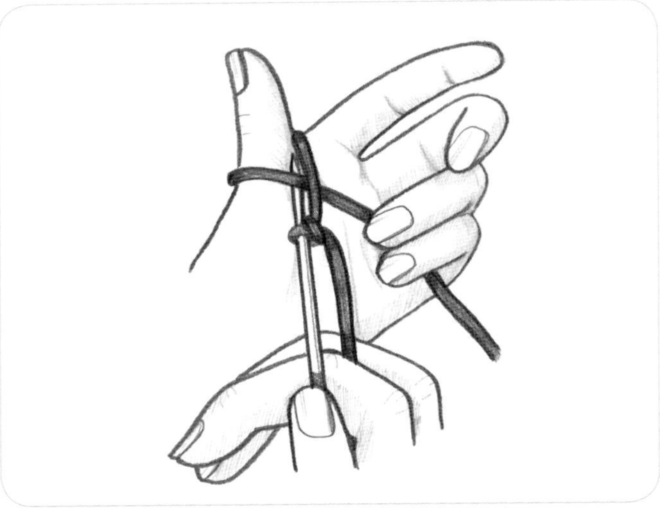

2 Insert the point of the needle under the first strand of yarn on your thumb.

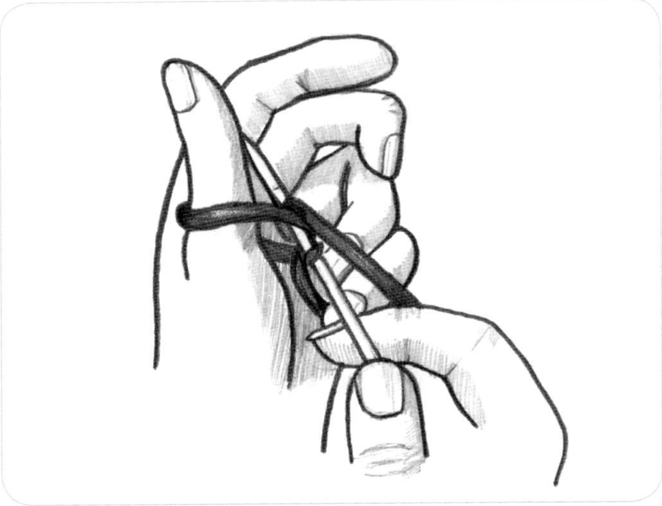

3 With your right index finger, take the ball end of the yarn over the point of the needle.

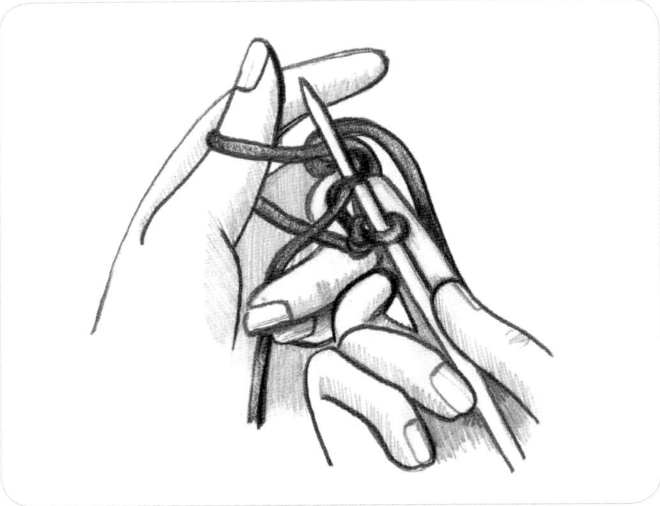

4 Pull a loop through to form the first stitch. Remove your left thumb from the yarn. Pull the loose end to secure the stitch. Repeat until all stitches have been cast on.

Knit stitch

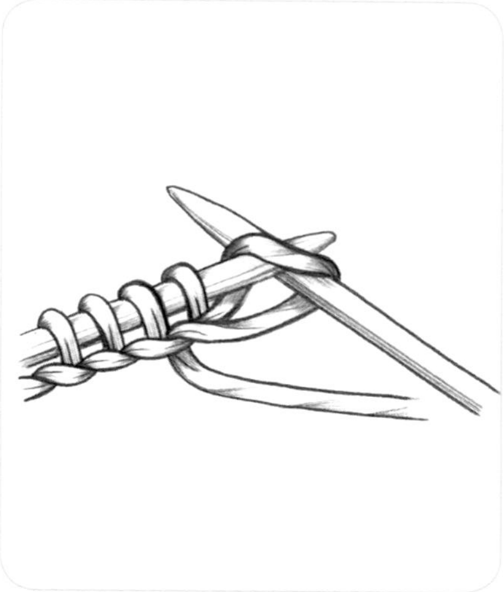

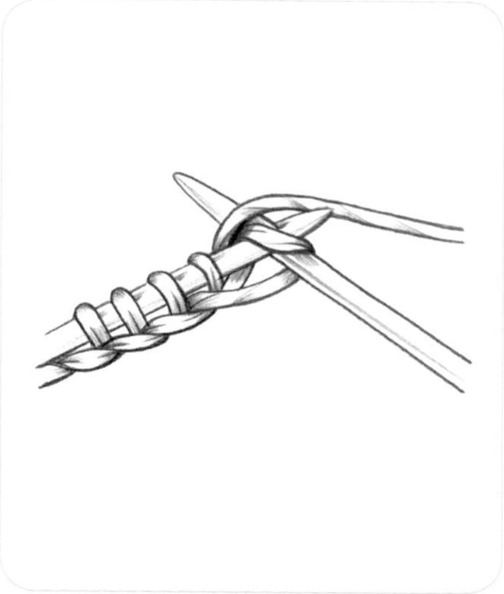

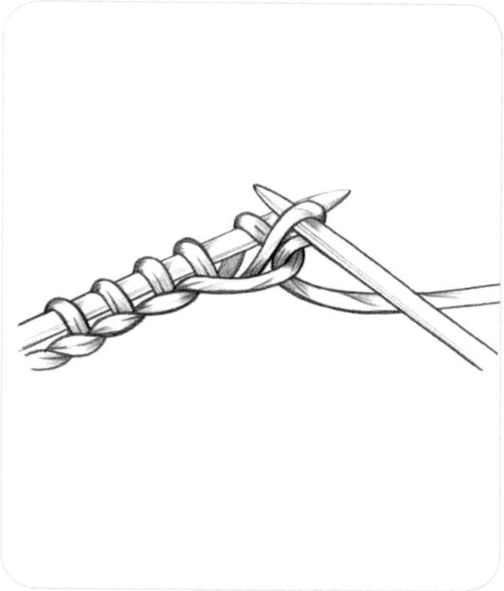

1 Hold the needle with the cast-on stitches in your left hand, with the loose yarn at the back of the work. Insert the right-hand needle from left to right through the front of the first stitch on the left-hand needle.

2 Wind the yarn from left to right over the point of the right-hand needle.

3 Draw the yarn through the stitch, thus forming a new stitch on the right-hand needle.

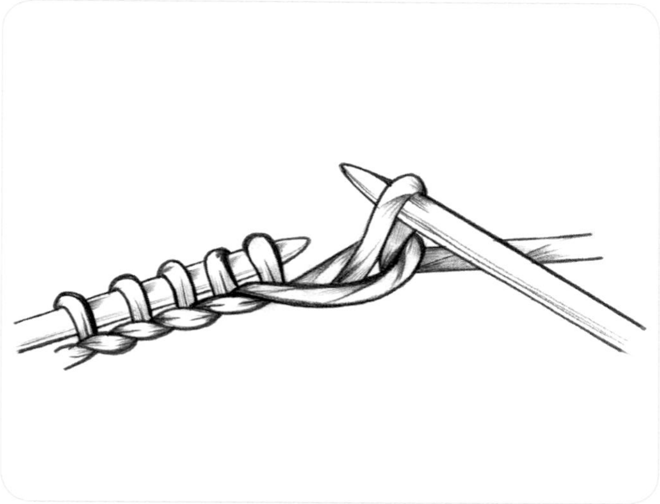

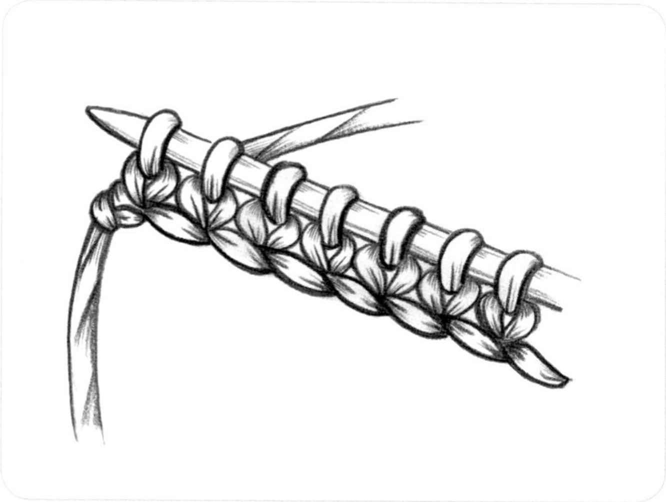

4 Slip the original stitch off the left-hand needle, keeping the new stitch on the right-hand needle.

5 To knit a row, repeat steps 1 to 4 until all the stitches have been transferred from the left-hand needle to the right-hand needle. Turn the work, transferring the needle that holds the stitches to your left hand to work the next row.

Purl stitch

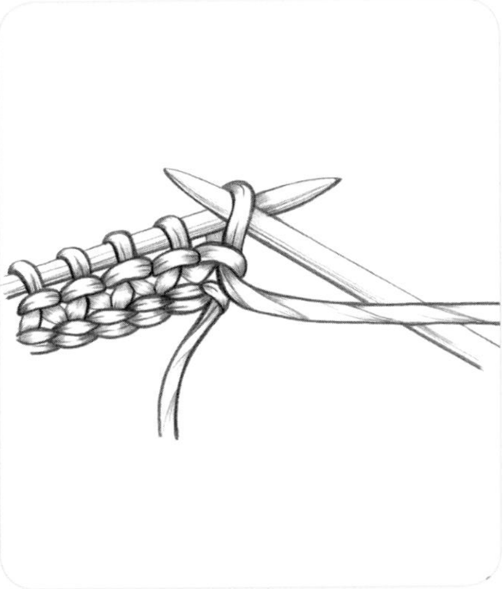

1 Hold the needle with the stitches in your left hand, with the loose yarn at the front of the work. Insert the right-hand needle from right to left into the front of the first stitch on the left-hand needle.

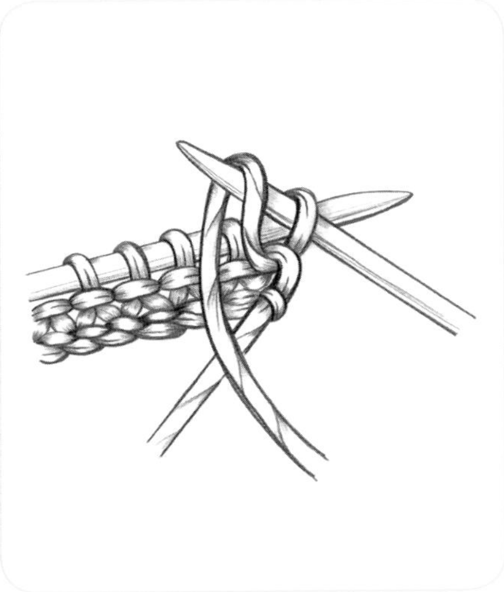

2 Wind the yarn from right to left over the point of the right-hand needle.

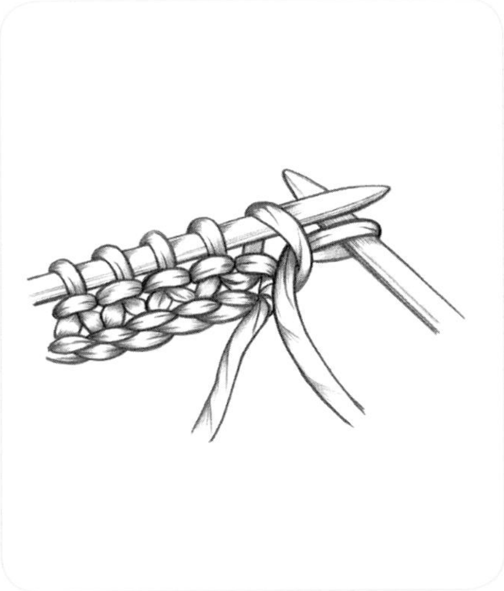

3 Draw the yarn through the stitch, thus forming a new stitch on the right-hand needle.

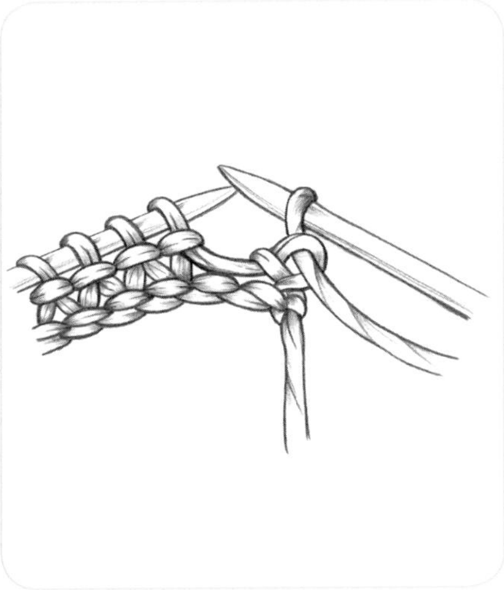

4 Slip the original stitch off the left-hand needle, keeping the new stitch on the right-hand needle.

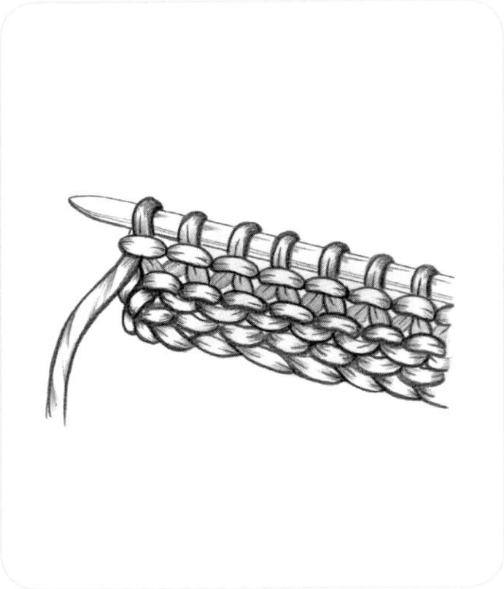

5 To purl a row, repeat steps 1 to 4 until all the stitches have been transferred from the left-hand needle to the right-hand needle. Turn the work, transferring the needle that holds the stitches into your left hand to work the next row.

Binding off

There is one simple, most commonly used method of securing stitches once you have finished a piece of knitting—binding off. The bound-off edge should always have the same "give" or elasticity as the fabric, and you should always bind off in the stitch pattern used for the main fabric unless the pattern directs otherwise.

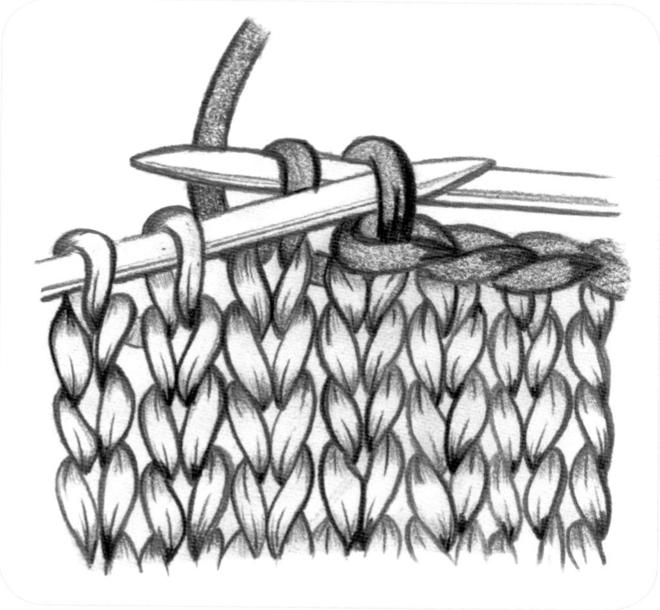

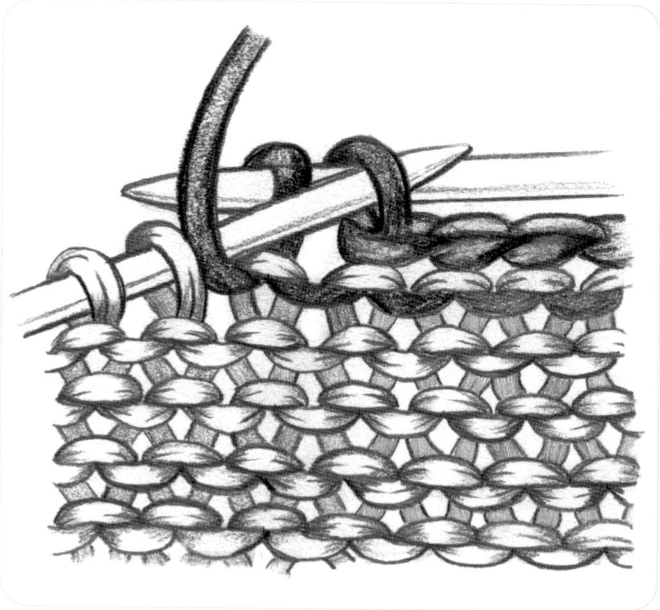

Knitwise

Knit two stitches. *Using the point of the left-hand needle, lift the first stitch on the right-hand needle over the second, then drop it off the needle. Knit the next stitch and repeat from * until all stitches have been worked off the left-hand needle and only one stitch remains on the right-hand needle. Cut the yarn (leaving enough to weave in the end), thread the end through the stitch, and then slip it off the needle. Draw the yarn up firmly to fasten off.

Purlwise

Purl two stitches. *Using the point of the left-hand needle, lift the first stitch on the right-hand needle over the second and drop it off the needle. Purl the next stitch and repeat from * until all the stitches have been worked off the left-hand needle and only one stitch remains on the right-hand needle. Secure the last stitch as described for binding off knitwise.

Increasing

The simplest method of increasing one stitch is to work into the front and back of the same stitch.

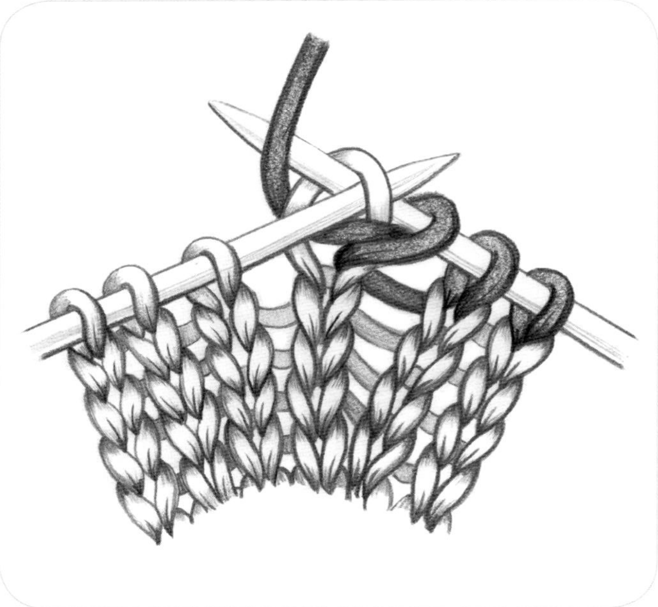

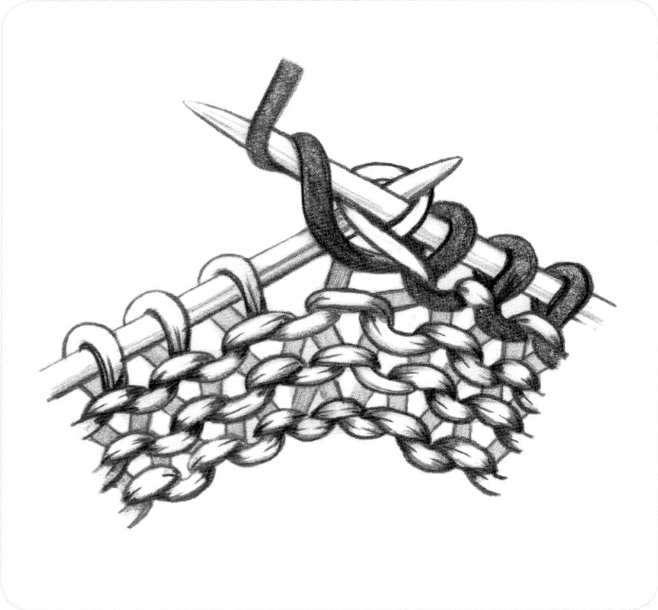

On a knit row

Knit into the front of the stitch to be increased into; then, before slipping it off the needle, place the right-hand needle behind the left-hand needle and knit again into the back of the same stitch. Slip the original stitch off the left-hand needle.

On a purl row

Purl into the front of the stitch to be increased into; then, before slipping it off the needle, purl again into the back of the same stitch. Slip the original stitch off the left-hand needle.

Tip

In this book, you will most often find that increases and decreases are used to create the lace and eyelet patterns. With lace stitches, it is commonplace for sets of increases and decreases to be paired together. This creates the open, "holey" nature of the pattern while keeping the overall stitch count consistent.

Decreasing

The simplest method of decreasing one stitch is to work two stitches together.

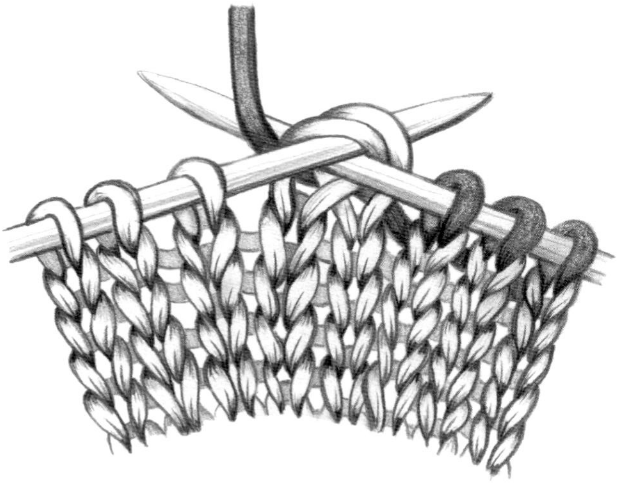

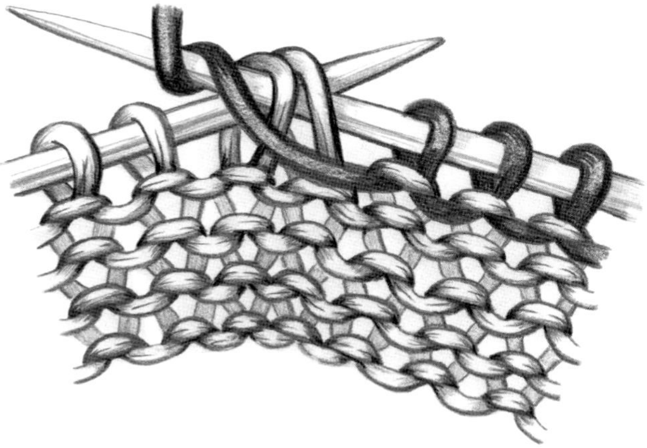

On a knit row

Insert the right-hand needle from left to right through two stitches instead of one, then knit them together as one stitch. This is called knit two together (k2tog).

On a purl row

Insert the right-hand needle from right to left through two stitches instead of one, then purl them together as one stitch. This is called purl two together (p2tog).

Joining in a new color on a knit row

When working Fair Isle, it is better to join in a new color at the beginning of a row, but in some cases, you may have to join a new yarn in the middle of a row. This is how you join in a new color mid-row on a knit row.

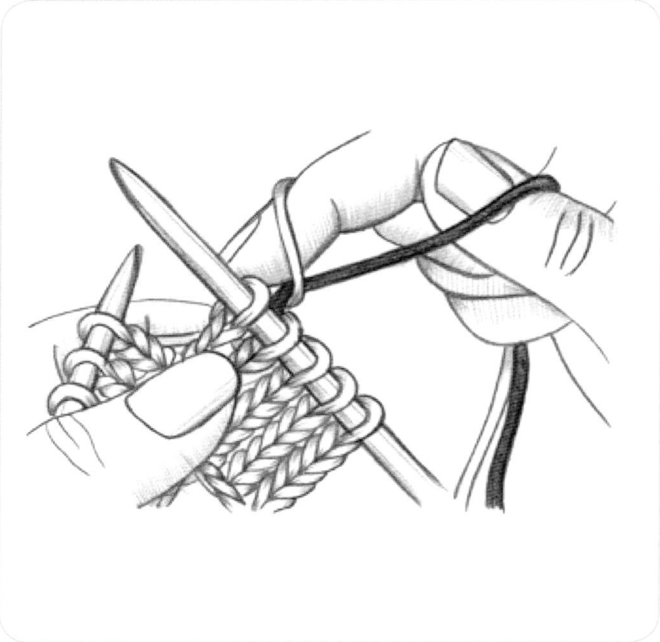

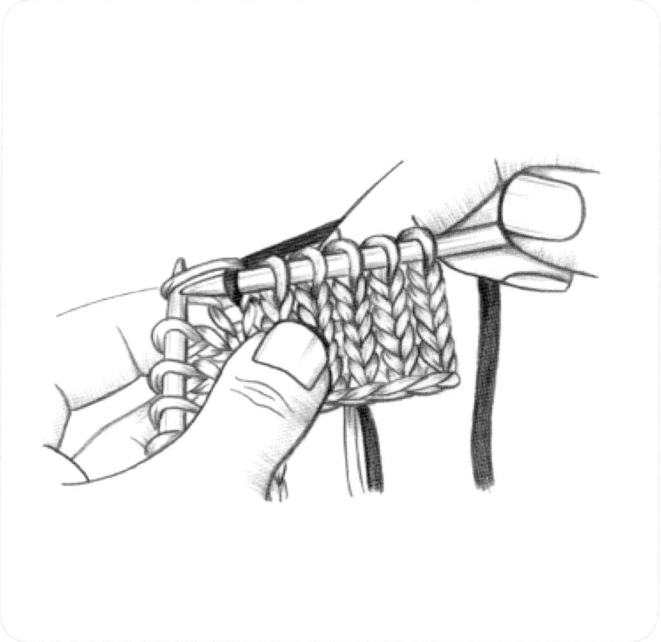

1 Lay the new color (B) over the original color (A). Twist the yarns over themselves and hold them in place.

2 Knit with the new color (B). You can always go back and tighten the join after a couple of stitches.

The Plowed furrows design (see page 193) requires you to join yarn in the middle of a row.

Joining in a new color on a purl row

This is how you join in a new color mid-row on a purl row.

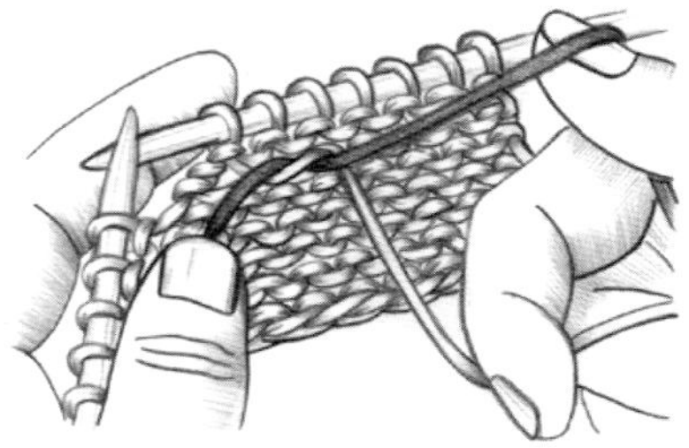

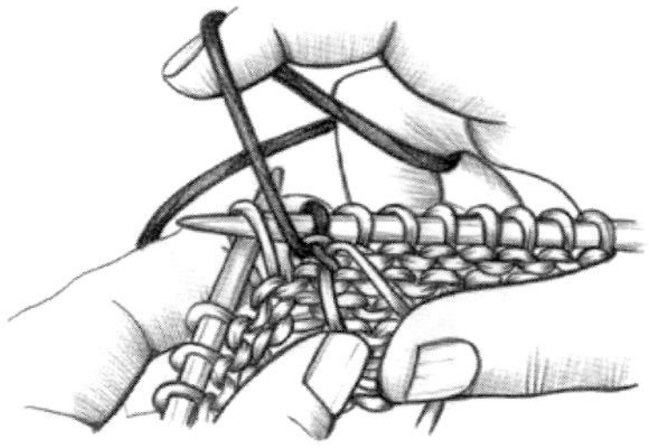

1 Lay the new color (B) over the original color (A). Twist the yarns over themselves and hold them in place.

2 Purl with the new color (B).

Joining in a new color in the middle of a row

When working in intarsia you will find yourself needing to join in a new color in the middle of a row.

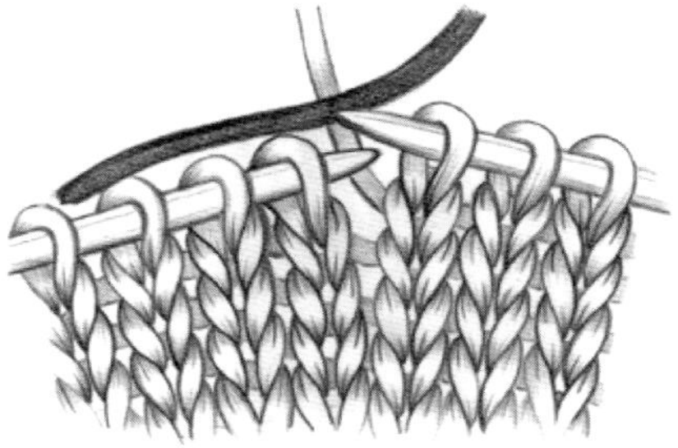

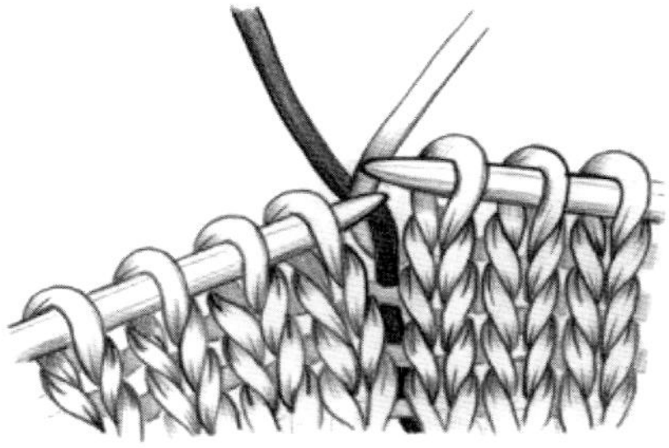

1 On a knit row, knit to the change in color. Lay the new color over the existing color and between the two needles, with the tail to the left.

2 Bring the new color under and then over the existing color.

3 Knit the stitch with the new color. Go back and pull gently on the tail to tighten up the first stitch in the new color after you have knitted a couple more stitches.

Changing colors in a straight vertical line

Once you have joined in a new color, you may need to work for a number of rows, changing these colors on both the knit rows and purl rows. This is often confusingly referred to as "twisting" the yarns, but it is a link rather than a twist. It is a common mistake to overtwist the yarns at this point, with the result that the fabric will not lie flat.

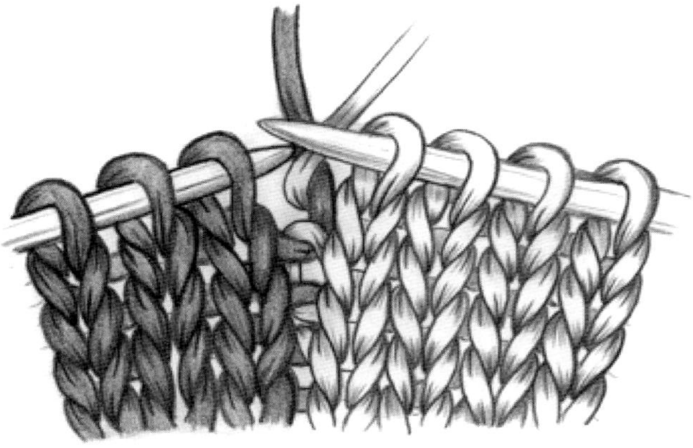

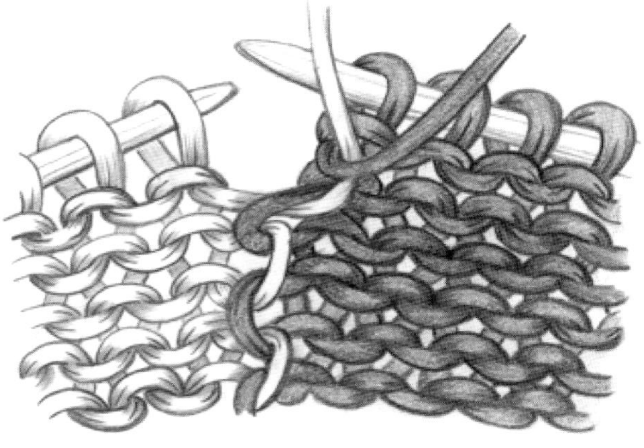

1 On a knit row, knit to the change in color. Bring the new color up from under the old color and drop the old color so that the new color is ready to work with.

2 On a purl row, purl to the change in color. Bring the new color from the left under the old color and up to the top. Drop the old color and continue with the new color.

Tip

When working blocks of color in an intarsia pattern, you may find it easiest to wind a small skein of yarn, called a bobbin, for each color section, rather than working off a full ball of yarn. This makes the process less fiddly, and you are less likely to get your various yarns tangled.

Eliminating ends

If you are working a complex design, it is always best to look for ways of eliminating ends so that you can cut down the amount of time that will be needed to weave them all in. Look for shapes that perhaps have an outline, as with a diamond motif.

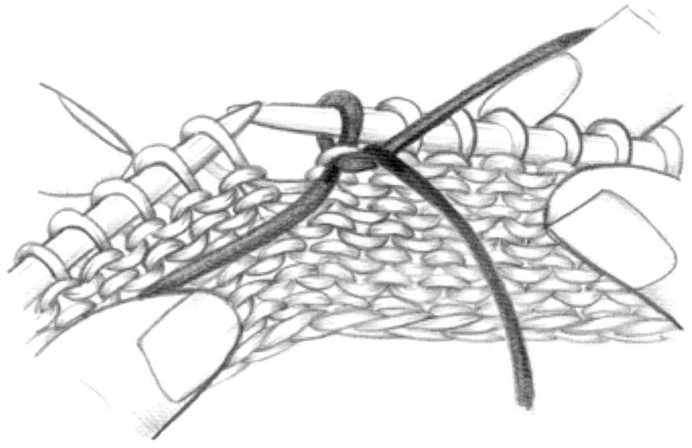

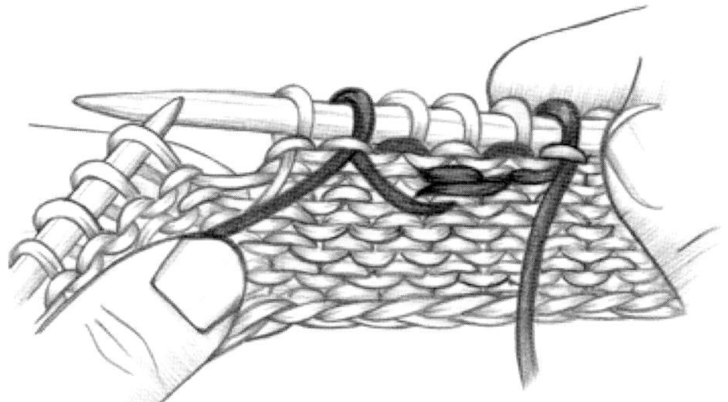

1 Take a length of the yarn required to work the whole motif and fold it in half. On the center stitch of the motif, loop the fold over the right-hand needle.

2 On the next row, take one end of the yarn to the right and the other to the left, linking the outline and background colors on each row. If the motif is very small and the background color remains the same, it is best to carry the background color across the back of the motif, weaving it in if necessary.

How to read charts

Charts are featured in many of the instructions for the cable and Aran stitches (pages 80–131) and for the colorwork designs (pages 182–233).

Charts are read exactly as the knitting is worked—from the bottom to the top. After the last row at the top has been worked, repeat the sequence from row 1 if required.

Each symbol represents an instruction. Symbols have been designed to resemble the actual appearance of the knitting. This is more difficult to do with multicolor slip-stitch patterns, which have to be knitted before the mosaic effects become obvious.

Before starting to knit, look up all the symbols on your chosen chart (see page 24 for a key to the stitch diagrams) so that you are familiar with the techniques involved. These may be shown with the pattern as a special abbreviation. The most common abbreviations that are not shown as special abbreviations are listed on page 26. Make sure that you understand the difference between working similar symbols on a right-side and on a wrong-side row.

Each square represents a stitch and each horizontal line represents a row. Place a ruler above the line you are working and work the symbols one by one. If you are new to reading charts, try comparing the charted instructions with the written ones.

For knitters who wish to follow the written directions, it is still a good idea to look at the chart (where one is available) before starting, to see what the repeat looks like and how the pattern has been balanced.

Right-side and wrong-side rows

"Right-side rows" are where the right side of the fabric is facing you when you work; "wrong-side rows" are where the wrong side is facing you when you work. Row numbers are shown at the side of the charts at the beginning of the row. Right-side rows are always read from right to left. Wrong-side rows are always read from left to right.

Symbols on charts are shown as they appear from the right side of the work. Therefore, a horizontal dash stands for a purl "bump" on the right side, regardless of whether it was achieved by purling on a right-side row or by knitting on a wrong-side row. To make things clearer, symbols on right-side rows are slightly darker than those on wrong-side rows.

Pattern repeats and multiples

The "multiple" or repeat of the pattern is given with each set of instructions—for example, "multiple of 7 + 4." This means you can cast on any number of stitches that is a multiple of 7, plus 4 balancing stitches—for instance, 14 + 4, 21 + 4, 28 + 4, and so on.

In written instructions, the 7 stitches are shown in parentheses or follow an asterisk *. These stitches are repeated across the row the required number of times. In charted instructions, the pattern repeat is contained between heavier vertical lines. The extra stitches not included in the pattern repeat are there to "balance" the row or make it symmetrical, and are only worked once.

Some patterns require a foundation row that is worked once before commencing the pattern, but does not form part of the repeat. On charts, this row is marked by a letter "F" and is separated from the pattern repeat by a heavier horizontal line.

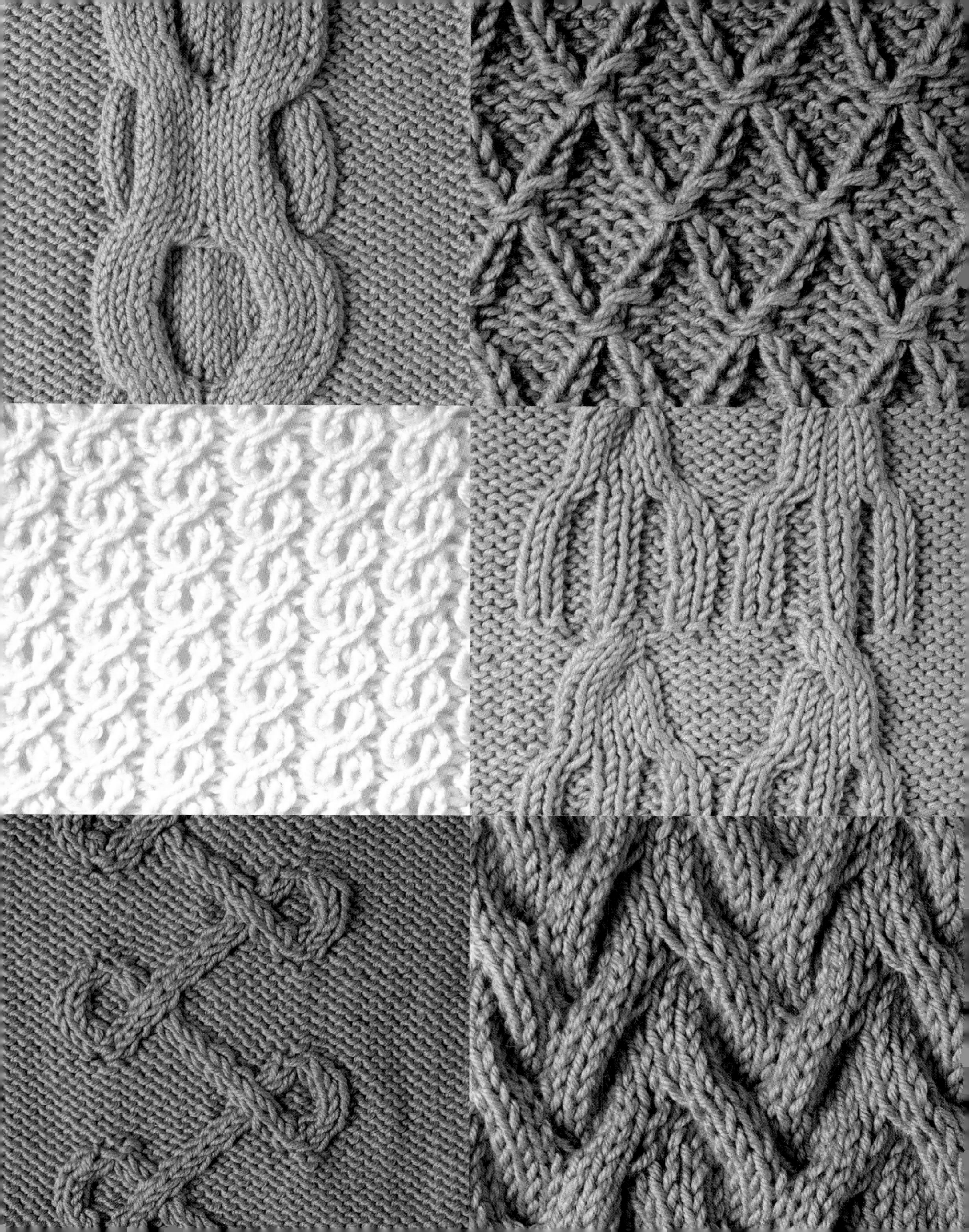

Advice on knitting lace

Lace knitting can be used in many different ways—as an allover pattern, as a horizontal or vertical panel, or as single or random motifs. Lace stitch patterns are most effective when worked in plain yarns, because fluffy or textured yarns do not show the detail of the pattern. Finer yarns are also more suitable than bulky yarns, because they give the stitch a more delicate appearance. Lace knitting is especially popular for baby garments, such as heirloom shawls and christening blankets.

Lace patterns are produced by using the eyelet method of increasing. These increases are usually worked in conjunction with decreases, so that the number of stitches remains constant at the end of each row. However, some of the most beautiful lace effects are achieved by increasing stitches on one or more rows and decreasing the extra stitches on subsequent rows. Circular shawls are produced by continually increasing stitches on every round (or every alternate round), while working the increases into the lace pattern.

The yarnover method of increasing is used in lace patterns to form an eyelet hole. The exact way that the yarn is taken over the needle depends on the stitches at either side of the eyelet—whether they are knitted, purled, or a combination of both. The yarnovers are then accompanied by one of the decrease methods, depending on whether the slant is to be toward the left or the right.

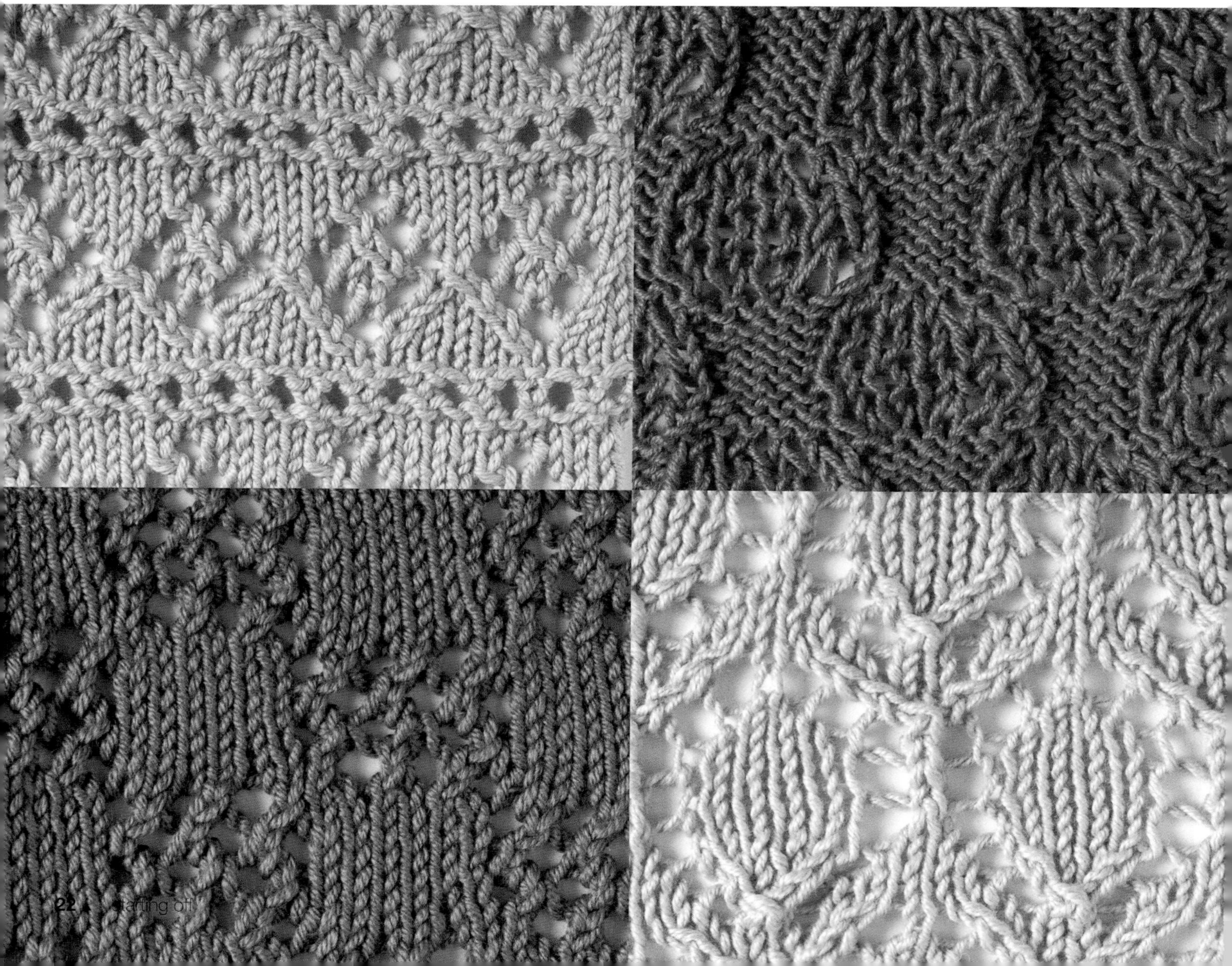

Advice on knitting edgings

If an edging is worked lengthwise, then the instruction at the start of the pattern will say, for example, "Worked lengthwise over 10 sts." This means that you cast on 10 stitches to work the first row. Once you have worked all the pattern rows, you simply repeat them until the edging is the required length.

The instructions may tell you to finish the final repeat on a particular row. This is usually so that if the ends of the knitted edging are joined to form a circle, the pattern will run as evenly as possible across the join. If a particular row is not given, end the last repeat with the last pattern row.

Depending on the pattern, the number of stitches on the needle may vary on some rows. When the number changes, a stitch count is given in brackets at the end of the row. This count includes all loops on the needle, whether they are full stitches or yarnovers. If no stitch count is given, then the number of stitches has not changed since the last count. So, a lengthwise pattern with no stitch counts at all has the same number of stitches on every row as originally cast on.

Some patterns need a foundation row that does not form part of the repeat. These are marked as such in the patterns.

Edgings that are worked from the top down or bottom up have different instructions. The "multiple" or repeat of the pattern is given at the start—for example, "Starts with multiple of 7 + 4." This means you can cast on any number of stitches that is a multiple of 7, plus 4 balancing stitches—for instance, 14 + 4, 21 + 4, 28 + 4, and so on. These patterns do not have stitch counts at the ends of the rows, so you will need to follow the increases and decreases carefully to keep the pattern correct.

The number of times the pattern rows need to be repeated to make the edging shown in the swatch will be specified, though on many of the patterns you could work the repeat more often to create a deeper edging if required.

If you are going to work a bottom-up edging and then continue knitting the project, you need to make sure that the number of stitches the edging finishes with—for example, "Ends with multiple of 6 + 2"—can be multiplied to make the correct number of stitches for the first row of the project. So, in this example, the first row of the project needs to be any multiple of 6 stitches, plus 2 balancing stitches.

For a top-down edging worked on the lower edge of a project, check the multiple that the edging starts with. Edging patterns will not work without the correct multiple, so you will usually need to adjust the number of project stitches.

However, if the number of project stitches is just one or two more than is needed for the edging, then you can add one or two selvage stitches to the end of the edging pattern, but remember they are there and do not try to work them into the pattern. Make careful notes of any changes and consider how they might affect other areas of the project. Of course, both bottom-up and top-down edgings can be worked as strips and sewn on afterward if preferred.

Attaching edgings

Lengthwise edgings need to be sewn to the finished project. Usually it is best to use a tapestry needle and matching yarn, and then whip stitch the top edge of the edging to the knitted fabric. To attach an edging to cloth fabric, use a sewing needle and matching sewing thread.

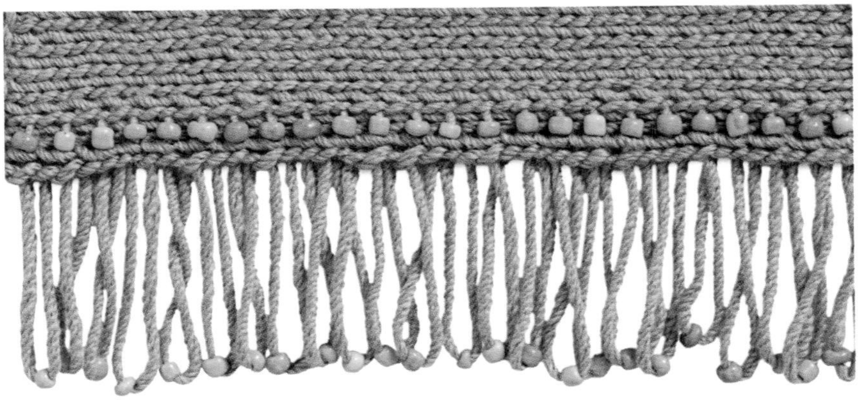

Key to stitch diagrams

C2B (CROSS 2 BACK)
Slip next st onto cable needle and hold at back of work, knit next st from left-hand needle, then knit st from cable needle.

C2BW (CROSS 2 BACK ON WRONG SIDE)
Slip next st onto cable needle and hold at back (right side) of work, purl next st from left-hand needle, then purl st from cable needle.

C2F (CROSS 2 FRONT)
Slip next st onto cable needle and hold at front of work, knit next st from left-hand needle, then knit st from cable needle.

C2FW (CROSS 2 FRONT ON WRONG SIDE)
Slip next st onto cable needle and hold at front (wrong side) of work, purl next st from left-hand needle, then purl st from cable needle.

C3B (CABLE 3 BACK)
Slip next st onto cable needle and hold at back of work, knit next 2 sts from left-hand needle, then knit st from cable needle.

C3F (CABLE 3 FRONT)
Slip next 2 sts onto cable needle and hold at front of work, knit next st from left-hand needle, then knit 2 sts from cable needle.

C3L (CABLE 3 LEFT)
Slip next st onto cable needle and hold at front of work, knit next 2 sts from left-hand needle, then knit st from cable needle.

C3R (CABLE 3 RIGHT)
Slip next 2 sts onto cable needle and hold at back of work, knit next st from left-hand needle, then knit 2 sts from cable needle.

C4B (CABLE 4 BACK)
Slip next 2 sts onto cable needle and hold at back of work, knit next 2 sts from left-hand needle, then knit 2 sts from cable needle.

C4F (CABLE 4 FRONT)
Slip next 2 sts onto cable needle and hold at front of work, knit next 2 sts from left-hand needle, then knit 2 sts from cable needle.

C5B (CABLE 5 BACK)
Slip next 3 sts onto cable needle and hold at back of work, knit next 2 sts from left-hand needle, then knit 3 sts from cable needle.

C5F (CABLE 5 FRONT)
Slip next 2 sts onto cable needle and hold at front of work, knit next 3 sts from left-hand needle, then knit 2 sts from cable needle.

C6B (CABLE 6 BACK)
Slip next 3 sts onto cable needle and hold at back of work, knit next 3 sts from left-hand needle, then knit 3 sts from cable needle.

C6F (CABLE 6 FRONT)
Slip next 3 sts onto cable needle and hold at front of work, knit next 3 sts from left-hand needle, then knit 3 sts from cable needle.

C7B (CABLE 7 BACK)
Slip next 4 sts onto cable needle and hold at back of work, knit next 3 sts from left-hand needle, then knit 4 sts from cable needle.

C8B (CABLE 8 BACK)
Slip next 4 sts onto cable needle and hold at back of work, knit next 4 sts from left-hand needle, then knit 4 sts from cable needle.

C8F (CABLE 8 FRONT)
Slip next 4 sts onto cable needle and hold at front of work, knit next 4 sts from left-hand needle, then knit 4 sts from cable needle.

C10B (CABLE 10 BACK)
Slip next 5 sts onto cable needle and hold at back of work, knit next 5 sts from left-hand needle, then knit 5 sts from cable needle.

C10F (CABLE 10 FRONT)
Slip next 5 sts onto cable needle and hold at front of work, knit next 5 sts from left-hand needle, then knit 5 sts from cable needle.

C12B (CABLE 12 BACK)
Slip next 6 sts onto cable needle and hold at back of work, knit next 6 sts from left-hand needle, then knit 6 sts from cable needle.

T2B (TWIST 2 BACK)
Slip next st onto cable needle and hold at back of work, knit next st from left-hand needle, then purl st from cable needle.

T2F (TWIST 2 FRONT)
Slip next st onto cable needle and hold at front of work, purl next st from left-hand needle, then knit st from cable needle.

T3B (TWIST 3 BACK)
Slip next st onto cable needle and hold at back of work, knit next 2 sts from left-hand needle, then purl st from cable needle.

T3F (TWIST 3 FRONT)
Slip next 2 sts onto cable needle and hold at front of work, purl next st from left-hand needle, then knit 2 sts from cable needle.

T4B (TWIST 4 BACK)
Slip next 2 sts onto cable needle and hold at back of work, knit next 2 sts from left-hand needle, then purl 2 sts from cable needle.

T4BP (TWIST 4 BACK PURL)
Slip next 2 sts onto cable needle and hold at back of work, knit next 2 sts from left-hand needle, then p1, k1 from cable needle.

T4F (TWIST 4 FRONT)
Slip next 2 sts onto cable needle and hold at front of work, purl next 2 sts from left-hand needle, then knit 2 sts from cable needle.

T4FP (TWIST 4 FRONT PURL)
Slip next 2 sts onto cable needle and hold at front of work, k1, p1 from left-hand needle, then knit 2 sts from cable needle.

T5B (TWIST 5 BACK)
Slip next 3 sts onto cable needle and hold at back of work, knit next 2 sts from left-hand needle, then purl 3 sts from cable needle.

T5BP (TWIST 5 BACK PURL)
Slip next 3 sts onto cable needle and hold at back of work, knit next 2 sts from left-hand needle, then p1, k2 from cable needle.

T5L (TWIST 5 LEFT)
Slip next 3 sts onto cable needle and hold at front of work, purl next 2 sts from left-hand needle, then knit 3 sts from cable needle.

T5R (TWIST 5 RIGHT)
Slip next 2 sts onto cable needle and hold at back of work, knit next 3 sts from left-hand needle, then purl 2 sts from cable needle.

T6B (TWIST 6 BACK)
Slip next 3 sts onto cable needle and hold at back of work, knit next 3 sts from left-hand needle, then purl 3 sts from cable needle.

K
Knit on right-side rows.

K
Knit on wrong-side rows.

K2tog
Knit two sts together.

KB1
Knit into back of st on wrong-side rows.

KB1
Knit into back of st on right-side rows.

M3 (Make 3 sts)
(K1, p1, k1) into next st.

P
Purl on right-side rows.

P
Purl on wrong-side rows.

P2tog
Purl two sts together.

PB1
Purl into back of st on wrong-side rows.

Sl 1
Slip one st with yarn at back (wrong side) of work.

Skpo
Slip one st knitwise, knit one st, pass the slipped st over.

Sk2po
Slip one st knitwise, knit two sts together, pass the slipped st over.

Sl 2tog knitwise, k1, p2sso
Slip two sts together knitwise, knit one st, pass the two slipped sts over.

Abbreviations

Knitting patterns are usually written with abbreviated instructions in order to save space. Below is an explanation of all the abbreviations that are used in this book.

[ ]	work instructions within brackets as many times as directed
( )	work instructions within parentheses in the place directed
*	repeat instructions following the single asterisk as directed
* *	repeat instructions within the asterisks as directed
alt	alternate
beg	begin(s)(ning)
C2B	cross 2 back—slip next st onto cable needle and hold at back, knit next st from LH needle, knit st from cable needle
C2BW	cross 2 back on wrong side—slip next st onto cable needle and hold at back (RS), purl next st from LH needle, purl next st from cable needle
C2F	cross 2 front—slip next st onto cable needle and hold at front, knit next st from LH needle, knit st from cable needle
C2FW	cross 2 front on wrong side—slip next st onto cable needle and hold at front (WS), purl next st from LH needle, purl st from cable needle
C2L	cross 2 left—slip next st onto cable needle and hold at front, knit next st from LH needle, knit st from cable needle
C2R	cross 2 right—slip next st onto cable needle and hold at back, knit next st from LH needle, knit st from cable needle
C3B	cable 3 back—slip next st onto cable needle and hold at back, knit next 2 sts from LH needle, knit st from cable needle
C3F	cable 3 front—slip next 2 sts onto cable needle and hold at front, knit next st from LH needle, knit 2 sts from cable needle
C3L	cable/cross 3 left—slip next st onto cable needle and hold at front, knit next 2 sts from LH needle, knit st from cable needle
C3R	cable/cross 3 right—slip next 2 sts onto cable needle and hold at back, knit next st from LH needle, knit 2 sts from cable needle
C4B	cable 4 back—slip next 2 sts onto cable needle and hold at back, knit next 2 sts from LH needle, knit 2 sts from cable needle
C4F	cable 4 front—slip next 2 sts onto cable needle and hold at front, knit next 2 sts from LH needle, knit 2 sts from cable needle
C5B	cable 5 back—slip next 3 sts onto cable needle and hold at back, knit next 2 sts from LH needle, knit 3 sts from cable needle
C5F	cable 5 front—slip next 2 sts onto cable needle and hold at front, knit next 3 sts from LH needle, knit 2 sts from cable needle
C6	cross 6—slip next 4 sts onto cable needle and hold at front, knit next 2 sts from LH needle, slip 2 purl sts from cable needle back onto LH needle. Pass cable needle with 2 rem knit sts to back of work, purl 2 sts from LH needle, knit 2 sts from cable needle
C6B	cable 6 back—slip next 3 sts onto cable needle and hold at back, knit next 3 sts from LH needle, knit 3 sts from cable needle
C6F	cable 6 front—slip next 3 sts onto cable needle and hold at front, knit next 3 sts from LH needle, knit 3 sts from cable needle
C7B	cable 7 back—slip next 4 sts onto cable needle and hold at back, knit next 3 sts from LH needle, knit 4 sts from cable needle
C7F	cable 7 front—slip next 3 sts onto cable needle and hold at front, knit next 4 sts from LH needle, knit 3 sts from cable needle
C8B	cable 8 back—slip next 4 sts onto cable needle and hold at back, knit next 4 sts from LH needle, knit 4 sts from cable needle
C8F	cable 8 front—slip next 4 sts onto cable needle and hold at front, knit next 4 sts from LH needle, knit 4 sts from cable needle
C9	cross 9—slip next 4 sts onto cable needle and hold at front, knit next 5 sts from LH needle, knit 4 sts from cable needle
C10B	cable 10 back—slip next 5 sts onto cable needle and hold at back, knit next 5 sts from LH needle, knit 5 sts from cable needle
C10F	cable 10 front—slip next 5 sts onto cable needle and hold at front, knit next 5 sts from LH needle, knit 5 sts from cable needle
cm	centimeter(s)
cont	continue
foll(s)	follow(s)(ing)

in	inch(es)
inc	increase 1—work into front and back of next st
inc 2	increase 2—work into front, back, and front of next st
k	knit
K1B	knit 1 below—insert point of RH needle into st one row below next st on LH needle and knit it
k2tog	knit 2 sts (or number specified) together
K5W	knit next 5 sts winding yarn twice around needle for each st
KB1	knit into back of next st
LH	left hand
M1	make 1
M1K	make 1 knitwise
M1P	make 1 purlwise
M5K	make 5 knitwise
MB	make bobble—use this method unless specified otherwise: knit into front, back, and front of next st, [turn and knit these 3 sts] 3 times, then turn and sk2po to complete bobble
ML	make loop—use this method unless specified otherwise: k1 but do not slip st off LH needle, bring yarn between needles to front, take it under and over your left thumb, take yarn between needles to back, knit st on LH needle again, then slip second st on RH needle over first st
p	purl
p2tog	purl 2 sts (or number specified) together
PB1	purl into back of next st
psso	pass slipped st over
p2sso	pass 2 slipped sts over
p3sso	pass 3 slipped sts over
rem	remain(ing)
rep	repeat(s)
rev st st	reverse stockinette stitch
RH	right hand
RS	right side
skpo	slip one st knitwise, knit one st, pass slipped st over
sk2po	slip one st knitwise, knit two sts together, pass slipped st over
sl	slip
ssk	slip one st knitwise, slip next st knitwise, insert LH needle through fronts of slipped sts and knit the two sts together
st(s)	stitch(es)
st st	stockinette stitch
T2B	twist 2 back—slip next st onto cable needle and hold at back, knit next st from LH needle, purl st from cable needle
T2F	twist 2 front—slip next st onto cable needle and hold at front, purl next st from LH needle, knit st from cable needle
T3B	twist 3 back—slip next st onto cable needle and hold at back, knit next 2 sts from LH needle, purl st from cable needle
T3F	twist 3 front—slip next 2 sts onto cable needle and hold at front, purl next st from LH needle, knit 2 sts from cable needle
T4B	twist 4 back—slip next 2 sts onto cable needle and hold at back, knit 2 sts, purl 2 sts from cable needle
T4BR	twist 4 back right—slip next st onto cable needle and hold at back, knit next 3 sts from LH needle, purl st from cable needle
T4F	twist 4 front—slip next 2 sts onto cable needle and hold at front, purl next 2 sts from LH needle, knit 2 sts from cable needle
T4FL	twist 4 front left—slip next 3 sts onto cable needle and hold at front, purl next st from LH needle, knit 3 sts from cable needle
T4FP	twist 4 front purl—slip next 2 sts onto cable needle and hold at front, k1, p1 from LH needle, knit 2 sts from cable needle
T5BP	twist 5 back purl—slip next 3 sts onto cable needle and hold at back, knit next 2 sts from LH needle, p1, k2 from cable needle
T5L	twist 5 left—slip next 3 sts onto cable needle and hold at front, purl next 2 sts from LH needle, knit 3 sts from cable needle
T5R	twist 5 right—slip next 2 sts onto cable needle and hold at back, knit next 3 sts from LH needle, purl 2 sts from cable needle
T6B	twist 6 back—slip next 3 sts onto cable needle and hold at back, knit next 3 sts from LH needle, purl 3 sts from cable needle
T6F	twist 6 front—slip next 3 sts onto cable needle and hold at front, knit next 3 sts from LH needle, purl 3 sts from cable needle
tbl	through back of loop
tog	together
WS	wrong side
wyib	with yarn in back
wyif	with yarn in front
yb	yarn to the back
yf	yarn to the front
yo	yarn over needle
yo2	yarn over needle twice
yo3	yarn over needle 3 times

Garter stitch

Knit every row.

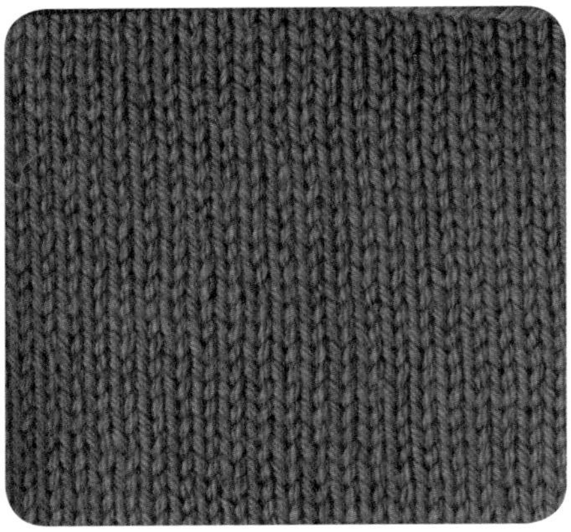

Stockinette stitch

Any number of stitches.

Row 1 (RS): Knit.

Row 2: Purl.

Rep these 2 rows.

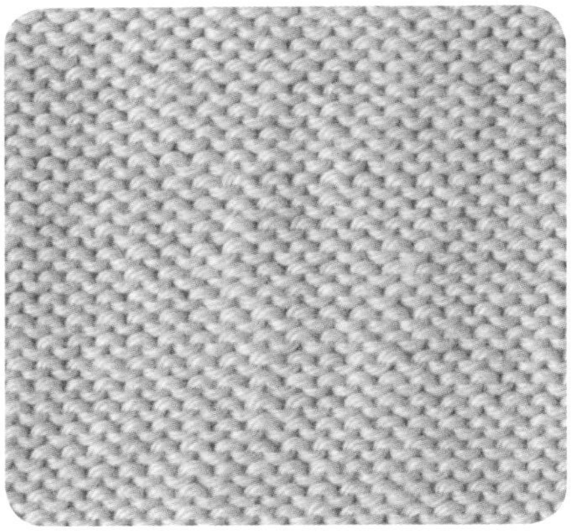

Reverse stockinette stitch

Any number of stitches.

Row 1 (RS): Purl.

Row 2: Knit.

Rep these 2 rows.

Linen stitch

Multiple of 2.

Row 1: *K1, yf, sl 1, yb; rep from * to end.

Row 2: *P1, yb, sl 1, yf; rep from * to end.

Rep these 2 rows.

K1, p1 rib

On an even number of sts:

*K1, p1; rep from * to end.

Rep this row.

On an odd number of sts:

Row 1: K1, *p1, k1; rep from * to end.

Row 2: P1, *k1, p1; rep from * to end.

Rep these 2 rows.

K2, p2 rib

Multiple of 4.

Row 1: *K2, p2; rep from * to end.

Rep this row.

Multiple of 4 + 2.

Row 1: K2, *p2, k2; rep from * to end.

Row 2: P2, *k2, p2; rep from * to end.

Rep these 2 rows.

Cartridge stitch

Any number of stitches.

Rows 1 (RS), 3, 4, and 6: Knit.

Rows 2 and 5: Purl.

Rep these 6 rows.

Alternated smooth stitch and tier

Any number of stitches.

Rows 1 (RS), 3, and 4: Knit.

Row 2: Purl.

Rep these 4 rows.

Texture stitch

Multiple of 2 + 1.

Row 1 (RS): Purl.

Row 2: K1, *yf, sl 1 purlwise, yb, k1; rep from * to end.

Rep these 2 rows.

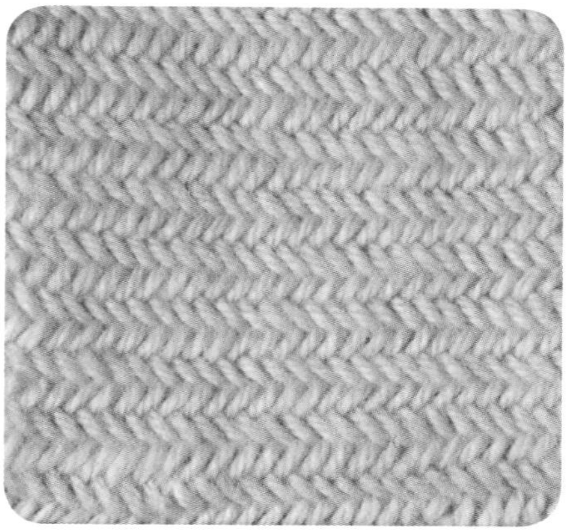

Herringbone I

Multiple of 2.

Row 1: K2tog tbl dropping only first loop off left needle, *k2tog tbl (rem st and next st) again dropping only first loop off needle*, KB1.

Row 2: P2tog dropping only first loop off left needle, *p2tog (rem st and next stitch) again dropping only first loop off needle*, p1.

Rep these 2 rows.

Gathered stitch

Any number of stitches.

Rows 1–6: Knit.

Row 7: Knit into front and back of each st.

Rows 8, 10, and 12: Purl.

Rows 9 and 11: Knit.

Row 13: [K2tog] to end.

Rep from row 2.

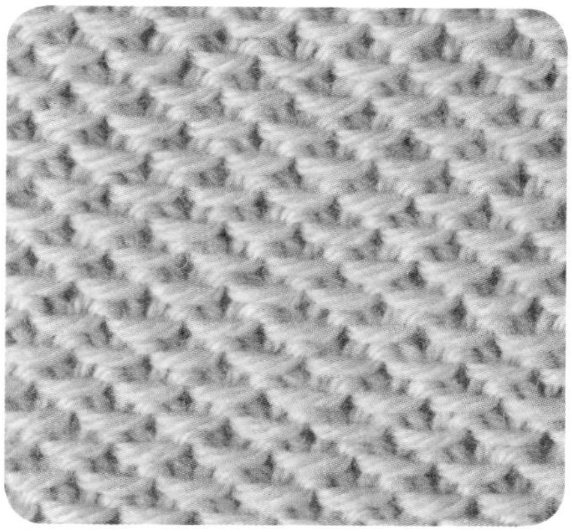

Loop pattern

Multiple of 2 + 2.

Row 1 (RS): Knit.

Row 2: *K1, sl 1; rep from * to last 2 sts, k2.

Row 3: Knit.

Row 4: K2, *sl 1, k1; rep from * to end.

Rep these 4 rows.

Bobble stitch

Multiple of 12 + 11.

Special abbreviation:

MB (make bobble) = [Knit into front and back] twice into next st, then into front again, turn, on these 5 sts work 4 rows in st st starting with purl, then with left-hand needle lift 2nd, 3rd, 4th, and 5th sts over first st.

Row 1 (RS): Knit.

Row 2: Purl.

Row 3: K5, *MB, k11; rep from * to last 6 sts, MB, k5.

Rows 4–14: Work 11 rows in st st, starting with purl.

Row 15: K11, *MB, k11; rep from * to end.

Rows 16–26: Work 11 rows in st st, starting with purl.

Rep rows 3–26.

Fur stitch

Multiple of 2 + 2.

Special abbreviation:

ML (make loop) = K1 leaving st on left-hand needle, yf, wrap yarn around left thumb to make a loop approx. 1½ in. (4 cm) long, yb, knit same st again and slip it off left-hand needle, yo, pass the 2 sts just worked over the yarnover.

Row 1 (WS): Knit.

Row 2: *K1, ML; rep from * to last 2 sts, k2.

Row 3: Knit.

Row 4: K2, *ML, k1; rep from * to end.

Rep these 4 rows.

Whelk pattern

Multiple of 4 + 3.

Row 1 (RS): K3, *sl 1 purlwise, k3; rep from * to end.

Row 2: K3, *yf, sl 1 purlwise, yb, k3; rep from * to end.

Row 3: K1, *sl 1 purlwise, k3; rep from * to last 2 sts, sl 1 purlwise, k1.

Row 4: P1, sl 1 purlwise, *p3, sl 1 purlwise; rep from * to last st, p1.

Rep these 4 rows.

Diagonal ridge I

Multiple of 4 + 2.

Row 1: 1 edge st, *p1, k3; rep from * to last st, 1 edge st.

Row 2: 1 edge st, p2, *k1, p3; rep from * to last 3 sts, k1, p1, 1 edge st.

Row 3: 1 edge st, k2, *p1, k3; rep from * to last 3 sts, p1, k1, 1 edge st.

Row 4: 1 edge st, *k1, p3; rep from * to last st, 1 edge st.

Rep these 4 rows.

This pattern can be used on either side.

Bowknot

Multiple of 10 + 7.

Special abbreviation:

Bowknot = Slip right needle under 3 strands, then knit next st pulling the loop through under the strands.

Rows 1 (WS) and 3: Purl.

Rows 2, 4, 6, and 8: Knit.

Rows 5, 7, and 9: P6, *yb, sl 5, yf, p5; rep from* to last st, p1.

Row 10: K8, *bowknot, k8; rep from * to end.

Rows 11 and 13: Purl.

Rows 12, 14, 16, and 18: Knit.

Rows 15, 17, and 19: P1, *yb, sl 5, yf, p5; rep from * to last 6 sts, yb, sl 5, yf, p1.

Row 20: K3, *bowknot, k9; rep from * to last 4 sts, bowknot, k3.

Rep these 20 rows.

Ornamental stitches

Multiple of 10 + 8.

Special abbreviation:

Daisy = Insert needle into loop 3 rows below 2nd st on left-hand needle, draw up a loop, k2, draw 2nd loop through same st, k2, draw 3rd loop through same st.

Rows 1, 3, and 5: Knit.

Rows 2, 4, and 6: Purl.

Row 7: K2, daisy, *k6, daisy; rep from * to last 2 sts, k2.

Row 8: P2, *[p2tog, p1] twice, p2tog, p5; rep from * to last 9 sts, [p2tog, p1] twice, p2tog, p1.

Rows 9, 11, and 13: Knit.

Rows 10, 12, and 14: Purl.

Row 15: K7, *daisy, k6; rep from * to last st, k1.

Row 16: P2, *p5, [p2tog, p1] twice, p2tog; rep from * to last 6 sts, p6.

Rep these 16 rows.

Pleats

Multiple of 2 +1 + 2 sts each edge.

Row 1 (RS): 1 edge st, *k1, p1; rep from * to last 2 sts, k1, 1 edge st.

Row 2: 1 edge st, p1, *k1, p1; rep from * to last st, 1 edge st.

Rows 3, 5, 7, and 9: 1 edge st, *k1, yf, sl 1 purlwise, yb; rep from * to * last 2 sts, k1, 1 edge st.

Rows 4, 6, 8, and 10: 1 edge st, *yf, sl 1 purlwise, yb, k1; rep from * to last 2 sts, yf, sl 1 purlwise, yb, 1 edge st.

Rep these 10 rows.

Ribbed extended stitches

Multiple of 8 + 4 + 2 edge sts.

Row 1 (RS): 1 edge st, *p4, k4 (winding yarn around needle 3 times for each st); rep from * to last st, 1 edge st.

Rows 2 and 4: 1 edge st, k4, *yf, sl 4 purlwise dropping extra loops off needle, yb, k4; rep from * to last st, 1 edge st.

Row 3: 1 edge st, *p4, yb, sl 4 knitwise, yf; rep from * to last st, 1 edge st.

Rep these 4 rows.

Diagonal ridge II

Multiple of 18 + 2 edge sts.

Row 1: 1 edge st, *p4, k4, p1, k4, p1, k4; rep from * to last st, 1 edge st.

Row 2: 1 edge st, *k1, p4, k4, p4, k1, p4; rep from * to last st, 1 edge st.

Row 3: 1 edge st, k5, *p1, k10, p1, k6; rep from * to last 14 sts, p1, k10, p1, k1, 1 edge st.

Row 4: 1 edge st, p2, *k1, p8, k1, p8; rep from * to last 17 sts, k1, p8, k1, p6, 1 edge st.

Row 5: 1 edge st, k7, *p1, k6, p1, k10; rep from * to last 12 sts, p1, k6, p1, k3, 1 edge st.

Row 6: 1 edge st, *p4, k1, p4, k1, p4, k4; rep from * to last st, 1 edge st.

Row 7: 1 edge st, *k4, p1, k4, p4, k4, p1; rep from * to last st, 1 edge st.

Row 8: 1 edge st, p1, *k1, p10, k1, p6; rep from * to last 18 sts, k1, p10, k1, p5, 1 edge st.

Row 9: 1 edge st, k6, *p1, k8, p1, k8; rep from * to last 13 sts, p1, k8, p1, k2, 1 edge st.

Row 10: 1 edge st, p3, *k1, p6, k1, p10; rep from * to last 16 sts, k1, p6, k1, p7, 1 edge st.

Rep these 10 rows.

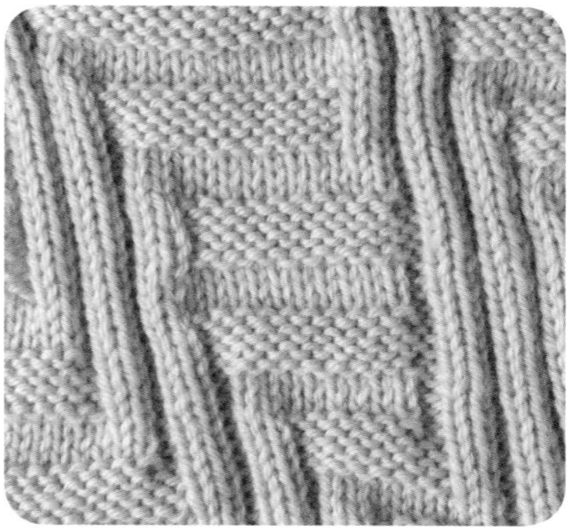

Labyrinth

Panel of 40 sts.

Rows 1 (RS) and 3: [K2, p2] twice, k2, p8, k2, p2, k2, p16.

Row 2 and every alt row: Knit all k sts and purl all p sts.

Rows 5 and 7: [K2, p2] 3 times, k8, p2, k2, p2, k14.

Rows 9 and 11: [K2, p2] 4 times, p6, k2, p2, k2, p12.

Rows 13 and 15: [K2, p2] 4 times, k8, p2, k2, p2, k10.

Rows 17 and 19: [K2, p2] 4 times, p10, k2, p2, k2, p8.

Rows 21 and 23: [K2, p2] 4 times, k12, p2, k2, p2, k6.

Rows 25 and 27: K6, [p2, k2] twice, p12, k2, [p2, k2] twice, p4.

Rows 29 and 31: P8, [k2, p2] twice, k12, [p2, k2] 3 times.

Rows 33 and 35: K10, [p2, k2] twice, p12, k2, [p2, k2] twice.

Rows 37 and 39: P12, k2, p2, k16, p2, k12, p2, k2.

Rows 41 and 43: K14, p2, k2, p16, k2, p2, k2.

Rows 45 and 47: P12, k2, p2, k20, p2, k2.

Row 48: As row 2.

Rep these 48 rows.

Plain diamonds

Multiple of 9.

Row 1 (RS): K4, *p1, k8; rep from * to last 5 sts, p1, k4.

Row 2: P3, *k3, p6; rep from * to last 6 sts, k3, p3.

Row 3: K2, *p5, k4; rep from * to last 7 sts, p5, k2.

Row 4: P1, *k7, p2; rep from * to last 8 sts, k7, p1.

Row 5: Purl.

Row 6: As row 4.

Row 7: As row 3.

Row 8: As row 2.

Rep these 8 rows.

Embossed diamonds

Multiple of 10 + 3.

Row 1 (RS): P1, k1, p1, *[k3, p1] twice, k1, p1; rep from * to end.

Row 2: P1, k1, *p3, k1, p1, k1, p3, k1; rep from * to last st, p1.

Row 3: K4, *[p1, k1] twice, p1, k5; rep from * to last 9 sts, [p1, k1] twice, p1, k4.

Row 4: P3, *[k1, p1] 3 times, k1, p3; rep from * to end.

Row 5: As row 3.

Row 6: As row 2.

Row 7: As row 1.

Row 8: P1, k1, p1, *k1, p5, [k1, p1] twice; rep from * to end.

Row 9: [P1, k1] twice, *p1, k3, [p1, k1] 3 times; rep from * to last 9 sts, p1, k3, [p1, k1] twice, p1.

Row 10: As row 8.

Rep these 10 rows.

Pleat pattern

Multiple of 5 + 1.
Row 1 (RS): K1B, *p1, k2, p1, k1B; rep from * to end.
Row 2: P1, *k1, p2, k1, p1; rep from * to end.
Row 3: K1B, *p4, k1B; rep from * to end.
Row 4: P1, *k4, p1; rep from * to end.
Rep these 4 rows.

Vertical bar lines

Multiple of 4 + 2.
Row 1 (RS): P2, *k2, p2; rep from * to end.
Row 2: K2, *sl 2 purlwise, k2; rep from * to end.
Rep these 2 rows.

Openwork mullions

Multiple of 5 + 1.
Row 1 (RS): P1, *k4, p1; rep from * to end.
Row 2: K1, *knit twice into st below st on needle, k2tog, knit into st below st on needle, p1; rep from * to end.
Rep these 2 rows.

Supple rib

Multiple of 3 + 1.
Row 1 (RS): K1, *knit next st but do not slip it off left-hand needle, then purl the same st and the next st tog, k1; rep from * to end.
Row 2: Purl.
Rep these 2 rows.

Dot stitch

Multiple of 4 + 3.
Row 1 (RS): K1, *p1, k3; rep from * to last 2 sts, p1, k1.
Row 2: Purl.
Row 3: *K3, p1; rep from * to last 3 sts, k3.
Row 4: Purl.
Rep these 4 rows.

Farrow rib

Multiple of 3 + 1.
Row 1 (RS): *K2, p1; rep from * to last st, k1.
Row 2: P1, *k2, p1; rep from * to end.
Rep these 2 rows.

Box stitch

Multiple of 4 + 2.

Row 1: K2, *p2, k2; rep from * to end.

Row 2: P2, *k2, p2; rep from * to end.

Row 3: As row 2.

Row 4: As row 1.

Rep these 4 rows.

Seed stitch

Multiple of 2 + 1.

Row 1: K1, *p1, k1; rep from * to end.

Rep this row.

Double seed stitch

Multiple of 2 + 1.

Row 1: K1, *p1, k1; rep from * to end.

Row 2: P1, *k1, p1; rep from * to end.

Row 3: As row 2.

Row 4: As row 1.

Rep these 4 rows.

Oblique rib

Multiple of 4.

Row 1 (RS): *K2, p2; rep from * to end.

Row 2: K1, *p2, k2; rep from * to last 3 sts, p2, k1.

Row 3: *P2, k2; rep from * to end.

Row 4: P1, *k2, p2; rep from * to last 3 sts, k2, p1.

Rep these 4 rows.

Lizard lattice

Multiple of 6 + 3.

Work 4 rows in st st, starting with knit.

Row 5 (RS): P3, *k3, p3; rep from * to end.

Row 6: Purl.

Rep the last 2 rows once more, then row 5 again.

Work 4 rows in st st, starting with purl.

Row 14: P3, *k3, p3; rep from * to end.

Rep these 14 rows.

Stockinette stitch triangles

Multiple of 5.

Row 1 (RS): Knit.

Row 2: *K1, p4; rep from * to end.

Row 3: *K3, p2; rep from * to end.

Row 4: *K3, p2; rep from * to end.

Row 5: *K1, p4; rep from * to end.

Row 6: Knit.

Rep these 6 rows.

Cross motif pattern

Multiple of 12.

Row 1 (RS): P1, k10, *p2, k10; rep from * to last st, p1.
Row 2: K1, p10, *k2, p10; rep from * to last st, k1.
Rep the last 2 rows once more.
Row 5: P3, k6, *p6, k6; rep from * to last 3 sts, p3.
Row 6: K3, p6, *k6, p6; rep from * to last 3 sts, k3.
Row 7: As row 1.
Row 8: As row 2.
Rep the last 2 rows once more.
Row 11: Knit.
Row 12: Purl.
Row 13: K5, p2, *k10, p2; rep from * to last 5 sts, k5.
Row 14: P5, k2, *p10, k2; rep from * to last 5 sts, p5.
Rep the last 2 rows once more.
Row 17: K3, p6, *k6, p6; rep from * to last 3 sts, k3.
Row 18: P3, k6, *p6, k6; rep from * to last 3 sts, p3.
Row 19: K5, p2, *k10, p2; rep from * to last 5 sts, k5.
Row 20: P5, k2, *p10, k2; rep from * to last 5 sts, p5.
Rep the last 2 rows once more.
Row 23: Knit.
Row 24: Purl.
Rep these 24 rows.

Pyramids I

Multiple of 15 + 7.

Row 1 (RS): *P1, [KB1] 5 times, p1, k8; rep from * to last 7 sts, p1, [KB1] 5 times, p1.
Row 2: *K1, [PB1] 5 times, k1, p8; rep from * to last 7 sts, k1, [PB1] 5 times, k1.
Row 3: P1, *[KB1] 5 times, p10; rep from * to last 6 sts, [KB1] 5 times, p1.
Row 4: K1, *[PB1] 5 times, k10; rep from * to last 6 sts, [PB1] 5 times, k1.
Row 5: P2, *[KB1] 3 times, p3, k6, p3; rep from * to last 5 sts, [KB1] 3 times, p2.
Row 6: K2, *[PB1] 3 times, k3, p6, k3; rep from * to last 5 sts, [PB1] 3 times, k2.
Row 7: P2, *[KB1] 3 times, p12; rep from * to last 5 sts, [KB1] 3 times, p2.
Row 8: K2, *[PB1] 3 times, k12; rep from * to last 5 sts, [PB1] 3 times, k2.
Row 9: P3, *KB1, p5, k4, p5; rep from * to last 4 sts, KB1, p3.
Row 10: K3, *PB1, k5, p4, k5; rep from * to last 4 sts, PB1, k3.
Row 11: P3, *KB1, p14; rep from * to last 4 sts, KB1, p3.
Row 12: K3, *PB1, k14; rep from * to last 4 sts, PB1, k3.
Rep these 12 rows.

Seed stitch parallelograms

Multiple of 10.

Row 1 (RS): *K5, [p1, k1] twice, p1; rep from * to end.
Row 2: [P1, k1] 3 times, *p5, [k1, p1] twice, k1; rep from * to last 4 sts, p4.
Row 3: K3, *[p1, k1] twice, p1, k5; rep from * to last 7 sts, [p1, k1] twice, p1, k2.
Row 4: P3, *[k1, p1] twice, k1, p5; rep from * to last 7 sts, [k1, p1] twice, k1, p2.
Row 5: [K1, p1] 3 times, *k5, [p1, k1] twice, p1; rep from * to last 4 sts, k4.
Row 6: Purl.
Rep these 6 rows.

Woven horizontal herringbone

Multiple of 4.

Row 1 (RS): K3, *yf, sl 2, yb, k2; rep from * to last st, k1.
Row 2: P2, *yb, sl 2, yf, p2; rep from * to last 2 sts, p2.
Row 3: K1, yf, sl 2, yb, *k2, yf, sl 2, yb; rep from * to last st, k1.
Row 4: P4, *yb, sl 2, yf, p2; rep from * to end.
Rep the last 4 rows twice more.
Row 13: As row 3.
Row 14: As row 2.
Rep these 14 rows.

Seed stitch triangles

Multiple of 8.

Row 1 (RS): *P1, k7; rep from * to end.
Row 2: P6, *k1, p7; rep from * to last 2 sts, k1, p1.
Row 3: *P1, k1, p1, k5; rep from * to end.
Row 4: P4, *k1, p1, k1, p5; rep from * to last 4 sts, [k1, p1] twice.
Row 5: *[P1, k1] twice, p1, k3; rep from * to end.
Row 6: P2, *[k1, p1] twice, k1, p3; rep from * to last 6 sts, [k1, p1] 3 times.
Row 7: *P1, k1; rep from * to end.
Row 8: As row 6.
Row 9: As row 5.
Row 10: As row 4.
Row 11: As row 3.
Row 12: As row 2.
Rep these 12 rows.

Seed stitch squares

Multiple of 12 + 3.

Row 1 (RS): Knit.

Row 2: Purl.

Row 3: K4, *[p1, k1] 3 times, p1, k5; rep from * to last 11 sts, [p1, k1] 3 times, p1, k4.

Row 4: P3, *[k1, p1] 4 times, k1, p3; rep from * to end.

Row 5: K4, *p1, k5; rep from * to last 5 sts, p1, k4.

Row 6: P3, *k1, p7, k1, p3; rep from * to end.

Rep the last 2 rows twice more, then row 5 again.

Row 12: As row 4.

Row 13: As row 3.

Row 14: Purl.

Rep these 14 rows.

Little birds

Multiple of 14 + 8.

Row 1 (RS): Knit.

Row 2: Purl.

Row 3: K10, *sl 2 purlwise, k12; rep from * to last 12 sts, sl 2 purlwise, k10.

Row 4: P10, *sl 2 purlwise, p12; rep from * to last 12 sts, sl 2 purlwise, p10.

Row 5: K8, *C3R, C3L, k8; rep from * to end.

Row 6: Purl.

Rows 7–8: As rows 1–2.

Row 9: K3, *sl 2, k12; rep from * to last 5 sts, sl 2, k3.

Row 10: P3, *sl 2, p12; rep from * to last 5 sts, sl 2, p3.

Row 11: K1, *C3R, C3L, k8; rep from * to last 7 sts, C3R, C3L, k1.

Row 12: Purl.

Rep these 12 rows.

Chevron stripes

Multiple of 18 + 9.

Row 1 (RS): P4, k1, p4, *k4, p1, k4, p4, k1, p4; rep from * to end.

Row 2: K3, *p3, k3; rep from * to end.

Row 3: P2, k5, p2, *k2, p5, k2, p2, k5, p2; rep from * to end.

Row 4: K1, p7, k1, *p1, k7, p1, k1, p7, k1; rep from * to end.

Row 5: K4, p1, k4, *p4, k1, p4, k4, p1, k4; rep from * to end.

Row 6: P3, *k3, p3; rep from * to end.

Row 7: K2, p5, k2, *p2, k5, p2, k2, p5, k2; rep from * to end.

Row 8: P1, k7, p1, *k1, p7, k1, p1, k7, p1; rep from * to end.

Rep these 8 rows.

Hexagon stitch

Multiple of 10 + 1.

Row 1 (RS): Knit.

Row 2: Purl.

Row 3: K4, *p1, k1, p1, k7; rep from * to last 7 sts, p1, k1, p1, k4.

Row 4: P3, *[k1, p1] twice, k1, p5; rep from * to last 8 sts, [k1, p1] twice, k1, p3.

Row 5: K2, *[p1, k1] 3 times, p1, k3, rep from * to last 9 sts, [p1, k1] 3 times, p1, k2.

Rep the last 2 rows once more.

Row 8: As row 4.

Row 9: As row 3.

Row 10: Purl.

Row 11: Knit.

Row 12: Purl.

Row 13: K1, p1, *k7, p1, k1, p1; rep from * to last 9 sts, k7, p1, k1.

Row 14: K1, p1, k1, *p5, [k1, p1] twice, k1; rep from * to last 8 sts, p5, k1, p1, k1.

Row 15: [K1, p1] twice, *k3, [p1, k1] 3 times, p1; rep from * to last 7 sts, k3, [p1, k1] twice.

Rep the last 2 rows once more.

Row 18: As row 14.

Row 19: As row 13.

Row 20: Purl.

Rep these 20 rows.

Open chain ribbing

Multiple of 6 + 2.

Row 1 (WS): K2, *p4, k2; rep from * to end.

Row 2: P2, *k2tog, yo2, skpo, p2; rep from * to end.

Row 3: K2, *p1, purl into front of first yo, purl into back of 2nd yo, p1, k2; rep from * to end.

Row 4: P2, *yo, skpo, k2tog, yo, p2; rep from * to end.

Rep these 4 rows.

Seed stitch diagonal

Multiple of 8 + 3.

Row 1 (RS): K4, *p1, k1, p1, k5; rep from * to last 7 sts, p1, k1, p1, k4.

Row 2: P3, *[k1, p1] twice, k1, p3; rep from * to end.

Row 3: K2, *p1, k1, p1, k5; rep from * to last st, p1.

Row 4: P1, k1, *p3, [k1, p1] twice, k1; rep from * to last st, p1.

Row 5: *P1, k1, p1, k5; rep from * to last 3 sts, p1, k1, p1.

Row 6: *[P1, k1] twice, p3, k1; rep from * to last 3 sts, p1, k1, p1.

Row 7: P1, *k5, p1, k1, p1; rep from * to last 2 sts, k2.

Row 8: [P1, k1] 3 times, *p3, [k1, p1] twice, k1; rep from * to last 5 sts, p3, k1, p1.

Rep these 8 rows.

Seed stitch checks

Multiple of 10 + 5.

Row 1 (RS): K5, *[p1, k1] twice, p1, k5; rep from * to end.

Row 2: P6, *k1, p1, k1, p7; rep from * to last 9 sts, k1, p1, k1, p6.

Rep the last 2 rows once more, then row 1 again.

Row 6: *[K1, p1] twice, k1, p5; rep from * to last 5 sts, [k1, p1] twice, k1.

Row 7: [K1, p1] twice, *k7, p1, k1, p1; rep from * to last st, k1.

Rep the last 2 rows once more, then row 6 again.

Rep these 10 rows.

Alternate bobble stripe

Multiple of 10 + 5.

Special abbreviation:

MB (make bobble) = (K1, p1, k1, p1, k1) into next st, turn, k5, turn, k5tog.

Row 1 (RS): P2, k1, *p4, k1; rep from * to last 2 sts, p2.

Row 2: K2, p1, *k4, p1; rep from * to last 2 sts, k2.

Row 3: P2, *MB, p4, k1, p4; rep from * to last 3 sts, MB, p2.

Row 4: As row 2.

Rep the last 4 rows 4 times more.

Row 21: As row 1.

Row 22: As row 2.

Row 23: P2, *k1, p4, MB, p4; rep from * to last 3 sts, k1, p2.

Row 24: As row 2.

Rep the last 4 rows 4 times more.

Rep these 40 rows.

Seed stitch panes

Multiple of 10 + 3.

Row 1 (RS): P1, *k1, p1; rep from * to end.

Row 2: P1, *k1, p1; rep from * to end.

Row 3: P1, k1, p1, *k7, p1, k1, p1; rep from * to end.

Row 4: P1, k1, p9, *k1, p9; rep from * to last 2 sts, k1, p1.

Rep the last 2 rows 3 times more.

Rep these 10 rows.

Vertical zigzag seed stitch

Multiple of 7.

Row 1 (RS): *P1, k1, p1, k4; rep from * to end.

Row 2: *P4, k1, p1, k1; rep from * to end.

Row 3: *[K1, p1] twice, k3; rep from * to end.

Row 4: *P3, [k1, p1] twice; rep from * to end.

Row 5: K2, p1, k1, p1, *k4, p1, k1, p1; rep from * to last 2 sts, k2.

Row 6: P2, k1, p1, k1, *p4, k1, p1, k1; rep from * to last 2 sts, p2.

Row 7: K3, p1, k1, p1, *k4, p1, k1, p1; rep from * to last st, k1.

Row 8: [P1, k1] twice, *p4, k1, p1, k1; rep from * to last 3 sts, p3.

Row 9: *K4, p1, k1, p1; rep from * to end.

Row 10: *K1, p1, k1, p4; rep from * to end.

Rows 11–12: As rows 7–8.

Rows 13–14: As rows 5–6

Rows 15–16: As rows 3–4.

Rep these 16 rows.

Top hat pattern

Multiple of 6 + 4.

Row 1 (RS): K4, *p2, k4; rep from * to end.

Row 2: P4, *k2, p4; rep from * to end.

Rep the last 2 rows once more.

Row 5: P1, k2, *p4, k2; rep from * to last st, p1.

Row 6: K1, p2, *k4, p2; rep from * to last st, k1.

Rep the last 2 rows once more.

Row 9: Purl.

Row 10: Knit.

Rep these 10 rows.

Diagonal garter ribs

Multiple of 5 + 2.

Row 1 (RS) and every alt row: Knit.

Row 2: *P2, k3; rep from * to last 2 sts, p2.

Row 4: K1, *p2, k3; rep from * to last st, p1.

Row 6: K2, *p2, k3; rep from * to end.

Row 8: *K3, p2; rep from * to last 2 sts, k2.

Row 10: P1, *k3, p2; rep from * to last st, k1.

Rep these 10 rows.

Double rice stitch

Multiple of 2 + 1.

Row 1 (WS): P1, *KB1, p1; rep from * to end.

Row 2: Knit.

Row 3: *KB1, p1; rep from * to last st, KB1.

Row 4: Knit.

Rep these 4 rows.

Checkerboard

Multiple of 8 + 4.

Row 1: K4, *p4, k4; rep from * to end.

Row 2: P4, *k4, p4; rep from * to end.

Rep the last 2 rows once more.

Row 5: As row 3.

Row 6: As row 1.

Rep the last 2 rows once more.

Rep these 8 rows.

Woven stitch I

Multiple of 2 + 1.

Row 1 (RS): K1, *yf, sl 1, yb, k1; rep from * to end.

Row 2: Purl.

Row 3: K2, *yf, sl 1, yb, k1; rep from * to last st, k1.

Row 4: Purl.

Rep these 4 rows.

Beaded rib

Multiple of 5 + 2.

Row 1 (RS): P2, *k1, p1, k1, p2; rep from * to end.

Row 2: K2, *p3, k2; rep from * to end.

Rep these 2 rows.

Double woven stitch

Multiple of 4.

Row 1 (RS): K3, *yf, sl 2, yb, k2; rep from * to last st, k1.

Row 2: Purl.

Row 3: K1, *yf, sl 2, yb, k2; rep from * to last 3 sts, yf, sl 2, yb, k1.

Row 4: Purl.

Rep these 4 rows.

Two-stitch ribs

Multiple of 4 + 2.

Row 1: K2, *p2, k2; rep from * to end.

Rep this row.

Four-stitch ribs

Multiple of 8 + 4.

Row 1: K4, *p4, k4; rep from * to end.

Rep this row.

Eyelet mock cable ribbing

Multiple of 5 + 2.

Row 1 (RS): P2, *sl 1, k2, psso, p2; rep from * to end.

Row 2: K2, *p1, yo, p1, k2; rep from * to end.

Row 3: P2, *k3, p2; rep from * to end.

Row 4: K2, *p3, k2; rep from * to end.

Rep these 4 rows.

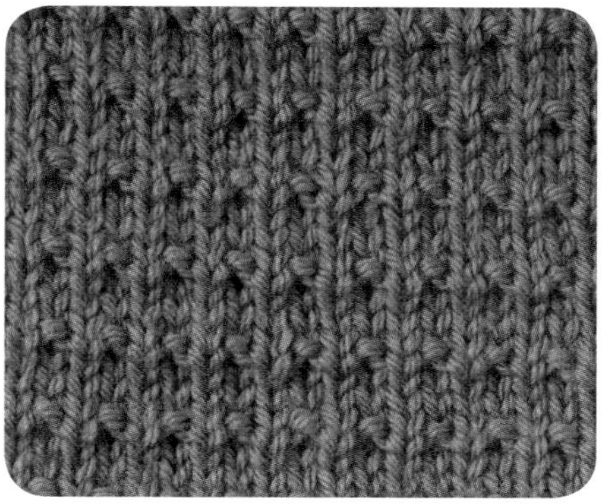

Fleck stitch

Multiple of 2 + 1.

Row 1 (RS): Knit.

Row 2: Purl.

Row 3: K1, *p1, k1; rep from * to end.

Row 4: Purl.

Rep these 4 rows.

Large eyelet rib

Multiple of 6 + 2.

Row 1 (RS): *P2, k2tog, yo2, skpo; rep from * to last 2 sts, p2.

Row 2: K2, *p1, knit into first yo, purl into 2nd yo, p1, k2; rep from * to end.

Row 3: *P2, k4; rep from * to last 2 sts, p2.

Row 4: K2, *p4, k2; rep from * to end.

Rep these 4 rows.

Double basketweave

Multiple of 4 + 3.

Row 1 (RS) and every alt row: Knit.

Row 2: *K3, p1; rep from * to last 3 sts, k3.

Row 4: As row 3.

Row 6: K1, *p1, k3; rep from * to last 2 sts, p1, k1.

Row 8: As row 6.

Rep these 8 rows.

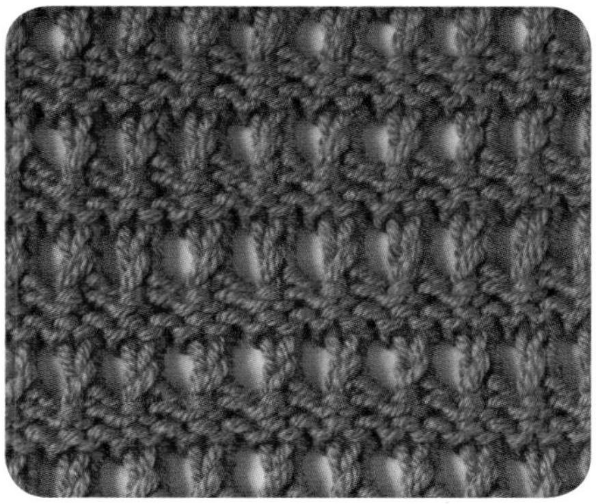

Open check stitch

Multiple of 2.

Row 1 (RS): Purl.

Row 2: Knit.

Row 3: K2, *sl 1, k1; rep from * to end.

Row 4: *K1, yf, sl 1, yb; rep from * to last 2 sts, k2.

Row 5: K1, *yo, k2tog; rep from * to last st, k1.

Row 6: Purl.

Rep these 6 rows.

Maze pattern

Multiple of 13.

Row 1 (RS): Knit.

Row 2: Purl.

Row 3: Knit.

Row 4: P1, k11, *p2, k11; rep from * to last st, p1.

Row 5: K1, p11, *k2, p11; rep from * to last st, k1.

Row 6: As row 4.

Row 7: K1, p2, k7, p2, *k2, p2, k7, p2; rep from * to last st, k1.

Row 8: P1, k2, p7, k2, *p2, k2, p7, k2; rep from * to last st, p1.

Row 9: As row 7.

Row 10: P1, k2, p2, k3, *[p2, k2] twice, p2, k3; rep from * to last 5 sts, p2, k2, p1.

Row 11: K1, p2, k2, p3, *[k2, p2] twice, k2, p3; rep from * to last 5 sts, k2, p2, k1.

Rep the last 2 rows once more.

Row 14: As row 8.

Row 15: As row 7.

Row 16: As row 8.

Row 17: As row 5.

Row 18: As row 4.

Row 19: As row 5.

Row 20: As row 3.

Rep these 20 rows.

Double parallelogram stitch

Multiple of 10.

Row 1 (RS): *P5, k5; rep from * to end.

Row 2: K1, *p5, k5; rep from * to last 9 sts, p5, k4.

Row 3: P3, *k5, p5; rep from * to last 7 sts, k5, p2.

Row 4: K3, *p5, k5; rep from * to last 7 sts, p5, k2.

Row 5: P1, *k5, p5; rep from * to last 9 sts, k5, p4.

Row 6: P4, *k5, p5; rep from * to last 6 sts, k5, p1.

Row 7: K2, *p5, k5; rep from * to last 8 sts, p5, k3.

Row 8: P2, *k5, p5; rep from * to last 8 sts, k5, p3.

Row 9: K4, *p5, k5; rep from * to last 6 sts, p5, k1.

Row 10: *K5, p5; rep from * to end.

Rep these 10 rows.

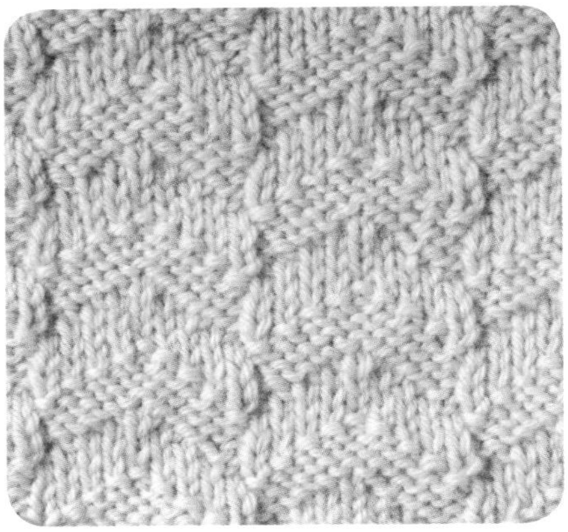

Double signal check

Multiple of 18 + 9.

Row 1 (RS): K1, p7, k1, *p1, k7, p1, k1, p7, k1; rep from * to end.

Row 2: P2, k5, p2, *k2, p5, k2, p2, k5, p2; rep from * to end.

Row 3: K3, *p3, k3; rep from * to end.

Row 4: P4, k1, p4, *k4, p1, k4, p4, k1, p4; rep from * to end.

Row 5: P1, k7, p1, *k1, p7, k1, p1, k7, p1; rep from * to end.

Row 6: K2, p5, k2, *p2, k5, p2, k2, p5, k2; rep from * to end.

Row 7: P3, *k3, p3; rep from * to end.

Row 8: K4, p1, k4, *p4, k1, p4, k4, p1, k4; rep from * to end.

Rep these 8 rows.

King Charles brocade

Multiple of 12 + 1.

Row 1 (RS): K1, *p1, k9, p1, k1; rep from * to end.

Row 2: K1, p1, k1, *p7, [k1, p1] twice, k1; rep from * to last 10 sts, p7, k1, p1, k1.

Row 3: [K1, p1] twice, *k5, [p1, k1] 3 times, p1; rep from * to last 9 sts, k5, [p1, k1] twice.

Row 4: P2, *k1, p1, k1, p3; rep from * to last 5 sts, k1, p1, k1, p2.

Row 5: K3, *[p1, k1] 3 times, p1, k5; rep from * to last 10 sts, [p1, k1] 3 times, p1, k3.

Row 6: P4, *[k1, p1] twice, k1, p7; rep from * to last 9 sts, [k1, p1] twice, k1, p4.

Row 7: K5, *p1, k1, p1, k9; rep from * to last 8 sts, p1, k1, p1, k5.

Row 8: As row 6.

Row 9: As row 5.

Row 10: As row 4.

Row 11: As row 3.

Row 12: As row 2.

Rep these 12 rows.

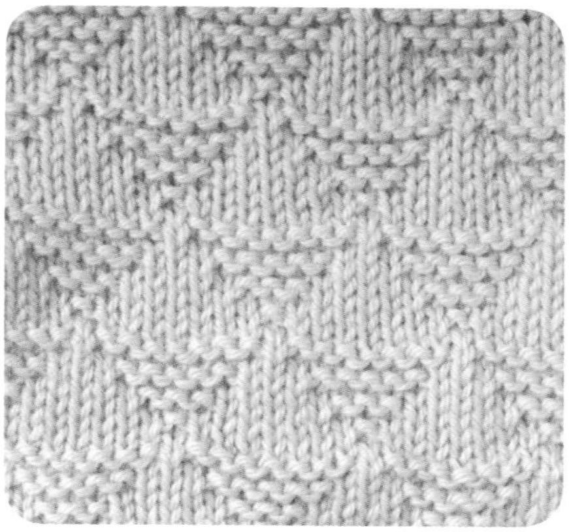

Garter stitch triangles

Multiple of 8 +1.

Row 1 (RS): P1, *k7, p1; rep from * to end.

Row 2 and every alt row: Purl.

Row 3: P2, *k5, p3; rep from * to last 7 sts, k5, p2.

Row 5: P3, *k3, p5; rep from * to last 6 sts, k3, p3.

Row 7: P4, *k1, p7; rep from * to last 5 sts, k1, p4.

Row 9: K4, *p1, k7; rep from * to last 5 sts, p1, k4.

Row 11: K3, *p3, k5; rep from * to last 6 sts, p3, k3.

Row 13: K2, *p5, k3; rep from * to last 7 sts; p5, k2.

Row 15: K1, *p7, k1; rep from * to end.

Row 16: Purl.

Rep these 16 rows.

Diagonals

Multiple of 8 + 6.

Row 1 (RS): P3, *k5, p3; rep from * to last 3 sts, k3.

Row 2: P4, *k3, p5; rep from * to last 2 sts, k2.

Row 3: P1, k5, *p3, k5; rep from * to end.

Row 4: K1, p5, *k3, p5; rep from * to end.

Row 5: K4, *p3, k5; rep from * to last 2 sts, p2.

Row 6: K3, *p5, k3; rep from * to last 3 sts, p3.

Row 7: K2, p3, *k5, p3; rep from * to last st, k1.

Row 8: P2, k3, *p5, k3; rep from * to last st, p1.

Rep these 8 rows.

Diamond and block

Multiple of 14 + 5.

Row 1 (RS): P5, *k4, p1, k4, p5; rep from * to end.

Row 2: K5, *p3, k3, p3, k5; rep from * to end.

Row 3: K7, p5, *k9, p5; rep from * to last 7 sts, k7.

Row 4: P6, k7, *p7, k7; rep from * to last 6 sts, p6.

Row 5: K5, *p9, k5; rep from * to end.

Row 6: As row 4.

Row 7: As row 3.

Row 8: As row 2.

Rep these 8 rows.

Divided triangles

Multiple of 14 + 1.

Row 1 (WS): Knit.

Row 2: Knit.

Row 3: K1, *p13, k1; rep from * to end.

Row 4: K1, *p1, k11, p1, k1; rep from * to end.

Row 5: P1, *k2, p9, k2, p1; rep from * to end.

Row 6: K1, *p3, k7, p3, k1; rep from * to end.

Row 7: P1, *k4, p5, k4, p1; rep from * to end.

Row 8: K1, *p5, k3, p5, k1; rep from * to end.

Row 9: P1, *[k6, p1] twice; rep from * to end.

Rows 10–11: Purl.

Row 12: K7, p1, *k13, p1; rep from * to last 7 sts, k7.

Row 13: P6, k1, p1, k1, *p11, k1, p1, k1; rep from * to last 6 sts, p6.

Row 14: K5, p2, k1, p2, *k9, p2, k1, p2; rep from * to last 5 sts, k5.

Row 15: P4, k3, p1, k3, *p7, k3, p1, k3; rep from * to last 4 sts, p4.

Row 16: K3, p4, k1, p4, *k5, p4, k1, p4; rep from * to last 3 sts, k3.

Row 17: P2, k5, p1, k5, *p3, k5, p1, k5; rep from * to last 2 sts, p2.

Row 18: K1, *p6, k1; rep from * to end.

Rep these 18 rows.

Rib checks

Multiple of 10 + 5.

Row 1 (RS): P5, *[KB1, p1] twice, KB1, p5; rep from * to end.

Row 2: K5, *[PB1, k1] twice, PB1, k5; rep from * to end.

Rep the last 2 rows once more, then row 1 again.

Row 6: [PB1, k1] twice, PB1, *k5, [PB1, k1] twice, PB1; rep from * to end.

Row 7: [KB1, p1] twice, KB1, *p5, [KB1, p1] twice, KB1; rep from * to end.

Rep the last 2 rows once more, then row 6 again.

Rep these 10 rows.

Purl triangles

Multiple of 8 + 1.

Row 1 (RS): K1, *p7, k1; rep from * to end.

Row 2: P1, *k7, p1; rep from * to end.

Row 3: K2, *p5, k3; rep from * to last 7 sts, p5, k2.

Row 4: P2, *k5, p3; rep from * to last 7 sts, k5, p2.

Row 5: K3, *p3, k5; rep from * to last 6 sts, p3, k3.

Row 6: P3, *k3, p5; rep from * to last 6 sts, k3, p3.

Row 7: K4, *p1, k7; rep from * to last 5 sts, p1, k4.

Row 8: P4, *k1, p7; rep from * to last 5 sts, k1, p4.

Row 9: As row 8.

Row 10: As row 7.

Row 11: As row 6.

Row 12: As row 5.

Row 13: As row 4.

Row 14: As row 3.

Row 15: As row 2.

Row 16: K1, *p7, k1; rep from * to end.

Rep these 16 rows.

Textured triangle stack

Multiple of 10 + 1.

Row 1 (RS): P5, *k1, p9; rep from * to last 6 sts, k1, p5.

Row 2: K5, *p1, k9; rep from * to last 6 sts, p1, k5.

Row 3: P4, *k3, p7; rep from * to last 7 sts, p3, k4.

Row 4: K4, *p3, k7; rep from * to last 7 sts, k3, p4.

Row 5: P3, *k5, p5; rep from * to last 8 sts, k5, p3.

Row 6: K3, *p5, k5; rep from * to last 8 sts, p5, k3.

Row 7: P2, *k7, p3; rep from * to last 9 sts, k7, p2.

Row 8: K2, *p7, k3; rep from * to last 9 sts, p7, k2.

Row 9: P1, *k9, p1; rep from * to end.

Row 10: K1, *p9, k1; rep from * to end.

Rep these 10 rows.

Seed diamonds

Multiple of 10 + 9.

Row 1 (RS): K4, *p1, k9; rep from * to last 5 sts, p1, k4.

Row 2: P3, *k1, p1, k1, p7; rep from * to last 6 sts, k1, p1, k1, p3.

Row 3: K2, *[p1, k1] twice, p1, k5; rep from * to last 7 sts, [p1, k1] twice, p1, k2.

Row 4: [P1, k1] 4 times, *p3, [k1, p1] 3 times, k1; rep from * to last st, p1.

Row 5: P1, *k1, p1; rep from * to end.

Row 6: As row 4.

Row 7: As row 3.

Row 8: As row 2.

Row 9: As row 1.

Row 10: Purl.

Rep these 10 rows.

Check stitch

Multiple of 4 + 2.

Row 1: K2, *p2, k2; rep from * to end.

Row 2: P2, *k2, p2; rep from * to end.

Rep the last 2 rows once more.

Row 5: As row 2.

Row 6: As row 1.

Rep the last 2 rows once more.

Rep these 8 rows.

Horizontal herringbone

Multiple of 2.

Row 1 (RS): K1, *skpo but instead of dropping slipped st from left-hand needle knit into the back of it; rep from * to last st, k1.

Row 2: *P2tog, then purl first st again slipping both sts off needle tog; rep from * to end.

Rep these 2 rows.

Double fleck stitch

Multiple of 6 + 4.

Rows 1 (RS) and 3: Knit.

Row 2: P4, *k2, p4; rep from * to end.

Row 4: P1, *k2, p4; rep from * to last 3 sts, k2, p1.

Rep these 4 rows.

Woven rib

Multiple of 6 + 3.

Row 1 (RS): P3, *sl 1 purlwise, yb, k1, yf, sl 1 purlwise, p3; rep from * to end.

Row 2: K3, *p3, k3; rep from * to end.

Row 3: *P3, k1, yf, sl 1 purlwise, yb, k1; rep from * to last 3 sts, p3.

Row 4: As row 2.

Rep these 4 rows.

Garter stitch checks

Multiple of 10 + 5.

Row 1 (RS): K5, *p5, k5; rep from * to end.

Row 2: Purl.

Rep the last 2 rows once more, then row 1 again.

Row 6: K5, *p5, k5; rep from * to end.

Row 7: Knit.

Rep the last 2 rows once more, then row 6 again.

Rep these 10 rows.

Medallion rib

Multiple of 8 + 4.

Row 1 (RS): P4, *yb, sl 2 purlwise, C2B, p4; rep from * to end.

Row 2: K4, *yf, sl 2 purlwise, purl the 2nd st on left-hand needle, then the first st, slipping both sts off needle tog, k4; rep from * to end.

Row 3: Knit.

Row 4: Purl.

Rep these 4 rows.

Cactus ladder

Multiple of 10 + 7.

Row 1 (RS): P3, KB1, *p4, KB1; rep from * to last 3 sts, p3.

Row 2: K3, PB1, *k4, PB1; rep from * to last 3 sts, k3.

Row 3: P2, [KB1] 3 times, *p3, KB1, p3, [KB1] 3 times; rep from * to last 2 sts, p2.

Row 4: K2, [PB1] 3 times, *k3, PB1, k3, [PB1] 3 times; rep from * to last 2 sts, k2.

Rep the last 2 rows once more.

Rows 7–8: As rows 1–2.

Rep the last 2 rows once more.

Row 11: P3, KB1, p3, *[KB1] 3 times, p3, KB1, p3; rep from * to end.

Row 12: K3, PB1, k3, *[PB1] 3 times, k3, PB1, k3; rep from * to end.

Rep the last 2 rows once more.

Rows 15–16: As rows 1–2.

Rep these 16 rows.

Seed stitch double parallelograms

Multiple of 10.

Row 1 (RS): *K5, [p1, k1] twice, p1; rep from * to end.

Row 2: P1, *[k1, p1] twice, k1, p5; rep from * to last 9 sts, [k1, p1] twice, k1, p4.

Row 3: K3, *[p1, k1] twice, p1, k5; rep from * to last 7 sts, [p1, k1] twice, p1, k2.

Row 4: P3, *[k1, p1] twice, k1, p5; rep from * to last 7 sts, [k1, p1] twice, k1, p2.

Row 5: K1, *[p1, k1] twice, p1, k5; rep from * to last 9 sts, [p1, k1] twice, p1, k4.

Row 6: *[P1, k1] twice, p5, k1; rep from * to end.

Row 7: K1, p1, *k5, [p1, k1] twice, p1; rep from * to last 8 sts, k5, p1, k1, p1.

Row 8: P1, k1, *p5, [k1, p1] twice, k1, rep from * to last 8 sts, p5, k1, p1, k1.

Row 9: *[K1, p1] twice, k5, p1; rep from * to end.

Row 10: *P5, [k1, p1] twice, k1; rep from * to end.

Rep these 10 rows.

Flag pattern

Multiple of 11.

Row 1 (RS): *P1, k10; rep from * to end.

Row 2: *P9, k2; rep from * to end.

Row 3: *P3, k8; rep from * to end.

Row 4: *P7, k4; rep from * to end.

Row 5: *P5, k6; rep from * to end.

Row 6: As row 5.

Row 7: As row 5.

Row 8: As row 4.

Row 9: As row 3.

Row 10: As row 2.

Row 11: As row 1.

Row 12: *K1, p10; rep from * to end.

Row 13: *K9, p2; rep from * to end.

Row 14: *K3, p8; rep from * to end.

Row 15: *K7, p4; rep from * to end.

Row 16: *K5, p6; rep from * to end.

Row 17: As row 16.

Row 18: As row 16.

Row 19: As row 15.

Row 20: As row 14.

Row 21: As row 13.

Row 22: As row 12.

Rep these 22 rows.

Crosses

Multiple of 12 + 1.

Row 1 (RS): Purl.

Row 2: Knit.

Row 3: P5, *[KB1] 3 times, p9; rep from * to last 8 sts, [KB1] 3 times, p5.

Row 4: K5, *p3, k9; rep from * to last 8 sts, p3, k5.

Rep the last 2 rows once more.

Row 7: P2, *[KB1] 9 times, p3; rep from * to last 11 sts, [KB1] 9 times, p2.

Row 8: K2, *p9, k3; rep from * to last 11 sts, p9, k2.

Rep the last 2 rows once more.

Row 11: As row 3.

Row 12: As row 4.

Rep the last 2 rows once more.

Row 15: Purl.

Row 16: Knit.

Rep these 16 rows.

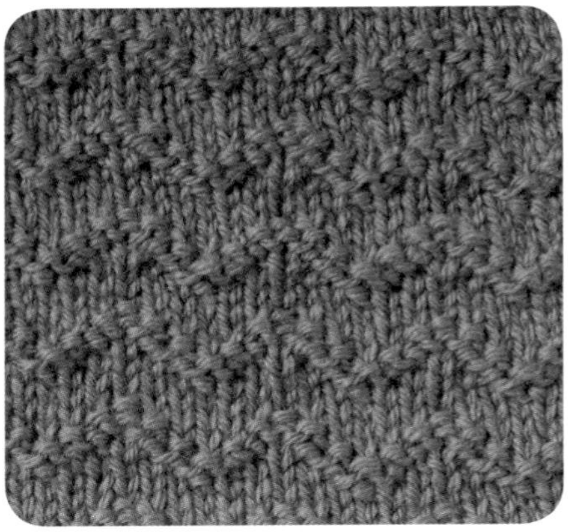

Reverse stockinette stitch chevrons

Multiple of 6 + 5.

Row 1 (RS): K5, *p1, k5; rep from * to end.

Row 2: K1, *p3, k3; rep from * to last 4 sts, p3, k1.

Row 3: P2, *k1, p2; rep from * to end.

Row 4: P1, *k3, p3; rep from * to last 4 sts, k3, p1.

Row 5: K2, *p1, k5; rep from * to last 3 sts, p1, k2.

Row 6: Purl.

Rep these 6 rows.

Twisted cable rib

Multiple of 4 + 2.

Row 1 (RS): P2, *k2, p2; rep from * to end.

Row 2: K2, *p2, k2; rep from * to end.

Row 3: P2, *k2tog but do not slip off left-hand needle, insert right-hand needle between these 2 sts and knit the first st again, slipping both sts off needle tog, p2; rep from * to end.

Row 4: As row 2.

Rep these 4 rows.

Ladder stitch

Multiple of 8 + 5.

Row 1 (RS): K5, *p3, k5; rep from * to end.

Row 2: P5, *k3, p5; rep from * to end.

Rep the last 2 rows once more.

Row 5: K1, *p3, k5; rep from * to last 4 sts, p3, k1.

Row 6: P1, *k3, p5; rep from * to last 4 sts, k3, p1.

Rep the last 2 rows once more.

Rep these 8 rows.

Small basket stitch

Multiple of 10 + 5.

Row 1 (RS): [K1, p1] twice, *k7, p1, k1, p1; rep from * to last st, k1.

Row 2: P1, [k1, p1] twice, *k5, [p1, k1] twice, p1; rep from * to end.

Rep the last 2 rows once more.

Row 5: K6, *p1, k1, p1, k7; rep from * to last 9 sts, p1, k1, p1, k6.

Row 6: *K5, [p1, k1] twice, p1; rep from * to last 5 sts, k5.

Rep the last 2 rows once more.

Rep these 8 rows.

Herringbone II

Multiple of 7 + 1.

Special abbreviation:

K1B Back = From the top, insert point of right-hand needle into back of st one row below next st on left-hand needle and knit it.

Row 1 (WS): Purl.

Row 2: *K2tog, k2, K1B Back then knit st above, k2; rep from * to last st, k1.

Row 3: Purl.

Row 4: K3, K1B Back then knit st above, k2, k2tog, *k2, K1B Back then knit st above, k2, k2tog; rep from * to end.

Rep these 4 rows.

Double seed stitch triangles

Multiple of 8 + 1.

Row 1 (RS): *K1, p7; rep from * to last st, k1.

Row 2: *P1, k7; rep from * to last st, p1.

Row 3: *P1, k1, p5, k1; rep from * to last st, p1.

Row 4: *K1, p1, k5, p1; rep from * to last st, k1.

Row 5: K1, p1, *k1, p3, [k1, p1] twice; rep from * to last 7 sts, k1, p3, k1, p1, k1.

Row 6: P1, k1, *p1, k3, [p1, k1] twice; rep from * to last 7 sts, p1, k3, p1, k1, p1.

Row 7: *P1, k1; rep from * to last st, p1.

Row 8: *K1, p1; rep from * to last st, k1.

Row 9: P4, *k1, p7; rep from * to last 5 sts, k1, p4.

Row 10: K4, *p1, k7; rep from * to last 5 sts, p1, k4.

Row 11: P3, *k1, p1, k1, p5; rep from * to last 6 sts, k1, p1, k1, p3.

Row 12: K3, *p1, k1, p1, k5; rep from * to last 6 sts, p1, k1, p1, k3.

Row 13: P2, *[k1, p1] twice, k1, p3; rep from * to last 7 sts, [k1, p1] twice, k1, p2.

Row 14: K2, *[p1, k1] twice, p1, k3; rep from * to last 7 sts, [p1, k1] twice, p1, k2.

Row 15: As row 7.

Row 16: As row 8.

Rep these 16 rows.

Spaced knots

Multiple of 6 + 5.

Special abbreviation:

Make knot = Sl 3, k1, pass 3 slipped sts one at a time over knitted st.

Note: Stitches should not be counted after row 5 or 11.

Work 4 rows in st st, starting with knit.

Row 5: K5, *[k1, p1] twice into next st, k5; rep from * to end.

Row 6: P5, *make knot, p5; rep from * to end.

Work 4 rows in st st, starting with knit.

Row 11: K2, *[k1, p1] twice into next st, k5; rep from * to last 3 sts, [k1, p1] twice into next st, k2.

Row 12: P2, *make knot, p5; rep from * to last 6 sts, make knot, p2.

Rep these 12 rows.

Twisted check

Multiple of 4 + 2.

Row 1 (RS): Knit into the back of every st.

Row 2: Purl.

Row 3: [KB1] twice, *p2, [KB1] twice; rep from * to end.

Row 4: P2, *k2, p2; rep from * to end.

Rows 5–6: As rows 1–2.

Row 7: P2, *[KB1] twice, p2; rep from * to end.

Row 8: K2, *p2, k2; rep from * to end.

Rep these 8 rows.

Dotted ladder stitch

Multiple of 8 + 5.

Row 1 (RS): K2, p1, k2, *p3, k2, p1, k2; rep from * to end.

Row 2: [P1, k1] twice, p1, *k3, [p1, k1] twice, p1; rep from * to end.

Rep the last 2 rows once more.

Row 5: K1, *p3, k2, p1, k2; rep from * to last 4 sts, p3, k1.

Row 6: P1, k3, p1, *[k1, p1] twice, k3, p1; rep from * to end.

Rep the last 2 rows once more.

Rep these 8 rows.

Tip

If you have made a number of swatches to see which stitch patterns you like most or which work best with your yarn, you can try turning a collection of your swatches into a project. You could make the front of a patchwork pillow, a baby blanket, or some scented sachets.

Knot pattern

Multiple of 6 + 5.

Special abbreviation:

Make knot = P3tog leaving sts on left-hand needle, then knit them tog, then purl them tog again, slipping sts off needle at end.

Work 2 rows in st st, starting with knit.

Row 3 (RS): K1, *make knot, k3; rep from * to last 4 sts, make knot, k1.

Work 3 rows in st st, starting with purl.

Row 7: K4, *make knot, k3; rep from * to last st, k1.

Row 8: Purl.

Rep these 8 rows.

Trellis stitch

Multiple of 6 + 5.

Row 1 (RS): K1, p3, *keeping yarn at front of work sl 3 purlwise, p3; rep from * to last st, k1.

Row 2: P1, k3, *keeping yarn at back of work sl 3 purlwise, k3; rep from * to last st, p1.

Row 3: K1, p3, *k3, p3; rep from * to last st, k1.

Row 4: P1, k3, *p3, k3; rep from * to last st, p1.

Row 5: K5, *insert point of right-hand needle upward under the 2 strands in front of the slipped sts and knit the next st, then lift the 2 strands off over the point of the right-hand needle (called "pull up loop"), k5; rep from * to end.

Row 6: As row 3.

Row 7: P1, *keeping yarn at front sl 3 purlwise, p3; rep from * to last 4 sts, sl 3 purlwise, p1.

Row 8: K1, *keeping yarn at back sl 3 purlwise, k3; rep from * to last 4 sts, sl 3 purlwise, k1.

Row 9: As row 4.

Row 10: As row 3.

Row 11: K2, *pull up loop, k5; rep from * to last 3 sts, pull up loop, k2.

Row 12: As row 4.

Rep these 12 rows.

Bud stitch

Multiple of 6 + 5.

Note: Stitches should only be counted after row 6 or 12.

Row 1 (RS): P5, *k1, yo, p5; rep from * to end.

Row 2: K5, *p2, k5; rep from * to end.

Row 3: P5, *k2, p5; rep from * to end.

Rep the last 2 rows once more.

Row 6: K5, *p2tog, k5; rep from * to end.

Row 7: P2, *k1, yo, p5; rep from * to last 3 sts, k1, yo, p2.

Row 8: K2, *p2, k5; rep from * to last 4 sts, p2, k2.

Row 9: P2, *k2, p5; rep from * to last 4 sts, k2, p2.

Rep the last 2 rows once more.

Row 12: K2, *p2tog, k5; rep from * to last 4 sts, p2tog, k2.

Rep these 12 rows.

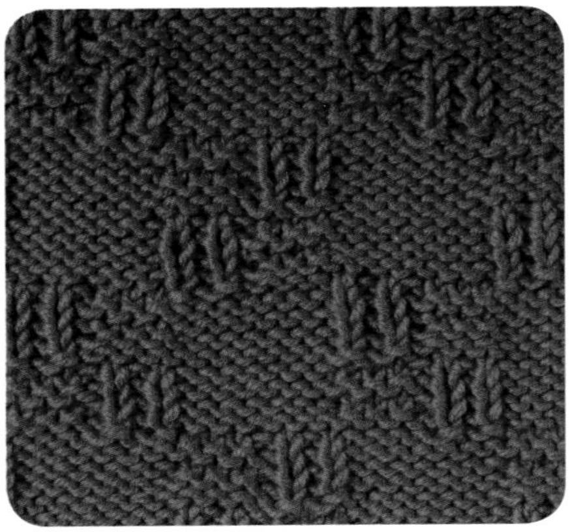

Compass check pattern

Multiple of 14 + 7.

Row 1 (WS): [P1, KB1] twice, *k10, [p1, KB1] twice; rep from * to last 3 sts, k3.

Row 2: K3, [PB1, k1] twice, *p7, k3, [PB1, k1] twice; rep from * to end.

Rep the last 2 rows once more.

Row 5: Knit.

Row 6: [K1, PB1] twice, *p10, [k1, PB1] twice; rep from * to last 3 sts, p3.

Row 7: P3, [KB1, p1] twice, *k7, p3, [KB1, p1] twice; rep from * to end.

Rep the last 2 rows once more.

Row 10: P7, *[k1, PB1] twice, p10; rep from * to end.

Row 11: K7, *p3, [KB1, p1] twice, k7; rep from * to end.

Rep the last 2 rows once more.

Row 14: Purl.

Row 15: K7, *[p1, KB1] twice, k10; rep from * to end.

Row 16: P7, *k3, [PB1, k1] twice, p7; rep from * to end.

Rep the last 2 rows once more.

Rep these 18 rows.

Mock cable on seed stitch

Multiple of 9 + 5.

Row 1 (RS): [K1, p1] twice, k1, *KB1, p2, KB1, [k1, p1] twice, k1; rep from * to end.

Row 2: *[K1, p1] 3 times, k2, p1; rep from * to last 5 sts, [k1, p1] twice, k1.

Rep the last 2 rows once more.

Row 5: [K1, p1] twice, k1, *yo, k1, p2, k1, lift yo over last 4 sts and off needle, [k1, p1] twice, k1; rep from * to end.

Row 6: As row 2.

Rep these 6 rows.

Puffed rib

Multiple of 3 + 2.
Note: Stitches should only be counted after row 4.
Row 1 (RS): P2, *yo, k1, yo, p2; rep from * to end.
Row 2: K2, *p3, k2; rep from * to end.
Row 3: P2, *k3, p2; rep from * to end.
Row 4: K2, *p3tog, k2; rep from * to end.
Rep these 4 rows.

Interrupted rib

Multiple of 2 + 1.
Row 1 (RS): P1, *k1, p1; rep from * to end.
Row 2: K1, *p1, k1; rep from * to end.
Row 3: Purl.
Row 4: Knit.
Rep these 4 rows.

Uneven rib

Multiple of 4 + 3.
Row 1: *K2, p2; rep from * to last 3 sts, k2, p1.
Rep this row.

Stockinette stitch checks

Multiple of 10 + 5.
Row 1 (RS): K5, *p5, k5; rep from * to end.
Row 2: P5, *k5, p5; rep from * to end.
Rep the last 2 rows once more, then row 1 again.
Row 6: K5, *p5, k5; rep from * to end.
Row 7: As row 2.
Rep the last 2 rows once more, then row 6 again.
Rep these 10 rows.

Ridged rib

Multiple of 2 + 1.
Rows 1–2: Knit.
Row 3 (RS): P1, *k1, p1; rep from * to end.
Row 4: K1, *p1, k1; rep from * to end.
Rep these 4 rows.

Garter slip stitch

Multiple of 2 + 1.
Row 1 (RS): Knit.
Row 2: Knit.
Row 3: K1, *sl 1 purlwise, k1; rep from * to end.
Row 4: K1, *yf, sl 1 purlwise, yb, k1; rep from * to end.
Knit 2 rows.
Row 7: K2, *sl 1 purlwise, k1; rep from * to last st, k1.
Row 8: K2, *yf, sl 1 purlwise, yb, k1; rep from * to last st, k1.
Rep these 8 rows.

Lattice stitch

Multiple of 6 + 1.

Row 1 (RS): K3, *p1, k5; rep from * to last 4 sts, p1, k3.

Row 2: P2, *k1, p1, k1, p3; rep from * to last 5 sts, k1, p1, k1, p2.

Row 3: K1, *p1, k3, p1, k1; rep from * to end.

Row 4: K1, *p5, k1; rep from * to end.

Row 5: As row 3.

Row 6: As row 2.

Rep these 6 rows.

Slanting diamonds

Multiple of 10.

Row 1 (RS): *K9, p1; rep from * to end.

Row 2: *K2, p8; rep from * to end.

Row 3: *K7, p3; rep from * to end.

Row 4: *K4, p6; rep from * to end.

Rows 5–6: *K5, p5; rep from * to end.

Row 7: K5, p4, *k6, p4; rep from * to last st, k1.

Row 8: P2, k3, *p7, k3; rep from * to last 5 sts, p5.

Row 9: K5, p2, *k8, p2; rep from * to last 3 sts, k3.

Row 10: P4, k1, *p9, k1; rep from * to last 5 sts, p5.

Row 11: K4, p1, *k9, p1; rep from * to last 5 sts, k5.

Row 12: P5, k2, *p8, k2; rep from * to last 3 sts, p3.

Row 13: K2, p3, *k7, p3; rep from * to last 5 sts, k5.

Row 14: P5, k4, *p6, k4; rep from * to last st, p1.

Rows 15–16: *P5, k5; rep from * to end.

Row 17: *P4, k6; rep from * to end.

Row 18: *P7, k3; rep from * to end.

Row 19: *P2, k8; rep from * to end.

Row 20: *P9, k1; rep from * to end.

Rep these 20 rows.

Steps

Multiple of 8 + 2.

Row 1 (RS): *K4, p4; rep from * to last 2 sts, k2.

Row 2: P2, *k4, p4; rep from * to end.

Rep the last 2 rows once more.

Row 5: K2, *p4, k4; rep from * to end.

Row 6: *P4, k4; rep from * to last 2 sts, p2.

Row 7: As row 5.

Row 8: As row 6.

Row 9: *P4, k4; rep from * to last 2 sts, p2.

Row 10: K2, *p4, k4; rep from * to end.

Rep the last 2 rows once more.

Row 13: As row 2.

Row 14: *K4, p4; rep from * to last 2 sts, k2.

Rep the last 2 rows once more.

Rep these 16 rows.

Harbor flag

Multiple of 10.

Row 1 (RS): P7, k2, *p8, k2; rep from * to last st, p1.
Row 2: *P1, k1, p2, k6; rep from * to end.
Row 3: *P5, k2, p1, k2; rep from * to end.
Row 4: *P3, k1, p2, k4; rep from * to end.
Row 5: *P3, k2, p1, k4; rep from * to end.
Row 6: *P5, k1, p2, k2; rep from * to end.
Row 7: *P1, k2, p1, k6; rep from * to end.
Row 8: As row 6.
Row 9: As row 5.
Row 10: As row 4.
Row 11: As row 3.
Row 12: As row 2.
Row 13: As row 1.
Row 14: *P2, k8; rep from * to end.
Rep these 14 rows.

Diagonal bobble stitch

Multiple of 6.

Special abbreviation:
MB (make bobble) = [Knit into front and back] 3 times into next st, then lift first, 2nd, 3rd, 4th, and 5th sts over 6th st.

Row 1 (RS): *K2, MB, p3; rep from * to end.
Row 2: *K3, p3; rep from * to end.
Row 3: P1, *k2, MB, p3; rep from * to last 5 sts, k2, MB, p2.
Row 4: K2, *p3, k3; rep from * to last 4 sts, p3, k1.
Row 5: P2, *k2, MB, p3; rep from * to last 4 sts, k2, MB, p1.
Row 6: K1, *p3, k3; rep from * to last 5 sts, p3, k2.
Row 7: *P3, k2, MB; rep from * to end.
Row 8: *P3, k3; rep from * to end.
Row 9: *MB, p3, k2; rep from * to end.
Row 10: P2, *k3, p3; rep from * to last 4 sts, k3, p1.
Row 11: K1, *MB, p3, k2; rep from * to last 5 sts, MB, p3, k1.
Row 12: P1, *k3, p3; rep from * to last 5 sts, k3, p2.
Rep these 12 rows.

Shingle stitch

Multiple of 10 + 5.

Row 1 (RS): K5, *KB1, [p1, KB1] twice, k5; rep from * to end.
Row 2: K5, *PB1, [k1, PB1] twice, k5; rep from * to end.
Rep the last 2 rows twice more.
Row 7: KB1, [p1, KB1] twice, *k5, KB1, [p1, KB1] twice; rep from * to end.
Row 8: PB1, [k1, PB1] twice, *k5, PB1, [k1, PB1] twice; rep from * to end.
Rep the last 2 rows twice more.
Rep these 12 rows.

Basket rib

Multiple of 2 + 1.

Row 1 (RS): Knit.

Row 2: Purl.

Row 3: K1, *sl 1 purlwise, k1; rep from * to end.

Row 4: K1, *yf, sl 1 purlwise, yb, k1; rep from * to end.

Rep these 4 rows.

Basketweave

Multiple of 4 + 3.

Rows 1 (RS) and 3: Knit.

Row 2: *K3, p1; rep from * to last 3 sts, k3.

Row 4: K1, *p1, k3; rep from * to last 2 sts, p1, k1.

Rep these 4 rows.

Mini bobble stitch

Multiple of 2 + 1.

Special abbreviation:

MB (make bobble) = (P1, k1, p1, k1) into next st, then lift 2nd, 3rd, and 4th sts over first st.

Row 1 (RS): Knit.

Row 2: K1, *MB, k1; rep from * to end.

Row 3: Knit.

Row 4: K2, *MB, k1; rep from * to last st, k1.

Rep these 4 rows.

Twisted stockinette stitch

Any number of stitches.

Row 1 (RS): Knit into the back of every st.

Row 2: Purl.

Rep these 2 rows.

Alternating triangles

Multiple of 5.

Row 1 (RS): *P1, k4; rep from * to end.

Rows 2–3: *P3, k2; rep from * to end.

Row 4: *P1, k4; rep from * to end.

Row 5: *K4, p1; rep from * to end.

Rows 6–7: *K2, p3; rep from * to end.

Row 8: As row 5.

Rep these 8 rows.

Bramble stitch

Multiple of 4 + 2.

Row 1 (RS): Purl.

Row 2: K1, *(k1, p1, k1) into next st, p3tog; rep from * to last st, k1.

Row 3: Purl.

Row 4: K1, *p3tog, (k1, p1, k1) into next st; rep from * to last st, k1.

Rep these 4 rows.

Slipped rib

Multiple of 4 + 3.
Row 1 (RS): K1, sl 1 purlwise, *k3, sl 1 purlwise; rep from * to last st, k1.
Row 2: P1, sl 1 purlwise, *p3, sl 1 purlwise; rep from * to last st, p1.
Row 3: *K3, sl 1 purlwise; rep from * to last 3 sts, k3.
Row 4: *P3, sl 1 purlwise; rep from * to last 3 sts, p3.
Rep these 4 rows.

Half brioche stitch (purl version)

Multiple of 2 + 1.
Row 1 (WS): Purl.
Row 2: K1, *K1B, k1; rep from * to end.
Row 3: Purl.
Row 4: K1B, *k1, K1B; rep from * to end.
Rep these 4 rows.

Seed slip stitch

Multiple of 2 + 1.
Row 1 (RS): K1, *sl 1 purlwise, k1; rep from * to end.
Row 2: K1, *yf, sl 1 purlwise, yb, k1; rep from * to end.
Row 3: K2, *sl 1 purlwise, k1; rep from * to last st, k1.
Row 4: K2, *yf, sl 1 purlwise, yb, k1; rep from * to last st, k1.
Rep these 4 rows.

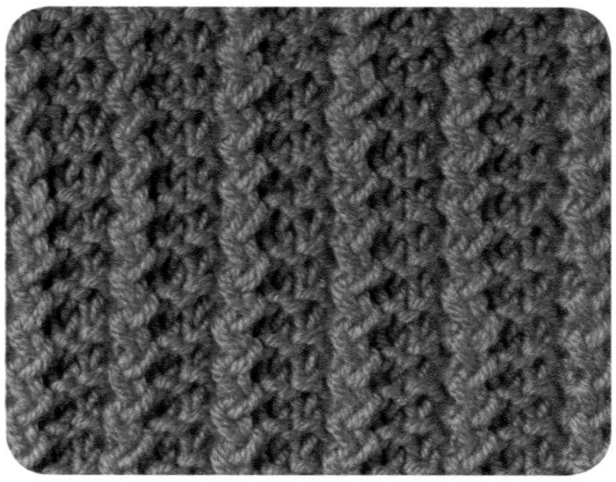

Garter stitch twisted rib

Multiple of 4.
Row 1 (RS): K1, *C2B, k2; rep from * to last 3 sts, C2B, k1.
Row 2: K1, *yf, C2P, yb, k2; rep from * to last 3 sts, yf, C2P, yb, k1.
Rep these 2 rows.

Knotted rib

Multiple of 5.
Note: Stitches should only be counted after row 2.
Row 1 (RS): P2, *knit into front and back of next st, p4; rep from * to last 3 sts, knit into front and back of next st, p2.
Row 2: K2, *p2tog, k4; rep from * to last 4 sts, p2tog, k2.
Rep these 2 rows.

Three-stitch twisted rib

Multiple of 5 + 2.
Row 1 (WS): K2, *p3, k2; rep from * to end.
Row 2: P2, *C3, p2; rep from * to end.
Rep these 2 rows.

Triple wave

Worked over 14 sts on a background of st st.

Row 1 (RS): P3, k8, p3.
Row 2: [K1, p1] twice, k2, p2, k2, [p1, k1] twice.
Row 3: P3, k3, p2, k3, p3.
Row 4: K1, p1, k1, p8, k1, p1, k1.
Row 5: P3, k1, p2, k2, p2, k1, p3.
Row 6: K1, p1, k1, p3, k2, p3, k1, p1, k1.
Rep these 6 rows.

Linked ribs

Multiple of 8 + 4.

Row 1 (RS): P4, *k1, p2, k1, p4; rep from * to end.
Row 2: K4, *p1, k2, p1, k4; rep from * to end.
Rep the last 2 rows once more.
Row 5: P4, *C2L, C2R, p4; rep from * to end.
Row 6: K4, *p4, k4; rep from * to end.
Rep these 6 rows.

Purled ladder stitch

Multiple of 4 + 2.

Rows 1–2: Knit.
Row 3 (RS): P2, *k2, p2; rep from * to end.
Row 4: K2, *p2, k2; rep from * to end.
Rows 5–6: Knit.
Row 7: As row 4.
Row 8: P2, *k2, p2; rep from * to end.
Rep these 8 rows.

Broken rib

Multiple of 2 + 1.

Row 1 (RS): Knit.
Row 2: P1, *k1, p1; rep from * to end.
Rep these 2 rows.

Rose stitch

Multiple of 2 + 1.

Row 1 (WS): K2, *p1, k1; rep from * to last st, k1.
Row 2: K1, *K1B, k1; rep from * to end.
Row 3: K1, *p1, k1; rep from * to end.
Row 4: K2, *K1B, k1; rep from * to last st, k1.
Rep these 4 rows.

Seed stitch rib

Multiple of 4 + 1.

Row 1: K2, *p1, k3; rep from * to last 3 sts, p1, k2.
Row 2: P1, *k3, p1; rep from * to end.
Rep these 2 rows.

Embossed rib

Multiple of 6 + 2.

Row 1 (RS): P2, *KB1, k1, p1, KB1, p2; rep from * to end.

Row 2: K2, *PB1, k1, p1, PB1, k2; rep from * to end.

Row 3: P2, *KB1, p1, k1, KB1, p2; rep from * to end.

Row 4: K2, *PB1, p1, k1, PB1, k2; rep from * to end.

Rep these 4 rows.

Garter stitch steps

Multiple of 8.

Row 1 (RS) and every alt row: Knit.

Rows 2 and 4: *K4, p4; rep from * to end.

Rows 6 and 8: K2, *p4, k4; rep from * to last 6 sts, p4, k2.

Rows 10 and 12: *P4, k4; rep from * to end.

Rows 14 and 16: P2, *k4, p4; rep from * to last 6 sts, k4, p2.

Rep these 16 rows.

Ridge and furrow

Worked over 23 sts on a background of st st.

Row 1 (RS): P4, k7, p1, k7, p4.

Row 2: K1, p2, k1, p5, [k1, p1] twice, k1, p5, k1, p2, k1.

Row 3: P4, k4, [p1, k2] twice, p1, k4, p4.

Row 4: K1, p2, [k1, p3] 4 times, k1, p2, k1.

Row 5: P4, k2, [p1, k4] twice, p1, k2, p4.

Row 6: K1, p2, k1, p1, [k1, p5] twice, k1, p1, k1, p2, k1.

Rep these 6 rows.

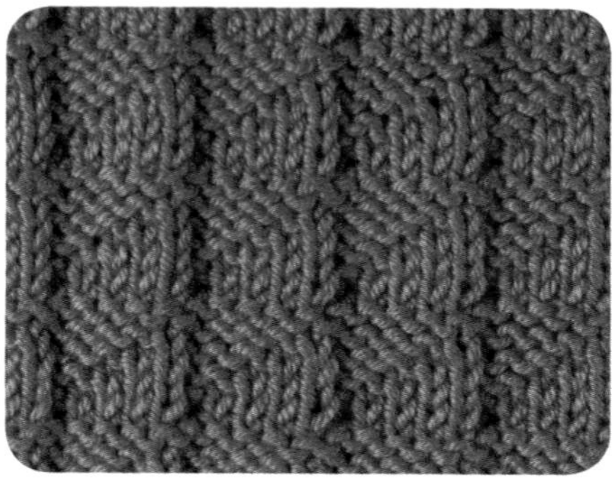

Divided boxes

Multiple of 5.

Row 1 (RS): Knit.

Row 2: *K1, p4; rep from * to end.

Row 3: *K3, p2; rep from * to end.

Row 4: As row 3.

Row 5: As row 2.

Row 6: Knit.

Rep these 6 rows.

Twisted seed stitch

Multiple of 2 + 1.

Row 1 (WS): Knit.

Row 2: K1, *K1B, k1; rep from * to end.

Row 3: Knit.

Row 4: K1B, *k1, K1B; rep from * to end.

Rep these 4 rows.

Tile stitch

Multiple of 6 + 4.

Row 1 (RS): K4, *p2, k4; rep from * to end.

Row 2: P4, *k2, p4; rep from * to end.

Rep the last 2 rows twice more.

Row 7: As row 2.

Row 8: K4, *p2, k4; rep from * to end.

Rep these 8 rows.

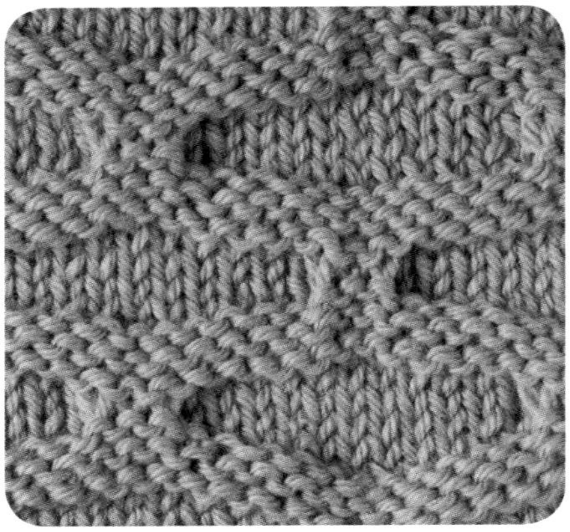

Biba trellis

Multiple of 14 + 5.

Note: Slip sts purlwise with yarn at WS of work.

Row 1 (RS): Purl.

Row 2: Knit.

Row 3: Purl.

Row 4: P8, sl 3, *p11, sl 3; rep from * to last 8 sts, p8.

Row 5: K8, sl 3, *k11, sl 3; rep from * to last 8 sts, k8.

Rep the last 2 rows once more, then row 4 again.

Rows 9–11: As rows 1–3.

Row 12: P1, sl 3, *p11, sl 3; rep from * to last st, p1.

Row 13: K1, sl 3, *k11, sl 3; rep from * to last st, k1.

Rep the last 2 rows once more, then row 12 again.

Rep these 16 rows.

Diagonal checks

Multiple of 5.

Row 1 (RS): *P1, k4; rep from * to end.

Row 2: *P3, k2; rep from * to end.

Row 3: As row 2.

Row 4: *P1, k4; rep from * to end.

Row 5: *K1, p4; rep from * to end.

Row 6: *K3, p2; rep from * to end.

Row 7: As row 6.

Row 8: As row 5.

Rep these 8 rows.

Diagonal rib I

Multiple of 4.

Row 1 (RS): *K2, p2; rep from * to end.

Row 2: As row 1.

Row 3: K1, *p2, k2; rep from * to last 3 sts, p2, k1.

Row 4: P1, *k2, p2; rep from * to last 3 sts, k2, p1.

Row 5: *P2, k2; rep from * to end.

Row 6: As row 5.

Row 7: As row 4.

Row 8: As row 3

Rep these 8 rows.

Tip

If you are designing a garment, take your swatches and pin them onto an old sweater or a shape you like to get a sense of scale and what the finished item might look like. Alternately, pin the swatch onto a stand or a tailor's dummy (a patient family member or friend will also do!) and calculate the number of stitches and rows required.

Diamond net mask

Worked over 19 sts on a background of st st.

Row 1 (RS): P3, k6, p1, k6, p3.
Row 2: K1, p1, k1, [p6, k1] twice, p1, k1.
Row 3: P3, k5, p1, k1, p1, k5, p3.
Row 4: K1, p1, k1, [p5, k1, p1, k1] twice.
Row 5: P3, k4, [p1, k1] twice, p1, k4, p3.
Row 6: K1, p1, k1, p4, [k1, p1] twice, k1, p4, k1, p1, k1.
Row 7: P3, k3, [p1, k1] 3 times, p1, k3, p3.
Row 8: K1, p1, k1, p3, [k1, p1] 3 times, k1, p3, k1, p1, k1.
Row 9: P3, k2, p1, k1, p1, k3, p1, k1, p1, k2, p3.
Row 10: K1, p1, k1, p2, k1, p1, k1, p3, k1, p1, k1, p2, k1, p1, k1.
Row 11: P3, [k1, p1] twice, k5, [p1, k1] twice, p3.
Row 12: [K1, p1] 3 times, k1, p5, [k1, p1] 3 times, k1.
Row 13: As row 9.
Row 14: As row 10.
Row 15: As row 7.
Row 16: As row 8.
Row 17: As row 5.
Row 18: As row 6.
Row 19: As row 3.
Row 20: As row 4.
Rep these 20 rows.

Seed stitch panels

Multiple of 8 + 7.

Row 1 (WS): K3, *p1, k3; rep from * to end.
Row 2: P3, *k1, p3; rep from * to end.
Row 3: K2, p1, k1, *[p1, k2] twice, p1, k1; rep from * to last 3 sts, p1, k2.
Row 4: P2, k1, p1, *[k1, p2] twice, k1, p1; rep from * to last 3 sts, k1, p2.
Row 5: K1, *p1, k1; rep from * to end.
Row 6: P1, *k1, p1; rep from * to end.
Row 7: As row 3.
Row 8: As row 4.
Row 9: As row 1.
Row 10: As row 2.
Rep these 10 rows.

Anchor

Worked over 17 sts on a background of st st.

Row 1 (RS): P3, k11, p3.
Row 2: K1, p1, [k1, p5] twice, k1, p1, k1.
Row 3: P3, k4, p1, k1, p1, k4, p3.
Row 4: K1, p1, k1, p3, [k1, p1] twice, k1, p3, k1, p1, k1.
Row 5: P3, k2, p1, k5, p1, k2, p3.
Row 6: [K1, p1] twice, [k1, p3] twice, [k1, p1] twice, k1.
Row 7: P3, k1, p1, k7, p1, k1, p3.
Row 8: K1, p1, [k1, p5] twice, k1, p1, k1.
Row 9: As row 1.
Rep the last 2 rows once more.
Row 12: K1, p1, k1, p3, k5, p3, k1, p1, k1.
Row 13: P3, k3, p5, k3, p3.
Row 14: As row 12.
Row 15: As row 1.
Row 16: As row 8.
Rep the last 2 rows once more.
Row 19: As row 3.
Row 20: K1, p1, [k1, p3] 3 times, k1, p1, k1.
Row 21: As row 3.
Row 22: As row 2.
Row 23: As row 1.
Row 24: K1, p1, k1, p11, k1, p1, k1.
Rep these 24 rows.

Topiary stitch

Multiple of 24 + 3.

Row 1 (RS): P1, KB1, *p5, KB1, [p1, KB1] 6 times, p5, KB1; rep from * to last st, p1.

Row 2: K1, p1, *k5, p1, [k1, p1] 6 times, k5, p1; rep from * to last st, k1.

Row 3: As row 1.

Row 4: K1, p1, *k7, p1, [k1, p1] 4 times, k7, p1; rep from * to last st, k1.

Row 5: P1, KB1, *p7, KB1, [p1, KB1] 4 times, p7, KB1; rep from * to last st, p1.

Row 6: K1, p1, k9, p1, [k1, p1] twice, *[k9, p1] twice, [k1, p1] twice; rep from * to last 11 sts, k9, p1, k1.

Row 7: P1, KB1, p9, KB1, [p1, KB1] twice, *[p9, KB1] twice, [p1, KB1] twice; rep from * to last 11 sts, p9, KB1, p1.

Row 8: K1, p1, *k11, p1; rep from * to last st, k1.

Row 9: P1, KB1, *p11, KB1; rep from * to last st, p1.

Row 10: *[K1, p1] twice, [k9, p1] twice; rep from * to last 3 sts, k1, p1, k1.

Row 11: *[P1, KB1] twice, [p9, KB1] twice; rep from * to last 3 sts, p1, KB1, p1.

Row 12: [K1, p1] 3 times, [k7, p1] twice, *[k1, p1] 4 times, [k7, p1] twice; rep from * to last 5 sts, k1, [p1, k1] twice.

Row 13: [P1, KB1] 3 times, [p7, KB1] twice, *[p1, KB1] 4 times, [p7, KB1] twice; rep from * to last 5 sts, p1, [KB1, p1] twice.

Row 14: [K1, p1] 4 times, [k5, p1] twice, *[k1, p1] 6 times, [k5, p1] twice; rep from * to last 7 sts, k1, [p1, k1] 3 times.

Row 15: [P1, KB1] 4 times, [p5, KB1] twice, *[p1, KB1] 6 times, [p5, KB1] twice; rep from * to last 7 sts, p1, [KB1, p1] 3 times.

Rep the last 2 rows twice more.

Rows 20–21: As rows 12–13.

Rows 22–23: As rows 10–11.

Rows 24–25: As rows 8–9.

Rows 26–27: As rows 6–7.

Rows 28–29: As rows 4–5.

Row 30: As row 2.

Rows 31–32: As rows 1–2.

Rep these 32 rows.

Seed stitch diamonds

Multiple of 10 + 7.

Row 1 (RS): *[K3, p1] twice, k1, p1; rep from * to last 7 sts, k3, p1, k3.

Row 2: *[P3, k1] twice, p1, k1; rep from * to last 7 sts, p3, k1, p3.

Row 3: K2, p1, k1, p1, *[k3, p1] twice, k1, p1; rep from * to last 2 sts, k2.

Row 4: P2, k1, p1, k1, *[p3, k1] twice, p1, k1; rep from * to last 2 sts, p2.

Row 5: [K1, p1] 3 times, *[k2, p1] twice, [k1, p1] twice; rep from * to last st, k1.

Row 6: [P1, k1] 3 times, *[p2, k1] twice, [p1, k1] twice; rep from * to last st, p1.

Row 7: As row 3.

Row 8: As row 4.

Row 9: As row 1.

Row 10: As row 2.

Row 11: K3, p1, *k2, [p1, k1] twice, p1, k2, p1; rep from * to last 3 sts, k3.

Row 12: P3, k1, *p2, [k1, p1] twice, k1, p2, k1; rep from * to last 3 sts, p3.

Rep these 12 rows.

Pyramid triangles

Multiple of 14 + 1.

Row 1 (RS): K7, p1, *k13, p1; rep from * to last 7 sts, k7.

Row 2 and every alt row: Purl.

Row 3: K6, p3, *k11, p3; rep from * to last 6 sts, k6.

Row 5: K5, p5, *k9, p5; rep from * to last 5 sts, k5.

Row 7: K4, p7, *k7, p7; rep from * to last 4 sts, k4.

Row 9: K3, p9, *k5, p9; rep from * to last 3 sts, k3.

Row 11: K2, p11, *k3, p11; rep from * to last 2 sts, k2.

Row 13: K1, *p13, k1; rep from * to end.

Row 15: P1, *k13, p1; rep from * to end.

Row 17: P2, k11, *p3, k11; rep from * to last 2 sts, p2.

Row 19: P3, k9, *p5, k9; rep from * to last 3 sts, p3.

Row 21: P4, k7, *p7, k7; rep from * to last 4 sts, p4.

Row 23: P5, k5, *p9, k5; rep from * to last 5 sts, p5.

Row 25: P6, k3, *p11, k3; rep from * to last 6 sts, p6.

Row 27: P7, k1, *p13, k1; rep from * to last 7 sts, p7.

Row 28: Purl.

Rep these 28 rows.

Unusual pattern check

Multiple of 8.

Row 1 (RS): Knit.

Row 2: *K4, p4; rep from * to end.

Row 3: P1, *k4, p4; rep from * to last 7 sts, k4, p3.

Row 4: K2, *p4, k4; rep from * to last 6 sts, p4, k2.

Row 5: P3, *k4, p4; rep from * to last 5 sts, k4, p1.

Row 6: *P4, k4; rep from * to end.

Row 7: Knit.

Row 8: *K4, p4; rep from * to end.

Rep the last row 3 times more.

Row 12: Purl.

Row 13: As row 6.

Row 14: K1, *p4, k4; rep from * to last 7 sts, p4, k3.

Row 15: P2, *k4, p4; rep from * to last 6 sts, k4, p2.

Row 16: K3, *p4, k4; rep from * to last 5 sts, p4, k1.

Row 17: As row 2.

Row 18: Purl.

Row 19: *P4, k4; rep from * to end.

Rep the last row 3 times more.

Rep these 22 rows.

Chevron rib

Multiple of 18 + 1.

Row 1 (RS): P1, *k1, p2, k2, p2, k1, p1; rep from * to end.

Row 2: *K3, p2, k2, p2, k1, [p2, k2] twice; rep from * to last st, k1.

Row 3: *[P2, k2] twice, p3, k2, p2, k2, p1; rep from * to last st, p1.

Row 4: *K1, p2, k2, p2, k5, p2, k2, p2; rep from * to last st, k1.

Rep these 4 rows.

Woven stitch II

Multiple of 4 + 2.

Row 1 (RS): Knit.

Row 2: Purl.

Row 3: K2, *p2, k2; rep from * to end.

Row 4: P2, *k2, p2; rep from * to end.

Row 5: Knit.

Row 6: Purl.

Row 7: As row 4.

Row 8: As row 3.

Rep these 8 rows.

Stockinette stitch ridge

Multiple of 2.

Note: Stitches should not be counted after row 2.

Row 1 (RS): Knit.

Row 2: P1, *k2tog; rep from * to last st, p1.

Row 3: K1, *knit into front and back of next st; rep from * to last st, k1.

Row 4: Purl.

Rep these 4 rows.

Centipede stitch

Multiple of 6 + 4.

Row 1 (RS): Knit.

Row 2: P1, k2, *p4, k2; rep from * to last st, p1.

Rep the last 2 rows 5 times more.

Row 13: Knit.

Row 14: P4, *k2, p4; rep from * to end.

Rep the last 2 rows 5 times more.

Rep these 24 rows.

Caterpillar stitch

Multiple of 8 + 6.

Row 1 (RS): K4, p2, *k6, p2; rep from * to end.

Row 2: P1, k2, *p6, k2; rep from * to last 3 sts, p3.

Row 3: K2, p2, *k6, p2; rep from * to last 2 sts, k2.

Row 4: P3, k2, *p6, k2; rep from * to last st, p1.

Row 5: P2, *k6, p2; rep from * to last 4 sts, k4.

Row 6: Purl.

Rep these 6 rows.

Little chevron rib

Multiple of 10 + 1.

Row 1 (RS): P1, *k1, p1, [k2, p1] twice, k1, p1; rep from * to end.

Row 2: K1, *p2, [k1, p1] twice, k1, p2, k1; rep from * to end.

Row 3: P1, *k3, p3, k3, p1; rep from * to end.

Row 4: K2, *p3, k1, p3, k3; rep from * to last 9 sts, p3, k1, p3, k2.

Rep these 4 rows.

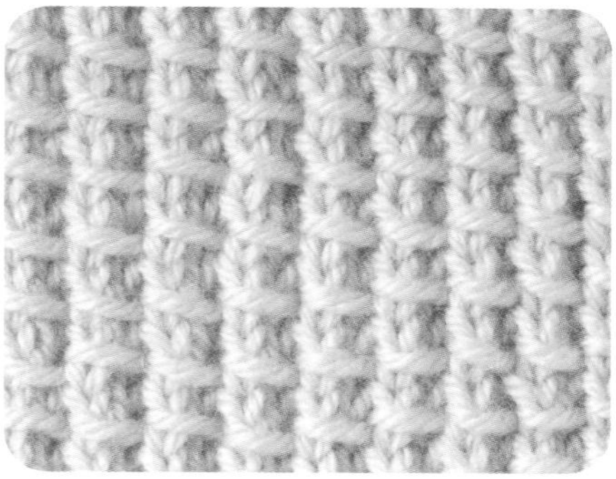

Pillar stitch

Multiple of 2.
Row 1 (WS): Purl.
Row 2: K1, *yo, k2, pass yo over k2; rep from * to last st, k1.
Rep these 2 rows.

Waffle stitch

Multiple of 3 + 1.
Row 1 (RS): P1, *k2, p1; rep from * to end.
Row 2: K1, *p2, k1; rep from * to end.
Row 3: As row 1.
Row 4: Knit.
Rep these 4 rows.

Tweed stitch

Multiple of 2 + 1.
Row 1 (RS): K1, *yf, sl 1 purlwise, yb, k1; rep from * to end.
Row 2: P2, *yb, sl 1 purlwise, yf, p1; rep from * to last st, p1.
Rep these 2 rows.

Horizontal dash stitch

Multiple of 10 + 6.
Row 1 (RS): P6, *k4, p6; rep from * to end.
Row 2 and every alt row: Purl.
Row 3: Knit.
Row 5: P1, *k4, p6; rep from * to last 5 sts, k4, p1.
Row 7: Knit.
Row 8: Purl.
Rep these 8 rows.

Open twisted rib

Multiple of 5 + 3.
Note: Stitches should not be counted after row 2 or 3.
Row 1 (WS): K1, PB1, k1, *p2, k1, PB1, k1; rep from * to end.
Row 2: P1, KB1, p1, *k1, yo, k1, p1, KB1, p1; rep from * to end.
Row 3: K1, PB1, k1, *p3, k1, PB1, k1; rep from * to end.
Row 4: P1, KB1, p1, *k3, pass 3rd st on right-hand needle over first 2 sts, p1, KB1, p1; rep from * to end.
Rep these 4 rows.

Diagonal rib II

Multiple of 4.
Rows 1–2: *K2, p2; rep from * to end.
Row 3 (RS): K1, *p2, k2; rep from * to last 3 sts, p2, k1.
Row 4: P1, *k2, p2; rep from * to last 3 sts, k2, p1.
Rows 5–6: *P2, k2; rep from * to end.
Row 7: As row 4.
Row 8: As row 3.
Rep these 8 rows.

Large basketweave

Multiple of 6 + 2.

Row 1 (RS): Knit.

Row 2: Purl.

Row 3: K2, *p4, k2; rep from * to end.

Row 4: P2, *k4, p2; rep from * to end.

Rep the last 2 rows once more.

Row 7: Knit.

Row 8: Purl.

Row 9: P3, *k2, p4; rep from * to last 5 sts, k2, p3.

Row 10: K3, *p2, k4; rep from * to last 5 sts, p2, k3.

Rep the last 2 rows once more.

Rep these 12 rows.

Broken rib diagonal

Multiple of 6.

Row 1 (RS): *K4, p2; rep from * to end.

Row 2: *K2, p4; rep from * to end.

Row 3: As row 1.

Row 4: As row 2.

Row 5: K2, *p2, k4; rep from * to last 4 sts, p2, k2.

Row 6: P2, *k2, p4; rep from * to last 4 sts, k2, p2.

Row 7: As row 5.

Row 8: As row 6.

Row 9: *P2, k4; rep from * to end.

Row 10: *P4, k2; rep from * to end.

Row 11: As row 9.

Row 12: As row 10.

Rep these 12 rows.

Stripe pillars

Multiple of 6 + 3.

Work 4 rows in st st, starting with knit.

Row 5 (RS): K1, *p1, k1; rep from * to end.

Row 6: P1, *k1, p1; rep from * to end.

Rep the last 2 rows once more.

Row 9: K1, p1, k1, *p3, k1, p1, k1; rep from * to end.

Row 10: P1, k1, p1, *k3, p1, k1, p1; rep from * to end.

Rep the last 2 rows once more.

Rep these 12 rows.

Tip

When creating a garment design, think about assembling the swatches on a mood board. Consider adding the trims, buttons, ribbons, and edging you may wish to use. You could also sew buttons onto the swatch to make sure that they work with the design and don't get lost.

Diamond panels

Multiple of 8 + 1.

Row 1 (RS): Knit.

Row 2: K1, *p7, k1; rep from * to end.

Row 3: K4, *p1, k7; rep from * to last 5 sts, p1, k4.

Row 4: K1, *p2, k1, p1, k1, p2, k1; rep from * to end.

Row 5: K2, *[p1, k1] twice, p1, k3; rep from * to last 7 sts, [p1, k1] twice, p1, k2.

Row 6: As row 4.

Row 7: As row 3.

Row 8: As row 2.

Rep these 8 rows.

Textured tiles

Multiple of 10 + 6.

Row 1 (RS): P1, *k4, p1; rep from * to end.

Row 2: K1, *p4, k1; rep from * to end.

Rep the last 2 rows once more, then row 1 again.

Row 6: K6, *p4, k6; rep from * to end.

Row 7: As row 1.

Rep the last 2 rows twice more.

Row 12: As row 2.

Row 13: As row 1.

Rep the last 2 rows once more.

Row 16: K1, p4, *k6, p4; rep from * to last st, k1.

Row 17: As row 1.

Rep the last 2 rows once more, then row 16 again.

Rep these 20 rows.

Enlarged basket stitch

Multiple of 18 + 10.

Row 1 (RS): K11, *p2, k2, p2, k12; rep from * to last 17 sts, p2, k2, p2, k11.

Row 2: P1, *k8, [p2, k2] twice, p2; rep from * to last 9 sts, k8, p1.

Row 3: K1, *p8, [k2, p2] twice, k2; rep from * to last 9 sts, p8, k1.

Row 4: P11, *k2, p2, k2, p12; rep from * to last 17 sts, k2, p2, k2, p11.

Rep the last 4 rows once more.

Row 9: Knit.

Row 10: [P2, k2] twice, p12, *k2, p2, k2, p12; rep from * to last 8 sts, [k2, p2] twice.

Row 11: [K2, p2] twice, k2, *p8, [k2, p2] twice, k2; rep from * to end.

Row 12: [P2, k2] twice, p2, *k8, [p2, k2] twice, p2; rep from * to end.

Row 13: [K2, p2] twice, k12, *p2, k2, p2, k12; rep from * to last 8 sts, [p2, k2] twice.

Rep the last 4 rows once more.

Row 18: Purl.

Rep these 18 rows.

Garter and slip stitch

Multiple of 6 + 4.

Row 1 (RS): Knit.

Row 2: K1, *yf, sl 2 purlwise, yb, k4; rep from * to last 3 sts, yf, sl 2 purlwise, yb, k1.

Row 3: K1, *keeping yarn at back sl 2 purlwise, k4; rep from * to last 3 sts, sl 2 purlwise, k1.

Rep the last 2 rows once more.

Row 6: As row 2.

Row 7: Knit.

Row 8: K4, *yf, sl 2 purlwise, yb, k4; rep from * to end.

Row 9: K4, *keeping yarn at back sl 2 purlwise, k4; rep from * to end.

Rep the last 2 rows once more.

Row 12: As row 8.

Rep these 12 rows.

Chevron

Multiple of 8 + 1.

Row 1 (RS): K1, *p7, k1; rep from * to end.

Row 2: P1, *k7, p1; rep from * to end.

Row 3: K2, *p5, k3; rep from * to last 7 sts, p5, k2.

Row 4: P2, *k5, p3; rep from * to last 7 sts, k5, p2.

Row 5: K3, *p3, k5; rep from * to last 6 sts, p3, k3.

Row 6: P3, *k3, p5; rep from * to last 6 sts, k3, p3.

Row 7: K4, *p1, k7; rep from * to last 5 sts, p1, k4.

Row 8: P4, *k1, p7; rep from * to last 5 sts, k1, p4.

Row 9: As row 2.

Row 10: As row 1.

Row 11: As row 4.

Row 12: As row 3.

Row 13: As row 6.

Row 14: As row 5.

Row 15: As row 8.

Row 16: As row 7.

Rep these 16 rows.

Intertwined texture stitch

Multiple of 15 + 2.

Row 1 (RS): *P13, k2; rep from * to last 2 sts, p2.

Row 2: K2, *p2, k13; rep from * to end.

Row 3: As row 1.

Row 4: Purl.

Row 5: P2, *k2, p1, [k1, p1] 4 times, k2, p2; rep from * to end.

Row 6: K2, *p3, k1, [p1, k1] 3 times, p3, k2; rep from * to end.

Rep the last 2 rows 4 times more.

Row 15: P2, *k2, p13; rep from * to end.

Row 16: *K13, p2; rep from * to last 2 sts, k2.

Row 17: As row 15.

Row 18: Purl.

Rep these 18 rows.

Bobble rib

Multiple of 8 + 3.

Special abbreviation:

MB (make bobble) = [P1, k1] twice into next st, then lift first 3 of these sts one at a time over 4th st.

Row 1 (RS): K3, *p2, MB, p2, k3; rep from * to end.

Row 2: P3, *k2, p1, k2, p3; rep from * to end.

Row 3: K3, *p2, k1, p2, k3; rep from * to end.

Row 4: As row 2.

Rep these 4 rows.

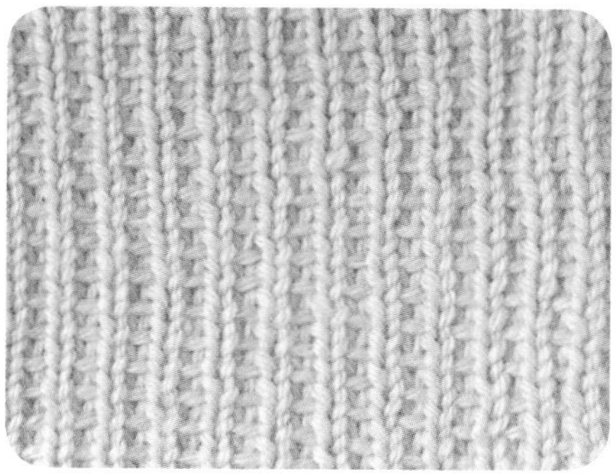

Slip stitch rib

Multiple of 2 + 1.

Row 1 (WS): Purl.

Row 2: K1, *yf, sl 1 purlwise, yb, k1; rep from * to end.

Rep these 2 rows.

Granite rib

Multiple of 8 + 2.

Row 1 (RS): K2, *[C2F] 3 times, k2; rep from * to end.

Row 2: Purl.

Row 3: K2, *[knit 3rd st from left-hand needle, then 2nd st, then first stitch, slipping all 3 sts off needle tog] twice, k2; rep from * to end.

Row 4: Purl.

Rep these 4 rows.

Basketweave rib

Multiple of 15 + 8.

Row 1 (RS): *P3, k2, p3, k1, [C2F] 3 times; rep from * to last 8 sts, p3, k2, p3.

Row 2: *K3, purl 2nd st on needle then purl first st, slipping both sts off needle tog (called "C2P"), k3, p1, [C2P] 3 times; rep from * to last 8 sts, k3, C2P, k3.

Rep these 2 rows.

Garter stitch ridges

Any number of stitches.

Row 1 (RS): Knit.

Row 2: Purl.

Rep the last 2 rows once more.

Purl 6 rows.

Rep these 10 rows.

Piqué rib

Multiple of 10 + 3.

Row 1 (RS): K3, *p3, k1, p3, k3; rep from * to end.

Row 2: P3, *k3, p1, k3, p3; rep from * to end.

Row 3: As row 1.

Row 4: Knit.

Rep these 4 rows.

Ladder tile

Multiple of 12.

Row 1 (RS): K4, p1, *k11, p1; rep from * to last 7 sts, k7.

Row 2 and every alt row: Purl.

Rows 3 and 5: K4, p2, *k10, p2; rep from * to last 6 sts, k6.

Row 7: K4, p7, *k5, p7; rep from * to last st, k1.

Row 9: *K4, p8; rep from * to end.

Row 11: K1, p7, *k5, p7; rep from * to last 4 sts, k4.

Row 13: *P8, k4; rep from * to end.

Rows 15 and 17: K6, p2, *k10, p2; rep from * to last 4 sts, k4.

Row 19: K7, p1, *k11, p1; rep from * to last 4 sts, k4.

Row 20: Purl.

Rep these 20 rows.

Spiral rib

Multiple of 6 + 3.

Row 1 (RS): K3, *p3, k3; rep from * to end.

Row 2: P3, *k3, p3; rep from * to end.

Row 3: As row 1.

Row 4: K1, *p3, k3; rep from * to last 2 sts, p2.

Row 5: K2, *p3, k3; rep from * to last st, p1.

Row 6: As row 4.

Row 7: As row 4.

Row 8: As row 5.

Row 9: As row 4.

Row 10: K3, *p3, k3; rep from * to end.

Row 11: As row 2.

Row 12: As row 10.

Row 13: P2, *k3, p3; rep from * to last st, k1.

Row 14: P1, *k3, p3; rep from * to last 2 sts, k2.

Row 15: As row 13.

Row 16: As row 13.

Row 17: As row 14.

Row 18: As row 13.

Rep these 18 rows.

Dotted chevron

Multiple of 18.

Row 1 (RS): K8, *p2, k16; rep from * to last 10 sts, p2, k8.

Row 2: P7, *k4, p14; rep from * to last 11 sts, k4, p7.

Row 3: P1, *k5, p2, k2, p2, k5, p2; rep from * to last 17 sts, k5, p2, k2, p2, k5, p1.

Row 4: K2, *p3, k2, p4, k2, p3, k4; rep from * to last 16 sts, p3, k2, p4, k2, p3, k2.

Row 5: P1, *k3, p2, k6, p2, k3, p2; rep from * to last 17 sts, k3, p2, k6, p2, k3, p1.

Row 6: P3, *k2, [p3, k2] twice, p6; rep from * to last 15 sts, k2, [p3, k2] twice, p3.

Row 7: K2, *p2, k3, p4, k3, p2, k4; rep from * to last 16 sts, p2, k3, p4, k3, p2, k2.

Row 8: P1, *k2, [p5, k2] twice, p2; rep from * to last 17 sts, k2, [p5, k2] twice, p1.

Row 9: P2, *k14, p4; rep from * to last 16 sts, k14, p2.

Row 10: K1, *p16, k2; rep from * to last 17 sts, p16, k1.

Rep these 10 rows.

Tweed pattern

Multiple of 6 + 3.

Row 1 (RS): K3, *p3, k3; rep from * to end.

Rep the last row twice more.

Row 4: Knit.

Row 5: Purl.

Row 6: Knit.

Row 7: K3, *p3, k3; rep from * to end.

Rep the last row twice more.

Row 10: Purl.

Row 11: Knit.

Row 12: Purl.

Rep these 12 rows.

Chain stitch rib

Multiple of 3 + 2.

Row 1 (WS): K2, *p1, k2; rep from * to end.

Row 2: P2, *k1, p2; rep from * to end.

Row 3: As row 1.

Row 4: P2, *yb, insert needle through center of st 3 rows below next st on needle and knit this in the usual way slipping st above off needle at the same time, p2; rep from * to end.

Rep these 4 rows.

Diamond pattern

Multiple of 8 + 1.

Row 1 (RS): P1, *k7, p1; rep from * to end.

Row 2: K2, p5, *k3, p5; rep from * to last 2 sts, k2.

Row 3: K1, *p2, k3, p2, k1; rep from * to end.

Row 4: P2, k2, p1, k2, *p3, k2, p1, k2; rep from * to last 2 sts, p2.

Row 5: K3, p3, *k5, p3; rep from * to last 3 sts, k3.

Row 6: P4, k1, *p7, k1; rep from * to last 4 sts, p4.

Row 7: As row 5.

Row 8: As row 4.

Row 9: As row 3.

Row 10: As row 2.

Rep these 10 rows.

Mock cable rib

Multiple of 7 + 2.

Row 1 (RS): P2, *C2B, k3, p2; rep from * to end.

Row 2 and every alt row: K2, *p5, k2; rep from * to end.

Row 3: P2, *k1, C2B, k2, p2; rep from * to end.

Row 5: P2, *k2, C2B, k1, p2; rep from * to end.

Row 7: P2, *k3, C2B, p2; rep from * to end.

Row 8: K2, *p5, k2; rep from * to end.

Rep these 8 rows.

Brick stitch

Multiple of 4 + 1.

Row 1 (RS): K4, *k1 winding yarn twice around needle, k3; rep from * to last st, k1.

Row 2: P4, *sl 1 purlwise dropping extra loop, p3; rep from * to last st, p1.

Row 3: K4, *sl 1 purlwise, k3; rep from * to last st, k1.

Row 4: K4, *yf, sl 1 purlwise, yb, k3; rep from * to last st, k1.

Row 5: K2, *k1 winding yarn twice around needle, k3; rep from * to last 3 sts, k1 winding yarn twice around needle, k2.

Row 6: P2, *sl 1 purlwise dropping extra loop, p3; rep from * to last 3 sts, sl 1 purlwise, p2.

Row 7: K2, *sl 1 purlwise, k3; rep from * to last 3 sts, sl 1 purlwise, k2.

Row 8: K2, *yf, sl 1 purlwise, yb, k3, rep from * to last 3 sts, yf, sl 1 purlwise, yb, k2.

Rep these 8 rows.

Pyramids II

Multiple of 8 + 1.

Row 1 (WS): P1, *k1, p1; rep from * to end.

Row 2: K1, *p1, k1; rep from * to end.

Rep the last 2 rows once more.

Row 5: P2, *[k1, p1] twice, k1, p3; rep from * to last 7 sts, [k1, p1] twice, k1, p2.

Row 6: K2, *[p1, k1] twice, p1, k3; rep from * to last 7 sts, [p1, k1] twice, p1, k2.

Rep the last 2 rows once more.

Row 9: P3, *k1, p1, k1, p5; rep from * to last 6 sts, k1, p1, k1, p3.

Row 10: K3, *p1, k1, p1, k5; rep from * to last 6 sts, p1, k1, p1, k3.

Rep the last 2 rows once more.

Row 13: P4, *k1, p7; rep from * to last 5 sts, k1, p4.

Row 14: K4, *p1, k7; rep from * to last 5 sts, p1, k4.

Rep the last 2 rows once more.

Rep these 16 rows.

Zigzag stitch

Multiple of 6.

Row 1 (RS): *K3, p3; rep from * to end.

Row 2 and every alt row: Purl.

Row 3: P1, *k3, p3; rep from * to last 5 sts, k3, p2.

Row 5: P2, *k3, p3; rep from * to last 4 sts, k3, p1.

Row 7: *P3, k3; rep from * to end.

Row 9: As row 5.

Row 11: As row 3.

Row 12: Purl.

Rep these 12 rows.

Spaced checks

Multiple of 10 + 1.

Row 1 (WS): Purl.

Row 2: K4, *p3, k7; rep from * to last 7 sts, p3, k4.

Row 3: P4, *k3, p7; rep from * to last 7 sts, k3, p4.

Row 4: As row 2.

Row 5: Purl.

Row 6: Knit.

Row 7: K2, *p7, k3; rep from * to last 9 sts, p7, k2.

Row 8: P2, *k7, p3; rep from * to last 9 sts, k7, p2.

Row 9: As row 7.

Row 10: Knit.

Rep these 10 rows.

Fancy diamond

Multiple of 15.

Row 1 (RS): K1, *p13, k2; rep from * to last 14 sts, p13, k1.

Row 2: P2, *k11, p4; rep from * to last 13 sts, k11, p2.

Row 3: K3, *p9, k6; rep from * to last 12 sts, p9, k3.

Row 4: P4, *k7, p8; rep from * to last 11 sts, k7, p4.

Row 5: K5, *p5, k10; rep from * to last 10 sts, p5, k5.

Row 6: K1, *p5, k3, p5, k2; rep from * to last 14 sts, p5, k3, p5, k1.

Row 7: P2, *k5, p1, k5, p4; rep from * to last 13 sts, k5, p1, k5, p2.

Row 8: As row 3.

Row 9: As row 7.

Row 10: As row 6.

Row 11: As row 5.

Row 12: As row 4.

Row 13: As row 3.

Row 14: As row 2.

Rep these 14 rows.

Berry ladder

Multiple of 20 + 10.

Row 1 (RS): P2, *k2, p2; rep from * to end.

Row 2: K2, *p2, k2; rep from * to end.

Row 3: [K2, p2] twice, *k4, p2, k2, p2; rep from * to last 2 sts, k2.

Row 4: [P2, k2] twice, *p4, k2, p2, k2; rep from * to last 2 sts, p2.

Rep the last 4 rows once more, then rows 1–2 again.

Row 11: As row 2.

Row 12: P2, *k2, p2; rep from * to end.

Row 13: [K2, p2] 3 times, [k4, p2] twice, *[k2, p2] twice, [k4, p2] twice; rep from * to last 6 sts, k2, p2, k2.

Row 14: [P2, k2] twice, *[p4, k2] twice, [p2, k2] twice; rep from * to last 2 sts, p2.

Rep the last 4 rows once more, then rows 11–12 again.

Rep these 20 rows.

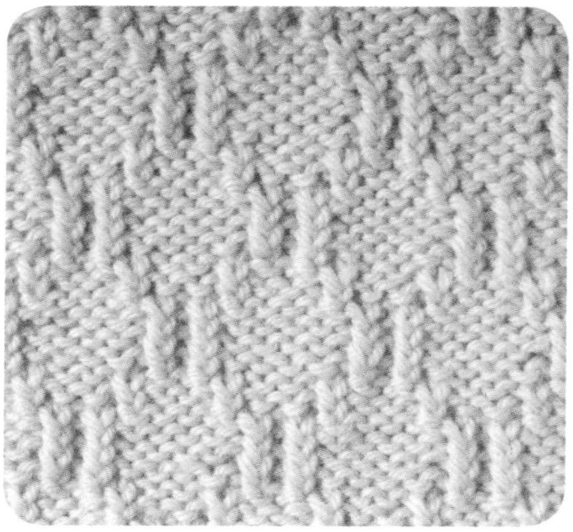

Embossed lozenge stitch

Multiple of 8 + 1.

Row 1 (RS): P3, *KB1, p1, KB1, p5; rep from * to last 6 sts, KB1, p1, KB1, p3.

Row 2: K3, *PB1, k1, PB1, k5; rep from * to last 6 sts, PB1, k1, PB1, k3.

Rep the last 2 rows once more.

Row 5: P2, *KB1, p3; rep from * to last 3 sts, KB1, p2.

Row 6: K2, *PB1, k3; rep from * to last 3 sts, PB1, k2.

Row 7: P1, *KB1, p5, KB1, p1; rep from * to end.

Row 8: K1, *PB1, k5, PB1, k1; rep from * to end.

Row 9: As row 7.

Row 10: As row 8.

Row 11: As row 5.

Row 12: As row 6.

Rep these 12 rows.

Slanted bamboo

Multiple of 8.

Row 1 (RS): P1, k6, *p2, k6; rep from * to last st, p1.

Row 2: K1, p5, *k3, p5; rep from * to last 2 sts, k2.

Row 3: P3, k4, *p4, k4; rep from * to last st, p1.

Row 4: K1, p3, k2, p1, *k2, p3, k2, p1; rep from * to last st, k1.

Row 5: P1, k2, *p2, k2; rep from * to last st, p1.

Row 6: K1, p1, k2, p3, *k2, p1, k2, p3; rep from * to last st, k1.

Row 7: P1, k4, *p4, k4; rep from * to last 3 sts, p3.

Row 8: K2, p5, *k3, p5; rep from * to last st, k1.

Row 9: As row 1.

Row 10: K1, p6, *k2, p6; rep from * to last st, k1.

Rep these 10 rows.

Squares

Multiple of 10 + 2.

Row 1 (RS): Knit.

Row 2: Purl.

Row 3: K2, *p8, k2; rep from * to end.

Row 4: P2, *k8, p2; rep from * to end.

Row 5: K2, *p2, k4, p2, k2; rep from * to end.

Row 6: P2, *k2, p4, k2, p2; rep from * to end.

Rep the last 2 rows twice more.

Row 11: As row 3.

Row 12: As row 4.

Rep these 12 rows.

Crossroad squares

Multiple of 12 + 2.

Row 1 (RS): K4, p6, *k6, p6; rep from * to last 4 sts, k4.

Row 2: P4, k6, *p6, k6; rep from * to last 4 sts, p4.

Row 3: K2, *p2, k6, p2, k2; rep from * to end.

Row 4: P2, *k2, p6, k2, p2; rep from * to end.

Rep the last 2 rows 3 times more.

Rows 11–12: As rows 1–2.

Row 13: Knit.

Row 14: Purl.

Rep these 14 rows.

Triangle ribs

Multiple of 8.

Row 1 (RS): *P2, k6; rep from * to end.

Row 2: *P6, k2; rep from * to end.

Row 3: *P3, k5; rep from * to end.

Row 4: *P4, k4; rep from * to end.

Row 5: *P5, k3; rep from * to end.

Row 6: *P2, k6; rep from * to end.

Row 7: *P7, k1; rep from * to end.

Row 8: *P2, k6; rep from * to end.

Row 9: As row 5.

Row 10: As row 4.

Row 11: As row 3.

Row 12: As row 2.

Rep these 12 rows.

Ocean wave

Multiple of 12 + 1.

Row 1 (RS) and every alt row: Knit.
Row 2: P5, k3, *p9, k3; rep from * to last 5 sts, p5.
Row 4: P4, k5, *p7, k5; rep from * to last 4 sts, p4.
Row 6: P3, k3, p1, k3, *p5, k3, p1, k3; rep from * to last 3 sts, p3.
Row 8: P2, k3, *p3, k3; rep from * to last 2 sts, p2.
Row 10: P1, *k3, p5, k3, p1; rep from * to end.
Row 12: Purl.
Rep these 12 rows.

Elongated chevron

Multiple of 18 + 1.

Row 1 (RS): P1, *[k2, p2] twice, k1, [p2, k2] twice, p1; rep from * to end.
Row 2: K1, *[p2, k2] twice, p1, [k2, p2] twice, k1; rep from * to end.
Rep the last 2 rows once more.
Row 5: [P2, k2] twice, *p3, k2, p2, k2; rep from * to last 2 sts, p2.
Row 6: [K2, p2] twice, *k3, p2, k2, p2; rep from * to last 2 sts, k2.
Rep the last 2 rows once more.
Row 9: As row 2.
Row 10: As row 1.
Row 11: As row 2.
Row 12: As row 1.
Row 13: As row 6.
Row 14: As row 5.
Row 15: As row 6.
Row 16: As row 5.
Rep these 16 rows.

Seed stitch zigzag

Multiple of 9.

Row 1 (RS): *[K1, p1] twice, k4, p1; rep from * to end.
Row 2: *P4, [k1, p1] twice, k1; rep from * to end.
Row 3: [K1, p1] 3 times, *k4, [p1, k1] twice, p1; rep from * to last 3 sts, k3.
Row 4: P2, *[k1, p1] twice, k1, p4; rep from * to last 7 sts, [k1, p1] twice, k1, p2.
Row 5: K3, *[p1, k1] twice, p1, k4; rep from * to last 6 sts, [p1, k1] 3 times.
Row 6: *[K1, p1] twice, k1, p4; rep from * to end.
Row 7: As row 5.
Row 8: As row 4.
Row 9: As row 3.
Row 10: As row 2.
Rep these 10 rows.

Single eyelet rib

Multiple of 5 + 2.

Row 1 (RS): P2, *k3, p2; rep from * to end.

Row 2 and every alt row: K2, *p3, k2; rep from * to end.

Row 3: P2, *k2tog, yo, k1, p2; rep from * to end.

Row 5: As row 1.

Row 7: P2, *k1, yo, skpo, p2; rep from * to end.

Row 8: As row 2.

Rep these 8 rows.

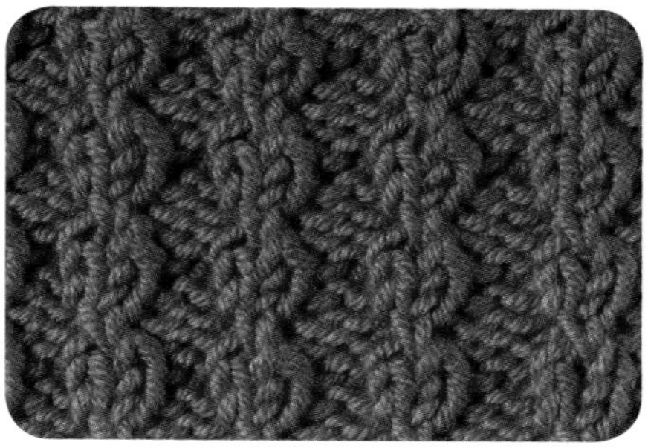

Double eyelet rib

Multiple of 7 + 2.

Row 1 (RS): P2, *k5, p2; rep from * to end.

Row 2: K2, *p5, k2; rep from * to end.

Row 3: P2, *k2tog, yo, k1, yo, skpo, p2; rep from * to end.

Row 4: As row 2.

Rep these 4 rows.

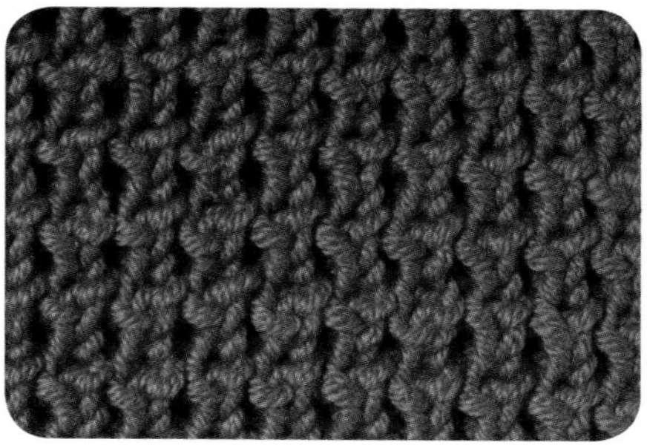

Square rib

Multiple of 2 + 1.

Row 1 (RS): K2, p1, *k1, p1; rep from * to last 2 sts, k2.

Row 2: K1, *p1, k1; rep from * to end.

Row 3: As row 1.

Row 4: K1, p1, *yb, insert needle through center of st 2 rows below next st on needle and knit this in the usual way slipping st above off needle at the same time, p1; rep from * to last st, k1.

Rep these 4 rows.

Diagonal knot stitch

Multiple of 3 + 1.

Special abbreviation:

Make knot = P3tog leaving sts on needle, yo, purl same 3 sts together again.

Row 1 (RS) and every alt row: Knit.

Row 2: *Make knot; rep from * to last st, p1.

Row 4: P2, *make knot; rep from * to last 2 sts, p2.

Row 6: P1, *make knot; rep from * to end.

Rep these 6 rows.

Close checks

Multiple of 6 + 3.

Row 1 (RS): K3, *p3, k3; rep from * to end.

Row 2: P3, *k3, p3; rep from * to end.

Rep the last 2 rows once more.

Row 5: As row 2.

Row 6: As row 1.

Rep the last 2 rows once more.

Rep these 8 rows.

Mock cable—left

Multiple of 4 + 2.

Row 1 (RS): P2, *k2, p2; rep from * to end.

Row 2: K2, *p2, k2; rep from * to end.

Row 3: P2, *C2B, p2; rep from * to end.

Row 4: As row 2.

Rep these 4 rows.

Small cable with grooves

Multiple of 12.

Row 1 (RS): *K2, p1, k6, p1, k2; rep from * to end.

Row 2: *P2, k1, p6, k1, p2; rep from * to end.

Rows 3, 5, 7, and 9: *K2, p2, k4, p2, k2; rep from * to end.

Rows 4, 6, and 8: *P2, k2, p4, k2, p2; rep from * to end.

Row 10: *P2, slip next 2 sts onto cable needle and hold at front of work, p2, k2 from cable needle, slip next 2 sts onto cable needle and hold at front of work, k2, p2 from cable needle, p2; rep from * to end.

Row 11: Knit.

Row 12: As row 2.

Rep these 12 rows.

Baby cable and garter ridges

Multiple of 25.

Row 1 (RS): *P9, k4, p12; rep from * to end.

Row 2: *[P3, k1] 3 times, p4, k1, [p3, k1] twice; rep from * to end.

Row 3: *[P1, k3] twice, p1, C4F, [p1, k3] 3 times; rep from * to end.

Row 4: As row 2.

Rep these 4 rows.

Twists with knotted pattern

Multiple of 20.

Row 1 (RS): *P2, k5, p5, k5, p3; rep from * to end.

Row 2 and every alt row: *K3, p5, k5, p5, k2; rep from * to end.

Row 3: As row 1.

Row 5: *P2, using another ball of yarn k5, turn, p5, work another 12 rows in st st on these 5 sts, place on stitch holder, slip next 5 sts onto cable needle and hold at back of work, using another ball of yarn k5, turn, p5, work another 12 rows in st st on these 5 sts, place on stitch holder, knot the 2 strips as follows: put 2nd strip underneath first then over first, k5 from 2nd strip, p5 from cable needle, k5 from first strip, p3; rep from * to end.

Row 7, 9, 11, 13, and 15: As row 1.

Row 16: As row 2.

Rep these 16 rows.

Sand wind

Multiple of 12 + 6 + 1 st for the rim on each edge.

Rows 1 (RS) and 5: Knit.

Rows 2, 4, and 6: Purl.

Row 3: 1 edge st, *C6F, k6; rep from * to last st, 1 edge st.

Row 7: 1 edge st, *k6, C6B; rep from * to last st, 1 edge st.

Row 8: Knit.

Rep these 8 rows.

Rhombus

Panel of 12 sts on a background of st st.

Rows 1 (RS) and 5: Knit.

Row 2 and every alt row: Purl.

Row 3: C4B, k4, C4F.

Row 7: K2, C4F, C4B, k2.

Row 8: Purl.

Rep these 8 rows.

20-stitch twisted candle

Panel of 20 sts on a background of rev st st.

Rows 1 (RS), 5, 7, 9, and 11: Knit.

Row 2 and every alt row: Purl.

Row 3: C10B, C10F.

Row 12: Purl.

Rep these 12 rows.

Woven cable stitch

Multiple of 4.

Row 1 (RS): *C4F; rep from * to end.

Row 2: Purl.

Row 3: K2, *C4B; rep from * to last 2 sts, k2.

Row 4: Purl.

Rep these 4 rows.

Knotted cable

Panel of 6 sts on a background of rev st st.

Row 1 (RS): K2, p2, k2.

Row 2 and every alt row: P2, k2, p2.

Row 3: C6.

Rows 5, 7, and 9: As row 1.

Row 10: As row 2.

Rep these 10 rows.

Little pearl

Panel of 4 sts on a background of st st.

Row 1 (RS): C2F, C2B.

Row 2: Purl.

Row 3: C2B, C2F.

Row 4: Purl.

Rep these 4 rows.

Big twisted candle

Panel of 9 sts on a background of rev st st.

Row 1 (RS): Knit.
Row 2 and every alt row: Purl.
Rows 3, 5, 7, 11, 13, 15, and 17: Knit.
Row 9: C9 (slip next 4 sts onto cable needle and hold at front of work, k5, k4 from cable needle).
Row 18: Purl.
Rep these 18 rows.

Sloping diamonds

Multiple of 10.

Row 1 (RS): *K2, p5, C3B; rep from * to end.
Row 2: *P3, k5, p2; rep from * to end.
Row 3: *K2, p4, C3B, k1; rep from * to end.
Row 4: *P4, k4, p2; rep from * to end.
Row 5: *K2, p3, T3B, k2; rep from * to end.
Row 6: *P2, k1, p2, k3, p2; rep from * to end.
Row 7: *K2, p2, T3B, p1, k2; rep from * to end.
Row 8: *P2, [k2, p2] twice; rep from * to end.
Row 9: *K2, p1, T3B, p2, k2; rep from * to end.
Row 10: *P2, k3, p2, k1, p2; rep from * to end.
Row 11: *K2, T3B, p3, k2; rep from * to end.
Row 12: *P2, k4, p4; rep from * to end.
Row 13: *K1, T3B, p4, k2; rep from * to end.
Row 14: *P2, k5, p3; rep from * to end.
Row 15: *T3B, p5, k2; rep from * to end.
Row 16: *P2, k6, p2; rep from * to end.
Rep these 16 rows.

Dramatic curves

Multiple of 47 sts on row 1; 62 sts thereafter.

Row 1 (RS): P8, *(k1, p1) in each of next 5 sts, p8; rep from * to end.
Row 2: K8 *p10, place point of left-hand needle into st one row below last knit st worked, knit it together with next st on left-hand needle, k7; rep from * to end.
Row 3: P8, *k10, p8; rep from * to end.
Row 4: As row 2.
Rep the last 2 rows 4 times more.
Row 13: P8, slip next 10 sts onto cable needle and hold at front of work, slip next 8 sts onto 2nd cable needle and hold at back of work, k10, p8 from 2nd cable needle, k10 from first cable needle, p8, k10, p8.
Row 14: As row 2.
Rep rows 3–4, 5 times more.
Row 25: P8, k10, p8, slip next 10 sts onto cable needle and hold at back of work, slip next 8 sts onto 2nd cable needle and hold at back of work, k10, p8 from 2nd cable needle, k10 from first cable needle, p8.
Row 26: As row 2.
Rep rows 3–26.

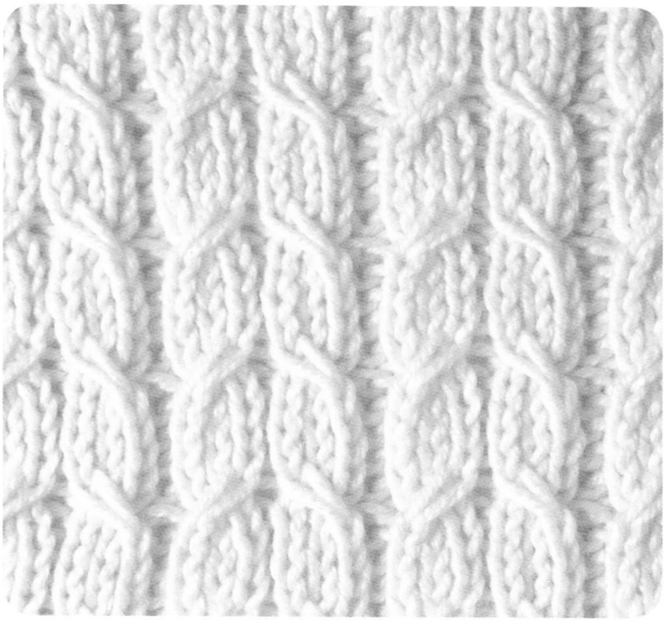

Alternating twists

Multiple of 9 + 2.

Row 1 (WS): K2, *p3, k1, p3, k2; rep from * to end.

Row 2: *P2, wyib sl 1, k2, p1, k2, wyib sl 1; rep from * to last 2 sts, p2.

Row 3: K2, *wyif sl 1, p2, k1, p2, wyif sl 1, k2; rep from * to end.

Row 4: *P2, drop slipped st off needle to front of work, k2, pick up dropped st and knit it, p1, wyib slip next 2 sts, drop slipped st off needle to front of work, slip same 2 sts back onto left-hand needle, pick up dropped st and knit it; rep from * to last 2 sts, p2.

Row 5: K2, *p3, k1, p3, k2; rep from * to end.

Row 6: *P2, k3, p1, k3; rep from * to last 2 sts, p2.

Rep these 6 rows.

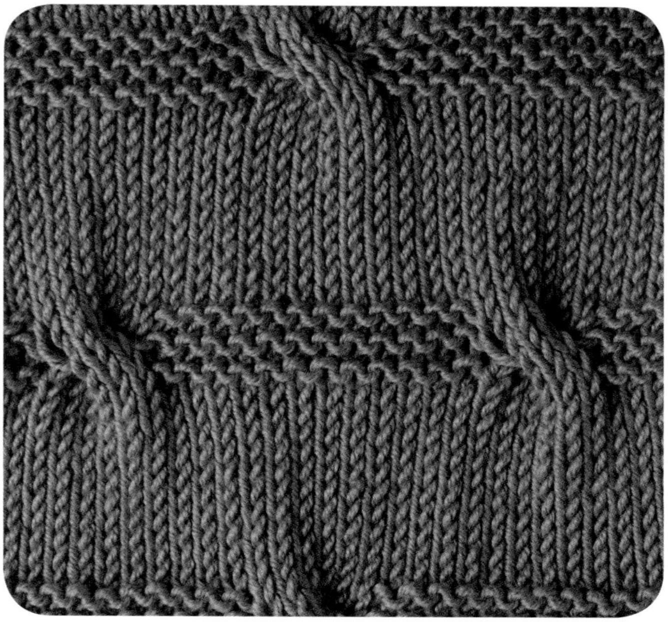

Twisted candles

Multiple of 18 + 8 + 1 st for the rim on each edge.

Row 1 (RS): Knit.

Row 2: Purl.

Rows 3 and 5: Knit.

Row 4: Purl.

Row 6: 1 edge st, k1, p6, k1, *k11, p6, k1; rep from * to last st, 1 edge st.

Row 7: Knit.

Row 8: As row 6.

Row 9: 1 edge st, *k1, C6F, k11; rep from * to last 9 sts, k1, C6F, k1, 1 edge st.

Row 10: As row 6.

Rows 11–21: As rows 1–2.

Row 22: 1 edge st, *k10, p6, k10; rep from * to last st, 1 edge st.

Row 23: As row 1.

Row 24: As row 22.

Row 25: 1 edge st, *k10, C6F, k10; rep from * to last st, 1 edge st.

Row 26: As row 22.

Rep these 26 rows.

Geometric twisted candles

Multiple of 10 + 6 + 1 st for the rim on each edge.

Row 1 (RS): 1 edge st, *p1, k4, p5; rep from * to last 7 sts, p1, k4, p1, 1 edge st.

Row 2 and every alt row: Knit all k sts and purl all p sts.

Row 3: Knit all k sts and purl all p sts.

Row 5: 1 edge st, *p1, C4B, p5; rep from * to last 6 sts, p1, C4B, 1 edge st.

Row 7: As row 3.

Row 9: 1 edge st, *p6, k4; rep from * to last 7 sts, p6, 1 edge st.

Row 11: As row 3.

Row 13: 1 edge st, *p6, C4B; rep from * to last 7 sts, p6, 1 edge st.

Row 15: As row 3.

Row 16: As row 2.

Rep these 16 rows.

Crossed grooves

Multiple of 8 + 2 + 1 st for the rim on each edge.

Special abbreviation:

C6 = Slip next 4 sts onto cable needle and hold at back of work, k2, slip 3rd and 4th sts from cable needle onto left-hand needle, [PB1] twice, k2 from cable needle.

Rows 1 (RS), 3, 5, 9, 11, and 13: 1 edge st, *k2, p2; rep from * to last 3 sts, k2, 1 edge st.

Row 2 and every alt row: Knit all k sts and purl all p sts.

Row 7: 1 edge st, *C6, p2; rep from * to last 3 sts, k2, 1 edge st.

Row 15: 1 edge st, k2, *p2, C6; rep from * to last st, 1 edge st.

Row 16: As row 2.

Rep these 16 rows.

Rhombus delight

Multiple of 10.

Row 1 (RS): *P1, KB1, p1, KB1, p1, T2B, k1, T2F; rep from * to end.

Row 2: *P5, k1, PB1, k1, PB1, k1; rep from * to end.

Row 3: *P1, KB1, p1, KB1, p1, T2B, k1, T2F; rep from * to end.

Row 4: *K1, p3, k2, PB1, k1, PB1, k1; rep from * to end.

Row 5: *P1, KB1, p1, KB1, p2, knit 3rd st on left-hand needle, knit 2nd st, then knit first st, then slip all 3 sts off left-hand needle together, p1; rep from * to end.

Row 6: As row 4.

Rep these 6 rows.

Floating snake pattern

Multiple of 10 + 5.

Special abbreviations:

3-st RC (3-stitch right cross) = Slip next 2 sts onto cable needle and hold at back of work, k1, k2 from cable needle.

3-st LC (3-stitch left cross) = Slip next st onto cable needle and hold at front of work, k2, k1 from cable needle.

Row 1 (RS): *P2, k1, p2, KB1, 3-st RC, KB1; rep from * to last 5 sts, p2, k1, p2.

Rows 2 and 4: *K2, p1, k2, wyif sl 1, p3, wyif sl 1; rep from * to last 5 sts, k2, p1, k2.

Row 3: *P2, k1, p2, KB1, 3-st LC, KB1; rep from * to last 5 sts, p2, k1, p2.

Rep these 4 rows.

Open honeycomb

Multiple of 4 + 1 st for the rim on each edge.

Row 1 (RS): 1 edge st, *T2B, T2F; rep from * to last st, 1 edge st.

Row 2 and every alt row: Purl.

Rows 3 and 7: Knit.

Row 5: 1 edge st, *T2F, T2B; rep from * to last st, 1 edge st; rep from * to end.

Row 8: Purl.

Rep these 8 rows.

Ray of honey

Multiple of 4 + 1 st for the rim on each edge.

Row 1 (RS): 1 edge st, *T2B, T2F; rep from * to last st, 1 edge st.

Rows 2 and 4: Purl.

Row 3: 1 edge st, *T2F, T2B; rep from * to last st, 1 edge st.

Rep these 4 rows.

Arched cables

Multiple of 24 + 2.

Row 1 (RS): Knit.

Rows 2 and every alt row: K1, p to last st, k1.

Row 3: K1, *C4B, k4, C4F; rep from * to last st, k1.

Row 5: Knit.

Row 7: K3, C4F, C4B, *k4, C4F, C4B; rep from * to last 3 sts, k3.

Row 8: As row 2.

Rep these 8 rows.

Mock cable wide rib

Multiple of 13 + 8.

Row 1 (WS): P8, *k1, p3, k1, p8; rep from * to end.

Row 2: K8, *p1, sl 2, knit 3rd st on left-hand needle, knit 2nd st, then knit first st, then slip all 3 sts off left-hand needle together, p1, k8; rep from * to end.

Rep these 2 rows.

Centered cables

Panel of 16 sts on a background of rev st st.

Special abbreviations:

T8B rib (twist 8 back rib) = Slip next 4 sts onto cable needle and hold at back of work, k1, p2, k1 from left-hand needle, then k1, p2, k1 from cable needle.

T8F rib (twist 8 front rib) = Slip next 4 sts onto cable needle and hold at front of work, k1, p2, k1 from left-hand needle, then k1, p2, k1 from cable needle.

Row 1 (RS): K1, p2, [k2, p2] 3 times, k1.

Row 2: P1, k2, [p2, k2] 3 times, p1.

Row 3: T8B rib, T8F rib.

Row 4: As row 2.

Rep rows 1–2, 5 times more.

Row 15: T8F rib, T8B rib.

Row 16: As row 2.

Rep rows 1–2, 4 times more.

Rep these 24 rows.

Slipped three-stitch cable

Panel of 3 sts on a background of rev st st.

Slipped to the left:

Row 1 (RS): Sl 1 purlwise, k2.

Row 2: P2, sl 1 purlwise.

Row 3: C3L.

Row 4: Purl.

Rep these 4 rows.

Slipped to the right:

Row 1 (RS): K2, sl 1 purlwise.

Row 2: Sl 1 purlwise, p2.

Row 3: C3R.

Row 4: Purl.

Rep these 4 rows.

Divided circles

Multiple of 28 + 18.

Row 1 (RS): P6, k6, *p4, [k2, p4] 3 times, k6; rep from * to last 6 sts, p6.

Row 2: K6, p6, *k4, p14, k4, p6; rep from * to last 6 sts, k6.

Row 3: P4, T4B, k2, *[T4F, p2] twice, k2, [p2, T4B] twice, k2; rep from * to last 8 sts, T4F, p4.

Row 4: K4, *p10, k4; rep from * to end.

Row 5: P2, T4B, p2, k2, *[p2, T4F] twice, k2, [T4B, p2] twice, k2; rep from * to last 8 sts, p2, T4F, p2.

Row 6: K2, p14, *k4, p6, k4, p14; rep from * to last 2 sts, k2.

Row 7: P2, *[k2, p4] 3 times, k6, p4; rep from * to last 16 sts, k2, [p4, k2] twice, p2.

Row 8: As row 6.

Row 9: P2, T4F, p2, k2, *[p2, T4B] twice, k2, [T4F, p2] twice, k2; rep from * to last 8 sts, p2, T4B, p2.

Row 10: As row 4.

Row 11: P4, T4F, k2, *[T4B, p2] twice, k2, [p2, T4F] twice, k2; rep from * to last 8 sts, T4B, p4.

Row 12: As row 2.

Rep these 12 rows.

Sloping cable

Panel of 10 sts on a background of rev st st.

Note: Increases should be made by knitting into front and back of next st.

Row 1 (WS): K1, p8, k1.

Row 2: P1, skpo, k4, inc, k1, p1.

Rep the last 2 rows 3 times more, then row 1 again.

Row 10: P1, C8F, p1.

Row 11: As row 1.

Row 12: P1, inc, k5, k2tog, p1.

Rep the last 2 rows 3 times more, then row 11 again.

Row 20: P1, C8B, p1.

Rep these 20 rows.

Eight-stitch cable

Panel of 8 sts on a background of rev st st.

Row 1 (RS): Knit.

Row 2: Purl.

Row 3: C8B.

Row 4: Purl.

Rep rows 1–2 twice more.

Row 9: C8F.

Row 10: Purl.

Rows 11–12: As rows 1–2.

Rep these 12 rows.

Cable with bobbles

Panel of 9 sts on a background of rev st st.

Row 1 (RS): P2, T5BP, p2.
Row 2: K2, p2, k1, p2, k2.
Row 3: P1, T3B, p1, T3F, p1.
Row 4: K1, p2, k3, p2, k1.
Row 5: T3B, p3, T3F.
Row 6: P2, k5, p2.
Row 7: K2, p2, MB, p2, k2.
Row 8: As row 6.
Row 9: T3F, p3, T3B.
Row 10: As row 4.
Row 11: P1, T3F, p1, T3B, p1.
Row 12: As row 2.
Rep these 12 rows.

Pillar cable

Panel of 5 sts on a background of rev st st.

Row 1 (RS): K1, [C2F] twice.
Row 2: P1, [C2BW] twice.
Rep these 2 rows.

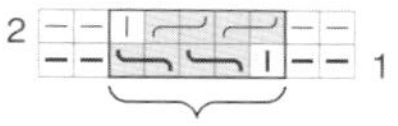

5-stitch panel

Horn cable

Panel of 16 sts on a background of rev st st.

Row 1 (RS): K4, C4B, C4F, k4.
Row 2: Purl.
Row 3: K2, C4B, k4, C4F, k2.
Row 4: Purl.
Row 5: C4B, k8, C4F.
Row 6: Purl.
Rep these 6 rows.

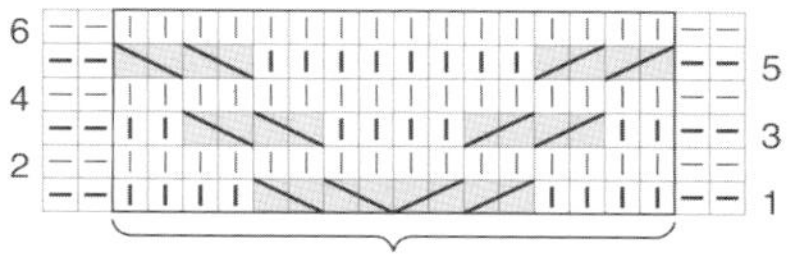

16-stitch panel

Textured cable

Panel of 13 sts on a background of rev st st.

Row 1 (RS): P3, C3B, p1, C3F, p3.
Row 2: K3, p3, k1, p3, k3.
Row 3: P2, C3B, p1, k1, p1, C3F, p2.
Row 4: K2, p3, k1, p1, k1, p3, k2.
Row 5: P1, C3B, p1, [k1, p1] twice, C3F, p1.
Row 6: K1, p3, k1, [p1, k1] twice, p3, k1.
Row 7: C3B, p1, [k1, p1] 3 times, C3F.
Row 8: P3, k1, [p1, k1] 3 times, p3.
Row 9: K2, p1, [k1, p1] 4 times, k2.
Row 10: P2, k1, [p1, k1] 4 times, p2.
Row 11: T3F, p1, [k1, p1] 3 times, T3B.
Row 12: K1, p2, k1, [p1, k1] 3 times, p2, k1.
Row 13: P1, T3F, p1, [k1, p1] twice, T3B, p1.
Row 14: K2, p2, k1, [p1, k1] twice, p2, k2.
Row 15: P2, T3F, p1, k1, p1, T3B, p2.
Row 16: K3, p2, k1, p1, k1, p2, k3.
Row 17: P3, T3F, p1, T3B, p3.
Row 18: K4, p2, k1, p2, k4.
Row 19: P4, C5B, p4.
Row 20: K4, p5, k4.
Rep these 20 rows.

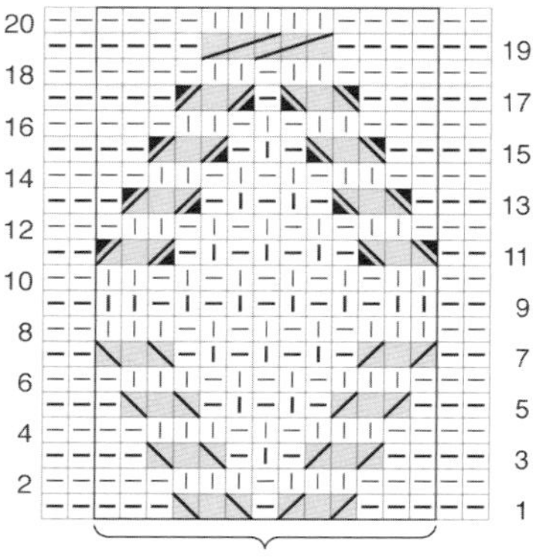

13-stitch panel

Crossroads cable

Panel of 12 sts on a background of rev st st.

Row 1 (RS): P3, T3B, T3F, p3.
Row 2: K3, p2, k2, p2, k3.
Row 3: P2, T3B, p2, T3F, p2.
Row 4: K2, p2, k4, p2, k2.
Row 5: P1, T3B, p4, T3F, p1.
Row 6: K1, p2, k6, p2, k1.
Row 7: T3B, p6, T3F.
Row 8: P2, k8, p2.
Row 9: T3F, p6, T3B.
Row 10: As row 6.
Row 11: P1, T3F, p4, T3B, p1.
Row 12: As row 4.
Row 13: P2, T3F, p2, T3B, p2.
Row 14: As row 2.
Row 15: P3, T3F, T3B, p3.
Row 16: K4, p4, k4.
Row 17: P4, C4B, p4.
Row 18: K4, p4, k4.
Rep these 18 rows.

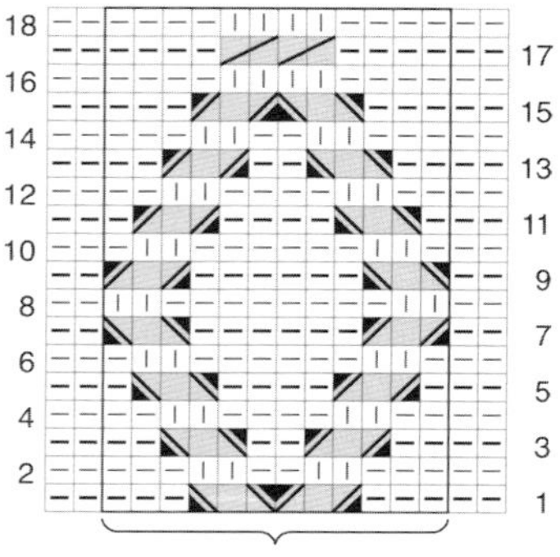

12-stitch panel

Framed cross cable

Panel of 16 sts on a background of rev st st.

Row 1 (RS): K2, p3, T3B, T3F, p3, k2.
Row 2: P2, k3, p2, k2, p2, k3, p2.
Row 3: K2, p2, T3B, p2, T3F, p2, k2.
Row 4: P2, k2, p2, k4, p2, k2, p2.
Row 5: K2, p1, T3B, p4, T3F, p1, k2.
Row 6: P2, k1, p2, k6, p2, k1, p2.
Row 7: K2, T3B, p6, T3F, k2.
Row 8: P4, k8, p4.
Row 9: C4F, p8, C4B.
Row 10: As row 8.
Row 11: K2, T3F, p6, T3B, k2.
Row 12: As row 6.
Row 13: K2, p1, T3F, p4, T3B, p1, k2.
Row 14: As row 4.
Row 15: K2, p2, T3F, p2, T3B, p2, k2.
Row 16: As row 2.
Row 17: K2, p3, T3F, T3B, p3, k2.
Row 18: P2, k4, p4, k4, p2.
Row 19: K2, p4, C4B, p4, k2.
Row 20: As row 18.
Rep these 20 rows.

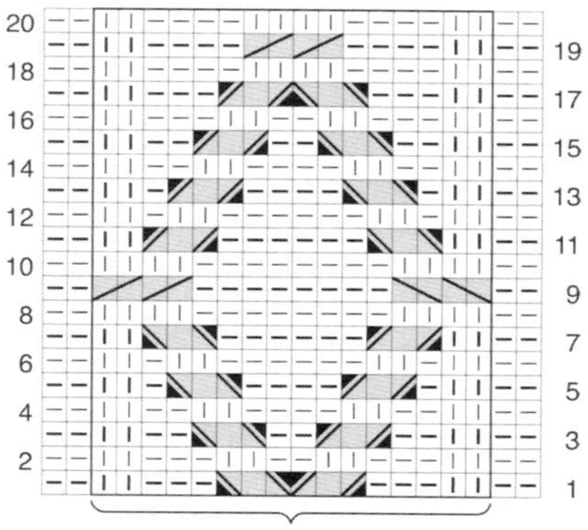

16-stitch panel

Open and closed cable I

Panel of 8 sts on a background of rev st st.

Special abbreviations:

T6F rib (twist 6 front rib) = Slip next 3 sts onto cable needle and hold at front of work, k1, p1, k1 from left-hand needle, then k1, p1, k1 from cable needle.

T4R rib (twist 4 right rib) = Slip next st onto cable needle and hold at back of work, k1, p1, k1 from left-hand needle, then p1 from cable needle.

T4L rib (twist 4 feft rib) = Slip next 3 sts onto cable needle and hold at front of work, p1 from left-hand needle, then k1, p1, k1 from cable needle.

Row 1 (RS): P1, k1, p1, k2, p1, k1, p1.
Row 2: K1, p1, k1, p2, k1, p1, k1.
Row 3: P1, T6F rib, p1.
Row 4: As row 2.
Row 5: T4R rib, T4L rib.
Row 6: P1, k1, p1, k2, p1, k1, p1.
Row 7: K1, p1, k1, p2, k1, p1, k1.
Rep the last 2 rows twice more, then row 6 again.
Row 13: T4L rib, T4R rib.
Rows 14–16: As rows 2–4.
Rows 17–18: As rows 1–2.
Rep these 18 rows.

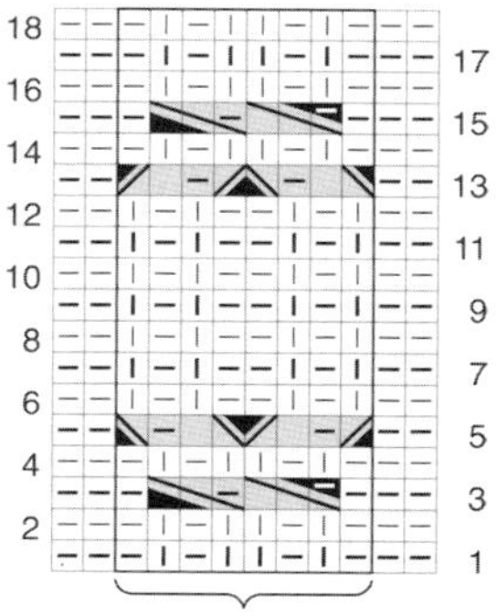

8-stitch panel

Smocking stitch pattern

Multiple of 8 + 7.

Special abbreviation:

S5 (smock 5) = Slip next 5 sts onto cable needle and hold at front of work, wind yarn twice around sts on cable needle in a counterclockwise direction, then work sts from cable needle as follows: k1, p3, k1.

Row 1 (RS): P1, k1, *p3, k1; rep from * to last st, p1.

Row 2: K1, p1, *k3, p1; rep from * to last st, k1.

Row 3: P1, S5, *p3, S5; rep from * to last st, p1.

Rep row 2 once more, then rows 1–2 twice more.

Row 9: P1, k1, p3, *S5, p3; rep from * to last 2 sts, k1, p1.

Row 10: As row 2.

Rows 11–12: As rows 1–2.

Repeat these 12 rows.

Note: This method creates a small gap in the work at either side of the smocked stitches. The technique can be adapted to any rib pattern, provided the stitches on the cable needle begin and end with a knit stitch. The number of rows between the smocked stitches can also be varied as required.

Fuchsia stitch

Multiple of 6.

Note: Stiches should only be counted after row 11 or 12.

Row 1 (RS): P2, *k2, yo, p4; rep from * to last 4 sts, k2, yo, p2.

Row 2: K2, *p3, k4; rep from * to last 5 sts, p3, k2.

Row 3: P2, *k3, yo, p4; rep from * to last 5 sts, k3, yo, p2.

Row 4: K2, *p4, k4; rep from * to last 6 sts, p4, k2.

Row 5: P2, *k4, yo, p4; rep from * to last 6 sts, k4, yo, p2.

Row 6: K2, *p5, k4; rep from * to last 7 sts, p5, k2.

Row 7: P2, *k3, k2tog, p4; rep from * to last 7 sts, k3, k2tog, p2.

Row 8: As row 4.

Row 9: P2, *k2, k2tog, p4; rep from * to last 6 sts, k2, k2tog, p2.

Row 10: As row 2.

Row 11: P2, *k1, k2tog, p4; rep from * to last 5 sts, k1, k2tog, p2.

Row 12: K2, *p2, k4; rep from * to last 4 sts, p2, k2.

Rep these 12 rows.

Defined diamonds

Multiple of 8 + 10.

Row 1 (RS): P3, C4B, *p4, C4B; rep from * to last 3 sts, p3.

Row 2: K3, p4, *k4, p4; rep from * to last 3 sts, k3.

Row 3: P1, *T4B, T4F; rep from * to last st, p1.

Row 4: K1, p2, k4, *p4, k4; rep from * to last 3 sts, p2, k1.

Row 5: P1, k2, p4, *C4B, p4; rep from * to last 3 sts, k2, p1.

Row 6: As row 4.

Row 7: P1, *T4F, T4B; rep from * to last st, p1.

Row 8: As row 2.

Rep these 8 rows.

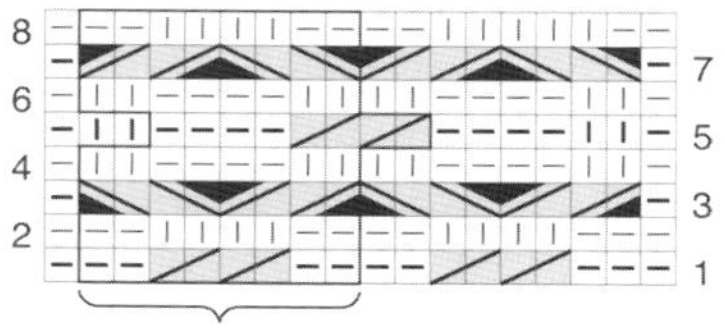

8-stitch repeat

Cable with stripes

Multiple of 13 + 1.

Row 1 (RS): P1, [k1, p1] twice, T2B, T2F, *p1, [k1, p1] 4 times, T2B, T2F; rep from * to last 5 sts, p1, [k1, p1] twice.

Row 2: [K1, p1] 3 times, k2, *p1, [k1, p1] 5 times, k2; rep from * to last 6 sts, [p1, k1] 3 times.

Row 3: P1, [k1, p1] twice, T2F, T2B, *p1, [k1, p1] 4 times, T2F, T2B; rep from * to last 5 sts, p1, [k1, p1] twice.

Row 4: [K1, p1] twice, k2, p2, k2, *p1, [k1, p1] 3 times, k2, p2, k2; rep from * to last 4 sts, [p1, k1] twice.

Row 5: [P1, k1] twice, p2, C2B, p2, *k1, [p1, k1] 3 times, p2, C2B, p2; rep from * to last 4 sts, [k1, p1] twice.

Row 6: As row 4.

Rep these 6 rows.

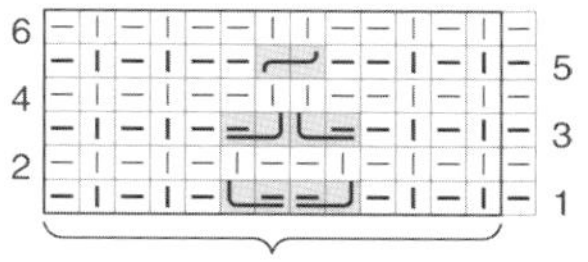

13-stitch repeat

Four-section cable

Panel of 7 sts on a background of rev st st.

Special abbreviation:

T7B rib (twist 7 back rib) = Slip next 4 sts onto cable needle and hold at back of work, k1, p1, k1 from left-hand needle, then [p1, k1] twice from cable needle.

Row 1 (RS): K1, [p1, k1] 3 times.

Row 2: PB1, [k1, PB1] 3 times.

Row 3: T7B rib.

Row 4: As row 2.

Rep rows 1–2, 3 times more.

Rep these 10 rows.

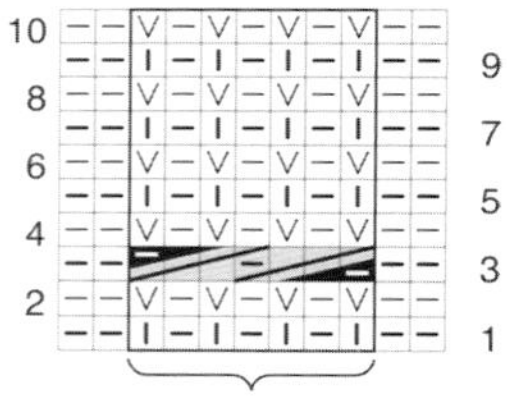

7-stitch panel

Medallion seed stitch cable

Panel of 13 sts on a background of rev st st.

Row 1 (RS): K4, [p1, k1] 3 times, k3.

Row 2: P3, [k1, p1] 4 times, p2.

Rows 3–4: As rows 1–2.

Row 5: C6F, k1, C6B.

Row 6: Purl.

Row 7: Knit.

Rep the last 2 rows twice more.

Row 12: Purl.

Row 13: C6B, k1, C6F.

Row 14: As row 2.

Row 15: As row 1.

Row 16: As row 2.

Rep these 16 rows.

Bold cable

Panel of 6 sts on a background of rev st st.

Row 1 (RS): Knit.

Row 2: Purl.

Row 3: C6B.

Row 4: Purl.

Rep rows 1–2 twice more.

Row 9: C6F.

Row 10: Purl.

Rows 11–12: As rows 1–2.

Rep these 12 rows.

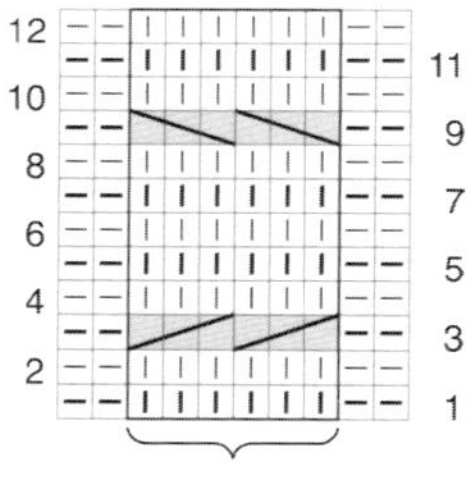

6-stitch panel

Six-stitch spiral cable

Panel of 6 sts on a background of rev st st.

Row 1 (RS): [C2F] 3 times.

Row 2: Purl.

Row 3: K1, [C2F] twice, k1.

Row 4: Purl.

Rep these 4 rows.

Climbing cable

Panel of 4 sts on a background of rev st st.

Row 1 (RS): Knit.

Row 2: Purl.

Row 3: C4B.

Row 4: Purl.

Rep the last 4 rows once more, then rows 1–2 twice again.

Rep these 12 rows.

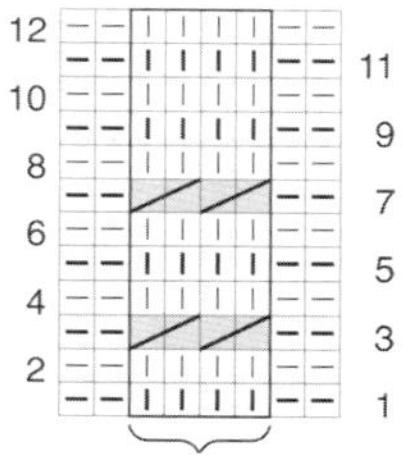

4-stitch panel

Alternated cable

Worked over 10 sts on a background of rev st st.

Row 1 (RS): P1, k8, p1.

Row 2: K1, p8, k1.

Row 3: P1, C4B, C4F, p1.

Row 4: K1, p2, k4, p2, k1.

Row 5: T3B, p4, T3F.

Row 6: P2, k6, p2.

Row 7: K2, p6, k2.

Rep the last 2 rows once more, then row 6 again.

Row 11: T3F, p4, T3B.

Row 12: As row 4.

Row 13: P1, C4F, C4B, p1.

Row 14: K1, p8, k1.

Row 15: P1, C4B, C4F, p1.

Row 16: K1, p8, k1.

Row 17: P1, k8, p1.

Rows 18–20: As rows 14–16.

Rep these 20 rows.

Honeycomb pattern

Worked over a multiple of 8 sts. The example shown is worked over 24 sts.

Row 1 (RS): *C4B, C4F; rep from * to end of panel.

Row 2: Purl.

Row 3: Knit.

Row 4: Purl.

Row 5: *C4F, C4B; rep from * to end of panel.

Row 6: Purl.

Row 7: Knit.

Row 8: Purl.

Rep these 8 rows.

Chunky cable

Panel of 10 sts on a background of rev st st.

Row 1 (RS): Knit.

Row 2: Purl.

Row 3: C10F.

Row 4: Purl.

Rep rows 1–2, 3 times more.

Rep these 10 rows.

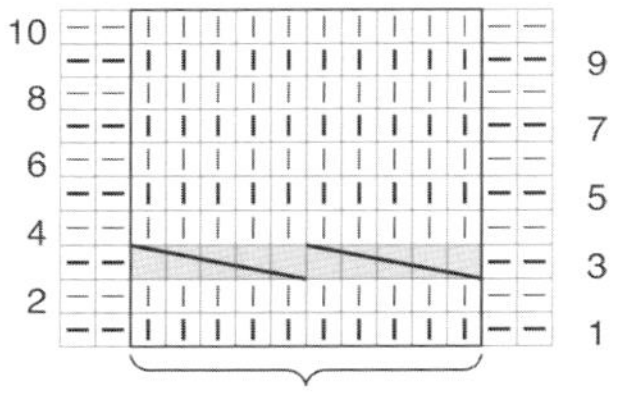

10-stitch panel

Slipped double chain

Worked over 7 sts.

Row 1 (RS): Sl 1 purlwise, k5, sl 1 purlwise.

Row 2: Sl 1 purlwise, p5, sl 1 purlwise.

Row 3: C3L, k1, C3R.

Row 4: Purl.

Row 5: K2, sl 1 purlwise, k1, sl 1 purlwise, k2.

Row 6: P2, sl 1 purlwise, p1, sl 1 purlwise, p2.

Row 7: C3R, k1, C3L.

Row 8: Purl.

Rep these 8 rows.

Small seed stitch cable

Panel of 5 sts on a background of rev st st.

Row 1 (WS): [P1, k1] twice, p1.

Row 2: K2, p1, k2.

Rep the last 2 rows once more, then row 1 again.

Row 6: Slip next st onto cable needle and hold at front of work, slip next 3 sts onto 2nd cable needle and hold at back of work, k1 from left-hand needle, k3 from 2nd cable needle, k1 from first cable needle.

Work 5 rows in st st, starting with purl.

Row 12: As row 6.

Rep rows 1–2 twice more.

Rep these 16 rows.

Roman cable

Panel of 4 sts on a background of rev st st.

Row 1 (RS): C2B, C2F.

Row 2: Purl.

Rep these 2 rows.

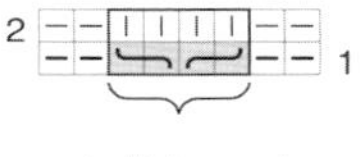

4-stitch panel

Tulip cable

Panel of 12 sts on a background of rev st st.

Row 1 (RS): Knit.

Row 2: Purl.

Row 3: C12B.

Row 4: Purl.

Rep rows 1–2, 4 times more.

Rep these 12 rows.

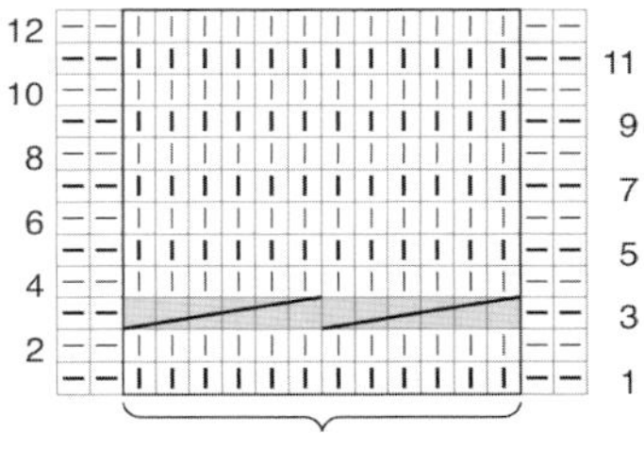

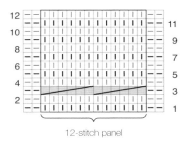

12-stitch panel

Garden path cable

Panel of 6 sts on a background of rev st st.

Row 1 (RS): K2, C4F.

Row 2: Purl.

Row 3: Knit.

Row 4: Purl.

Rows 5–6: As rows 1–2.

Row 7: C4B, k2.

Row 8: Purl.

Rows 9–10: As rows 3–4.

Rows 11–12: As rows 7–8.

Rep these 12 rows.

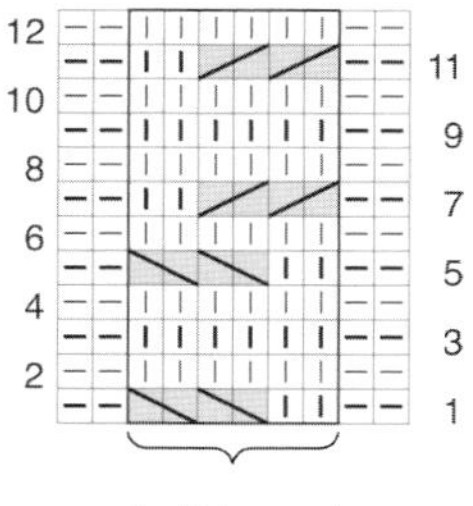

6-stitch panel

Country lane cable

Panel of 10 sts on a background of rev st st.

Row 1 (RS): Knit.

Row 2: Purl.

Row 3: C10F.

Row 4: Purl.

Rep rows 1–2, 4 times more.

Row 13: C10B.

Row 14: Purl.

Rep rows 1–2, 3 times more.

Rep these 20 rows.

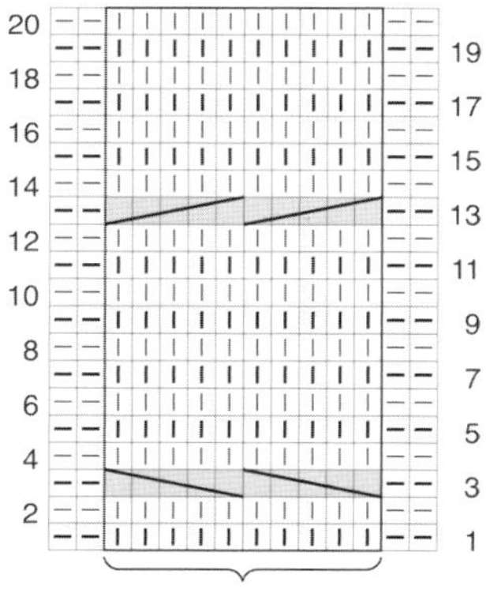

10-stitch panel

Stacked cable

Panel of 8 sts on a background of rev st st.

Row 1 (RS): Knit.

Row 2: Purl.

Row 3: C4B, C4F.

Row 4: Purl.

Rep these 4 rows.

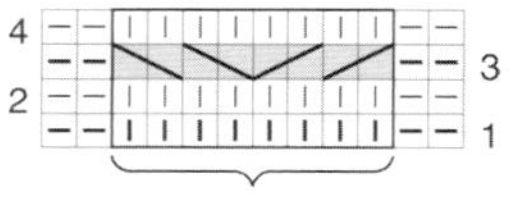

8-stitch panel

Cabled seed stitch

Panel of 13 sts on a background of rev st st.

Row 1 (RS): P3, T3B, k1, T3F, p3.
Row 2: K3, p2, k1, p1, k1, p2, k3.
Row 3: P2, T3B, k1, p1, k1, T3F, p2.
Row 4: K2, p2, [k1, p1] twice, k1, p2, k2.
Row 5: P1, T3B, [k1, p1] twice, k1, T3F, p1.
Row 6: K1, p2, [k1, p1] 3 times, k1, p2, k1.
Row 7: T3B, [k1, p1] 3 times, k1, T3F.
Row 8: P2, [k1, p1] 4 times, k1, p2.
Row 9: K3, [p1, k1] 3 times, p1, k3.
Row 10: P3, [k1, p1] 3 times, k1, p3.
Row 11: T3F, [k1, p1] 3 times, k1, T3B.
Row 12: K1, p3, [k1, p1] twice, k1, p3, k1.
Row 13: P1, T3F, [k1, p1] twice, k1, T3B, p1.
Row 14: K2, p3, k1, p1, k1, p3, k2.
Row 15: P2, T3F, k1, p1, k1, T3B, p2.
Row 16: K3, p3, k1, p3, k3.
Row 17: P3, T3F, k1, T3B, p3.
Row 18: K4, p5, k4.
Row 19: P4, T5R, p4.
Row 20: K4, p2, k1, p2, k4.
Row 21: P3, T3B, p1, T3F, p3.
Row 22: [K3, p2] twice, k3.
Row 23: [P3, k2] twice, p3.
Row 24: As row 22.
Row 25: P3, T3F, p1, T3B, p3.
Row 26: As row 20.
Row 27: As row 19.
Row 28: As row 20.
Rep these 28 rows.

Open and closed cable II

Panel of 18 sts on a background of rev st st.

Row 1 (RS): P5, C4B, C4F, p5.
Row 2: K5, p2, k4, p2, k5.
Row 3: P4, T3B, p4, T3F, p4.
Row 4: K4, p2, k6, p2, k4.
Row 5: P3, T3B, p6, T3F, p3.
Row 6: K3, p2, k8, p2, k3.
Row 7: P2, T3B, p8, T3F, p2.
Row 8: K2, p2, k10, p2, k2.
Row 9: P1, T3B, p10, T3F, p1.
Row 10: K1, p2, k12, p2, k1.
Row 11: T3B, p12, T3F.
Row 12: P2, k14, p2.
Row 13: K2, p14, k2.
Rep the last 2 rows once more, then row 12 again.
Row 17: T3F, p12, T3B.
Row 18: As row 10.
Row 19: P1, T3F, p10, T3B, p1.
Row 20: As row 8.
Row 21: P2, T3F, p8, T3B, p2.
Row 22: As row 6.
Row 23: P3, T3F, p6, T3B, p3.
Row 24: As row 4.
Row 25: P4, T3F, p4, T3B, p4.
Row 26: As row 2.
Row 27: P5, C4F, C4B, p5.
Row 28: K5, p8, k5.
Row 29: P5, C4B, C4F, p5.
Row 30: As row 28.
Row 31: P5, k8, p5.
Rep the last 4 rows twice more.
Row 40: As row 28.
Rep these 40 rows.

Twisted eyelet cable

Panel of 8 sts on a background of rev st st.

Row 1 (RS): Knit.

Row 2 and every alt row: Purl.

Row 3: K2, yo, slip next 2 sts onto cable needle and hold at front of work, k2tog from left-hand needle, then k2tog from cable needle, yo, k2.

Row 5: Knit.

Row 7: C3F, k2, C3B.

Row 9: K1, C3F, C3B, k1.

Row 10: Purl.

Rep these 10 rows.

Cable with horn detail

Panel of 6 sts on a background of rev st st.

Row 1 (RS): K1, C2B, C2F, k1.

Row 2: Purl.

Row 3: C2B, k2, C2F.

Row 4: Purl.

Rep these 4 rows.

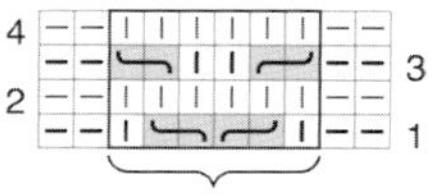

6-stitch panel

Large woven cable

Panel of 20 sts on a background of rev st st.

Row 1 (RS): Knit.

Row 2: Purl.

Row 3: K4, [C8F] twice.

Row 4: Purl.

Rep rows 1–2 twice more.

Row 9: [C8B] twice, k4.

Row 10: Purl.

Rows 11–12: As rows 1–2.

Rep these 12 rows.

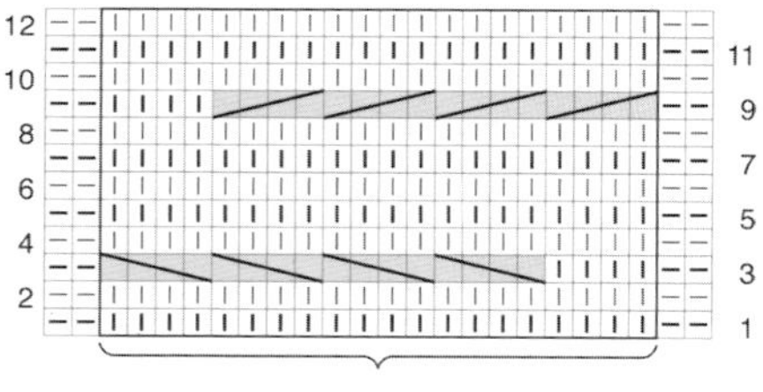

20-stitch panel

Cable and dot

Panel of 15 sts on a background of rev st st.

Row 1 (WS): K2, k into front, back, front, back, and front of next st (bobble made), k2, p2, k1, p2, k2, make bobble in next st as before, k2.

Row 2: P2, k5tog tbl (completing bobble), p2, C5F, p2, k5tog tbl, p2.

Row 3: K5, p2, k1, p2, k5.

Row 4: P4, T3B, p1, T3F, p4.

Row 5: K4, p2, k3, p2, k4.

Row 6: P3, T3B, p3, T3F, p3.

Row 7: K3, p2, k2, make bobble (as on row 1), k2, p2, k3.

Row 8: P2, T3B, p2, k5tog tbl, p2, T3F, p2.

Row 9: K2, p2, k7, p2, k2.

Row 10: P1, T3B, p7, T3F, p1.

Row 11: K1, p2, k2, make bobble, k3, make bobble, k2, p2, k1.

Row 12: T3B, p2, k5tog tbl, p3, k5tog tbl, p2, T3F.

Row 13: P2, k11, p2.

Row 14: K2, p11, k2.

Row 15: P2, k3, make bobble, k3, make bobble, k3, p2.

Row 16: T3F, p2, k5tog tbl, p3, k5tog tbl, p2, T3B.

Row 17: K1, p2, k9, p2, k1.

Row 18: P1, T3F, p7, T3B, p1.

Row 19: K2, p2, k3, make bobble, k3, p2, k2.

Row 20: P2, T3F, p2, k5tog tbl, p2, T3B, p2.

Row 21: K3, p2, k5, p2, k3.

Row 22: P3, T3F, p3, T3B, p3.

Row 23: K4, p2, k3, p2, k4.

Row 24: P4, T3F, p1, T3B, p4.

Rep these 24 rows.

Note: The cable as given here twists to the left. To work the cable twisted to the right, work C5B instead of C5F on row 2.

Free cable

Panel of 7 sts on a background of rev st st.

Row 1 (RS): [T2F] twice, p3.

Row 2: K3, [PB1, k1] twice.

Row 3: P1, [T2F] twice, p2.

Row 4: K2, PB1, k1, PB1, k2.

Row 5: P2, [T2F] twice, p1.

Row 6: [K1, PB1] twice, k3.

Row 7: P3, [T2F] twice.

Row 8: PB1, k1, PB1, k4.

Row 9: P4, k1, p1, k1.

Row 10: As row 8.

Row 11: P3, [T2B] twice.

Row 12: As row 6.

Row 13: P2, [T2B] twice, p1.

Row 14: As row 4.

Row 15: P1, [T2B] twice, p2.

Row 16: As row 2.

Row 17: [T2B] twice, p3.

Row 18: K4, PB1, k1, PB1.

Row 19: K1, p1, k1, p4.

Row 20: As row 18.

Rep these 20 rows.

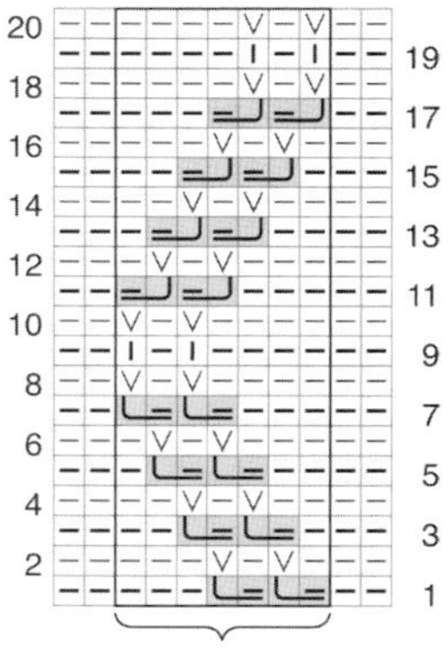

7-stitch panel

Raised circle cable

Panel of 4 sts on a background of rev st st.

Row 1 (RS): C2B, C2F.

Row 2: Purl.

Row 3: C2F, C2B.

Row 4: Purl.

Rep these 4 rows.

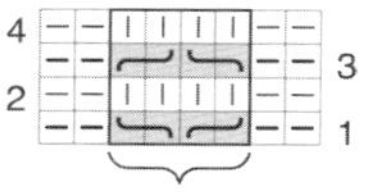

4-stitch panel

Small raised circle cable

Panel of 4 sts on a background of rev st st.

Row 1 (RS): C2B, C2F.

Row 2: Purl.

Rows 3–4: As rows 1–2.

Row 5: C2F, C2B.

Row 6: Purl.

Rows 7–8: As rows 5–6.

Rep these 8 rows.

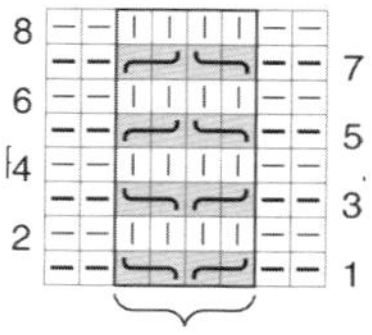

4-stitch panel

Tip

When working on complex patterns, you may find it helpful to place markers to denote the beginning and end of pattern repeats (or every 20 stitches or so if a single repeat contains a lot of stiches). This may be particularly helpful, for example, when setting a cable panel against an otherwise plain knitted background.

Tight braid cable

Panel of 10 sts on a background of rev st st.

Row 1 (WS): Purl.

Row 2: K2, [C4F] twice.

Row 3: Purl.

Row 4: [C4B] twice, k2.

Rep these 4 rows.

Folded cable

Panel of 10 sts on a background of rev st st.

Row 1 (RS): Knit.

Row 2: Purl.

Row 3: C10B.

Row 4: Purl.

Rep rows 1–2 twice more.

Row 9: K2, C6B, k2.

Row 10: Purl.

Rep rows 1–2 twice more.

Rows 15–16: As rows 9–10.

Rows 17–18: As rows 1–2.

Rep these 18 rows.

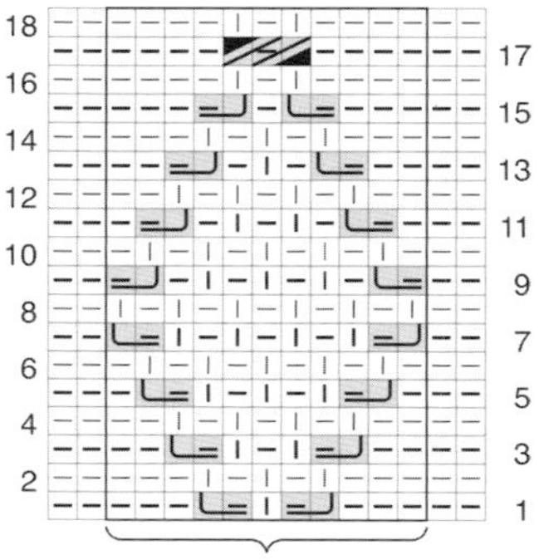

10-stitch panel

Linking ovals

Panel of 8 sts on a background of rev st st.

Row 1 (RS): P2, C4B, p2.

Row 2: K2, p4, k2.

Row 3: P1, T3B, T3F, p1.

Row 4: K1, p2, k2, p2, k1.

Row 5: T3B, p2, T3F.

Row 6: P2, k4, p2.

Row 7: K2, p4, k2.

Row 8: P2, k4, p2.

Row 9: T3F, p2, T3B.

Row 10: K1, p2, k2, p2, k1.

Row 11: P1, T3F, T3B, p1.

Row 12: K2, p4, k2.

Rep these 12 rows.

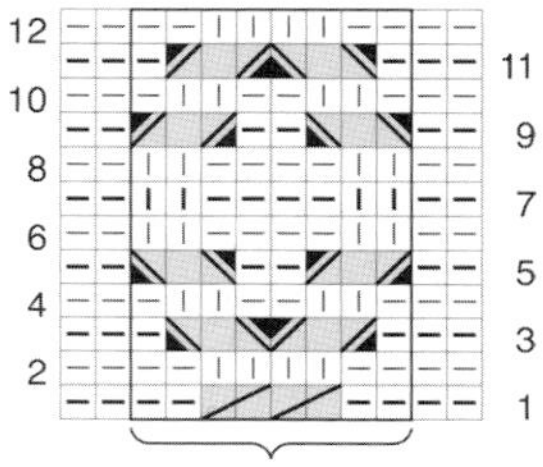

8-stitch panel

Propellor cable

Panel of 6 sts on a background of rev st st.

Row 1 (RS): Knit.

Row 2: Purl.

Row 3: C6F.

Row 4: Purl.

Rep rows 1–2 once more, then rows 1–4 once more.

Rep rows 1–2, 5 times more.

Rep these 20 rows.

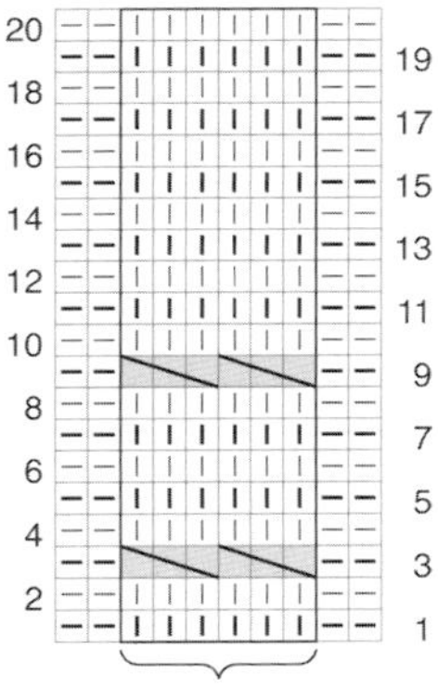

6-stitch panel

Lace cable pattern

Panel of 8 sts on a background of rev st st.

Row 1 (RS): K2, yo, skpo, k4.

Row 2 and every alt row: Purl.

Row 3: K3, yo, skpo, k3.

Row 5: K4, yo, skpo, k2.

Row 7: K5, yo, skpo, k1.

Row 9: C6B, yo, skpo.

Row 10: Purl.

Rep these 10 rows.

Cable with braid

Panel of 6 sts on a background of rev st st.

Row 1 (RS): K2, C4F.

Row 2: Purl.

Row 3: C4B, k2.

Row 4: Purl.

Rep these 4 rows.

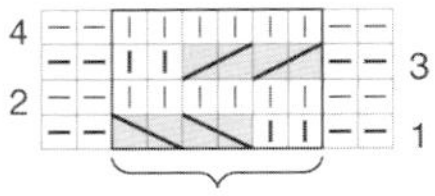

6-stitch panel

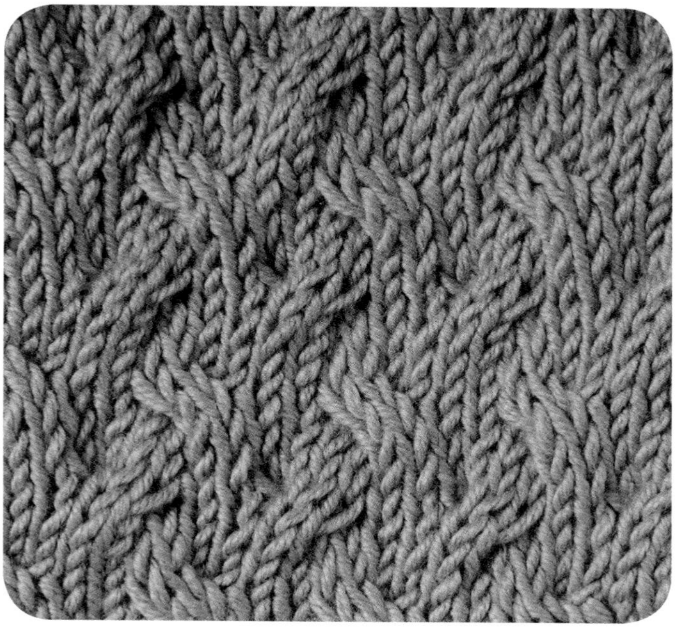

Cable fabric

Multiple of 6.
Row 1 (RS): Knit.
Row 2 and every alt row: Purl.
Row 3: *K2, C4B; rep from * to end.
Row 5: Knit.
Row 7: *C4F, k2; rep from * to end.
Row 8: Purl.
Rep these 8 rows.

Sweeping cable

Panel of 8 sts on a background of rev st st.
Row 1 (RS): Knit.
Row 2: Purl.
Row 3: C8B.
Row 4: Purl.
Rep rows 1–2 twice more.
Rep these 8 rows.

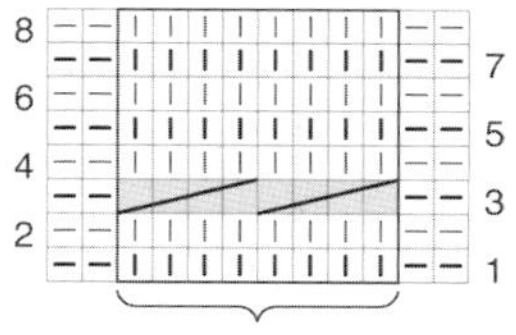

8-stitch panel

Tip

Cable patterns are very attractive, so why not make your gauge swatches into a feature by framing them? Cast on an additional 8 stitches to your swatch, keeping 4 stitches at the beginning and end of each row in garter stitch. This will will give a border to the swatch and prevent it from rolling. It also makes measuring the swatch easier.

Open cable

Panel of 7 sts on a background of rev st st.

Row 1 (RS): Knit.

Row 2: Purl.

Row 3: C3R, k1, C3L.

Row 4: Purl.

Rep these 4 rows.

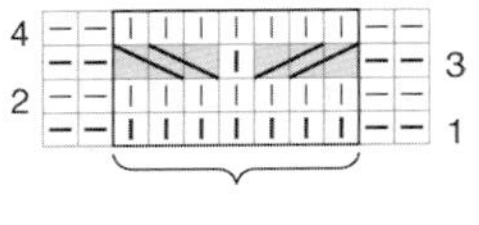

7-stitch panel

Medium circle cable

Panel of 8 sts on a background of rev st st.

Row 1 (RS): Knit.

Row 2 and every alt row: Purl.

Row 3: C4B, C4F.

Row 5: Knit.

Row 7: C4F, C4B.

Row 8: Purl.

Rep these 8 rows.

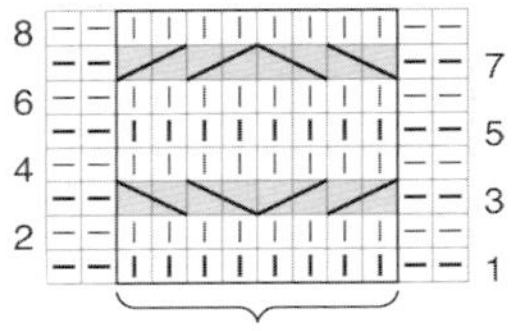

8-stitch panel

Vine cable

Panel of 9 sts on a background of rev st st.

Row 1 (RS): Knit.

Row 2: Purl.

Row 3: K3, C6F.

Row 4: Purl.

Rep rows 1–2 twice more, then rows 3–4 once more.

Rows 11–12: As rows 1–2.

Row 13: C6B, k3.

Row 14: Purl.

Rep rows 1–2 twice more.

Rows 19–20: As rows 13–14.

Rep these 20 rows.

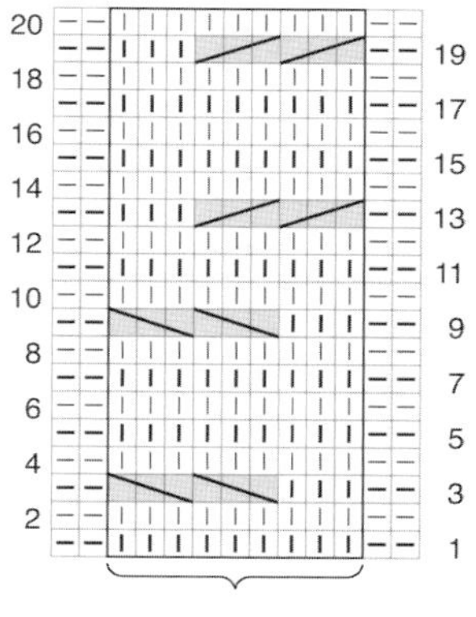

9-stitch panel

Divided cable I

Panel of 12 sts on a background of rev st st.

Row 1 (RS): [K1, p1] 4 times, T4B.

Row 2: K1, p3, [k1, p1] 4 times.

Row 3: [K1, p1] 3 times, T4B, T2F.

Row 4: P1, k2, p3, [k1, p1] 3 times.

Row 5: [K1, p1] twice, T4B, T2F, T2B.

Row 6: K1, C2BW, k2, p3, [k1, p1] twice.

Row 7: K1, p1, T4B, T2F, T2B, T2F.

Row 8: P1, k2, C2FW, k2, p3, k1, p1.

Row 9: T4B, [T2F, T2B] twice.

Row 10: K1, C2BW, k2, C2BW, k3, p2.

Row 11: T4FP, [T2B, T2F] twice.

Row 12: As row 8.

Row 13: K1, p1, T4FP, T2B, T2F, T2B.

Row 14: As row 6.

Row 15: [K1, p1] twice, T4FP, T2B, T2F.

Row 16: As row 4.

Row 17: [K1, p1] 3 times, T4FP, T2B.

Row 18: As row 2.

Row 19: [K1, p1] 4 times, T4FP.

Row 20: P2, [k1, p1] 5 times.

Rep these 20 rows.

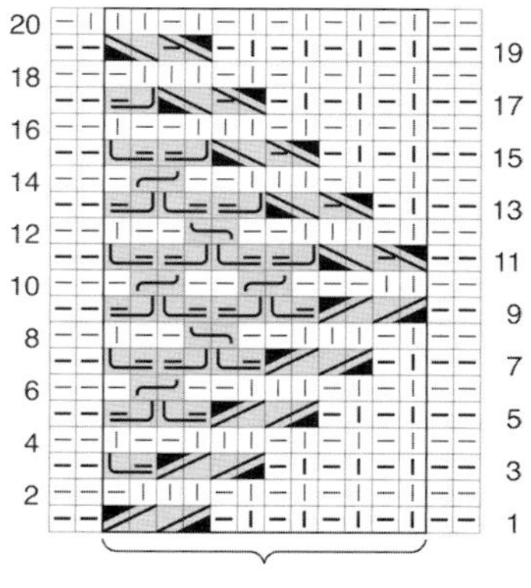

12-stitch panel

Overlapping cable

Panel of 6 sts on a background of rev st st.

Row 1 (RS): Knit.
Row 2: Purl.
Row 3: C6B.
Row 4: Purl.
Rows 5–6: As rows 1–2.
Row 7: K1, C4B, k1.
Row 8: Purl.
Rows 9–12: As rows 5–8.
Rep these 12 rows.

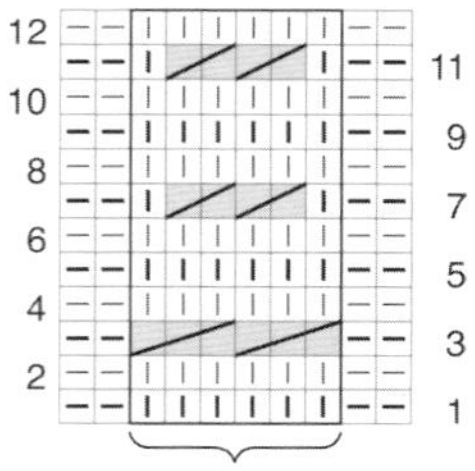

6-stitch panel

Raised curve cable

Panel of 4 sts on a background of rev st st.

Row 1 (RS): Knit.
Row 2 and every alt row: Purl.
Row 3: C4B.
Row 5: Knit.
Row 7: C4F.
Row 8: Purl.
Rep these 8 rows.

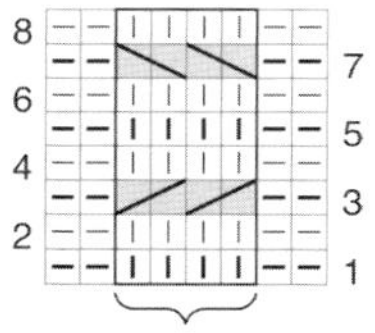

4-stitch panel

Large circle cable

Panel of 12 sts on a background of rev st st.

Row 1 (RS): Knit.
Row 2: Purl.
Row 3: C6B, C6F.
Row 4: Purl.
Rep rows 1–2 twice more.
Row 9: C6F, C6B.
Row 10: Purl.
Rows 11–12: As rows 1–2.
Rep these 12 rows.

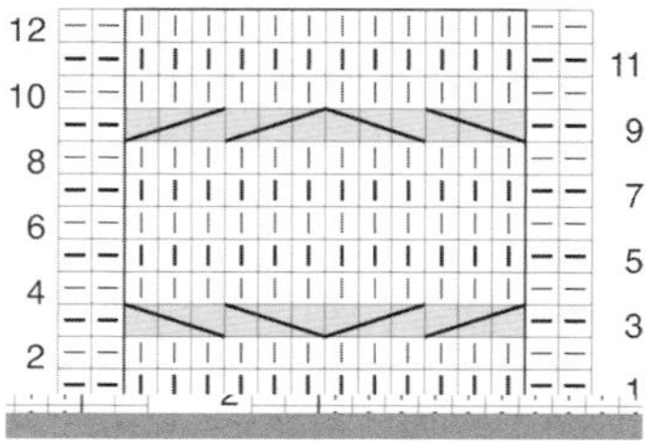

12-stitch panel

Disappearing cable

Panel of 18 sts on a background of rev st st.

Row 1 (RS): P6, k6, p6.
Row 2: K6, p6, k6.
Row 3: P3, k3, C6F, k3, p3.
Row 4: K3, p12, k3.
Row 5: P3, k12, p3.
Rep the last 2 rows once more, then row 4 again.
Row 9: K3, T6B, T6F, k3.
Row 10: P6, k6, p6.
Row 11: K6, p6, k6.
Rep the last 2 rows once more, then row 10 again.
Row 15: T6B, p6, T6F.
Row 16: P3, k12, p3.
Row 17: K3, p12, k3.
Rep the last 2 rows once more, then row 16 again.
Row 21: C6F, p6, C6B.
Rep rows 10–11 twice more, then row 10 again.
Row 27: P3, C6F, C6B, p3.
Rep rows 4–5 twice more, then row 4 again.
Row 33: P6, C6F, p6.
Row 34: As row 2.
Row 35: As row 1.
Row 36: As row 2.
Rep these 36 rows.

Divided cable II

Panel of 12 sts on a background of rev st st.

Row 1 (RS): T4F, [p1, k1] 4 times.
Row 2: [P1, k1] 4 times, p3, k1.
Row 3: T2B, T4F, [p1, k1] 3 times.
Row 4: [P1, k1] 3 times, p3, k2, p1.
Row 5: T2F, T2B, T4F, [p1, k1] twice.
Row 6: [P1, k1] twice, p3, k2, C2FW, k1.
Row 7: T2B, T2F, T2B, T4F, p1, k1.
Row 8: P1, k1, p3, k2, C2BW, k2, p1.
Row 9: [T2F, T2B] twice, T4F.
Row 10: P2, k3, C2FW, k2, C2FW, k1.
Row 11: [T2B, T2F] twice, T4BP.
Row 12: As row 8.
Row 13: T2F, T2B, T2F, T4BP, p1, k1.
Row 14: As row 6.
Row 15: T2B, T2F, T4BP, [p1, k1] twice.
Row 16: As row 4.
Row 17: T2F, T4BP, [p1, k1] 3 times.
Row 18: As row 2.
Row 19: T4BP, [p1, k1] 4 times.
Row 20: [P1, k1] 5 times, p2.
Rep these 20 rows.

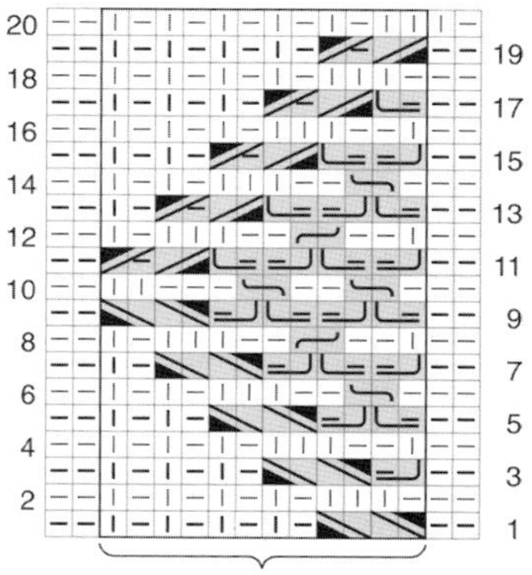

12-stitch panel

Bulky cable

Panel of 6 sts on a background of rev st st.

Row 1 (RS): Knit.
Row 2: Purl.
Row 3: C6B.
Row 4: Purl.
Rep these 4 rows.

6-stitch panel

Twelve-stitch braid

Panel of 12 sts on a background of rev st st.

Row 1 (RS): Knit.
Row 2: Purl.
Row 3: K4, C8B.
Row 4: Purl.
Rows 5–6: As rows 1–2.
Row 7: C8F, k4.
Row 8: Purl.
Rep these 8 rows.

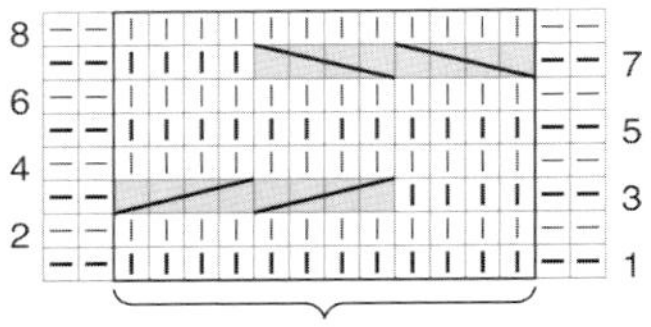

12-stitch panel

Checkered cable

Panel with a multiple of 4 + 2.
Example shown is worked over 10 sts on a background of rev st st.

Row 1 (RS): K2, *C4F; rep from * to end.
Row 2: Purl.
Row 3: *C4B; rep from * to last 2 sts, k2.
Row 4: Purl.
Rep these 4 rows.

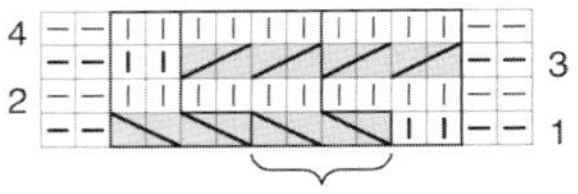

4-stitch panel

Tip

You will probably find a cable needle a very useful item when working with cable or Aran stitches (although you can make do with a straight double-pointed needle if you don't have a dedicated cable needle). The cable needle should be about the same size or smaller than the working needles. Don't use a larger size because this makes it difficult to knit from after the stitches are crossed.

Lattice pattern I

Multiple of 4 + 6.

Row 1 (RS): P1, *T2F, T2B; rep from * to last st, p1.

Row 2: K2, *C2BW, k2; rep from * to end.

Row 3: P1, *T2B, T2F; rep from * to last st, p1.

Row 4: K1, p1, k2, *C2FW, k2; rep from * to last 2 sts, p1, k1.

Rep these 4 rows.

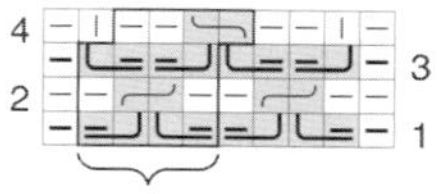

4-stitch repeat

Trophy cable I

Panel of 16 sts on a background of rev st st.

Row 1 (RS): Knit.

Row 2: Purl.

Row 3: C8B, C8F.

Row 4: Purl.

Rep rows 1–2 twice more.

Rep these 8 rows.

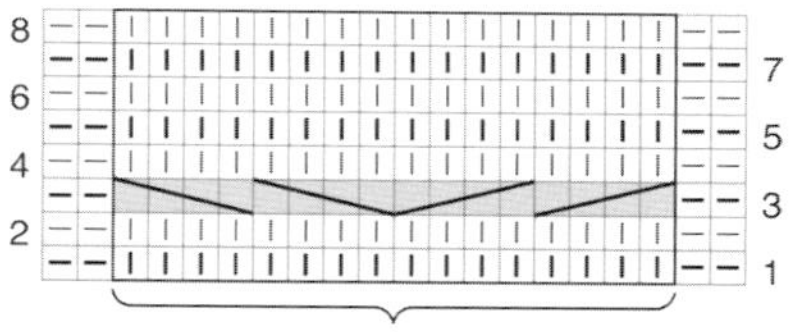

16-stitch panel

Open bobble pattern

Multiple of 4 +2.

Row 1 (RS): Purl.

Row 2: K1, *(k1, p1, k1) into next st, k3tog; rep from * to last st, k1.

Row 3: Purl.

Row 4: K1, *k3tog, (k1, p1, k1) into next st; rep from * to last st, k1.

Rep these 4 rows.

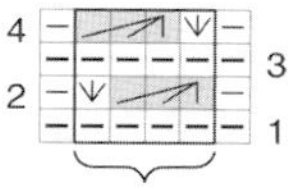

4-stitch repeat

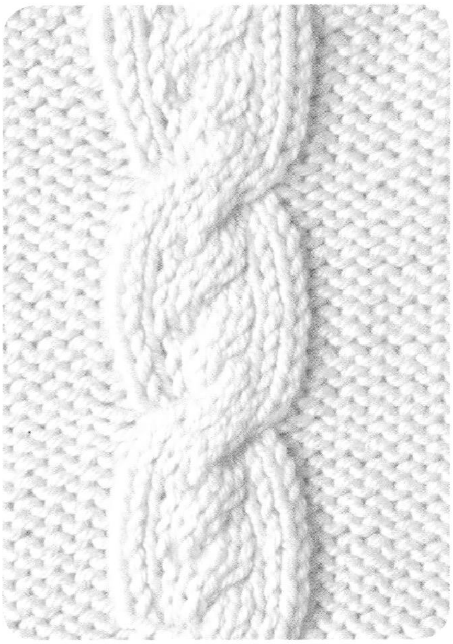

Filled oval cable

Panel of 8 sts on a background of rev st st.

Row 1 (RS): Knit.

Row 2: Purl.

Row 3: C8B.

Row 4: Purl.

Rows 5–6: As rows 1–2.

Row 7: K2, C4B, k2.

Row 8: Purl.

Rows 9–12: As rows 5–8.

Rep these 12 rows.

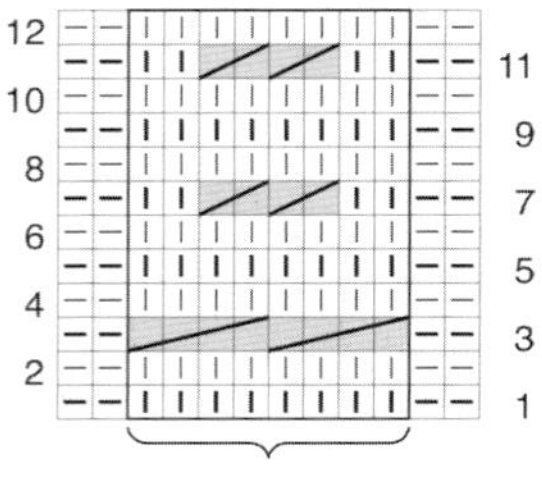

8-stitch panel

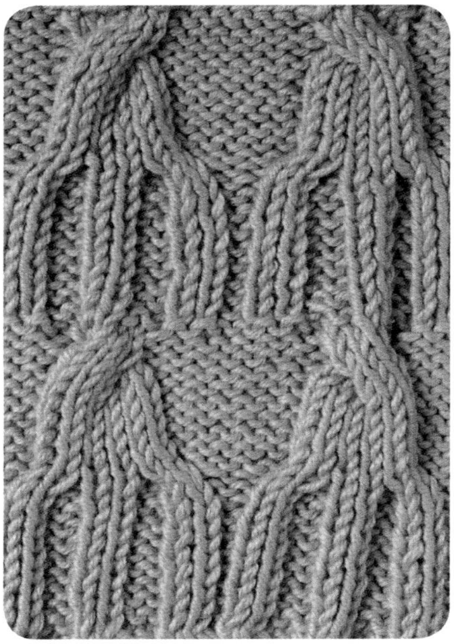

Bell cable

Worked over 26 sts on a background of rev st st.

Row 1 (RS): K2, [p3, k2] twice, p2, [k2, p3] twice, k2.

Row 2: P2, [k3, p2] twice, k2, p2, [k3, p2] twice.

Rep the last 2 rows 4 times more.

Row 11: T5L, k2, T5R, p2, T5L, k2, T5R.

Row 12: K3, p6, k8, p6, k3.

Row 13: P3, k6, p8, k6, p3.

Rep the last 2 rows twice more, then row 12 again.

Row 19: P3, C6F, p8, C6B, p3.

Row 20: K3, p6, k8, p6, k3.

Rep these 20 rows.

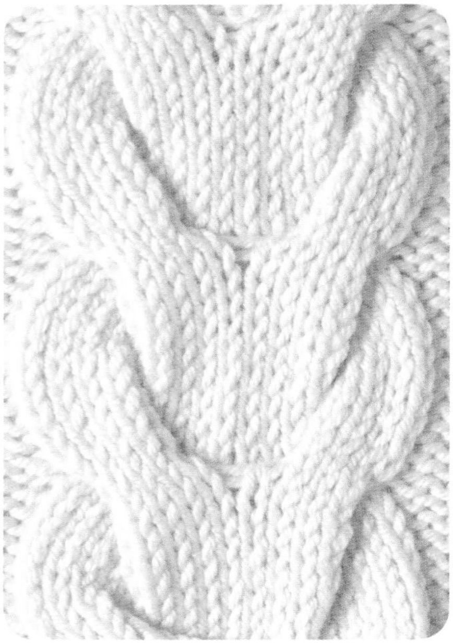

Trophy cable II

Panel of 20 sts on a background of rev st st.

Row 1 (RS): Knit.

Row 2: Purl.

Row 3: C10B, C10F.

Row 4: Purl.

Rep rows 1–2, 4 times more.

Rep these 12 rows.

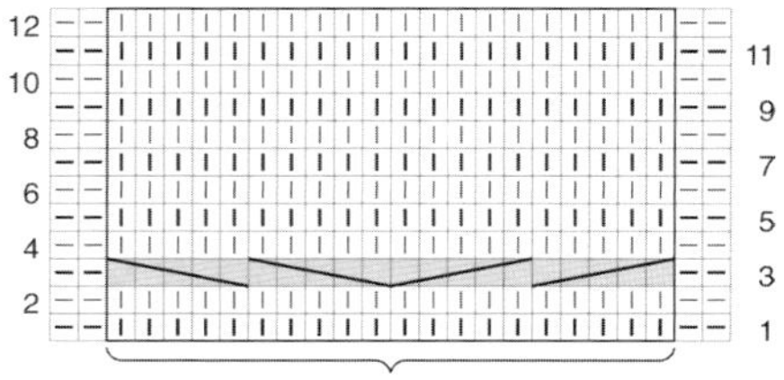

20-sttich panel

Touching paths

Panel of 9 sts on a background of rev st st.

Row 1 (RS): P3, T4B, k2.
Row 2: P2, k2, p2, k3.
Row 3: P1, T4B, p1, T3B.
Row 4: K1, p2, k3, p2, k1.
Row 5: T3B, p1, T4B, p1.
Row 6: K3, p2, k2, p2.
Row 7: K2, T4B, p3.
Row 8: K5, p4.
Row 9: C4B, p5.
Row 10: K5, p4.
Row 11: K2, T4F, p3.
Row 12: As row 6.
Row 13: T3F, p1, T4F, p1.
Row 14: As row 4.
Row 15: P1, T4F, p1, T3F.
Row 16: As row 2.
Row 17: P3, T4F, k2.
Row 18: P4, k5.
Row 19: P5, C4B.
Row 20: P4, k5.
Rep these 20 rows.

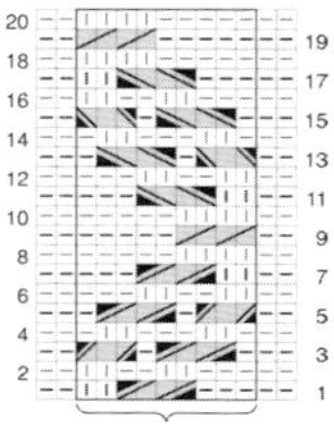

9-stitch panel

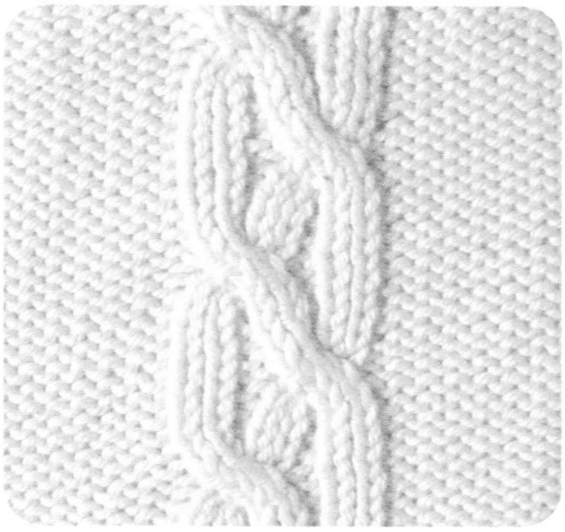

Crossing paths

Panel of 10 sts on a background of rev st st.

Special abbreviation:
T6L rib (twist 6 left rib) = Slip next 4 sts onto cable needle and hold at front of work, k2 from left-hand needle, slip 2 purl sts from cable needle back onto left-hand needle and purl them, then k2 from cable needle.

Row 1 (RS): K2, [p2, k2] twice.
Row 2: P2, [k2, p2] twice.
Row 3: T6L rib, p2, k2.
Row 4: As row 2.
Rep rows 1–2 twice more.
Row 9: K2, p2, T6L rib.
Row 10: As row 2.
Rows 11–12: As rows 1–2.
Rep these 12 rows.

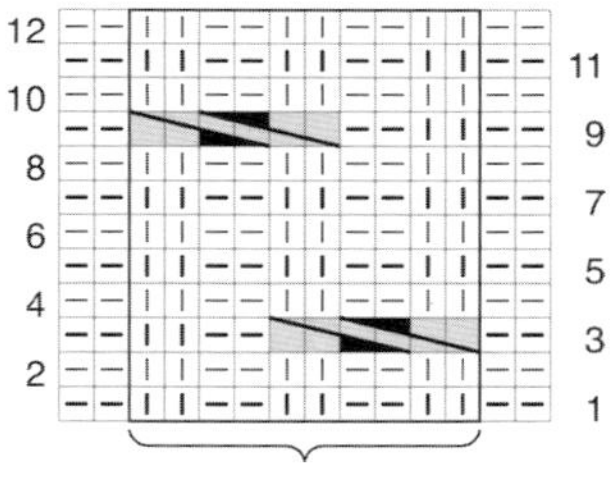

10-stitch panel

Interlocking cable

Panel of 12 sts on a background of rev st st.

Row 1 (RS): Knit.
Row 2: Purl.
Row 3: C6B, C6F.
Row 4: Purl.
Rep rows 1–2 twice more.
Rows 9–10: As rows 3–4.
Rep rows 1–2 twice more.
Row 15: C6F, C6B.
Row 16: Purl.
Rep rows 1–2 twice more.
Rows 21–22: As rows 15–16.
Rows 23–24: As rows 1–2.
Rep these 24 rows.

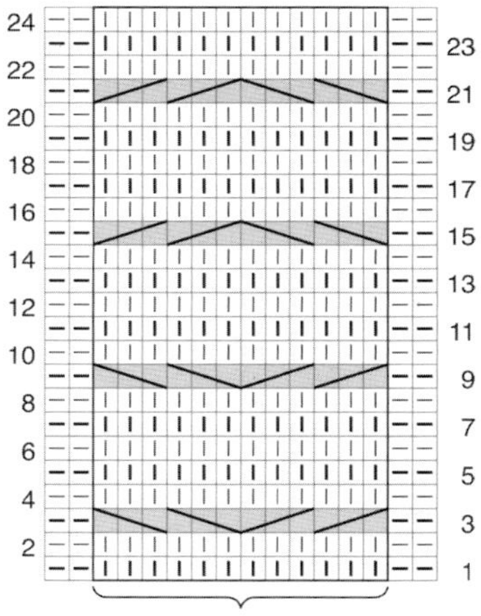

12-stitch panel

Inserted cable

Panel of 14 sts on a background of rev st st.

Row 1 (WS): K5, p4, k5.
Row 2: P5, C4F, p5.
Row 3: K5, p4, k5.
Row 4: P4, T3B, T3F, p4.
Row 5: K4, p2, k2, p2, k4.
Row 6: P3, T3B, p2, T3F, p3.
Row 7: K3, p2, k4, p2, k3.
Row 8: P2, T3B, p4, T3F, p2.
Row 9: K2, p2, k6, p2, k2.
Row 10: P1, [T3B] twice, [T3F] twice, p1.
Row 11: [K1, p2] twice, k2, [p2, k1] twice.
Row 12: [T3B] twice, p2, [T3F] twice.
Row 13: P2, k1, p2, k4, p2, k1, p2.
Row 14: K1, T2F, T3F, p2, T3B, T2B, k1.
Row 15: [P1, k1] twice, p2, k2, p2, [k1, p1] twice.
Row 16: K1, p1, T2F, T3F, T3B, T2B, p1, k1.
Row 17: P1, k2, p1, k1, p4, k1, p1, k2, p1.
Row 18: T2F, T2B, p1, C4F, p1, T2F, T2B.
Row 19: K1, C2B, k2, p4, k2, C2F, k1.
Rows 20–35: As rows 4–19.
Rep these 35 rows.

Dancing cable

Panel of 16 sts on a background of rev st st.

Row 1 (RS): P2, C4F, p4, C4F, p2.
Row 2: K2, p4, k4, p4, k2.
Row 3: P2, k4, p4, k4, p2.
Row 4: As row 2.
Rows 5–6: As rows 1–2.
Row 7: [T4B, T4F] twice.
Row 8: P2, k4, p4, k4, p2.
Row 9: K2, p4, C4F, p4, k2.
Row 10: As Row 8.
Row 11: K2, p4, k4, p4, k2.
Row 12: As row 8.
Rows 13–22: Rep the last 4 rows twice more, then rows 9–10 again.
Row 23: [T4F, T4B] twice.
Row 24: As row 2.
Rep these 24 rows.

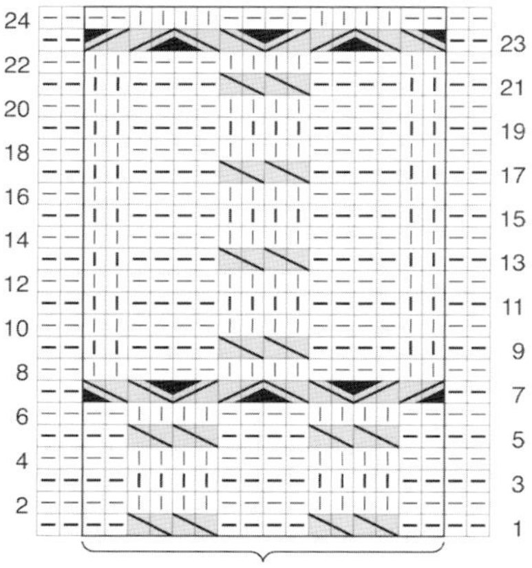

16-stitch panel

Open V-stitch

Panel of 12 sts on a background of rev st st.

Row 1 (RS): P3, C3B, C3F, p3.
Row 2: K3, p6, k3.
Row 3: P2, C3B, k2, C3F, p2.
Row 4: K2, p8, k2.
Row 5: P1, T3B, k4, T3F, p1.
Row 6: K1, p2, k1, p4, k1, p2, k1.
Row 7: T3B, p1, C4B, p1, T3F.
Row 8: P2, k2, p4, k2, p2.
Rep these 8 rows.

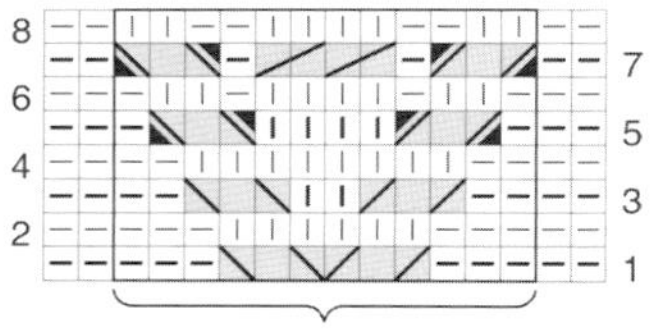

12-stitch panel

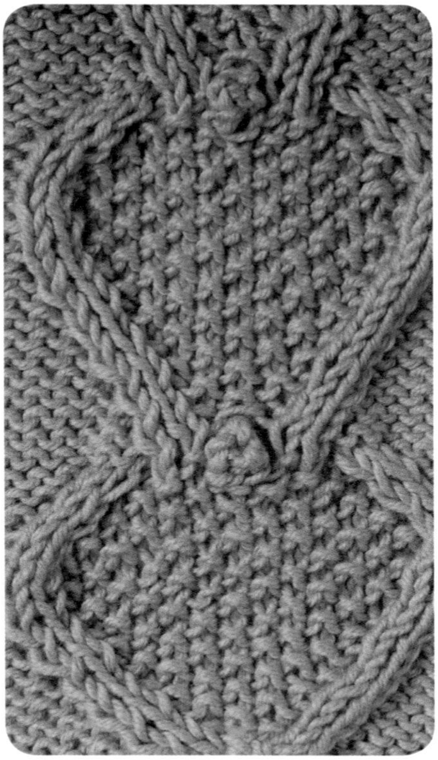

Seed stitch hearts

Worked over 19 sts.

Row 1 (RS): P6, T3B, k1, T3F, p6.

Row 2: K6, p3, k1, p3, k6.

Row 3: P5, C3B, p1, k1, p1, C3F, p5.

Row 4: K5, p2, [k1, p1] twice, k1, p2, k5.

Row 5: P4, T3B, [k1, p1] twice, k1, T3F, p4.

Row 6: K4, p3, [k1, p1] twice, k1, p3, k4.

Row 7: P3, C3B, [p1, k1] 3 times, p1, C3F, p3.

Row 8: K3, p2, [k1, p1] 4 times, k1, p2, k3.

Row 9: P2, T3B, [k1, p1] 4 times, k1, T3F, p2.

Row 10: K2, p3, [k1, p1] 4 times, k1, p3, k2.

Row 11: P1, C3B, [p1, k1] 5 times, p1, C3F, p1.

Row 12: K1, p2, [k1, p1] 6 times, k1, p2, k1.

Row 13: T3B, [k1, p1] 6 times, k1, T3F.

Row 14: P3, [k1, p1] 6 times, k1, p3.

Row 15: K2, [p1, k1] 7 times, p1, k2.

Row 16: As row 14.

Row 17: T4F, [p1, k1] 5 times, p1, T4B.

Row 18: K2, p3, [k1, p1] 4 times, k1, p3, k2.

Row 19: P2, T4F, [p1, k1] 3 times, p1, T4B, p2.

Row 20: K7, p2, k1, p2, k7.

Rep these 20 rows.

Note: Bobbles may be knitted into this pattern by working row 19 as follows: p2, T4F, p1, k1, p1, MB, p1, k1, p1, T4B, p2.

Bobble with cable

Panel of 9 sts on a background of rev st st.

Special abbreviation:

MB (make bobble) = [K1, p1] twice into next st, [turn and p4, turn and k4] twice, turn and p4, turn and sl 2, k2tog, p2sso.

Row 1 (RS): P1, T3B, p1, T3F, p1.

Row 2: K1, p2, k3, p2, k1.

Row 3: T3B, p3, T3F.

Row 4: P2, k5, p2.

Row 5: K2, p2, MB, p2, k2.

Row 6: P2, k5, p2.

Row 7: T3F, p3, T3B.

Row 8: As row 2.

Row 9: P1, T3F, p1, T3B, p1.

Row 10: K2, p5, k2.

Row 11: P2, T5BP, p2.

Row 12: K2, p5, k2.

Rep these 12 rows.

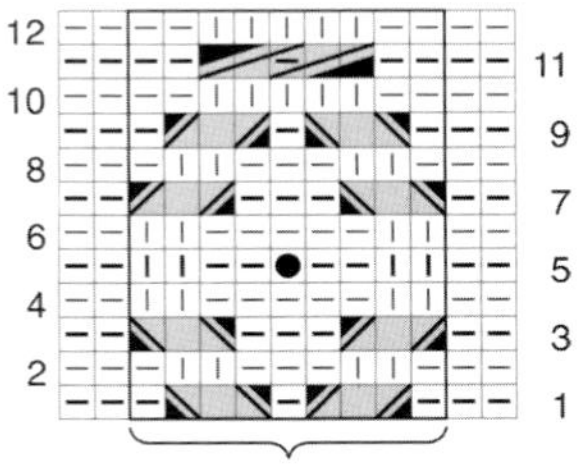

9-stitch panel

Double diamonds

Panel of 20 sts on a background of rev st st.

Row 1 (RS): P6, T4BP, T4FP, p6.
Row 2: K6, [p2, k1] twice, p2, k6.
Row 3: P4, T4B, p1, k2, p1, T4F, p4.
Row 4: K4, [p2, k3] twice, p2, k4.
Row 5: P2, T4B, p2, C2B, C2F, p2, T4F, p2.
Row 6: K2, p2, k4, p4, k4, p2, k2.
Row 7: T4B, p2, C4B, C4F, p2, T4F.
Row 8: P2, k4, p8, k4, p2.
Row 9: T4F, C4B, k4, C4F, T4B.
Row 10: K2, p16, k2.
Row 11: P2, C4B, k8, C4F, p2.
Row 12: K2, p16, k2.
Row 13: T4B, T4F, k4, T4B, T4F.
Row 14: As row 8.
Row 15: T4F, p2, T4F, T4B, p2, T4B.
Row 16: As row 6.
Row 17: P2, T4F, p2, T2F, T2B, p2, T4B, p2.
Row 18: As row 4.
Row 19: P4, T4F, p1, k2, p1, T4B, p4.
Row 20: As row 2.
Row 21: P6, T4F, T4B, p6.
Row 22: K8, p4, k8.
Row 23: P8, k4, p8.
Row 24: K8, p4, k8.
Rep these 24 rows.

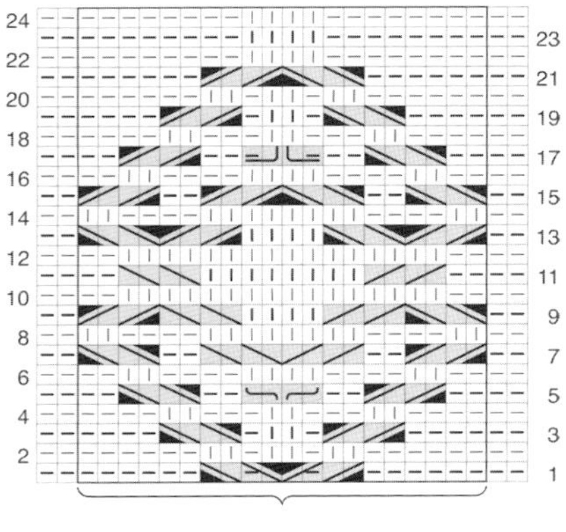

20-stitch panel

Cable with swirl

Panel of 22 sts on a background of rev st st.

Special abbreviation:
Work 5tog (work 5 sts together) = Wyib sl 3 purlwise, *pass 2nd st on right-hand needle over first (center) st, slip center st back onto left-hand needle, pass 2nd st on left-hand needle over*, slip center st back onto right-hand needle; rep from * to * once more, purl center st. (Note: Stitch referred to as "center st" is center one of 5 sts.)

Row 1 (RS): T4B, p1, T4F, T4B, p9.
Row 2: K11, p4, k5, p2.
Row 3: K2, p5, C4B, p11.
Row 4: As row 2.
Row 5: T4F, p1, T4B, T4F, p9.
Row 6: K9, p2, k4, p2, k1, p2, k2.
Row 7: P2, work 5tog, p4, T4F, p4, M5K, p2.
Row 8: K2, p2, k1, p2, k4, p2, k9.
Row 9: P9, T4F, T4B, p1, T4F.
Row 10: P2, k5, p4, k11.
Row 11: P11, C4F, p5, k2.
Row 12: As row 10.
Row 13: P9, T4B, T4F, p1, T4B.
Row 14: As row 8.
Row 15: P2, M5K, p4, T4B, p4, work 5tog, p2.
Row 16: As row 6.
Rep these 16 rows.

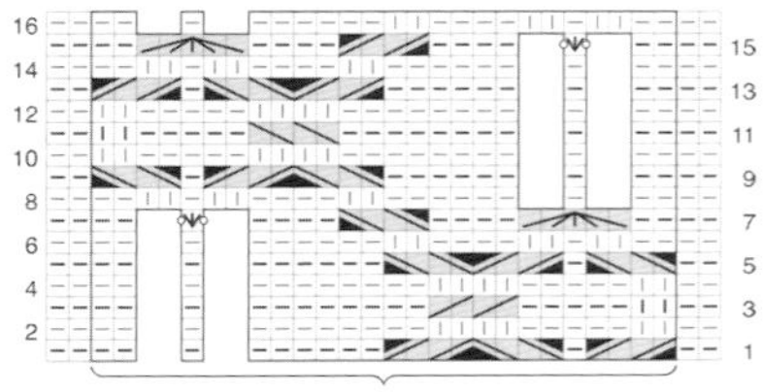

22-stitch panel

Slanting stripes

Multiple of 6 + 4.

Row 1 (RS): P1, *T3F, p3; rep from * to last 3 sts, p3.
Row 2: K6, p2, *k4, p2; rep from * to last 2 sts, k2.
Row 3: P2, *T3F, p3; rep from * to last 2 sts, p2.
Row 4: K5, p2, *k4, p2; rep from * to last 3 sts, k3.
Row 5: *P3, T3F; rep from * to last 4 sts, p4.
Row 6: K4, *p2, k4; rep from * to end.
Row 7: P4, *T3F, p3; rep from * to end.
Row 8: K3, *p2, k4; rep from * to last st, k1.
Row 9: P5, T3F, *p3, T3F; rep from * to last 2 sts, p2.
Row 10: K2, *p2, k4; rep from * to last 2 sts, k2.
Row 11: P6, T3F, *p3, T3F; rep from * to last st, p1.
Row 12: K1, *p2, k4; rep from * to last 3 sts, k3.
Rep these 12 rows.

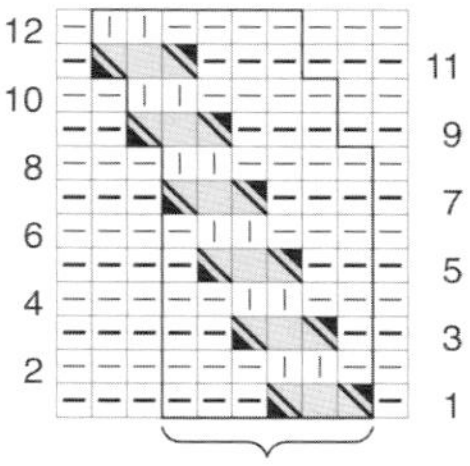

6-stitch repeat

Loose V-stitch

Panel of 12 sts on a background of rev st st.

Row 1 (RS): P3, T3B, T3F, p3.
Row 2: K3, p2, k2, p2, k3.
Row 3: P2, T3B, p2, T3F, p2.
Row 4: K2, p2, k4, p2, k2.
Row 5: P1, T3B, p4, T3F, p1.
Row 6: K1, p2, k6, p2, k1.
Row 7: T3B, p6, T3F.
Row 8: P2, k8, p2.
Rep these 8 rows.

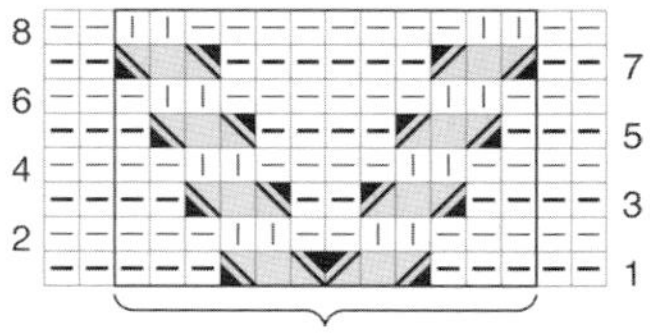

12-stitch panel

Woven cable

Worked over multiple of 8 + 4 on a background of rev st st (minimum 20 sts).
The example shown is worked over 28 sts.

Row 1 (RS): Knit.
Row 2 and every alt row: K2, purl to last 2 sts, k2.
Row 3: Knit.
Row 5: K2, *C8B; rep from * to last 2 sts, k2.
Row 7: Knit.
Row 9: Knit.
Row 11: K6, *C8F; rep from * to last 6 sts, k6.
Row 12: As row 2.
Rep these 12 rows.

Zigzag cable

Multiple of 4 + 2.

Row 1 (RS): P3, T2B, *p2, T2B; rep from * to last st, p1.
Row 2: K2, *p1, k3; rep from * to end.
Row 3: P2, *T2B, p2; rep from * to end.
Row 4: *K3, p1; rep from * to last 2 sts, k2.
Row 5: P1, T2B, *p2, T2B; rep from * to last 3 sts, p3.
Row 6: K4, p1, *k3, p1; rep from * to last st, k1.
Row 7: P1, T2F, *p2, T2F; rep from * to last 3 sts, p3.
Row 8: As row 4.
Row 9: P2, *T2F, p2; rep from * to end.
Row 10: As row 2.
Row 11: P3, T2F, *p2, T2F; rep from * to last st, p1.
Row 12: K1, p1, *k3, p1; rep from * to last 4 sts, k4.
Rep these 12 rows.

Note: This stitch is also very effective when worked as a panel of 4 sts on a background of rev st st.

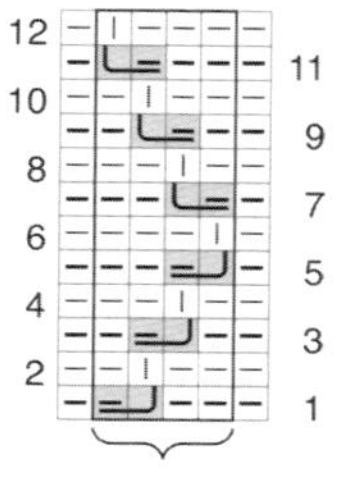

4-stitch repeat

Rippled diamonds

Panel of 11 sts on a background of rev st st.

Special abbreviation:

T3RP (twist 3 right purl) = Slip next 2 sts onto cable needle and hold at back of work, k1 from left-hand needle, then p1, k1 from cable needle.

Row 1 (RS): P3, T2B, k1, T2F, p3.
Row 2: K3, p1, [k1, p1] twice, k3.
Row 3: P2, T2B, k1, p1, k1, T2F, p2.
Row 4: K2, p1, [k1, p1] 3 times, k2.
Row 5: P1, T2B, k1, [p1, k1] twice, T2F, p1.
Row 6: K1, [p1, k1] 5 times.
Row 7: T2B, k1, [p1, k1] 3 times, T2F.
Row 8: P1, [k1, p1] 5 times.
Row 9: T2F, p1, [k1, p1] 3 times, T2B.
Row 10: As row 6.
Row 11: P1, T2F, p1, [k1, p1] twice, T2B, p1.
Row 12: As row 4.
Row 13: P2, T2F, p1, k1, p1, T2B, p2.
Row 14: As row 2.
Row 15: P3, T2F, p1, T2B, p3.
Row 16: K4, p1, k1, p1, k4.
Row 17: P4, T3RP, p4.
Row 18: As row 16.

Rep these 18 rows.

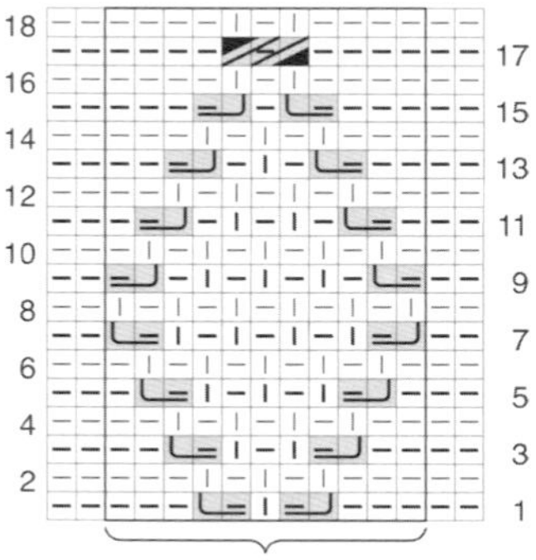

11-stitch panel

Lattice pattern II

Worked over a multiple of 16 + 1 on a background of rev st st (minimum 33 sts). The example shown is worked over 33 sts.

Row 1 (RS): K1, *yo, k2, skpo, p7, k2tog, k2, yo, k1; rep from * to end.

Row 2: P5, *k7, p9; rep from * to last 12 sts, k7, p5.

Row 3: K2, *yo, k2, skpo, p5, k2tog, k2, yo, k2tog, yo, k1; rep from * to last 15 sts, yo, k2, skpo, p5, k2tog, k2, yo, k2.

Row 4: P6, *k5, p11; rep from * to last 11 sts, k5, p6.

Row 5: *K2tog, yo, k1, yo, k2, skpo, p3, k2tog, k2, yo, k2tog, yo; rep from * to last st, k1.

Row 6: P7, *k3, p13; rep from * to last 10 sts, k3, p7.

Row 7: K1, *k2tog, yo, k1, yo, k2, skpo, p1, k2tog, k2, yo, [k2tog, yo] twice; rep from * to last 16 sts, k2tog, yo, k1, yo, k2, skpo, p1, k2tog, k2, yo, k2tog, yo, k2.

Row 8: P8, *k1, p15; rep from * to last 9 sts, k1, p8.

Row 9: P5, *C7B, p9; rep from * to last 12 sts, C7B, p5.

Row 10: K5, *p3, k1, p3, k9; rep from * to last 12 sts, p3, k1, p3, k5.

Row 11: P4, *k2tog, k2, yo, k1, yo, k2, skpo, p7; rep from * to last 13 sts, k2tog, k2, yo, k1, yo, k2, skpo, p4.

Row 12: K4, *p9, k7; rep from * to last 13 sts, p9, k4.

Row 13: P3, *k2tog, k2, yo, k2tog, yo, k1, yo, k2, skpo, p5; rep from * to last 14 sts, k2tog, k2, yo, k2tog, yo, k1, yo, k2, skpo, p3.

Row 14: K3, *p11, k5; rep from * to last 14 sts, p11, k3.

Row 15: P2, *k2tog, k2, yo, [k2tog, yo] twice, k1, yo, k2, skpo, p3; rep from * to last 15 sts, k2tog, k2, yo, [k2tog, yo] twice, k1, yo, k2, skpo, p2.

Row 16: K2, *p13, k3; rep from * to last 15 sts, p13, k2.

Row 17: P1, *k2tog, k2, yo, [k2tog, yo] 3 times, k1, yo, k2, skpo, p1; rep from * to end.

Row 18: K1, *p15, k1; rep from * to end.

Row 19: P1, k3, *p9, C7F; rep from * to last 13 sts, p9, k3, p1.

Row 20: K1, p3, *k9, p3, k1, p3; rep from * to last 13 sts, k9, p3, k1.

Rep these 20 rows.

Chunky braid

Panel with a multiple of 6 + 9.

Example shown is worked over 15 sts on a background of rev st st.

Row 1 (RS): Knit.

Row 2: Purl.

Row 3: K3, *C6F; rep from * to end.

Row 4: Purl.

Rows 5–6: As rows 1–2.

Row 7: *C6B; rep from * to last 3 sts, k3.

Row 8: Purl.

Rep these 8 rows.

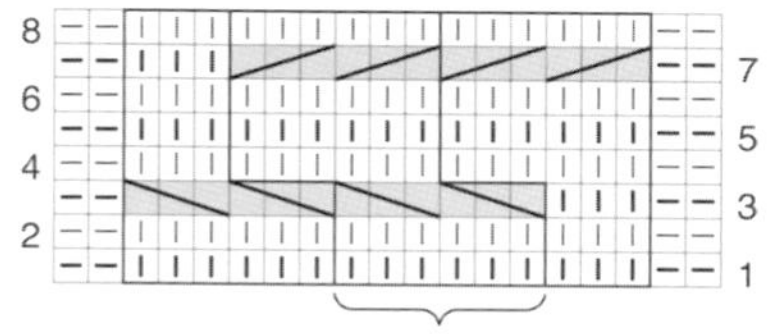

6-stitch repeat

Little cable fabric

Multiple of 4 + 1.

Row 1 (RS): K1, *sl 1 purlwise, k3; rep from * to end.

Row 2: *P3, sl 1 purlwise; rep from * to last st, p1.

Row 3: K1, *C3L, k1; rep from * to end.

Row 4: Purl.

Row 5: K5, *sl 1, k3; rep from * to end.

Row 6: *P3, sl 1; rep from * to last 5 sts, p5.

Row 7: K3, *C3R, k1; rep from * to last 2 sts, k2.

Row 8: Purl.

Rep these 8 rows.

Cable with segments

Panel of 16 sts on a background of rev st st.

Special abbreviations:

T8B rib (twist 8 back rib) = Slip next 4 sts onto cable needle and hold at back of work, k1, p2, k1 from left-hand needle, then k1, p2, k1 from cable needle.

T8F rib (twist 8 front rib) = Slip next 4 sts onto cable needle and hold at front of work, k1, p2, k1 from left-hand needle, then k1, p2, k1 from cable needle.

Row 1 (RS): K1, p2, [k2, p2] 3 times, k1.

Row 2: P1, k2, [p2, k2] 3 times, p1.

Row 3: T8B rib, T8F rib.

Row 4: As row 2.

Rep rows 1–2, 4 times more.

Rep these 12 rows.

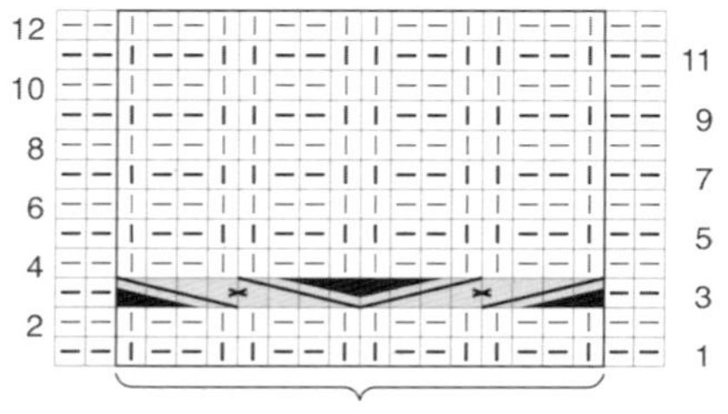

16-stitch panel

Bobbles and waves

Worked over 26 sts on a background of rev st st.

Special abbreviation:

MB (make bobble) = Knit into front, back, and front of next st, [turn and k3] 3 times, then turn and sk2po.

Row 1 (RS): P2, T3B, p5, C6B, p5, T3F, p2.

Row 2: K2, p2, k6, p6, k6, p2, k2.

Row 3: P1, T3B, p4, T5B, T5F, p4, T3F, p1.

Row 4: K1, p2, k5, p3, k4, p3, k5, p2, k1.

Row 5: T3B, p3, T5B, p4, T5F, p3, T3F.

Row 6: P2, k1, MB, k2, p3, k8, p3, k2, MB, k1, p2.

Row 7: T3F, p3, k3, p8, k3, p3, T3B.

Row 8: K1, p2, k3, p3, k8, p3, k3, p2, k1.

Row 9: P1, T3F, p2, T5F, p4, T5B, p2, T3B, p1.

Row 10: K2, p2, [k4, p3] twice, k4, p2, k2.

Row 11: P2, T3F, p3, T5F, T5B, p3, T3B, p2.

Row 12: K1, MB, k1, p2, k5, p6, k5, p2, k1, MB, k1.

Rep these 12 rows.

Internal diamonds

Panel of 14 sts on a background of rev st st.

Row 1 (RS): P4, C3B, C3F, p4.

Row 2: K4, [PB1] 6 times, k4.

Row 3: P3, T3B, C2B, T3F, p3.

Row 4: K3, *[PB1] twice, k1; rep from * to last 2 sts, k2.

Row 5: P2, T3B, p1, C2B, p1, T3F, p2.

Row 6: *K2, [PB1] twice; rep from * to last 2 sts, k2.

Row 7: P1, T3B, p1, T2B, T2F, p1, T3F, p1.

Row 8: K1, [PB1] twice, k2, [PB1, k2] twice, [PB1] twice, k1.

Row 9: T3B, p1, T2B, p2, T2F, p1, T3F.

Row 10: [PB1] twice, k2, PB1, k4, PB1, k2, [PB1] twice.

Row 11: K2, p2, k1, p4, k1, p2, k2.

Row 12: As row 10.

Row 13: T3F, p1, T2F, p2, T2B, p1, T3B.

Row 14: As row 8.

Row 15: P1, T3F, p1, T2F, T2B, p1, T3B, p1.

Row 16: As row 6.

Row 17: P2, T3F, p1, C2B, p1, T3B, p2.

Row 18: As row 4.

Row 19: P3, T3F, C2B, T3B, p3.

Row 20: As row 2.

Row 21: P4, T3F, T3B, p4.

Row 22: K5, [PB1] 4 times, k5.

Row 23: P5, C4B, p5.

Row 24: As row 22.

Rep these 24 rows.

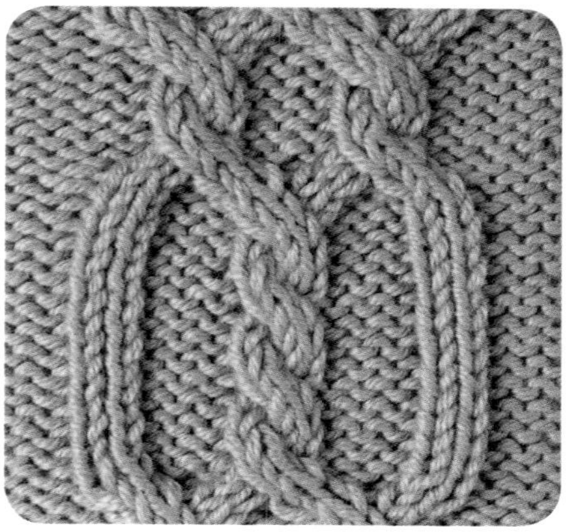

Criss-cross cable with twists

Panel of 16 sts on a background of rev st st.

Row 1 (RS): P2, C4F, p4, C4F, p2.
Row 2: K2, p4, k4, p4, k2.
Row 3: P2, k4, p4, k4, p2.
Row 4: As row 2.
Row 5: As row 1.
Row 6: As row 2.
Row 7: [T4B, T4F] twice.
Row 8: As row 3.
Row 9: K2, p4, C4F, p4, k2.
Row 10: As row 3.
Row 11: As row 2.
Row 12: As row 3.
Row 13: As row 9.
Rep the last 4 rows twice more.
Row 22: As row 3.
Row 23: [T4F, T4B] twice.
Row 24: As row 2.
Rep these 24 rows.

Wide cable panel

Panel of 20 sts on a background of rev st st.

Row 1 (WS) and every alt row: Purl.
Row 2: K6, C4B, C4F, k6.
Row 4: K4, C4B, k4, C4F, k4.
Row 6: K2, C4B, k8, C4F, k2.
Row 8: C4B, k12, C4F.
Rep these 8 rows.

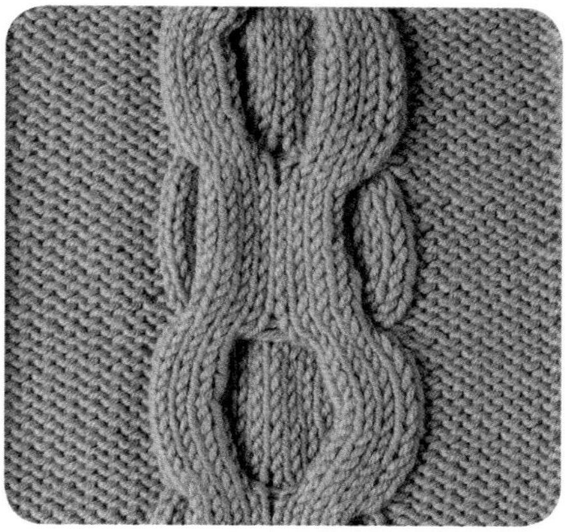

Padded cable

Panel of 20 sts on a background of rev st st.

Row 1 (RS): Knit.
Row 2: Purl.
Row 3: C10B, C10F.
Row 4: Purl.
Rep rows 1–2, 5 times more.
Row 15: C10F, C10B.
Row 16: Purl.
Rep rows 1–2, 4 times more.
Rep these 24 rows.

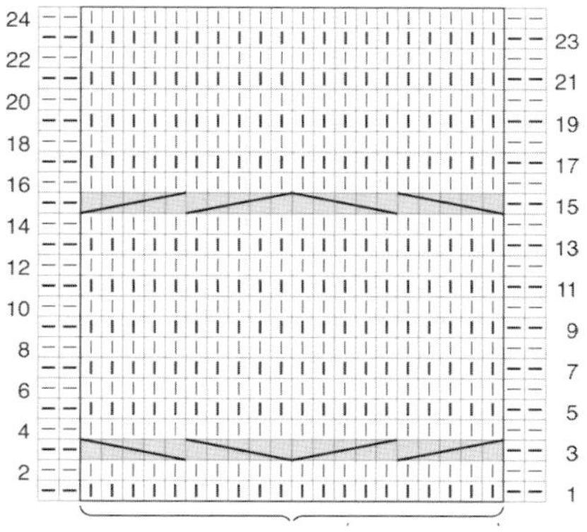

20-stitch panel

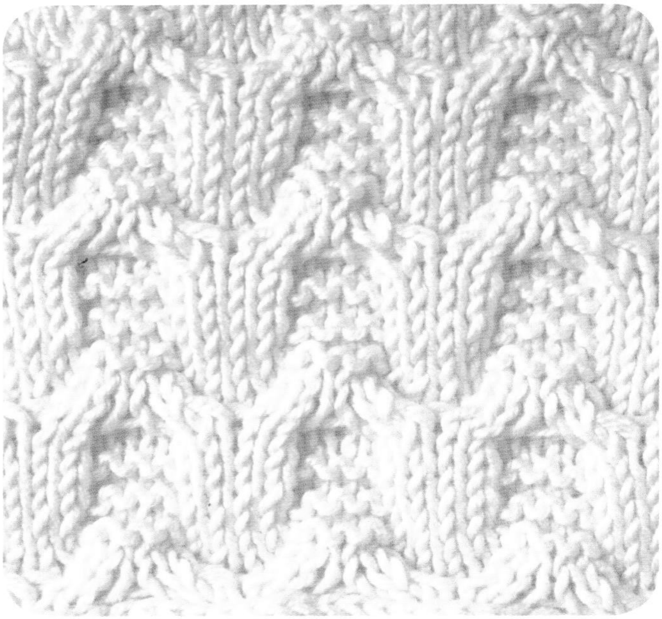

Cable stitch

Multiple of 12.

Row 1 (RS): *K2, p1, k6, p1, k2; rep from * to end.

Row 2: *P2, k1, p6, k1, p2; rep from * to end.

Rows 3, 5, 7, and 9: *K2, p2, k4, p2, k2; rep from * to end.

Rows 4, 6, and 8: *P2, k2, p4, k2, p2; rep from * to end.

Row 10: *P2, T4F, T4B, p2; rep from * to end.

Row 11: Knit.

Row 12: As row 2.

Rep these 12 rows.

Forked cable

Multiple of 8 + 2.

Row 1 (WS): Purl.

Row 2: P3, k4, *p4, k4; rep from * to last 3 sts, p3.

Rep the last 2 rows twice more, then row 1 again.

Row 8: K3, p4, *k4, p4; rep from * to last 3 sts, k3.

Row 9: Purl.

Row 10: K1, *C4F, C4B; rep from * to last st, k1.

Rep these 10 rows.

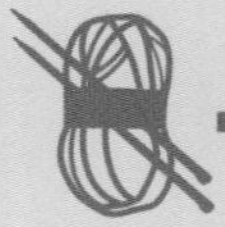

Tip

To avoid having a knot in the middle of the row where you have joined a new ball of yarn, check that you have enough yarn to complete the next row—you will need approximately three times the width of the swatch or garment. If you do not have sufficient yarn, tie the yarn off at the end of the row and join in the new ball. Weave the yarn tail into the seam at the end of the project.

Vine and twist

Worked over 17 sts on a background of rev st st.

Note: Increases are worked purlwise.

Row 1 (RS): P6, C5, p6.
Row 2: K6, p5, k6.
Row 3: P5, T3B, k1, T3F, p5.
Row 4: K5, p2, k1, p1, k1, p2, k5.
Row 5: P4, T3B, p1, k1, p1, T3F, p4.
Row 6: K4, p2, k2, p1, k2, p2, k4.
Row 7: P3, k2tog, k1, p2, yo, k1, yo, p2, k1, skpo, p3.
Row 8: K3, p2, k2, p3, k2, p2, k3.
Row 9: P2, k2tog, k1, p2, [k1, yo] twice, k1, p2, k1, skpo, p2.
Row 10: K2, p2, k2, p5, k2, p2, k2.
Row 11: P1, k2tog, k1, p2, k2, yo, k1, yo, k2, p2, k1, skpo, p1.
Row 12: K1, p2, k2, p7, k2, p2, k1.
Row 13: Inc, k2, p2, k2, sl 2tog knitwise, k1, p2sso, k2, p2, k2, inc.
Row 14: As row 10.
Row 15: P1, inc, k2, p2, k1, sl 2tog knitwise, k1, p2sso, k1, p2, k2, inc, p1.
Row 16: As row 8.
Row 17: P2, inc, k2, p2, sl 2tog knitwise, k1, p2sso, p2, k2, inc, p2.
Row 18: As row 6.
Row 19: P4, T3F, p1, k1, p1, T3B, p4.
Row 20: As row 4.
Row 21: P5, T3F, k1, T3B, p5.
Row 22: As row 2.
Row 23: As row 1.
Row 24: As row 2.
Row 25: P6, k5, p6.
Row 26: As row 2.
Rep these 26 rows.

Double spiral cable

Panel of 22 sts on a background of rev st st. The number of sts within the panel varies.

Special abbreviation:

Work 5tog (work 5 sts together) = Wyib sl 3 purlwise, *pass 2nd st on right-hand needle over first (center) st, slip center st back onto left-hand needle, pass 2nd st on left-hand needle over*, slip center st back onto right-hand needle; rep from * to * once more, purl center st. (Note: Stitch referred to as "center st" is center of 5 sts.)

Row 1 (RS): P9, k4, p9.
Row 2: K9, p4, k9.
Row 3: P9, C4B, p9.
Row 4: K9, p4, k9.
Row 5: P2, M5K, p4, T4B, T4F, p4, M5K, p2.
Row 6: K2, p2, k1, [p2, k4] 3 times, p2, k1, p2, k2.
Row 7: T4B, p1, T4F, T4B, p4, T4F, T4B, p1, T4F.
Row 8: P2, k5, p4, k8, p4, k5, p2.
Row 9: K2, p5, C4F, p8, C4B, p5, k2.
Row 10: As row 8.
Row 11: T4F, p1, T4B, T4F, p4, T4B, T4F, p1, T4B.
Row 12: As row 6.
Row 13: P2, work 5tog, p4, T4F, T4B, p4, work 5tog, p2.
Rows 14–16: As rows 2–4.
Rep these 16 rows.

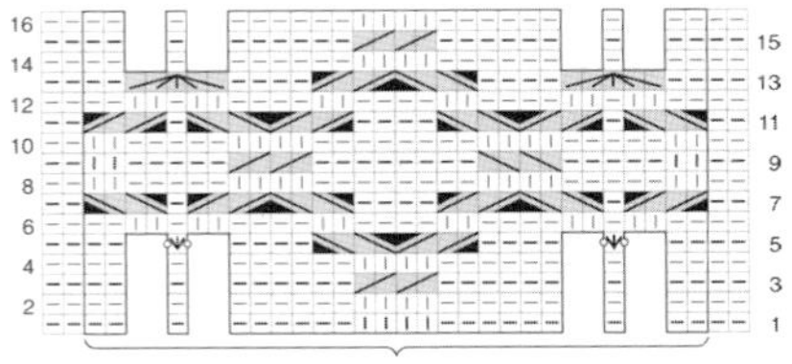

22-stitch panel

Ornamental cable

Panel of 30 sts on a background of rev st st.

Row 1 (RS): K9, C6B, C6F, k9.

Row 2 and every alt row: Purl.

Row 3: K6, C6B, k6, C6F, k6.

Row 5: K3, C6B, k12, C6F, k3.

Row 7: C6B, k18, C6F.

Row 8: Purl.

Rep these 8 rows.

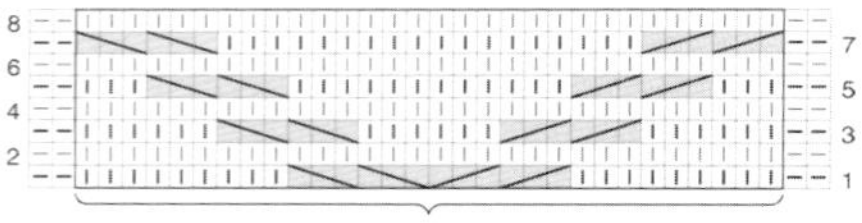

30-stitch panel

Small wavy cable

Multiple of 3 + 1.

Row 1 (RS): P1, *C2B, p1; rep from * to end.

Row 2: K1, *p2, k1; rep from * to end.

Row 3: P1, *C2F, p1; rep from * to end.

Row 4: As row 2.

Rep these 4 rows.

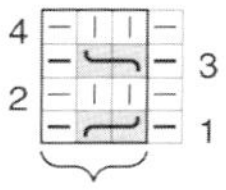

3-stitch repeat

Diagonal ripple

Multiple of 4 + 3.

Row 1 (RS): P4, T2B, *p2, T2B; rep from * to last st, p1.

Row 2: K2, p1, *k3, p1; rep from * to last 4 sts, k4.

Row 3: P3, *T2B, p2; rep from * to end.

Row 4: K3, *p1, k3; rep from * to end.

Row 5: *P2, T2B; rep from * to last 3 sts, p3.

Row 6: K4, p1, *k3, p1; rep from * to last 2 sts, k2.

Row 7: P1, T2B, *p2, T2B; rep from * to last 4 sts, p4.

Row 8: K5, p1, *k3, p1; rep from * to last st, k1.

Rep these 8 rows.

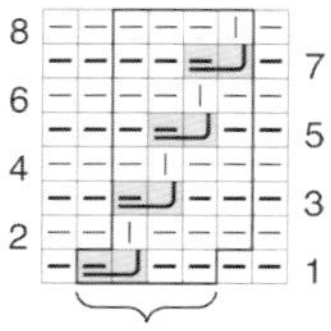

4-stitch repeat

Eyelet cable

Multiple of 8 + 1.

Special abbreviation:

C3tog (cross 3 together) = Slip next 2 sts onto cable needle and hold at back of work, k1 from left-hand needle, then k2tog from cable needle.

Row 1 (RS): P1, *C3tog, p1, k3, p1; rep from * to end.

Row 2: K1, *p3, k1, p1, yo, p1, k1; rep from * to end.

Row 3: P1, *k3, p1, C3tog, p1; rep from * to end.

Row 4: K1, *p1, yo, p1, k1, p3, k1; rep from * to end.

Rep these 4 rows.

Lace and cables

Multiple of 11 + 7.

Row 1 (RS): K1, *yo, skpo, k1, k2tog, yo, k6; rep from * to last 6 sts, yo, skpo, k1, k2tog, yo, k1.

Row 2 and every alt row: Purl.

Row 3: K2, *yo, sk2po, yo, k8; rep from * to last 5 sts, yo, sk2po, yo, k2.

Row 5: As row 1.

Row 7: K2, *yo, sk2po, yo, k1, C6B, k1; rep from * to last 5 sts, yo, sk2po, yo, k2.

Row 8: Purl.

Rep these 8 rows.

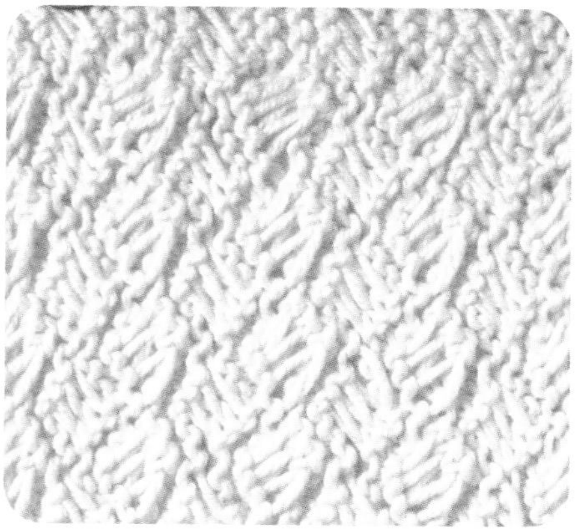

Loose woven cables

Multiple of 6 + 2.

Row 1 (RS): Knit.

Row 2: K1, knit to last st winding yarn twice around needle for each st, k1.

Row 3: K1, *C6B dropping extra loops; rep from * to last st, k1.

Work 2 rows in garter st.

Row 6: K4, *knit to last 4 sts wrapping yarn twice around needle for each st, k4.

Row 7: K4, *C6F dropping extra loops; rep from * to last 4 sts, k4.

Row 8: Knit.

Rep these 8 rows.

Diagonal tramline cable

Panel of 18 sts on a background of rev st st.

Row 1 (RS): K2, p3, k2, p4, k2, p3, k2.

Row 2: P2, k3, p2, k4, p2, k3, p2.

Row 3: As row 1.

Row 4: As row 2.

Row 5: [T3F, p2] twice, T3B, p2, T3B.

Row 6: K1, p2, k3, p2, k2, p2, k3, p2, k1.

Row 7: P1, T3F, p2, T3F, T3B, p2, T3B, p1.

Row 8: K2, p2, k3, p4, k3, p2, k2.

Row 9: P2, T3F, p2, C4B, p2, T3B, p2.

Row 10: K3, p2, k2, p4, k2, p2, k3.

Row 11: P3, [T3F, T3B] twice, p3.

Row 12: K4, p4, k2, p4, k4.

Row 13: P4, C4F, p2, C4F, p4.

Row 14: K4, p4, k2, p4, k4.

Row 15: P3, [T3B, T3F] twice, p3.

Row 16: K3, p2, k2, p4, k2, p2, k3.

Row 17: P2, T3B, p2, C4B, p2, T3F, p2.

Row 18: K2, p2, k3, p4, k3, p2, k2.

Row 19: P1, T3B, p2, T3B, T3F, p2, T3F, p1.

Row 20: K1, p2, k3, p2, k2, p2, k3, p2, k1.

Row 21: [T3B, p2] twice, T3F, p2, T3F.

Row 22: As row 2.

Row 23: As row 1.

Rep row 2 once more, then rows 1–2 once more.

Rep these 26 rows.

Simple cable

Panel of 2 sts on a background of rev st st.

Row 1 (RS): C2B

Row 2: Purl.

Rep these 2 rows.

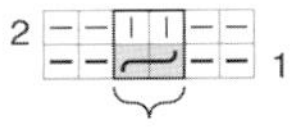

2-stitch panel

Twisted and crossed cable

Panel of 16 sts on a background of rev st st.

Row 1 (RS): P2, C4B, p4, C4F, p2.

Row 2: K2, p4, k4, p4, k2.

Row 3: P1, T3B, T3F, p2, T3B, T3F, p1.

Row 4: K1, [p2, k2] 3 times, p2, k1.

Row 5: [T3B, p2, T3F] twice.

Row 6: P2, k4, p4, k4, p2.

Row 7: K2, p4, C4B, p4, k2.

Row 8: As row 6.

Row 9: K2, p4, k4, p4, k2.

Row 10: As row 6.

Row 11: As row 7.

Row 12: As row 6.

Row 13: [T3F, p2, T3B] twice.

Row 14: As row 4.

Row 15: P1, T3F, T3B, p2, T3F, T3B, p1.

Row 16: As row 2.

Row 17: As row 1.

Row 18: As row 2.

Row 19: As row 3.

Row 20: As row 4.

Row 21: P1, [k2, p2] twice, k2, slip last 6 sts worked onto cable needle and wrap yarn 4 times counterclockwise around these 6 sts, then slip the 6 sts back onto right-hand needle, p2, k2, p1.

Row 22: As row 4.

Row 23: As row 15.

Row 24: As row 2.

Rep these 24 rows.

Repeated ovals

Multiple of 8 + 1.

Special abbreviation:

Work 5tog (work 5 sts together) = Wyif sl 3 purlwise, k2tog, p3sso.

Row 1 (RS): K1, *p5, k1, p1, k1; rep from * to end.

Row 2: P1, *k1, p1, k5, p1; rep from * to end.

Row 3: As row 1.

Row 4: P1, *M5K, p1, work 5tog, p1; rep from * to end.

Row 5: K1, *p1, k1, p5, k1; rep from * to end.

Row 6: P1, *k5, p1, k1, p1; rep from * to end.

Rep the last 2 rows once more, then row 5 again.

Row 10: P1, *work 5tog, p1, M5K, p1; rep from * to end.

Rows 11–12: As rows 1–2.

Rep these 12 rows.

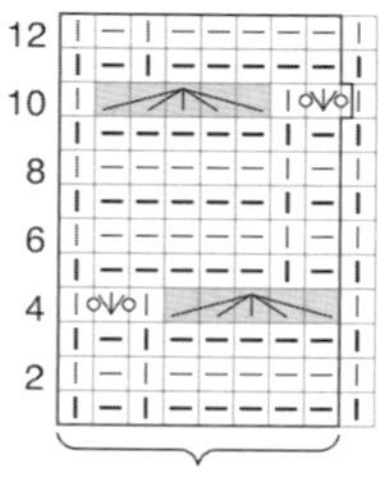

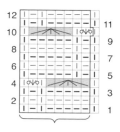

8-stitch repeat

Repeated circles

Multiple of 6 + 2.

Row 1 (RS): Knit.

Row 2: Purl.

Row 3: K1, *C3R, C3L; rep from * to last st, k1.

Row 4: Purl.

Rows 5–6: As rows 1–2.

Row 7: K1, *C3L, C3R; rep from * to last st, k1.

Row 8: Purl.

Rep these 8 rows.

Note: This stitch is also very effective when worked as a panel with a multiple of 6 sts on a background of rev st st.

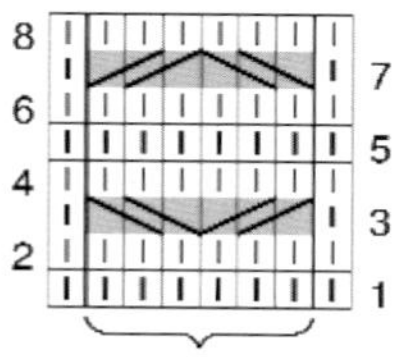

6-stitch repeat

Small circle cable

Multiple of 6 + 2.

Row 1 (RS): P2, *C2B, C2F, p2; rep from * to end.

Row 2: K2, *p4, k2; rep from * to end.

Row 3: P2, *C2F, C2B, p2; rep from * to end.

Row 4: As row 2.

Rep these 4 rows.

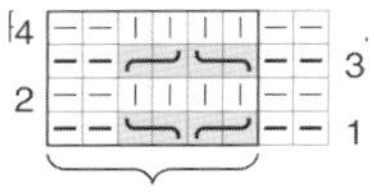

6-stitch repeat

Slanting diagonals

Multiple of 6 + 4.

Row 1 (RS): P6, T3B, *p3, T3B; rep from * to last st, p1.

Row 2: K2, *p2, k4; rep from * to last 2 sts, k2.

Row 3: P5, T3B, *p3, T3B; rep from * to last 2 sts, p2.

Row 4: K3, *p2, k4; rep from * to last st, k1.

Row 5: P4, *T3B, p3; rep from * to end.

Row 6: K4, *p2, k4; rep from * to end.

Row 7: *P3, T3B; rep from * to last 4 sts, p4.

Row 8: K5, p2, *k4, p2; rep from * to last 3 sts, k3.

Row 9: P2, *T3B, p3; rep from * to last 2 sts, p2.

Row 10: K6, p2, *k4, p2; rep from * to last 2 sts, k2.

Row 11: P1, *T3B, p3; rep from * to last 3 sts, p3.

Row 12: K7, p2, *k4, p2; rep from * to last st, k1.

Rep these 12 rows.

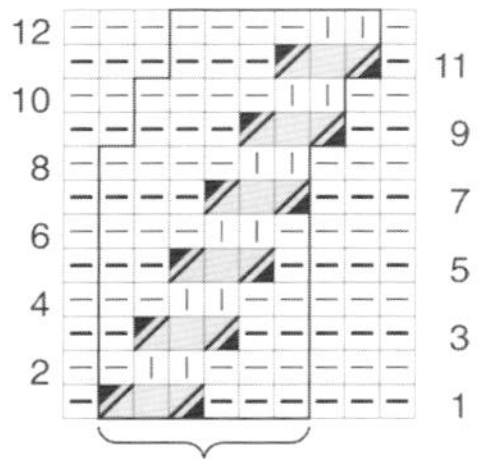

6-stitch repeat

Crossed cables

Multiple of 12 + 14.

Row 1 (RS): P3, T4B, T4F, *p4, T4B, T4F; rep from * to last 3 sts, p3.

Row 2: K3, p2, *k4, p2; rep from * to last 3 sts, k3.

Row 3: P1, *T4B, p4, T4F; rep from * to last st, p1.

Row 4: K1, p2, k8, *p4, k8; rep from * to last 3 sts, p2, k1.

Row 5: P1, k2, p8, *C4B, p8; rep from * to last 3 sts, k2, p1.

Row 6: As row 4.

Row 7: P1, *T4F, p4, T4B; rep from * to last st, p1.

Row 8: As row 2.

Row 9: P3, T4F, T4B, *p4, T4F, T4B; rep from * to last 3 sts, p3.

Row 10: K5, p4, *k8, p4; rep from * to last 5 sts, k5.

Row 11: P5, C4F, *p8, C4F; rep from * to last 5 sts, p5.

Row 12: As row 10.

Rep these 12 rows.

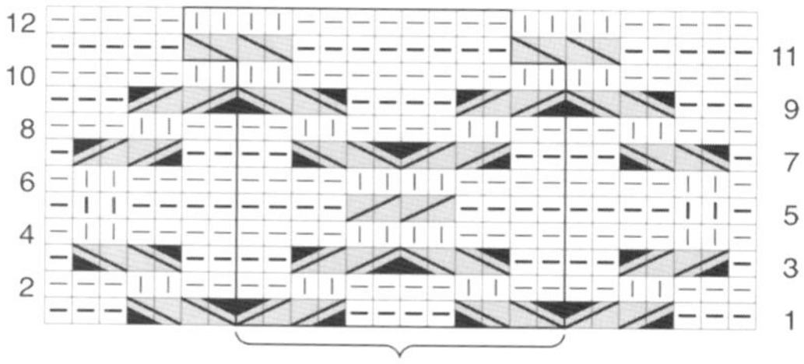

12-stitch repeat

Rose garden

Multiple of 9 + 5.

Row 1 (RS): P2, KB1, p2, *k4, p2, KB1, p2; rep from * to end.

Row 2: K2, PB1, k2, *p4, k2, PB1, k2; rep from * to end.

Row 3: P2, KB1, p2, *C4B, p2, KB1, p2; rep from * to end.

Row 4: As row 2.

Rep these 4 rows.

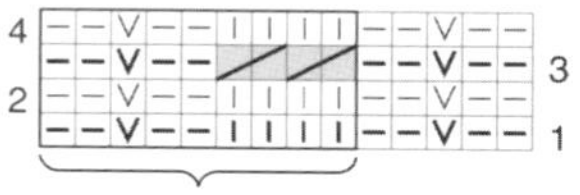

9-stitch repeat

Leafy trellis

Multiple of 10 + 3.

Row 1: 1 edge st, *KB1 (knit into back of st), p1, k1, K1B (knit 1 below), p1, KB1, p1, KB1, p1, KB1, p1; rep from * to last 2 sts, KB1, 1 edge st.

Row 2: 1 edge st, PB1 (purl into back of st), *k1, PB1, k1, PB1, k1, PB1, k1, p3, PB1; rep from * to last st, 1 edge st.

Row 3: 1 edge st, *KB1, K1B, wyib sl 1 purlwise, k2tog, psso, p1, KB1, p1, KB1, p1, KB1, p1; rep from * to last 2 sts, KB1, 1 edge st.

Row 4: As row 2.

Row 5: As row 3.

Row 6: As row 2.

Row 7: As row 3.

Rep these 7 rows.

Eyelet rib variation

Multiple of 8 + 2.

Note: Eyelet openwork is worked on WS rows to clearly indent the rib pattern.

Row 1 (RS): P2, *k6, p2; rep from * to end.

Row 2 (WS): K2, *p6, yo, k2tog; rep from * to last 8 sts, p6, k2.

Rep the last 2 rows until desired length, ending with RS row.

Next row (WS): K2, *p2, yo, k2tog; rep from * to last 4 sts, p2, k2.

Next row (RS): P2, *k2, p2; rep from * to end.

Rep the last 2 rows to cont patt, or work in a variation as desired.

Extended openwork stitches

Multiple of 6 + 2 sts for the rim on each edge.

Row 1 (RS): Knit.

Row 2: 1 edge st, *knit each st winding yarn around needle 3 times; rep from * to last st, k1.

Row 3: 1 edge st, *slip next 3 sts onto cable needle and hold at back of work, k3, k3 from cable needle; rep from * to last st, 1 edge st.

Row 4: Knit.

Rep these 4 rows.

Slanting openwork stitch

Even number of sts.

Row 1 (RS): 1 edge st, *yo, k2tog; rep from * to last st, 1 edge st.

Rows 2 and 4: Purl.

Row 3: K2, *yo, k2tog; rep from * to last 2 sts, k2tog.

Rep these 4 rows.

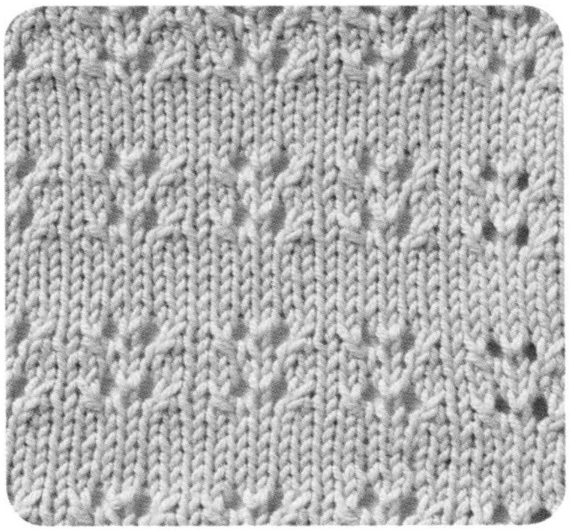

Eyelet quadrants

Multiple of 6 + 2.

Rows 1 (RS) and 5: 1 edge st, *k1, k2tog, yo, k1, yo, ssk; rep from * to last st, 1 edge st.

Row 2 and every alt row: 1 edge st, purl to last st, 1 edge st.

Rows 3, 7, 9, and 11: 1 edge st, knit to last st, 1 edge st.

Row 12: As row 2.

Rep these 12 rows.

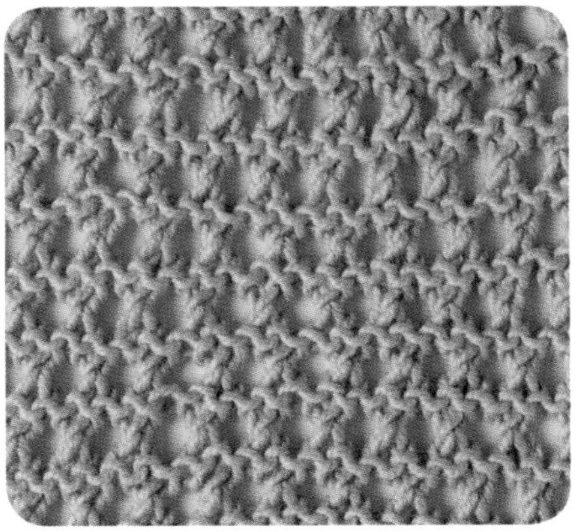

Ridged eyelet stitch

Multiple of 2.

Rows 1–3: Knit.

Row 4 (WS): P1, *yo, p2tog; rep from * to last st, p1.

Rows 5–7: Knit.

Row 8: P1, *p2tog, yo; rep from * to last st, p1.

Rep these 8 rows.

Feather openwork

Multiple of 5 + 2.

Row 1 (RS): K1, *k2tog, yo, k1, yo, skpo; rep from * to last st, k1.

Row 2: Purl.

Rep these 2 rows.

Single lace rib

Multiple of 4 + 1.

Row 1 (RS): K1, *yo, k2tog, p1, k1; rep from * to end.

Row 2: P1, *yo, p2tog, k1, p1; rep from * to end.

Rep these 2 rows.

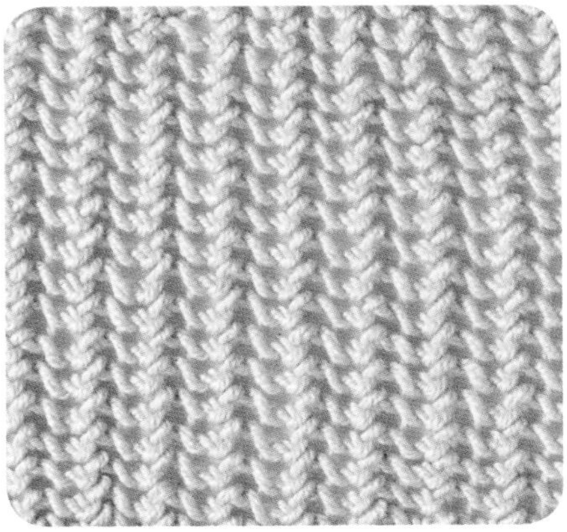

Purse stitch

Multiple of 2.

Row 1: P1, *yo, p2tog; rep from * to last st, p1.

Rep this row.

Angel wings lace panel

Worked over 19 sts.

Row 1 (RS): P2, skpo, k5, yo, k1, yo, k5, k2tog, p2.
Row 2: K2, p2tog, p5, yo, p1, yo, p5, p2tog tbl, k2.
Row 3: P2, skpo, k4, yo, k3, yo, k4, k2tog, p2.
Row 4: K2, p2tog, p4, yo, p3, yo, p4, p2tog tbl, k2.
Row 5: P2, skpo, k3, yo, k5, yo, k3, k2tog, p2.
Row 6: K2, p2tog, p3, yo, p5, yo, p3, p2tog tbl, k2.
Row 7: P2, skpo, k2, yo, k7, yo, k2, k2tog, p2.
Row 8: K2, p2tog, p2, yo, p7, yo, p2, p2tog tbl, k2.
Row 9: P2, skpo, k1, yo, k9, yo, k1, k2tog, p2.
Row 10: K2, p2tog, p1, yo, p9, yo, p1, p2tog tbl, k2.
Rep these 10 rows.

Mimosa shoot

Multiple of 20.

Special abbreviation:
MB (make bobble) = (K1, p1, k1, p1) into next st, turn, k4, turn, sl 1 purlwise, p3tog, psso.
Row 1 (RS): K6, yo, skpo, k2, MB, k9.
Row 2 and every alt row: Purl.
Row 3: K8, yo, skpo, k2, MB, k7.
Row 5: K10, yo, skpo, k2, MB, k5.
Row 7: K9, MB, k2, yo, skpo, k2, MB, k3.
Row 9: K7, MB, k2, k2tog, yo, k2, yo, skpo, k2, MB, k1.
Row 11: K5, MB, k2, k2tog, yo, k6, yo, skpo, k2.
Row 13: K3, MB, k2, k2tog, yo, k12.
Row 15: K1, MB, k2, k2tog, yo, k2, MB, k11.
Row 17: K2, k2tog, yo, k2, yo, skpo, k2, MB, k9.
Row 19: K8, yo, skpo, k2, MB, k7.
Row 20: Purl.
Rep rows 5–20.

Papyrus lace

Multiple of 8 + 1.

Row 1 (RS): K1, *yo, skpo, k3, k2tog, yo, k1; rep from * to end.

Row 2 and every alt row to 20: Purl.

Row 3: K1, *k1, yo, skpo, k1, k2tog, yo, k2; rep from * to end.

Row 5: K1, *k2, yo, sk2po, yo, k3; rep from * to end.

Row 7: Knit.

Rows 9 and 11: K1, *k1, k2tog, yo, k1, yo, skpo, k2; rep from * to end.

Row 13: As row 1.

Row 15: As row 3.

Row 17: As row 5.

Rows 19 and 21: As row 9.

Row 22: P1, *yo, p2tog, p3, p2tog tbl, yo, p1; rep from * to end.

Row 23: K1, *k1, yo, skpo, k1, k2tog, yo, k2; rep from * to end.

Row 24: P1, *yo, p2tog, yo, p3tog, yo, p2tog tbl, yo, p1; rep from * to end.

Row 25: K1, *k1, skpo, yo, k1, yo, k2tog, k2; rep from * to end.

Row 26: P1, *p1, p2tog, yo, p1, yo, p2tog tbl, p2; rep from * to end.

Rows 27–30: As rows 23–26.

Rep these 30 rows.

Lace and seed stitch

Multiple of 8 + 1.

Work 8 rows in seed st.

Lace pattern:

Row 1: K1, *yo, skpo, k3, k2tog, yo, k1; rep from * to end.

Row 2 and every alt row: Purl.

Row 3: *K2, yo, skpo, k1, k2tog, yo, k1; rep from * to last st, k1.

Row 5: *K3, yo, sk2po, yo, k2; rep from * to last st, k1.

Row 6: Purl.

Rep these 14 rows.

Slanting eyelet rib

Multiple of 10.

Row 1: K3, p2, k2tog, yo, C2B, p1.

Row 2: K2, p3, k2, p3.

Row 3: K3, p1, k2tog, yo, C2B, p2.

Row 4: K2, p4, k1, p3.

Row 5: K3, k2tog, yo, C2B, k1, p2.

Row 6: K2, p8.

Row 7: K2, k2tog, yo, C2B, k2, p2.

Row 8: K2, p8.

Row 9: K1, k2tog, yo, C2B, k3, p2.

Row 10: K2, p3, k1, p4.

Row 11: K2tog, yo, C2B, p1, k3, p2.

Row 12: K2, p3, k2, p3.

Rep these 12 rows.

Embossed leaf pattern

Multiple of 7 + 6.

Note: Stitches should only be counted after row 15 or 16.

Row 1 (RS): P6, *yo, k1, yo, p6; rep from * to end.
Row 2: K6, *p3, k6; rep from * to end.
Row 3: P6, *[k1, yo] twice, k1, p6; rep from * to end.
Row 4: K6, *p5, k6; rep from * to end.
Row 5: P6, *k2, yo, k1, yo, k2, p6; rep from * to end.
Row 6: K6, *p7, k6; rep from * to end.
Row 7: P6, *k3, yo, k1, yo, k3, p6; rep from * to end.
Row 8: K6, *p9, k6; rep from * to end.
Row 9: P6, *skpo, k5, k2tog, p6; rep from * to end.
Row 10: K6, *p7, k6; rep from * to end.
Row 11: P6, *skpo, k3, k2tog, p6; rep from * to end.
Row 12: K6, *p5, k6; rep from * to end.
Row 13: P6, *skpo, k1, k2tog, p6; rep from * to end.
Row 14: K6, *p3, k6; rep from * to end.
Row 15: P6, *sk2po, p6; rep from * to end.
Row 16: Knit.
Row 17: Purl.
Rep the last 2 rows once more, then row 16 again.
Rep these 20 rows.

Falling leaves

Multiple of 10 + 3.

Row 1 (RS): K1, k2tog, k3, *yo, k1, yo, k3, sk2po, k3; rep from * to last 7 sts, yo, k1, yo, k3, skpo, k1.
Row 2 and every alt row: Purl.
Row 3: K1, k2tog, k2, *yo, k3, yo, k2, sk2po, k2; rep from * to last 8 sts, yo, k3, yo, k2, skpo, k1.
Row 5: K1, k2tog, k1, *yo, k5, yo, k1, sk2po, k1; rep from * to last 9 sts, yo, k5, yo, k1, skpo, k1.
Row 7: K1, k2tog, yo, k7, *yo, sk2po, yo, k7; rep from * to last 3 sts, yo, skpo, k1.
Row 9: K2, yo, k3, *sk2po, k3, yo, k1, yo, k3; rep from * to last 8 sts, sk2po, k3, yo, k2.
Row 11: K3, yo, k2, *sk2po, k2, yo, k3, yo, k2; rep from * to last 8 sts, sk2po, k2, yo, k3.
Row 13: K4, yo, k1, *sk2po, k1, yo, k5, yo, k1; rep from * to last 8 sts, sk2po, k1, yo, k4.
Row 15: K5, *yo, sk2po, yo, k7; rep from * to last 8 sts, yo, sk2po, yo, k5.
Row 16: Purl.
Rep these 16 rows.

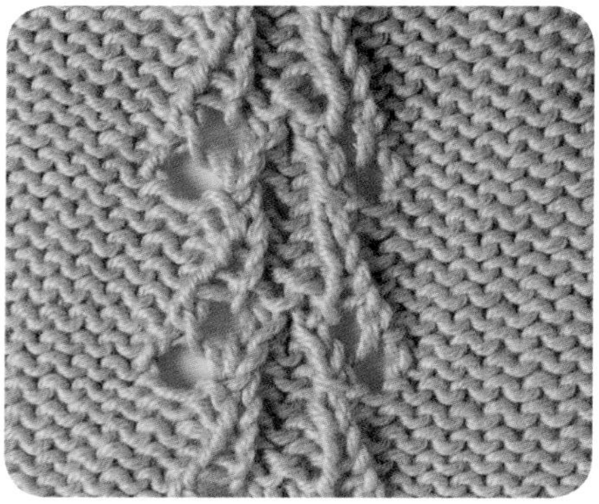

Bluebell insertion

Multiple of 8.

Row 1 (RS): P2, [k1, p2] twice.
Row 2: K2, [p1, k2] twice.
Rep the last 2 rows once more.
Row 5: P1, yo, skpo, p2, k2tog, yo, p1.
Row 6: K1, p2, k2, p2, k1.
Row 7: P2, yo, skpo, k2tog, yo, p2.
Row 8: K2, p4, k2.
Rep these 8 rows.

Eyelet twist panel

Multiple of 13.

Row 1 (WS) and every alt row: Purl.

Row 2: K1, [yo, skpo] twice, k3, [k2tog, yo] twice, k1.

Row 4: K2, [yo, skpo] twice, k1, [k2tog, yo] twice, k2.

Row 6: K3, yo, skpo, yo, sk2po, yo, k2tog, yo, k3.

Row 8: K4, yo, sk2po, yo, k2tog, yo, k4.

Row 10: K4, [k2tog, yo] twice, k5.

Row 12: K3, [k2tog, yo] twice, k1, yo, skpo, k3.

Row 14: K2, [k2tog, yo] twice, k1, [yo, skpo] twice, k2.

Row 16: K1, [k2tog, yo] twice, k3, [yo, skpo] twice, k1.

Row 18: [K2tog, yo] twice, k5, [yo, skpo] twice.

Rep these 18 rows.

Filigree cables pattern lace

Multiple of 12 + 8.

Row 1 (RS): P2, *k2, yo, k2tog, p2; rep from * to end.

Row 2: K2, *p2, yo, p2tog, k2; rep from * to end.

Rep the last 2 rows twice more.

Row 7: P2, k2, yo, k2tog, p2, *C4F, p2, k2, yo, k2tog, p2; rep from * to end.

Row 8: As row 2.

Rep rows 1–2, 3 times more.

Row 15: P2, C4F, p2, *k2, yo, k2tog, p2, C4F, p2; rep from * to end.

Row 16: As row 2.

Rep these 16 rows.

Tip

It is quite a common error when working lace or eyelet stitches to forget to make a yarnover. If you realize that you have forgotten to pass a slipped stitch, you can remedy this by working it on the wrong-side row when you come to the decreased stitch.

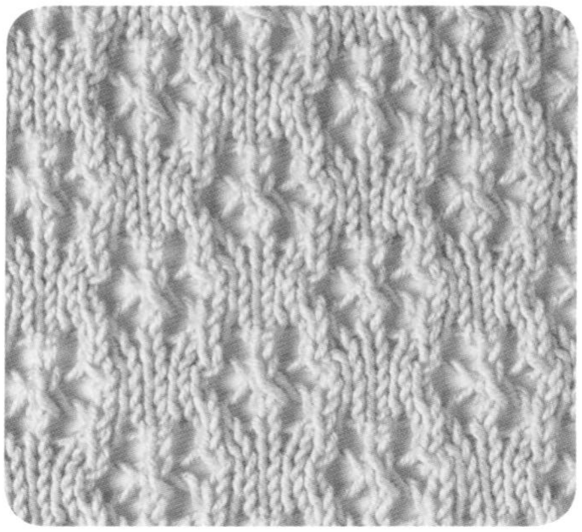

Lacy stars

Multiple of 8 + 5.

Row 1 (WS) and every alt row: Purl.

Row 2: K4, *ssk, yo, k1, yo, k2tog, k3; rep from * to last st, k1.

Row 4: K5, *yo, sl 2, k1, p2sso, yo, k5; rep from * to end.

Row 6: As row 2.

Row 8: Ssk, yo, k1, yo, k2tog, *k3, ssk, yo, k1, yo, k2tog; rep from * to end.

Row 10: K1, *yo, sl 2, k1, p2sso, yo, k5; rep from * to last 4 sts, yo, sl 2, k1, p2sso, yo, k1.

Row 12: As row 8.

Rep these 12 rows.

Dewdrop pattern

Multiple of 6 + 1.

Row 1 (WS): K2, *p3, k3; rep from * to last 5 sts, p3, k2.

Row 2: P2, *k3, p3; rep from * to last 5 sts, k3, p2.

Row 3: As row 1.

Row 4: K2, *yo, sk2po, yo, k3; rep from * to last 5 sts, yo, sk2po, yo, k2.

Row 5: As row 2.

Row 6: K2, *p3, k3; rep from * to last 5 sts, p3, k2.

Row 7: As row 2.

Row 8: K2tog, *yo, k3, yo, sk2po; rep from * to last 5 sts, yo, k3, yo, skpo.

Rep these 8 rows.

Garter stitch eyelet chevron

Multiple of 9 + 1.

Row 1 (RS): K1, *yo, skpo, k4, k2tog, yo, k1; rep from * to end.

Row 2: P2, *k6, p3; rep from * to last 8 sts, k6, p2.

Row 3: K2, *yo, skpo, k2, k2tog, yo, k3; rep from * to last 8 sts, yo, skpo, k2, k2tog, yo, k2.

Row 4: P3, *k4, p5; rep from * to last 7 sts, k4, p3.

Row 5: K3, *yo, skpo, k2tog, yo, k5; rep from * to last 7 sts, yo, skpo, k2tog, yo, k3.

Row 6: P4, *k2, p7; rep from * to last 6 sts, k2, p4.

Rep these 6 rows.

Fern lace

Multiple of 9 + 4.
Row 1 (WS): Purl.
Row 2: K3, *yo, k2, skpo, k2tog, k2, yo, k1; rep from * to last st, k1.
Row 3: Purl.
Row 4: K2, *yo, k2, skpo, k2tog, k2, yo, k1; rep from * to last 2 sts, k2.
Rep these 4 rows.

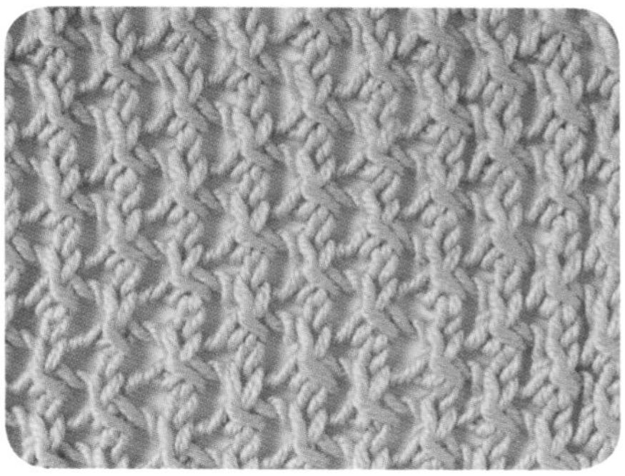

Cell stitch

Multiple of 4 + 3.
Row 1 (RS): K2, *yo, sk2po, yo, k1; rep from * to last st, k1.
Row 2: Purl.
Row 3: K1, k2tog, yo, k1, *yo, sk2po, yo, k1; rep from * to last 3 sts, yo, skpo, k1.
Row 4: Purl.
Rep these 4 rows.

Little arrowhead

Multiple of 6 + 1.
Row 1 (RS): K1, *yo, skpo, k1, k2tog, yo, k1; rep from * to end.
Row 2: Purl.
Row 3: K2, *yo, sk2po, yo, k3; rep from * to last 5 sts, yo, sk2po, yo, k2.
Row 4: Purl.
Rep these 4 rows.

Crowns I

Multiple of 5.
Work 4 rows in garter st.
Row 5: K1, *k1 winding yarn around needle 3 times; rep from * to end.
Row 6: *Sl 5 purlwise dropping extra loops, return same 5 sts to left-hand needle and work into them together as follows: k1, [p1, k1] twice; rep from * to end.
Work 2 rows in garter st.
Rep these 8 rows.

Foaming waves

Multiple of 12 + 1.
Work 4 rows in garter st.
Row 5 (RS): K1, *[k2tog] twice, [yo, k1] 3 times, yo, [skpo] twice, k1; rep from * to end.
Row 6: Purl.
Rep the last 2 rows 3 times more.
Rep these 12 rows.

Eyelets

Multiple of 3 + 2.
Work 2 rows in st st, starting with knit.
Row 3 (RS): K2, *yo, k2tog, k1; rep from * to end.
Row 4: Purl.
Rep these 4 rows.

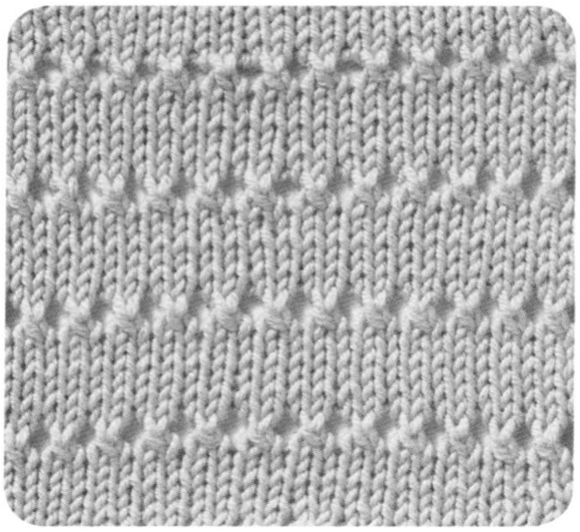

Eyelet rows

Multiple of 2 + 2.

Row 1 (RS): 1 edge st, knit to last st, 1 edge st.

Row 2 and every alt row: 1 edge st, purl to last st, 1 edge st.

Row 3: 1 edge st, *yo, ssk; rep from * to last st, 1 edge st.

Row 5, 7, 9, 13, and 15: As row 1.

Row 11: 1 edge st, k1, *yo, ssk; rep from * to last 2 sts, k1, 1 edge st.

Row 16: As row 2.

Rep these 16 rows.

Spiral and eyelet panel

Worked across 24 sts on a background of rev st st.

Row 1 (RS): K3, k2tog, k4, yo, p2, yo, k2tog, p2, yo, k4, skpo, k3.

Row 2 and every alt row: P9, k2, p2, k2, p9.

Row 3: K2, k2tog, k4, yo, k1, p2, k2tog, yo, p2, k1, yo, k4, skpo, k2.

Row 5: K1, k2tog, k4, yo, k2, p2, yo, k2tog, p2, k2, yo, k4, skpo, k1.

Row 7: K2tog, k4, yo, k3, p2, k2tog, yo, p2, k3, yo, k4, skpo.

Row 8: As row 2.

Rep these 8 rows.

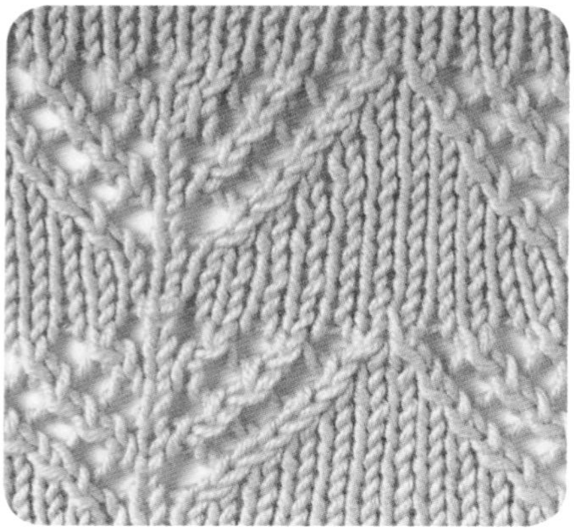

Candelabra panel

Worked over 13 sts on a background of st st.

Row 1 (RS): Knit.

Row 2 and every alt row: Purl.

Row 3: Knit.

Row 5: K4, k2tog, yo, k1, yo, skpo, k4.

Row 7: K3, k2tog, yo, k3, yo, skpo, k3.

Row 9: K2, [k2tog, yo] twice, k1, [yo, skpo] twice, k2.

Row 11: K1, [k2tog, yo] twice, k3, [yo, skpo] twice, k1.

Row 13: [K2tog, yo] 3 times, k1, [yo, skpo] 3 times.

Row 14: Purl.

Rep these 14 rows.

Zigzag panel

Worked over 9 sts on a background of st st.

Row 1 (RS): K3, skpo, yo, k2tog, yo, k2.

Row 2 and every alt row: Purl.

Row 3: K2, skpo, yo, k2tog, yo, k3.

Row 5: K1, skpo, yo, k2tog, yo, k4.

Row 7: Skpo, yo, k2tog, yo, k5.

Row 9: K2, yo, skpo, yo, k2tog, k3.

Row 11: K3, yo, skpo, yo, k2tog, k2.

Row 13: K4, yo, skpo, yo, k2tog, k1.

Row 15: K5, yo, skpo, yo, k2tog.

Row 16: Purl.

Rep these 16 rows.

Eyelet fan panel

Worked over 13 sts on a background of st st.

Work 4 rows in garter st.

Row 5 (RS): Skpo, k4, yo, k1, yo, k4, k2tog.

Row 6 and rem alt rows: Purl.

Row 7: Skpo, [k3, yo] twice, k3, k2tog.

Row 9: Skpo, k2, yo, k2tog, yo, k1, yo, skpo, yo, k2, k2tog.

Row 11: Skpo, k1, yo, k2tog, yo, k3, yo, skpo, yo, k1, k2tog.

Row 13: Skpo, [yo, k2tog] twice, yo, k1, [yo, skpo] twice, yo, k2tog.

Row 14: Purl.

Rep these 14 rows.

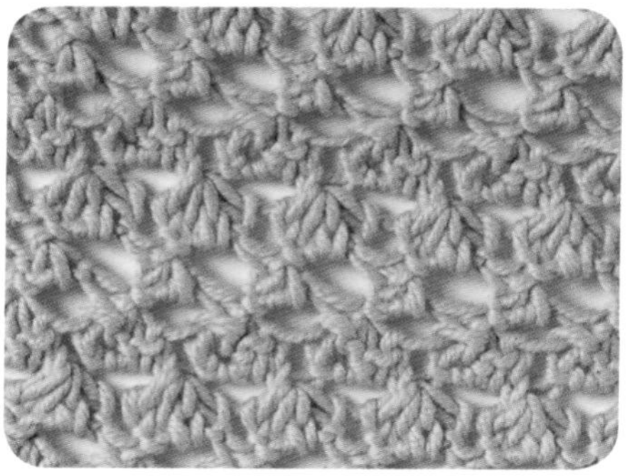

Grand eyelets

Multiple of 4.
Note: Stitches should not be counted after row 1.
Row 1: P2, *yo, p4tog; rep from * to last 2 sts, p2.
Row 2: K3, (k1, p1, k1) into next st, *k1, (k1, p1, k1) into next st; rep from * to last 2 sts, k2.
Row 3: Knit.
Rep these 3 rows.

Bluebell ribs

Multiple of 5 + 2.
Row 1 (RS): P2, *k3, p2; rep from * to end.
Row 2: K2, *p3, k2; rep from * to end.
Rep the last 2 rows once more.
Row 5: P2, *yo, sk2po, yo, p2; rep from * to end.
Row 6: As row 2.
Rep these 6 rows.

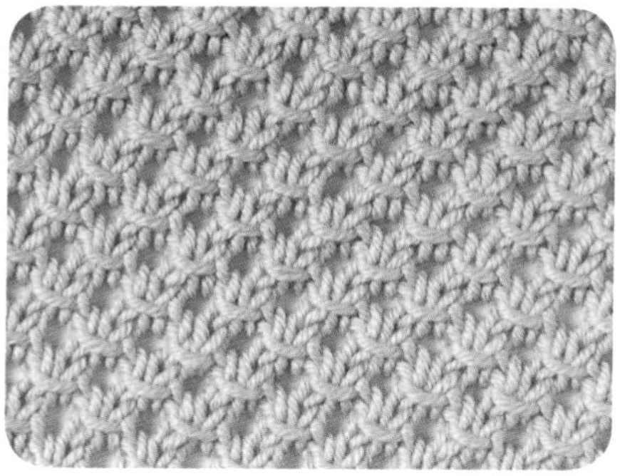

Knotted openwork

Multiple of 3.
Row 1 (WS): Purl.
Row 2: K2, *yo, k3, with left-hand needle lift first of 3 sts just knitted over last 2; rep from * to last st, k1.
Row 3: Purl.
Row 4: K1, *k3, with left-hand needle lift first of 3 sts just knitted over last 2, yo; rep from * to last 2 sts, k2.
Rep these 4 rows.

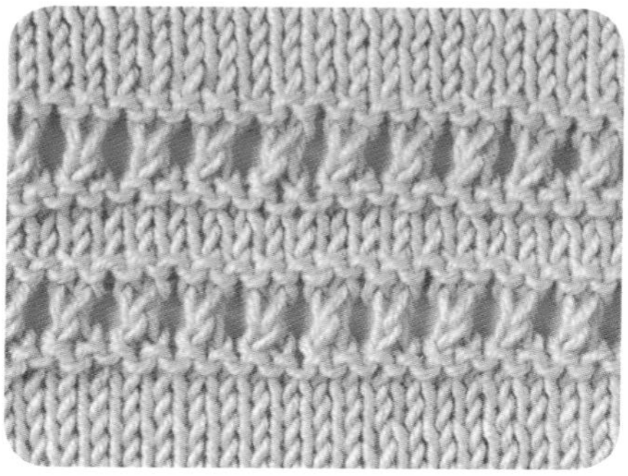

Ridged eyelet border

Multiple of 2 + 1.
Worked on a background of st st.
Rows 1–3: Knit.
Row 4 (WS): *P2tog, yo; rep from * to last st, p1.
Rows 5–7: Knit.
Row 8: Purl.
Rep the first 6 rows once more.

Simple garter stitch lace

Multiple of 4 + 2.
Row 1: K2, *yo, p2tog, k2; rep from * to end.
Rep this row.

Chevron and feather

Multiple of 13 + 1.
Row 1 (RS): *K1, yo, k4, k2tog, skpo, k4, yo; rep from * to last st, k1.
Row 2: Purl.
Rep these 2 rows.

Little flowers

Multiple of 6 + 3.

Row 1 (RS): Knit.

Row 2 and every alt row: Purl.

Row 3: Knit.

Row 5: *K4, yo, skpo; rep from * to last 3 sts, k3.

Row 7: K2, k2tog, yo, k1, yo, skpo, *k1, k2tog, yo, k1, yo, skpo; rep from * to last 2 sts, k2.

Rows 9–11: Knit.

Row 13: K1, yo, skpo, *k4, yo, skpo; rep from * to end.

Row 15: K2, yo, skpo, k1, k2tog, yo, *k1, yo, skpo, k1, k2tog, yo; rep from * to last 2 sts, k2.

Row 16: Purl.

Rep these 16 rows.

Little fountain pattern

Multiple of 4 + 1.

Note: Stitches should only be counted after row 3 or 4.

Row 1 (RS): K1, *yo, k3, yo, k1; rep from * to end.

Row 2: Purl.

Row 3: K2, sk2po, *k3, sk2po; rep from * to last 2 sts, k2.

Row 4: Purl.

Rep these 4 rows.

Butterfly lace

Multiple of 8 + 7.

Row 1 (RS): K1, *k2tog, yo, k1, yo, skpo, k3; rep from * to last 6 sts, k2tog, yo, k1, yo, skpo, k1.

Row 2: P3, *sl 1 purlwise, p7; rep from * to last 4 sts, sl 1 purlwise, p3.

Rep the last 2 rows once more.

Row 5: K5, *k2tog, yo, k1, yo, skpo, k3; rep from * to last 2 sts, k2.

Row 6: P7, *sl 1 purlwise, p7; rep from * to end.

Rep the last 2 rows once more.

Rep these 8 rows.

Tip

When slipping the first and last stitch of each row, be careful when you turn your work to avoid having a slipped loop down the side of your project.

Cable and lace check

Multiple of 12 + 8.
Row 1 (WS): K2, p2tog, yo, p2, k2, *p4, k2, p2tog, yo, p2, k2; rep from * to end.
Row 2: P2, k2tog, yo, k2, p2, *k4, p2, k2tog, yo, k2, p2; rep from * to end.
Row 3: As row 1.
Row 4: P2, k2tog, yo, k2, p2, *C4B, p2, k2tog, yo, k2, p2; rep from * to end.
Rows 5–7: As rows 1–3.
Row 8: P2, *C4B, p2; rep from * to end.
Row 9: K2, p4, k2, *p2tog, yo, p2, k2, p4, k2; rep from * to end.
Row 10: P2, k4, p2, *k2tog, yo, k2, p2, k4, p2; rep from * to end.
Row 11: As row 9.
Row 12: P2, C4B, p2, *k2tog, yo, k2, p2, C4B, p2; rep from * to end.
Rows 13–15: As rows 9–11.
Row 16: As row 8.
Rep these 16 rows.

Leafy lace

Multiple of 10 + 1.
Row 1 (RS): KB1, *p9, KB1; rep from * to end.
Row 2: P1, *k9, p1; rep from * to end.
Rep the last 2 rows once more.
Row 5: KB1, *p2, p2tog, yo, KB1, yo, p2tog, p2, KB1; rep from * to end.
Row 6: P1, *k4, PB1, k4, p1; rep from * to end.
Row 7: KB1, *p1, p2tog, yo, [KB1] 3 times, yo, p2tog, p1, KB1; rep from * to end.
Row 8: P1, *k3, [PB1] 3 times, k3, p1; rep from * to end.
Row 9: KB1, *p2tog, yo, [KB1] 5 times, yo, p2tog, KB1; rep from * to end.
Row 10: P1, *k2, [PB1] 5 times, k2, p1; rep from * to end.
Row 11: KB1, *p1, yo, [KB1] twice, sk2po, [KB1] twice, yo, p1, KB1; rep from * to end.
Row 12: As row 10.
Row 13: KB1, *p2, yo, KB1, sk2po, KB1, yo, p2, KB1; rep from * to end.
Row 14: As row 8.
Row 15: KB1, *p3, yo, sk2po, yo, p3, KB1; rep from * to end.
Row 16: As row 6.
Rep these 16 rows.

Cockleshells

Worked over 19 sts on a background of garter st.
Row 1 (RS): Knit.
Row 2: Knit.
Row 3: K1, yo2, p2tog tbl, k13, p2tog, yo2, k1.
Row 4: K2, p1, k15, p1, k2.
Rows 5–6: Knit.
Row 7: K1, yo2, p2tog tbl, yo2, p2tog tbl, k11, p2tog, yo2, p2tog, yo2, k1.
Row 8: [K2, p1] twice, k13, [p1, k2] twice.
Row 9: Knit.
Row 10: K5, k15 winding yarn 3 times around needle for each st, k5.
Row 11: K1, yo2, p2tog tbl, yo2, p2tog tbl, yo2, slip next 15 sts onto right-hand needle dropping extra loops, return same 15 sts to left-hand needle and purl all 15 sts tog, yo2, p2tog, yo2, p2tog, yo2, k1.
Row 12: K1, p1, [k2, p1] twice, k3, [p1, k2] twice, p1, k1.
Rep these 12 rows.

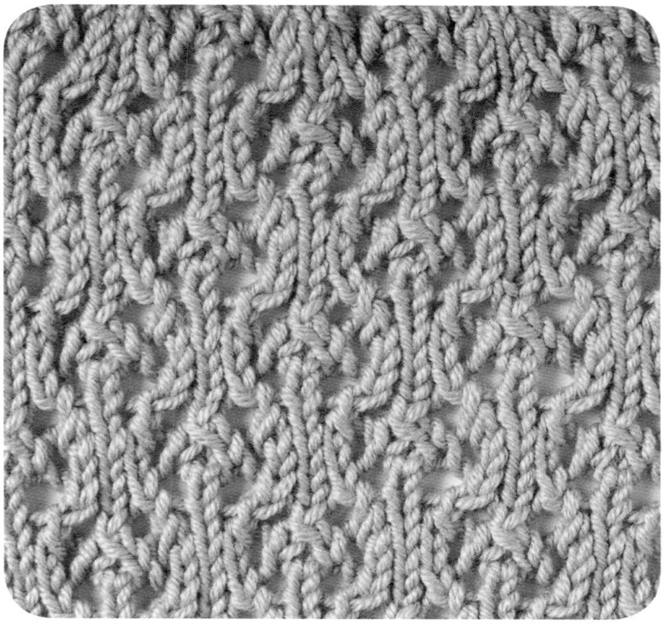

Eyelet panes

Multiple of 6 + 3.

Note: Stitches should not be counted after row 3, 4, 9, or 10.

Row 1 (RS): K2, *yo, skpo, k1, k2tog, yo, k1; rep from * to last st, k1.

Row 2 and every alt row: Purl.

Row 3: K3, *yo, k3; rep from * to end.

Row 5: K1, k2tog, *yo, skpo, k1, k2tog, yo, sk2po; rep from * to last 8 sts, yo, skpo, k1, k2tog, yo, skpo, k1.

Row 7: K2, *k2tog, yo, k1, yo, skpo, k1; rep from * to last st, k1.

Row 9: As row 3.

Row 11: K2, *k2tog, yo, sk2po, yo, skpo, k1; rep from * to last st, k1.

Row 12: Purl.

Rep these 12 rows.

Fern diamonds

Multiple of 10 + 1.

Row 1 (RS): K3, *k2tog, yo, k1, yo, skpo, k5; rep from * to last 8 sts, k2tog, yo, k1, yo, skpo, k3.

Row 2 and every alt row: Purl.

Row 3: K2, *k2tog, [k1, yo] twice, k1, skpo, k3; rep from * to last 9 sts, k2tog, [k1, yo] twice, k1, skpo, k2.

Row 5: K1, *k2tog, k2, yo, k1, yo, k2, skpo, k1; rep from * to end.

Row 7: K2tog, *k3, yo, k1, yo, k3, sk2po; rep from * to last 9 sts, k3, yo, k1, yo, k3, skpo.

Row 9: K1, *yo, skpo, k5, k2tog, yo, k1; rep from * to end.

Row 11: K1, *yo, k1, skpo, k3, k2tog, k1, yo, k1; rep from * to end.

Row 13: K1, *yo, k2, skpo, k1, k2tog, k2, yo, k1; rep from * to end.

Row 15: K1, *yo, k3, sk2po, k3, yo, k1; rep from * to end.

Row 16: Purl.

Rep these 16 rows.

Clover pattern

Multiple of 12 + 1.

Row 1 (RS): K2tog, k4, yo, k1, yo, k4, *sk2po, k4, yo, k1, yo, k4; rep from * to last 2 sts, skpo.

Row 2 and every alt row: Purl.

Row 3: K2tog, k3, [yo, k3] twice, *sk2po, k3, [yo, k3] twice; rep from * to last 2 sts, skpo.

Row 5: K2tog, k2, yo, k5, yo, k2, *sk2po, k2, yo, k5, yo, k2; rep from * to last 2 sts, skpo.

Row 7: K1, *yo, k4, sk2po, k4, yo, k1; rep from * to end.

Row 9: K2, yo, k3, sk2po, k3, *[yo, k3] twice, sk2po, k3; rep from * to last 2 sts, yo, k2.

Row 11: K3, yo, k2, sk2po, k2, *yo, k5, yo, k2, sk2po, k2; rep from * to last 3 sts, yo, k3.

Row 12: Purl.

Rep these 12 rows.

Lace diamond border

Multiple of 8.

Row 1 (RS): *K1, yo, k3, lift 3rd st on right-hand needle over first 2 sts; rep from * to end.

Row 2 and every alt row: Purl.

Row 3: Knit.

Row 5: K3, *yo, skpo, k6; rep from * to last 5 sts, yo, skpo, k3.

Row 7: K2, *[yo, skpo] twice, k4; rep from * to last 6 sts, [yo, skpo] twice, k2.

Row 9: K1, *[yo, skpo] 3 times, k2; rep from * to last 7 sts, [yo, skpo] 3 times, k1.

Row 11: As row 7.

Row 13: As row 5.

Row 15: Knit.

Row 17: As row 1.

Row 18: Purl.

Rep these 18 rows.

Bead stitch

Multiple of 7.

Row 1 (RS): K1, k2tog, yo, k1, yo, skpo, *k2, k2tog, yo, k1, yo, skpo; rep from * to last st, k1.

Row 2: *P2tog tbl, yo, p3, yo, p2tog; rep from * to end.

Row 3: K1, yo, skpo, k1, k2tog, yo, *k2, yo, skpo, k1, k2tog, yo; rep from * to last st, k1.

Row 4: P2, yo, p3tog, yo, *p4, yo, p3tog, yo; rep from * to last 2 sts, p2.

Rep these 4 rows.

Lacy lattice stitch

Multiple of 6 + 1.

Row 1 (RS): K1, *yo, p1, p3tog, p1, yo, k1; rep from * to end.

Row 2 and every alt row: Purl.

Row 3: K2, yo, sk2po, yo, *k3, yo, sk2po, yo; rep from * to last 2 sts, k2.

Row 5: P2tog, p1, yo, k1, yo, p1, *p3tog, p1, yo, k1, yo, p1; rep from * to last 2 sts, p2tog.

Row 7: K2tog, yo, k3, yo, *sk2po, yo, k3, yo; rep from * to last 2 sts, skpo.

Row 8: Purl.

Rep these 8 rows.

Parasol stitch

Worked over 17 sts on a background of st st.

Note: Stitches should only be counted after row 11 or 12.

Row 1 (RS): Yo, k1, [p3, k1] 4 times, yo.

Row 2 and every alt row: Purl.

Row 3: K1, yo, k1, [p3, k1] 4 times, yo, k1.

Row 5: K2, yo, k1, [p3, k1] 4 times, yo, k2.

Row 7: K3, yo, k1, [p2tog, p1, k1] 4 times, yo, k3.

Row 9: K4, yo, k1, [p2tog, k1] 4 times, yo, k4.

Row 11: K5, yo, k1, [k3tog, k1] twice, yo, k5.

Row 12: Purl.

Rep these 12 rows.

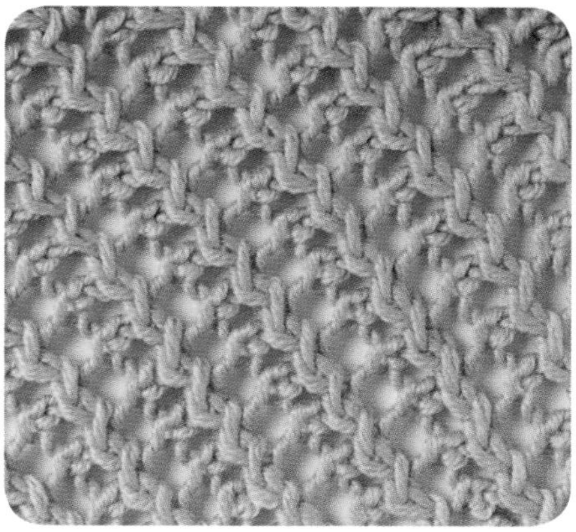

Diagonal openwork

Multiple of 4 + 2.

Row 1 (RS): *K1, yo, sk2po, yo; rep from * to last 2 sts, k2.

Row 2 and every alt row: Purl.

Row 3: K2, *yo, sk2po, yo, k1; rep from * to end.

Row 5: K2tog, yo, k1, yo, *sk2po, yo, k1, yo; rep from * to last 3 sts, skpo, k1.

Row 7: K1, k2tog, yo, k1, yo, *sk2po, yo, k1, yo; rep from * to last 2 sts, skpo.

Row 8: Purl.

Rep these 8 rows.

Little shell pattern

Multiple of 7 + 2.
Row 1 (RS): Knit.
Row 2: Purl.
Row 3: K2, *yo, p1, p3tog, p1, yo, k2; rep from * to end.
Row 4: Purl.
Rep these 4 rows.

Zigzag eyelet columns

Multiple of 6 + 4.
Row 1 (RS): *K4, yo, ssk; rep from * to last 4 sts, k4.
Row 2: Purl.
Row 3: *K4, k2tog, yo; rep from * to last 4 sts, k4.
Row 4: Purl.
Rep these 4 rows.

Faggoted panel

Worked over 9 sts on a background of st st.
Row 1 (RS): P1, k1, k2tog, yo, k1, yo, k2tog tbl, k1, p1.
Row 2: K1, p7, k1.
Row 3: P1, k2tog, yo, k3, yo, k2tog tbl, p1.
Row 4: As row 2.
Rep these 4 rows.

Astrakhan bobbles

Multiple of 12 + 3.
Row 1: K2, *yo, k4, p3tog, k4, yo, k1; rep from * to last st, k1.
Rep the last row 5 times more.
Row 7: K1, p2tog, *k4, yo, k1, yo, k4, p3tog; rep from * to last 12 sts, k4, yo, k1, yo, k4, p2tog, k1.
Rep the last row 5 times more.
Rep these 12 rows.
This pattern can be used on either side.

Pillar openwork

Multiple of 3 + 2.
Row 1 (RS): K1, *yo, sl 1 purlwise, k2, psso; rep from * to last st, k1.
Row 2: Purl.
Rep these 2 rows.

Ridged lace

Multiple of 2.
Row 1 (RS): K1, *yo, k2tog tbl; rep from * to last st, k1.
Row 2: P1, *yo, p2tog; rep from * to last st, p1.
Rep these 2 rows.

Crowns II

Multiple of 10 + 7.

Special abbreviations:

KW5 = Knit 5 sts winding yarn 3 times around needle for each st.

Twist 5 = Slip 5 sts purlwise dropping extra loops, return same 5 sts to left-hand needle, then k1, [p1, k1] twice into same 5 sts tog.

Row 1: K6, KW5, *k5, KW5; rep from * to last 6 sts, k6.

Row 2: P6, twist 5, *p5, twist 5; rep from * to last 6 sts, p6.

Row 3: Knit.

Row 4: K6, p5, *k5, p5; rep from * to last 6 sts, k6.

Row 5: K1, KW5, *k5, KW5; rep from * to last st, k1.

Row 6: P1, twist 5, *p5, twist 5; rep from * to last st, p1.

Row 7: Knit.

Row 8: K1, p5, *k5, p5; rep from * to last st, k1.

Rep these 8 rows.

King Charles lace

Worked over 11 sts on a background of st st.

Row 1 (RS): P2, k2tog, [k1, yo] twice, k1, skpo, p2.

Row 2 and every alt row: K2, p7, k2.

Row 3: P2, k2tog, yo, k3, yo, skpo, p2.

Row 5: P2, k1, yo, skpo, k1, k2tog, yo, k1, p2.

Row 7: P2, k2, yo, sk2po, yo, k2, p2.

Row 8: As row 2.

Rep these 8 rows.

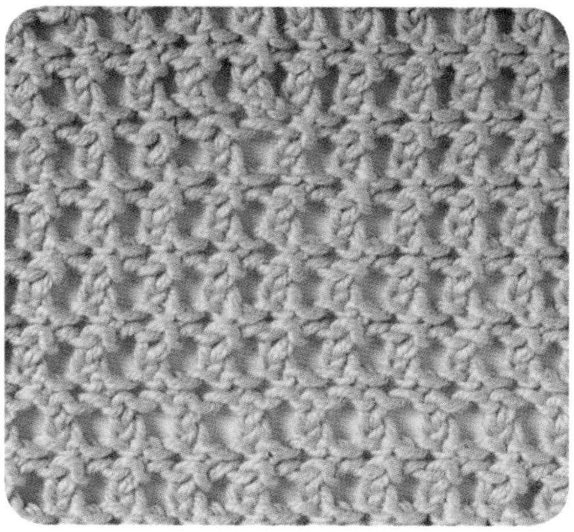

Ridge and hole pattern

Multiple of 2 + 1.

Note: Stitches should only be counted after row 1, 3, or 4.

Row 1 (RS): Purl.

Row 2: *P2tog; rep from * to last st, p1.

Row 3: P1, *purl through horizontal strand of yarn lying between stitch just worked and next st, p1; rep from * to end.

Row 4: P1, *yo, p2tog; rep from * to end.

Rep these 4 rows.

Bear paw panel

Worked over 23 sts on a background of st st.

Row 1 (RS): K2, [p4, k1] 3 times, p4, k2.
Row 2: P2, [k4, p1] 3 times, k4, p2.
Row 3: K1, yo, k1, p2, p2tog, [k1, p4] twice, k1, p2tog, p2, k1, yo, k1.
Row 4: P3, k2, p2, k4, p1, k4, p2, k2, p3.
Row 5: K2, yo, k1, p3, k1, p2, p2tog, k1, p2tog, p2, k1, p3, k1, yo, k2.
Row 6: P4, k3, p1, k2, p3, k2, p1, k3, p4.
Row 7: K3, yo, k1, p1, p2tog, [k1, p3] twice, k1, p2tog, p1, k1, yo, k3.
Row 8: P5, k1, p2, k3, p1, k3, p2, k1, p5.
Row 9: K4, yo, k1, p2, k1, p1, p2tog, k1, p2tog, p1, k1, p2, k1, yo, k4.
Row 10: P6, k2, p1, k1, p3, k1, p1, k2, p6.
Row 11: K5, yo, k1, p2tog, [k1, p2] twice, k1, p2tog, k1, yo, k5.
Row 12: P9, k2, p1, k2, p9.
Row 13: K6, yo, k1, p1, k1, [p2tog, k1] twice, p1, k1, yo, k6.
Row 14: P8, k1, p5, k1, p8.
Rep these 14 rows.

Arched windows

Worked over 13 sts on a background of rev st st.

Note: Stitches should not be counted after row 3, 4, 7, or 8.

T5R (twist 5 right) = Slip next 3 sts onto cable needle and hold at back of work, k2 from left-hand needle, then p1, k2 from cable needle.

Row 1 (RS): K2, p2, k2tog, yo, k1, yo, skpo, p2, k2.
Row 2: P2, k2, p5, k2, p2.
Row 3: K2, p2, k1, yo, k3, yo, k1, p2, k2.
Row 4: P2, k2, p7, k2, p2.
Row 5: K2, p2, skpo, yo, sk2po, yo, k2tog, p2, k2.
Row 6: As row 2.
Row 7: T3F, p1, k1, yo, k3, yo, k1, p1, T3B.
Row 8: K1, p2, k1, p7, k1, p2, k1.
Row 9: P1, T3F, skpo, yo, sk2po, yo, k2tog, T3B, p1.
Row 10: K2, p9, k2.
Row 11: P2, T3F, p3, T3B, p2.
Row 12: [K3, p2] twice, k3.
Row 13: P3, T3F, p1, T3B, p3.
Row 14: K4, p2, k1, p2, k4.
Row 15: P4, T5R, p4.
Row 16: Knit.
Rep these 16 rows.

Peacock plume

Multiple of 16 + 1.

Rows 1 (WS) and 3: Purl.
Row 2: Knit.
Row 4: [K1, yo] 3 times, [skpo] twice, sl 2, k1, p2sso, [k2tog] twice, *yo, [k1, yo] 5 times, [skpo] twice, sl 2, k1, p2sso, [k2tog] twice; rep from * to last 3 sts, [yo, k1] 3 times.
Rep the last 4 rows 3 times more.
Rows 17 and 19: Purl.
Row 18: Knit.
Row 20: [K2tog] 3 times, [yo, k1] 5 times, *yo, [skpo] twice, sl 2, k1, p2sso, [k2tog] twice, [yo, k1] 5 times; rep from * to last 6 sts, yo, [skpo] 3 times.
Rep the last 4 rows 3 times more.
Rep these 32 rows.

Canterbury bells

Multiple of 5.

Note: Stitches should only be counted after row 1, 2, or 10.

Row 1 (RS): P2, KB1, *p4, KB1; rep from * to last 2 sts, p2.

Row 2: K2, PB1, *k4, PB1; rep from * to last 2 sts, k2.

Row 3: P2, KB1, *p2, turn, cast on 8 sts using the cable method, turn, p2, KB1; rep from * to last 2 sts, p2.

Row 4: K2, PB1, *k2, p8, k2, PB1; rep from * to last 2 sts, k2.

Row 5: P2, KB1, *p2, k8, p2, KB1; rep from * to last 2 sts, p2.

Row 6: As row 4.

Row 7: P2, KB1, *p2, skpo, k4, k2tog, p2, KB1; rep from * to last 2 sts, p2.

Row 8: K2, PB1, *k2, p2tog, p2, p2tog tbl, k2, PB1; rep from * to last 2 sts, k2.

Row 9: P2, KB1, *p2, skpo, k2tog, p2, KB1; rep from * to last 2 sts, p2.

Row 10: K2, PB1, *k1, skpo, k2tog, k1, PB1; rep from * to last 2 sts, k2.

Rep these 10 rows.

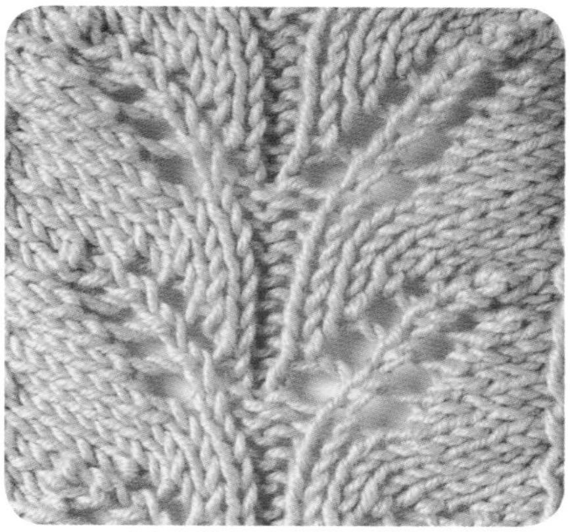

Leaf panel

Worked over 24 sts on a background of st st.

Row 1 (RS): Sk2po, k7, yo, k1, yo, p2, yo, k1, yo, k7, k3tog.

Row 2 and every alt row: P11, k2, p11.

Row 3: Sk2po, k6, [yo, k1] twice, p2, [k1, yo] twice, k6, k3tog.

Row 5: Sk2po, k5, yo, k1, yo, k2, p2, k2, yo, k1, yo, k5, k3tog.

Row 7: Sk2po, k4, yo, k1, yo, k3, p2, k3, yo, k1, yo, k4, k3tog.

Row 9: Sk2po, k3, yo, k1, yo, k4, p2, k4, yo, k1, yo, k3, k3tog.

Row 10: As row 2.

Rep these 10 rows.

Crowns of glory

Multiple of 14 + 1.

Note: Stitches should only be counted after row 7, 8, 9, 10, 11, or 12.

Row 1 (RS): K1, *skpo, k9, k2tog, k1; rep from * to end.

Row 2: P1, *p2tog, p7, p2tog tbl, p1; rep from * to end.

Row 3: K1, *skpo, k2, yo3, k3, k2tog, k1; rep from * to end.

Row 4: P1, *p2tog, p2, (k1, p1, k1, p1, k1) into yo3 to make 5 sts, p1, p2tog tbl, p1; rep from * to end.

Row 5: K1, *skpo, k6, k2tog, k1; rep from * to end.

Row 6: P1, *p2tog, p7; rep from * to end.

Row 7: K2, [yo, k1] 5 times, yo, *k3, [yo, k1] 5 times, yo; rep from * to last 2 sts, k2.

Row 8: Purl.

Rows 9–10: Knit.

Row 11: Purl.

Row 12: Knit.

Rep these 12 rows.

Garter stitch lacy diamonds

Multiple of 10 + 1.

Row 1 (RS) and every alt row: Knit.

Row 2: K3, *k2tog, yo, k1, yo, k2tog, k5; rep from * to last 8 sts, k2tog, yo, k1, yo, k2tog, k3.

Row 4: K2, *k2tog, yo, k3, yo, k2tog, k3; rep from * to last 9 sts, k2tog, yo, k3, yo, k2tog, k2.

Row 6: K1, *k2tog, yo, k5, yo, k2tog, k1; rep from * to end.

Row 8: K1, *yo, k2tog, k5, k2tog, yo, k1; rep from * to end.

Row 10: K2, *yo, k2tog, k3, k2tog, yo, k3; rep from * to last 9 sts, yo, k2tog, k3, k2tog, yo, k2.

Row 12: K3, *yo, k2tog, k1, k2tog, yo, k5; rep from * to last 8 sts, yo, k2tog, k1, k2tog, yo, k3.

Rep these 12 rows.

Seed stitch lace diamonds

Multiple of 8 + 1.

Row 1 (RS): K1, *p1, k1; rep from * to end.

Row 2: K1, *p1, k1; rep from * to end.

Rep the last 2 rows once more.

Row 5: K1, *yo, skpo, k3, k2tog, yo, k1; rep from * to end.

Row 6: Purl.

Row 7: K2, *yo, skpo, k1, k2tog, yo, k3; rep from * to last 7 sts, yo, skpo, k1, k2tog, yo, k2.

Row 8: Purl.

Row 9: K3, *yo, sk2po, yo, k5; rep from * to last 6 sts, yo, sk2po, yo, k3.

Row 10: Purl.

Row 11: K1, *p1, k1; rep from * to end.

Rep the last row 3 times more.

Row 15: K2, *k2tog, yo, k1, yo, skpo, k3; rep from * to last 7 sts, k2tog, yo, k1, yo, skpo, k2.

Row 16: Purl.

Row 17: *K1, k2tog, yo, k3, yo, skpo; rep from * to last st, k1.

Row 18: Purl.

Row 19: K2tog, *yo, k5, yo, sk2po; rep from * to last 7 sts, yo, k5, yo, skpo.

Row 20: Purl.

Rep these 20 rows.

Lace check

Multiple of 18 + 9.

Row 1 (WS): Purl.

Row 2: K1, *[yo, k2tog] 4 times, k10; rep from * to last 8 sts, [yo, k2tog] 4 times.

Row 3: Purl.

Row 4: *[Skpo, yo] 4 times, k10; rep from * to last 9 sts, [skpo, yo] 4 times, k1.

Rep the last 4 rows twice more.

Row 13: Purl.

Row 14: *K10, [yo, k2tog] 4 times; rep from * to last 9 sts, k9.

Row 15: Purl.

Row 16: K9, *[skpo, yo] 4 times, k10; rep from * to end.

Rep the last 4 rows twice more.

Rep these 24 rows.

Twisted openwork pattern

Multiple of 4 + 1.

Row 1 (RS): P1, *k3, p1; rep from * to end.

Row 2: K1, *p3, k1; rep from * to end.

Row 3: As row 1.

Row 4: K1, *yo, p3tog, yo, k1; rep from * to end.

Row 5: K2, p1, *k3, p1; rep from * to last 2 sts, k2.

Row 6: P2, k1, *p3, k1; rep from * to last 2 sts, p2.

Row 7: As row 5.

Row 8: P2tog, yo, k1, yo, *p3tog, yo, k1, yo; rep from * to last 2 sts, p2tog.

Rep these 8 rows.

Knotted boxes I

Multiple of 8 + 5.

Row 1 (RS): Knit.

Row 2: Purl.

Row 3: K1, p3, *k5, p3; rep from * to last st, k1.

Row 4: P1, k3, *p5, k3; rep from * to last st, p1.

Row 5: K1, yo, k3tog, yo, *k5, yo, k3tog, yo; rep from * to last st, k1.

Work 3 rows in st st, starting with purl.

Row 9: K5, *p3, k5; rep from * to end.

Row 10: P5, *k3, p5; rep from * to end.

Row 11: K5, *yo, k3tog, yo, k5; rep from * to end.

Row 12: Purl.

Rep these 12 rows.

Fishtail lace

Multiple of 8 + 1.

Row 1 (RS): K1, *yo, k2, sk2po, k2, yo, k1; rep from * to end.

Row 2: Purl.

Row 3: K2, *yo, k1, sk2po, k1, yo, k3; rep from * to last 7 sts, yo, k1, sk2po, k1, yo, k2.

Row 4: Purl.

Row 5: K3, *yo, sk2po, yo, k5; rep from * to last 6 sts, yo, sk2po, yo, k3.

Row 6: Purl.

Rep these 6 rows.

Fishtail lace panel

Worked over 11 sts on a background of st st.

Row 1 (RS): P1, k1, yo, k2, sk2po, k2, yo, k1, p1.
Row 2: K1, p9, k1.
Row 3: P1, k2, yo, k1, sk2po, k1, yo, k2, p1.
Row 4: As row 2.
Row 5: P1, k3, yo, sk2po, yo, k3, p1.
Row 6: As row 2.
Rep these 6 rows.

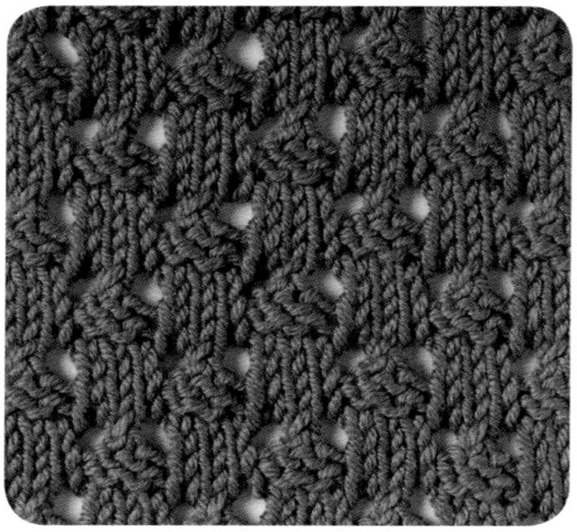

Knotted boxes II

Multiple of 6 + 5.
Row 1 (RS): K1, p3, *k3, p3; rep from * to last st, k1.
Row 2: P1, k3, *p3, k3; rep from * to last st, p1.
Row 3: K1, yo, k3tog, yo, *k3, yo, k3tog, yo; rep from * to last st, k1.
Row 4: Purl.
Row 5: K4, p3, *k3, p3; rep from * to last 4 sts, k4.
Row 6: P4, k3, *p3, k3; rep from * to last 4 sts, p4.
Row 7: K4, yo, k3tog, yo, *k3, yo, k3tog, yo; rep from * to last 4 sts, k4.
Row 8: Purl.
Rep these 8 rows.

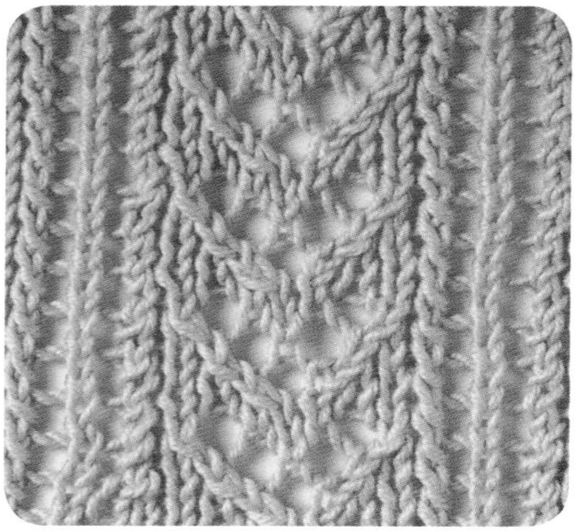

Vandyke lace panel I

Worked over 17 sts on a background of st st.

Row 1 (RS): *K2tog, yo, k1, yo, skpo*, k3, yo, skpo, k2; rep from * to * once more.
Row 2: Purl.
Row 3: [K2tog, yo, k1, yo, skpo, k1] twice, k2tog, yo, k1, yo, skpo.
Row 4: Purl.
Row 5: *K2tog, yo, k1, yo, skpo*, k2tog, yo, k3, yo, skpo; rep from * to * once more.
Row 6: Purl.
Rep these 6 rows.

Vandyke lace panel II

Worked over 9 sts on a background of st st.

Row 1 (RS): K4, yo, skpo, k3.

Row 2 and every alt row: Purl.

Row 3: K2, k2tog, yo, k1, yo, skpo, k2.

Row 5: K1, k2tog, yo, k3, yo, skpo, k1.

Row 7: K2tog, yo, k5, yo, skpo.

Row 8: Purl.

Rep these 8 rows.

Eyelet V-stitch

Multiple of 12 + 1.

Row 1 (RS): Knit.

Row 2 and every alt row: Purl.

Row 3: K4, yo, skpo, k1, k2tog, yo, *k7, yo, skpo, k1, k2tog, yo; rep from * to last 4 sts, k4.

Row 5: K5, yo, sk2po, yo, *k9, yo, sk2po, yo; rep from * to last 5 sts, k5.

Row 7: Knit.

Row 9: K1, *k2tog, yo, k7, yo, skpo, k1; rep from * to end.

Row 11: K2tog, yo, k9, *yo, sk2po, yo, k9; rep from * to last 2 sts, yo, skpo.

Row 12: Purl.

Rep these 12 rows.

Diamond lace I

Multiple of 8 + 7.

Row 1 (RS): Knit.

Row 2 and every alt row: Purl.

Row 3: K3, *yo, skpo, k6; rep from * to last 4 sts, yo, skpo, k2.

Row 5: K2, *yo, sk2po, yo, k5; rep from * to last 5 sts, yo, sk2po, yo, k2.

Row 7: As row 3.

Row 9: Knit.

Row 11: K7, *yo, skpo, k6; rep from * to end.

Row 13: K6, *yo, sk2po, yo, k5; rep from * to last st, k1.

Row 15: As row 11.

Row 16: Purl.

Rep these 16 rows.

Ridged lace pattern

Multiple of 2 + 1.
Purl 3 rows.
Row 4 (RS): K1, *yo, skpo; rep from * to end.
Purl 3 rows.
Row 8: K1, *yo, k2tog; rep from * to end.
Rep these 8 rows.

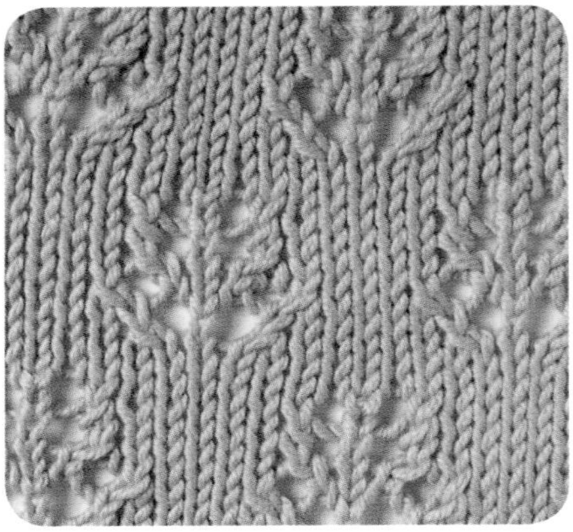

Pine cone pattern

Multiple of 10 + 1.
Row 1 (RS): Knit.
Row 2 and every alt row: Purl.
Row 3: K3, k2tog, yo, k1, yo, skpo, *k5, k2tog, yo, k1, yo, skpo; rep from * to last 3 sts, k3.
Row 5: K2, k2tog, yo, k3, yo, skpo, *k3, k2tog, yo, k3, yo, skpo; rep from * to last 2 sts, k2.
Rows 7 and 9: As row 3.
Row 11: Knit.
Row 13: K1, *yo, skpo, k5, k2tog, yo, k1; rep from * to end.
Row 15: K2, yo, skpo, k3, k2tog, yo, *k3, yo, skpo, k3, k2tog, yo; rep from * to last 2 sts, k2.
Rows 17 and 19: As row 13.
Row 20: Purl.
Rep these 20 rows.

Feather lace

Multiple of 6 + 1.
Row 1 (RS): K1, *yo, k2tog tbl, k1, k2tog, yo, k1; rep from * to end.
Row 2 and every alt row: Purl.
Row 3: K1, *yo, k1, sk2po, k1, yo, k1; rep from * to end.
Row 5: K1, *k2tog, yo, k1, yo, k2tog tbl, k1; rep from * to end.
Row 7: K2tog, *[k1, yo] twice, k1, sk2po; rep from * to last 5 sts, [k1, yo] twice, k1, k2tog tbl.
Row 8: Purl.
Rep these 8 rows.

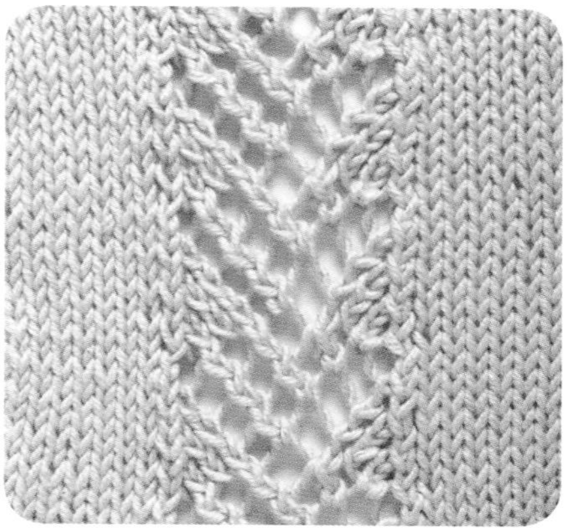

Fan lace panel

Worked over 11 sts on a background of st st.

Row 1 (RS): Skpo, [KB1] 3 times, yo, k1, yo, [KB1] 3 times, k2tog.

Row 2 and every alt row: Purl.

Row 3: Skpo, [KB1] twice, yo, k1, yo, skpo, yo, [KB1] twice, k2tog.

Row 5: Skpo, KB1, yo, k1, [yo, skpo] twice, yo, KB1, k2tog.

Row 7: Skpo, yo, k1, [yo, skpo] 3 times, yo, k2tog.

Row 8: Purl.

Rep these 8 rows.

Raindrops

Multiple of 6 + 5.

Row 1 (RS): P5, *yo, p2tog, p4; rep from * to end.

Row 2: K5, *p1, k5; rep from * to end.

Row 3: P5, *k1, p5; rep from * to end.

Rep the last 2 rows once more, then row 2 again.

Row 7: P2, yo, p2tog, *p4, yo, p2tog; rep from * to last st, p1.

Row 8: K2, p1, *k5, p1; rep from * to last 2 sts, k2.

Row 9: P2, k1, *p5, k1; rep from * to last 2 sts, p2.

Rep the last 2 rows once more, then row 8 again.

Rep these 12 rows.

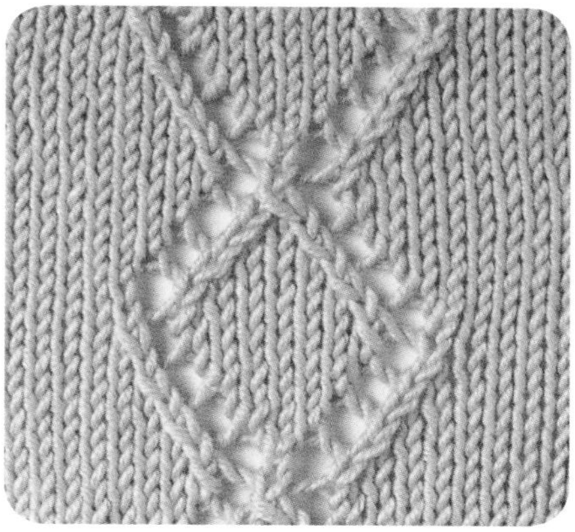

Lozenge lace panel

Worked over 11 sts on a background of st st.

Row 1 (RS): K1, yo, skpo, k5, k2tog, yo, k1.

Row 2 and every alt row: Purl.

Row 3: K2, yo, skpo, k3, k2tog, yo, k2.

Row 5: K3, yo, skpo, k1, k2tog, yo, k3.

Row 7: K4, yo, sk2po, yo, k4.

Row 9: K3, k2tog, yo, k1, yo, skpo, k3.

Row 11: K2, k2tog, yo, k3, yo, skpo, k2.

Row 13: K1, k2tog, yo, k5, yo, skpo, k1.

Row 15: K2tog, yo, k7, yo, skpo.

Row 16: Purl.

Rep these 16 rows.

Lace rib panel

Worked over 7 sts on a background of rev st st.

Row 1 (RS): P1, yo, skpo, k1, k2tog, yo, p1.

Row 2: K1, p5, k1.

Row 3: P1, k1, yo, sk2po, yo, k1, p1.

Row 4: K1, p5, k1.

Rep these 4 rows.

Bobble tree panel

Worked over 17 sts on a background of rev st st.

Special abbreviation:

MB (make bobble) = [K1, p1] twice into next st, turn and p4, turn and k4, turn and p4, turn and skpo, k2tog, turn and p2tog, turn and slip bobble st onto right-hand needle.

Row 1 (RS): P6, k2tog, yo, p1, yo, skpo, p6.

Row 2: K6, p1, k3, p1, k6.

Row 3: P5, k2tog, yo, p3, yo, skpo, p5.

Row 4: [K5, p1] twice, k5.

Row 5: P4, k2tog, yo, [p1, k1] twice, p1, yo, skpo, p4.

Row 6: K4, p1, k2, p1, k1, p1, k2, p1, k4.

Row 7: P3, k2tog, yo, p2, k1, p1, k1, p2, yo, skpo, p3.

Row 8: [K3, p1] twice, k1, [p1, k3] twice.

Row 9: P2, k2tog, yo, p2, k2tog, yo, p1, yo, skpo, p2, yo, skpo, p2.

Row 10: K2, [p1, k3] 3 times, p1, k2.

Row 11: P2, MB, p2, k2tog, yo, p3, yo, skpo, p2, MB, p2.

Row 12: [K5, p1] twice, k5.

Rep these 12 rows.

Lace and cable pattern

Worked over 21 sts on a background of st st.

Special abbreviation:

CB4F or CB4B (cable 4 front or back) = Slip next 2 sts onto cable needle and hold at front (or back) of work, knit into back of next 2 sts on left-hand needle, then knit into back of sts on cable needle.

Row 1 (RS): P2, [KB1] 4 times, k1, yo, k2tog tbl, k3, k2tog, yo, k1, [KB1] 4 times, p2.

Row 2 and every alt row: K2, [PB1] 4 times, k1, p7, k1, [PB1] 4 times, k2.

Row 3: P2, [KB1] 4 times, k2, yo, k2tog tbl, k1, k2tog, yo, k2, [KB1] 4 times, p2.

Row 5: P2, CB4F, k3, yo, sk2po, yo, k3, CB4B, p2.

Row 7: P2, [KB1] 4 times, k9, [KB1] 4 times, p2.

Row 8: As row 2.

Rep these 8 rows.

Catherine wheels

Worked over 13 sts on a background of st st.

Special abbreviations:

Inc 1 (increase 1) = Knit into front and back of next st.

Inc 2 (increase 2) = Knit into front, back, and front of next st.

Work 5tog = Skpo, k3tog, pass the st resulting from skpo over the st resulting from k3tog.

Row 1 (WS) and every alt row: Purl.

Row 2: K5, sl 3, yf, pass slipped sts back onto left-hand needle, yb, knit 3 slipped sts, k5.

Row 4: K3, k3tog, yo, inc 2, yo, k3tog tbl, k3.

Row 6: K1, k3tog, yo, k2tog, yo, inc 2, yo, skpo, yo, k3tog tbl, k1.

Row 8: [K2tog, yo] 3 times, KB1, [yo, skpo] 3 times.

Row 10: K1, [yo, k2tog] twice, yo, sk2po, [yo, skpo] twice, yo, k1.

Row 12: [Skpo, yo] 3 times, KB1, [yo, k2tog] 3 times.

Row 14: K1, inc 1, yo, skpo, yo, work 5tog, yo, k2tog, yo, inc 1, k1.

Row 16: K3, inc 1, yo, work 5tog, yo, inc 1, k3.

Rep these 16 rows.

Fishtails

Worked over 15 sts on a background of st st.

Row 1 (RS): K6, yo, sk2po, yo, k6.

Row 2 and every alt row: Purl.

Rep the last 2 rows 3 times more.

Row 9: [K1, yo] twice, skpo, k2, sk2po, k2, k2tog, [yo, k1] twice.

Row 11: K2, yo, k1, yo, skpo, k1, sk2po, k1, k2tog, yo, k1, yo, k2.

Row 13: K3, yo, k1, yo, skpo, sk2po, k2tog, yo, k1, yo, k3.

Row 15: K4, yo, skpo, yo, sk2po, yo, k2tog, yo, k4.

Row 16: Purl.

Rep these 16 rows.

Zigzag eyelet panel

Worked over 11 sts on a background of st st.

Row 1 (RS): K6, yo, skpo, k3.

Row 2 and every alt row: Purl.

Row 3: K7, yo, skpo, k2.

Row 5: K3, k2tog, yo, k3, yo, skpo, k1.

Row 7: K2, k2tog, yo, k5, yo, skpo.

Row 9: K1, k2tog, yo, k8.

Row 11: K2tog, yo, k9.

Row 12: Purl.

Rep these 12 rows.

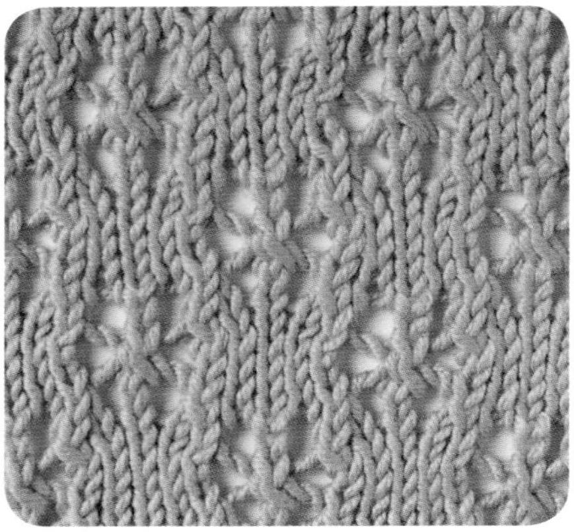

Snowflakes I

Multiple of 8 + 7.

Row 1 (WS) and every alt row: Purl.

Row 2: K5, skpo, yo, k1, yo, k2tog, *k3, skpo, yo, k1, yo, k2tog; rep from * to last 5 sts, k5.

Row 4: K6, yo, sl 2, k1, p2sso, yo, *k5, yo, sl 2, k1, p2sso, yo; rep from * to last 6 sts, k6.

Row 6: As row 2.

Row 8: K1, skpo, yo, k1, yo, k2tog, *k3, skpo, yo, k1, yo, k2tog; rep from * to last st, k1.

Row 10: K2, yo, sl 2, k1, p2sso, yo, *k5, yo, sl 2, k1, p2sso, yo; rep from * to last 2 sts, k2.

Row 12: As row 8.

Rep these 12 rows.

Trellis lace

Multiple of 6 + 5.

Row 1 (RS): K4, *yo, sk2po, yo, k3; rep from * to last st, k1.

Row 2: Purl.

Row 3: K1, *yo, sk2po, yo, k3; rep from * to last 4 sts, yo, sk2po, yo, k1.

Row 4: Purl.

Rep these 4 rows.

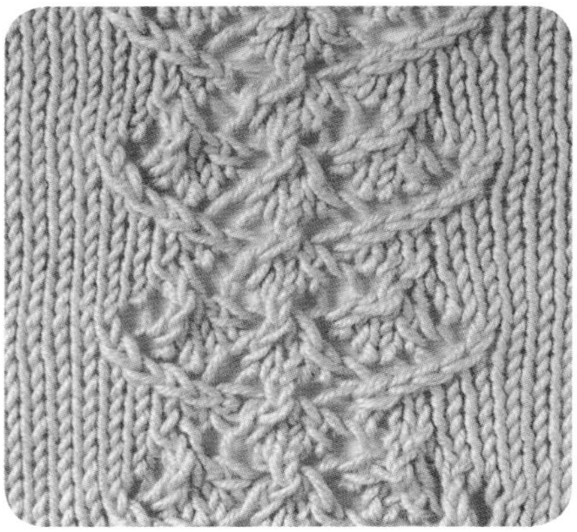

Quatrefoil panel

Worked over 15 sts on a background of st st.

Note: Stitches should not be counted after row 6, 7, 8, or 9.

Row 1 (RS): K5, k2tog, yo, k1, yo, skpo, k5.

Row 2: P4, p2tog tbl, yo, p3, yo, p2tog, p4.

Row 3: K3, k2tog, yo, k5, yo, skpo, k3.

Row 4: P2, p2tog tbl, yo, p1, yo, p2tog, p1, p2tog tbl, yo, p1, yo, p2tog, p2.

Row 5: K1, k2tog, yo, k3, yo, k3tog, yo, k3, yo, skpo, k1.

Row 6: P2, yo, p5, yo, p1, yo, p5, yo, p2.

Row 7: [K3, yo, skpo, k1, k2tog, yo] twice, k3.

Row 8: P4, p3tog, yo, p5, yo, p3tog, p4.

Row 9: K6, yo, skpo, k1, k2tog, yo, k6.

Row 10: P3, p2tog tbl, p2, yo, p3tog, yo, p2, p2tog, p3.

Rep these 10 rows.

Diamond and eyelet pattern

Multiple of 6 + 3.

Row 1 (WS): Knit.

Row 2: P1, *yo, p2tog; rep from * to end.

Rows 3–4: Knit.

Row 5 and rem alt rows: Purl.

Row 6: *K4, yo, skpo; rep from * to last 3 sts, k3.

Row 8: K2, *k2tog, yo, k1, yo, skpo, k1; rep from * to last st, k1.

Row 10: K1, k2tog, yo, *k3, yo, sk2po, yo; rep from * to last 6 sts, k3, yo, skpo, k1.

Row 12: K3, *yo, sk2po, yo, k3; rep from * to end.

Row 14: As row 6.

Row 16: Knit.

Rep these 16 rows.

Snowflakes II

Multiple of 6 + 1.

Note: Stitches should not be counted after row 3, 4, 9, or 10.

Row 1 (RS): K1, *yo, skpo, k1, k2tog, yo, k1; rep from * to end.

Row 2 and every alt row: Purl.

Row 3: K2, yo, *k3, yo; rep from * to last 2 sts, k2.

Row 5: K2tog, yo, skpo, k1, k2tog, yo, *sk2po, yo, skpo, k1, k2tog, yo; rep from * to last 2 sts, skpo.

Row 7: K1, *k2tog, yo, k1, yo, skpo, k1; rep from * to end.

Row 9: As row 3.

Row 11: K1, *k2tog, yo, sk2po, yo, skpo, k1; rep from * to end.

Row 12: Purl.

Rep these 12 rows.

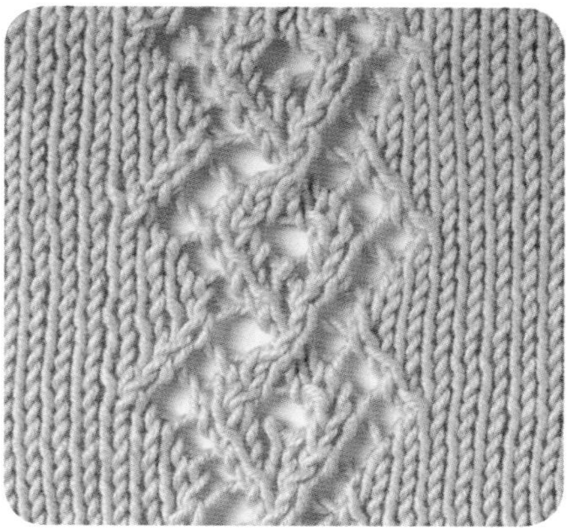

Lace chain panel

Worked over 10 sts on a background of st st.

Row 1 (RS): K2, k2tog, yo, k2tog but do not slip from needle, knit first of these 2 sts again then slip both sts off needle together, yo, skpo, k2.

Row 2: Purl.

Row 3: K1, k2tog, yo, k4, yo, skpo, k1.

Row 4: Purl.

Row 5: K2tog, yo, k1, k2tog, yo2, skpo, k1, yo, skpo.

Row 6: P4, knit into first yo, purl into 2nd yo, p4.

Row 7: K2, yo, skpo, k2, k2tog, yo, k2.

Row 8: Purl.

Row 9: K3, yo, skpo, k2tog, yo, k3.

Row 10: Purl.

Rep these 10 rows.

Eyelet diamonds

Multiple of 16 + 11.

Row 1 (RS): K10, yo, skpo, k3, k2tog, yo, *k9, yo, skpo, k3, k2tog, yo; rep from * to last 10 sts, k10.

Row 2 and every alt row: Purl.

Row 3: K3, k2tog, yo, k1, yo, skpo, *k3, yo, skpo, k1, k2tog, yo, k3, k2tog, yo, k1, yo, skpo; rep from * to last 3 sts, k3.

Row 5: K2, k2tog, yo, k3, yo, skpo, *k3, yo, sk2po, yo, k3, k2tog, yo, k3, yo, skpo; rep from * to last 2 sts, k2.

Row 7: K1, k2tog, yo, k5, yo, skpo, *k7, k2tog, yo, k5, yo, skpo; rep from * to last st, k1.

Row 9: K2, yo, skpo, k3, k2tog, yo, *k9, yo, skpo, k3, k2tog, yo; rep from * to last 2 sts, k2.

Row 11: K3, yo, skpo, k1, k2tog, yo, k3, *k2tog, yo, k1, yo, skpo, k3, yo, skpo, k1, k2tog, yo, k3; rep from * to end.

Row 13: K4, yo, sk2po, yo, *k3, k2tog, yo, k3, yo, skpo, k3, yo, sk2po, yo; rep from * to last 4 sts, k4.

Row 15: K9, k2tog, yo, k5, yo, skpo, *k7, k2tog, yo, k5, yo, skpo; rep from * to last 9 sts, k9.

Row 16: Purl.

Rep these 16 rows.

Ornamental tulip pattern

Multiple of 13.

Note: Stitches should only be counted after row 1, 2, 9, or 10.

Row 1 (RS): Purl.

Row 2: Knit.

Row 3: P6, [p1, k1] 3 times into next st, *p12, [p1, k1] 3 times into next st; rep from * to last 6 sts, p6.

Row 4: K6, p6, *k12, p6; rep from * to last 6 sts, k6.

Row 5: P6, k6, *p12, k6; rep from * to last 6 sts, p6.

Row 6: As row 4.

Row 7: [P2tog] twice, p2, [k2, yo] twice, k2, *p2, [p2tog] 4 times, p2, [k2, yo] twice, k2; rep from * to last 6 sts, p2, [p2tog] twice.

Row 8: K4, p8, *k8, p8; rep from * to last 4 sts, k4.

Row 9: [P2tog] twice, [k2tog, yo, k1, yo] twice, k2tog, *[p2tog] 4 times, [k2tog, yo, k1, yo] twice, k2tog; rep from * to last 4 sts, [p2tog] twice.

Row 10: K2, p9, *k4, p9; rep from * to last 2 sts, k2.

Rep these 10 rows.

Zigzag eyelets

Multiple of 9.

Row 1 (RS): K4, *yo, skpo, k7; rep from * to last 5 sts, yo, skpo, k3.

Row 2 and every alt row: Purl.

Row 3: K5, *yo, skpo, k7; rep from * to last 4 sts, yo, skpo, k2.

Row 5: K6, *yo, skpo, k7; rep from * to last 3 sts, yo, skpo, k1.

Row 7: *K7, yo, skpo; rep from * to end.

Row 9: K3, *k2tog, yo, k7; rep from * to last 6 sts, k2tog, yo, k4.

Row 11: K2, *k2tog, yo, k7; rep from * to last 7 sts, k2tog, yo, k5.

Row 13: K1, *k2tog, yo, k7; rep from * to last 8 sts, k2tog, yo, k6.

Row 15: *K2tog, yo, k7; rep from * to end.

Row 16: Purl.

Rep these 16 rows.

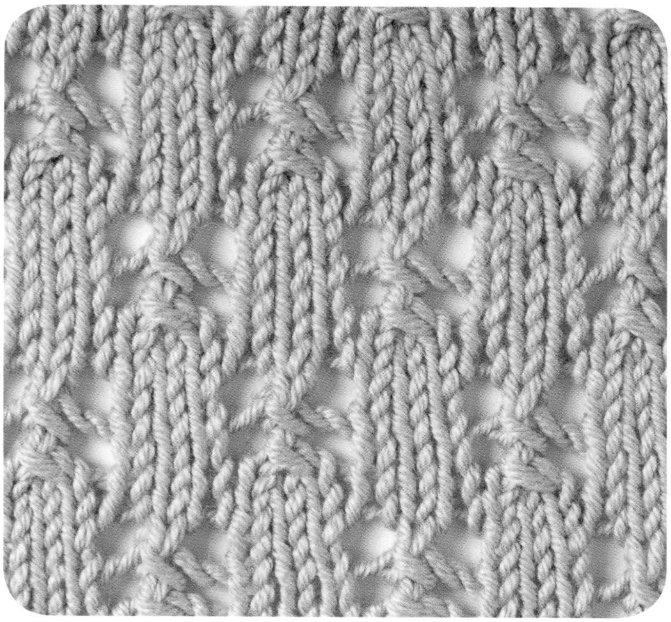

Lacy checks

Multiple of 6 + 5.

Row 1 (RS): K1, *yo, sk2po, yo, k3; rep from * to last 4 sts, yo, sk2po, yo, k1.

Row 2 and every alt row: Purl.

Row 3: As row 1.

Row 5: Knit.

Row 7: K4, *yo, sk2po, yo, k3; rep from * to last st, k1.

Row 9: As row 7.

Row 11: Knit.

Row 12: Purl.

Rep these 12 rows.

Little and large diamonds

Multiple of 12 + 1.

Row 1 (RS): K1, *yo, skpo, k7, k2tog, yo, k1; rep from * to end.

Row 2 and every alt row: Purl.

Row 3: K2, yo, skpo, k5, *k2tog, yo, k3, yo, skpo, k5; rep from * to last 4 sts, k2tog, yo, k2.

Row 5: K3, yo, skpo, k3, *k2tog, yo, k5, yo, skpo, k3; rep from * to last 5 sts, k2tog, yo, k3.

Row 7: *K1, k2tog, yo, k1, yo, skpo; rep from * to last st, k1.

Row 9: K2tog, yo, k3, *yo, sk2po, yo, k3; rep from * to last 2 sts, yo, skpo.

Row 11: K4, k2tog, yo, k1, yo, skpo, *k7, k2tog, yo, k1, yo, skpo; rep from * to last 4 sts, k4.

Row 13: K3, k2tog, yo, k3, yo, skpo, *k5, k2tog, yo, k3, yo, skpo; rep from * to last 3 sts, k3.

Row 15: K2, k2tog, yo, k5, yo, skpo, *k3, k2tog, yo, k5, yo, skpo; rep from * to last 2 sts, k2.

Row 17: As row 7.

Row 19: As row 9.

Row 20: Purl.

Rep these 20 rows.

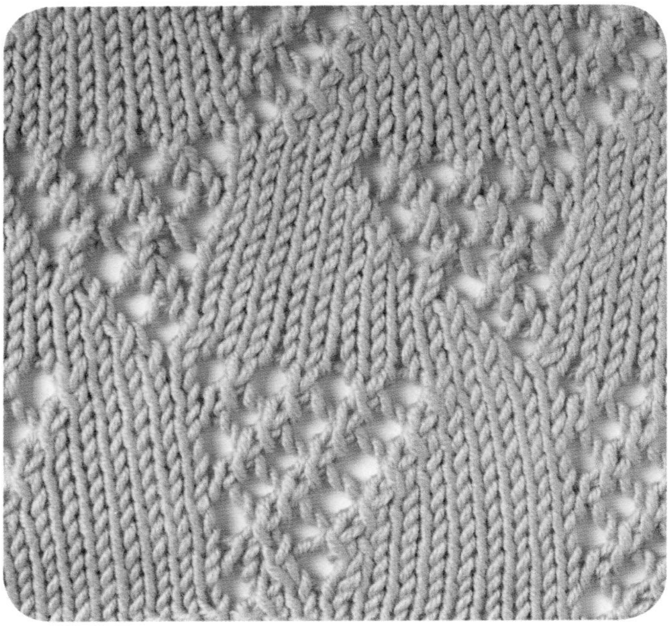

Swinging triangles

Multiple of 12 + 1.

Row 1 (WS) and every alt row: Purl.
Row 2: *K10, skpo, yo; rep from * to last st, k1.
Row 4: K9, skpo, yo, *k10, skpo, yo; rep from * to last 2 sts, k2.
Row 6: *K8, [skpo, yo] twice; rep from * to last st, k1.
Row 8: K7, [skpo, yo] twice, *k8, [skpo, yo] twice; rep from * to last 2 sts, k2.
Row 10: *K6, [skpo, yo] 3 times; rep from * to last st, k1.
Row 12: K5, [skpo, yo] 3 times, *k6, [skpo, yo] 3 times; rep from * to last 2 sts, k2.
Row 14: *K4, [skpo, yo] 4 times; rep from * to last st, k1.
Row 16: K1, *yo, k2tog, k10; rep from * to end.
Row 18: K2, yo, k2tog, *k10, yo, k2tog; rep from * to last 9 sts, k9.
Row 20: K1, *[yo, k2tog] twice, k8; rep from * to end.
Row 22: K2, [yo, k2tog] twice, *k8, [yo, k2tog] twice; rep from * to last 7 sts, k7.
Row 24: K1, *[yo, k2tog] 3 times, k6; rep from * to end.
Row 26: K2, [yo, k2tog] 3 times, *k6, [yo, k2tog] 3 times; rep from * to last 5 sts, k5.
Row 28: K1, *[yo, k2tog] 4 times, k4; rep from * to end.
Rep these 28 rows.

Chutes and ladders

Multiple of 8 + 2.

Row 1 (RS): K7, *k2tog, yo, k6; rep from * to last 3 sts, k2tog, yo, k1.
Row 2: K2, *yo, p2tog, k6; rep from * to end.
Row 3: K5, *k2tog, yo, k6; rep from * to last 5 sts, k2tog, yo, k3.
Row 4: K4, *yo, p2tog, k6; rep from * to last 6 sts, yo, p2tog, k4.
Row 5: K3, *k2tog, yo, k6; rep from * to last 7 sts, k2tog, yo, k5.
Row 6: *K6, yo, p2tog; rep from * to last 2 sts, k2.
Row 7: K1, *k2tog, yo, k6; rep from * to last st, k1.
Row 8: K7, *p2tog tbl, yo, k6; rep from * to last 3 sts, p2tog tbl, yo, k1.
Row 9: K2, *yo, k2tog tbl, k6; rep from * to end.
Row 10: K5, *p2tog tbl, yo, k6; rep from * to last 5 sts, p2tog tbl, yo, k3.
Row 11: K4, *yo, k2tog tbl, k6; rep from * to last 6 sts, yo, k2tog tbl, k4.
Row 12: K3, *p2tog tbl, yo, k6; rep from * to last 7 sts, p2tog tbl, yo, k5.
Row 13: *K6, yo, k2tog tbl; rep from * to last 2 sts, k2.
Row 14: K1, *p2tog tbl, yo, k6; rep from * to last st, k1.
Rep these 14 rows.

All-over eyelets

Multiple of 10 + 1.
Row 1 (RS): Knit.
Row 2 and every alt row: Purl.
Row 3: K3, *k2tog, yo, k1, yo, skpo, k5; rep from * to last 8 sts, k2tog, yo, k1, yo, skpo, k3.
Row 5: Knit.
Row 7: K1, *yo, skpo, k5, k2tog, yo, k1; rep from * to end.
Row 8: Purl.
Rep these 8 rows.

Little lace panel

Worked over 5 sts on a background of st st.
Note: Stitches should not be counted after row 1 or 2.
Row 1 (RS): K1, yo, k3, yo, k1.
Row 2: Purl.
Row 3: K2, sk2po, k2.
Row 4: Purl.
Rep these 4 rows.

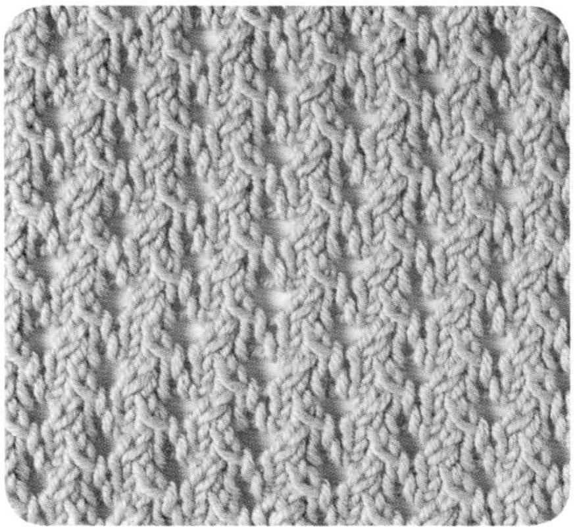

Eyelet lace

Multiple of 6 + 2.
Note: Stitches should only be counted after row 2 or 4.
Row 1 (RS): K1, yo, *k2tog tbl, k2, k2tog, yo; rep from * to last st, k1.
Row 2: K1, p5, *purl into front and back of next st, p4; rep from * to last 2 sts, p1, k1.
Row 3: K2, *k2tog, yo, k2tog tbl, k2; rep from * to end.
Row 4: K1, p2, *purl into front and back of next st, p4; rep from * to last 4 sts, purl into front and back of next st, p2, k1.
Rep these 4 rows.

Tip

A yarnover (yo) is the most common type of increase to be found in lace and eyelet stitch patterns. The increase is made by wrapping the yarn once around the right-hand needle, but without working any stitches on the left-hand needle. It is one of the easiest types of increases to make in knitting. The yarnover is nearly always paired with a decrease in order to keep the overall stitch count in a row consistent.

Trellis pattern

Multiple of 4 + 2.

Row 1 (RS): K1, yo, *skpo, k2tog, yo2; rep from * to last 5 sts, skpo, k2tog, yo, k1.

Row 2: K2, p2, *knit into front of first yo, knit into back of 2nd yo, p2; rep from * to last 2 sts, k2.

Row 3: K1, p1, *C2B, p2; rep from * to last 4 sts, C2B, p1, k1.

Row 4: K2, *p2, k2; rep from * to end.

Row 5: K1, k2tog, *yo2, skpo, k2tog; rep from * to last 3 sts, yo2, skpo, k1.

Row 6: K1, p1, knit into front of first yo, knit into back of 2nd yo, *p2, work into double yarnover as before; rep from * to last 2 sts, p1, k1.

Row 7: K2, *p2, C2B; rep from * to last 4 sts, p2, k2.

Row 8: K1, p1, k2, *p2, k2; rep from * to last 2 sts, p1, k1.

Rep these 8 rows.

Rhombus lace

Multiple of 8 + 2.

Row 1 (RS): K1, [k2tog, yo] twice, *k4, [k2tog, yo] twice; rep from * to last 5 sts, k5.

Row 2 and every alt row: Purl.

Row 3: [K2tog, yo] twice, *k4, [k2tog, yo] twice; rep from * to last 6 sts, k6.

Row 5: K1, k2tog, yo, k4, *[k2tog, yo] twice, k4; rep from * to last 3 sts, k2tog, yo, k1.

Row 7: K3, [k2tog, yo] twice, *k4, [k2tog, yo] twice; rep from * to last 3 sts, k3.

Row 9: K2, *[k2tog, yo] twice, k4; rep from * to end.

Row 11: As row 1.

Row 13: K5, [k2tog, yo] twice, *k4, [k2tog, yo] twice; rep from * to last st, k1.

Row 15: *K4, [k2tog, yo] twice; rep from * to last 2 sts, k2.

Row 17: As row 7.

Row 19: As row 5.

Row 21: K2tog, yo, k4, *[k2tog, yo] twice, k4; rep from * to last 4 sts, k2tog, yo, k2.

Row 23: As row 13.

Row 24: Purl.

Rep these 24 rows.

Fountains panel

Worked over 16 sts on a background of st st.

Row 1 (RS): K1, yo, k1, skpo, p1, k2tog, k1, yo, p1, skpo, p1, k2tog, [yo, k1] twice.
Row 2: P5, k1, p1, k1, p3, k1, p4.
Row 3: K1, yo, k1, skpo, p1, k2tog, k1, p1, sk2po, yo, k3, yo, k1.
Row 4: P7, k1, p2, k1, p4.
Row 5: [K1, yo] twice, skpo, p1, [k2tog] twice, yo, k5, yo, k1.
Row 6: P8, k1, p1, k1, p5.
Row 7: K1, yo, k3, yo, sk2po, p1, yo, k1, skpo, p1, k2tog, k1, yo, k1.
Row 8: P4, k1, p3, k1, p7.
Row 9: K1, yo, k5, yo, skpo, k1, skpo, p1, k2tog, k1, yo, k1.
Row 10: P4, k1, p2, k1, p8.
Rep these 10 rows.

Shetland fern panel

Worked over 13 sts on a background of st st.

Row 1 (RS): K6, yo, skpo, k5.
Row 2: Purl.
Row 3: K4, k2tog, yo, k1, yo, skpo, k4.
Row 4: Purl.
Row 5: K3, k2tog, yo, k3, yo, skpo, k3.
Row 6: Purl.
Row 7: K3, yo, skpo, yo, sk2po, yo, k2tog, yo, k3.
Row 8: Purl.
Row 9: K1, k2tog, yo, k1, yo, skpo, k1, k2tog, yo, k1, yo, skpo, k1.
Row 10: Purl.
Row 11: K1, [yo, skpo] twice, k3, [k2tog, yo] twice, k1.
Row 12: P2, [yo, p2tog] twice, p1, [p2tog tbl, yo] twice, p2.
Row 13: K3, yo, skpo, yo, sk2po, yo, k2tog, yo, k3.
Row 14: P4, yo, p2tog, p1, p2tog tbl, yo, p4.
Row 15: K5, yo, sk2po, yo, k5.
Row 16: Purl.
Rep these 16 rows.

Eyelet boxes

Multiple of 14 + 11.

Row 1 (RS): K2, p7, *k3, yo, skpo, k2, p7; rep from * to last 2 sts, k2.
Rows 2, 4, 6, 8, and 10: P2, k7, *p7, k7; rep from * to last 2 sts, p2.
Row 3: K2, p7, *k1, k2tog, yo, k1, yo, skpo, k1, p7; rep from * to last 2 sts, k2.
Row 5: K2, p7, *k2tog, yo, k3, yo, skpo, p7; rep from * to last 2 sts, k2.
Row 7: K2, p7, *k2, yo, sk2po, yo, k2, p7; rep from * to last 2 sts, k2.
Row 9: As row 1.
Row 11: P2, k3, yo, skpo, k2, *p7, k3, yo, skpo, k2; rep from * to last 2 sts, p2.
Rows 12, 14, 16, and 18: K2, p7, *k7, p7; rep from * to last 2 sts, k2.
Row 13: P2, k1, k2tog, yo, k1, yo, skpo, k1, *p7, k1, k2tog, yo, k1, yo, skpo, k1; rep from * to last 2 sts, p2.
Row 15: P2, k2tog, yo, k3, yo, skpo, *p7, k2tog, yo, k3, yo, skpo; rep from * to last 2 sts, p2.
Row 17: P2, k2, yo, sk2po, yo, k2, *p7, k2, yo, sk2po, yo, k2; rep from * to last 2 sts, p2.
Row 19: As row 11.
Row 20: K2, p7, *k7, p7; rep from * to last 2 sts, k2.
Rep these 20 rows.

Traveling vine

Multiple of 8 + 2.

Note: Stitches should only be counted after WS rows.

Row 1 (RS): K1, *yo, KB1, yo, k2tog tbl, k5; rep from * to last st, k1.

Row 2: P5, *p2tog tbl, p7; rep from * to last 6 sts, p2tog tbl, p4.

Row 3: K1, *yo, KB1, yo, k2, k2tog tbl, k3; rep from * to last st, k1.

Row 4: P3, *p2tog tbl, p7; rep from * to last 8 sts, p2tog tbl, p6.

Row 5: K1, *KB1, yo, k4, k2tog tbl, k1, yo; rep from * to last st, k1.

Row 6: P2, *p2tog tbl, p7; rep from * to end.

Row 7: K6, *k2tog, yo, KB1, yo, k5; rep from * to last 4 sts, k2tog, yo, KB1, yo, k1.

Row 8: P4, *p2tog, p7; rep from * to last 7 sts, p2tog, p5.

Row 9: K4, *k2tog, k2, yo, KB1, yo, k3; rep from * to last 6 sts, k2tog, k2, yo, KB1, yo, k1.

Row 10: P6, *p2tog, p7; rep from * to last 5 sts, p2tog, p3.

Row 11: K1, *yo, k1, k2tog, k4, yo, KB1; rep from * to last st, k1.

Row 12: *P7, p2tog; rep from * to last 2 sts, p2.

Rep these 12 rows.

Shadow triangles

Multiple of 10 + 3.

Row 1 (RS): K2, yo, skpo, k5, k2tog, yo, *k1, yo, skpo, k5, k2tog, yo; rep from * to last 2 sts, k2.

Row 2: P4, k5, *p5, k5; rep from * to last 4 sts, p4.

Row 3: K3, *yo, skpo, k3, k2tog, yo, k3; rep from * to end.

Row 4: P5, k3, *p7, k3; rep from * to last 5 sts, p5.

Row 5: K4, yo, skpo, k1, k2tog, yo, *k5, yo, skpo, k1, k2tog, yo; rep from * to last 4 sts, k4.

Row 6: P6, k1, *p9, k1; rep from * to last 6 sts, p6.

Row 7: K5, yo, sk2po, yo, *k7, yo, sk2po, yo; rep from * to last 5 sts, k5.

Row 8: Purl.

Row 9: K4, k2tog, yo, k1, yo, skpo, *k5, k2tog, yo, k1, yo, skpo; rep from * to last 4 sts, k4.

Row 10: K4, p5, *k5, p5; rep from * to last 4 sts, k4.

Row 11: K3, *k2tog, yo, k3, yo, skpo, k3; rep from * to end.

Row 12: K3, *p7, k3; rep from * to end.

Row 13: K2, k2tog, yo, k5, yo, skpo, *k1, k2tog, yo, k5, yo, skpo; rep from * to last 2 sts, k2.

Row 14: P1, k1, *p9, k1; rep from * to last st, p1.

Row 15: K1, k2tog, yo, k7, *yo, sk2po, yo, k7; rep from * to last 3 sts, yo, skpo, k1.

Row 16: Purl.

Rep these 16 rows.

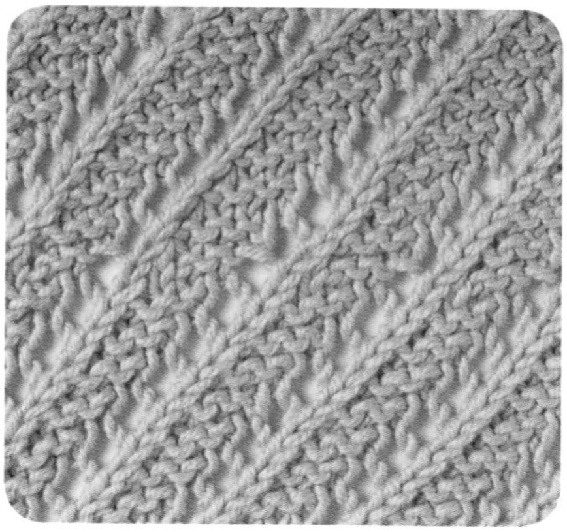

Diagonal ridges

Multiple of 5 + 2.

Row 1 (RS): K2tog, yo, *k3, k2tog, yo; rep from * to last 5 sts, k5.

Row 2: P2, *k3, p2; rep from * to end.

Row 3: K4, k2tog, yo, *k3, k2tog, yo; rep from * to last st, k1.

Row 4: K1, *p2, k3; rep from * to last st, p1.

Row 5: *K3, k2tog, yo; rep from * to last 2 sts, k2.

Row 6: K2, *p2, k3; rep from * to end.

Row 7: K2, *k2tog, yo, k3; rep from * to end.

Row 8: *K3, p2; rep from * to last 2 sts, k2.

Row 9: K1, k2tog, yo, *k3, k2tog, yo; rep from * to last 4 sts, k4.

Row 10: P1, *k3, p2; rep from * to last st, k1.

Rep these 10 rows.

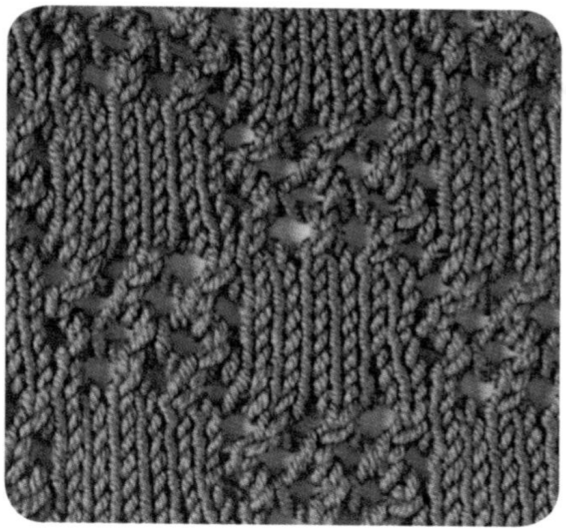

Checkerboard lace

Multiple of 12 + 8.

Row 1 (RS): K7, *[yo, k2tog] 3 times, k6; rep from * to last st, k1.

Row 2 and every alt row: Purl.

Row 3: K7, *[k2tog, yo] 3 times, k6; rep from * to last st, k1.

Row 5: As row 1.

Row 7: As row 3.

Row 9: K1, *[yo, k2tog] 3 times, k6; rep from * to last 7 sts, [yo, k2tog] 3 times, k1.

Row 11: K1, *[k2tog, yo] 3 times, k6; rep from * to last 7 sts, [k2tog, yo] 3 times, k1.

Row 13: As row 9.

Row 15: As row 11.

Row 16: Purl.

Rep these 16 rows.

Shetland eyelet panel

Worked over 9 sts on a background of st st.

Row 1 (RS): K2, k2tog, yo, k1, yo, skpo, k2.

Row 2 and every alt row: Purl.

Row 3: K1, k2tog, yo, k3, yo, skpo, k1.

Row 5: K1, yo, skpo, yo, sl 2, k1, p2sso, yo, k2tog, yo, k1.

Row 7: K3, yo, sl 2, k1, p2sso, yo, k3.

Row 8: Purl.

Rep these 8 rows.

Tip

It is always advisable to block a piece of knitting that features lace or eyelet stitches. This helps to open up and set the lacework or eyelets and even out the pattern, so that the intricacy of the design becomes really clear. There are various ways to block knitted work, but the process basically involves wetting or dampening the piece, pinning it out to the desired shape, and allowing it to dry.

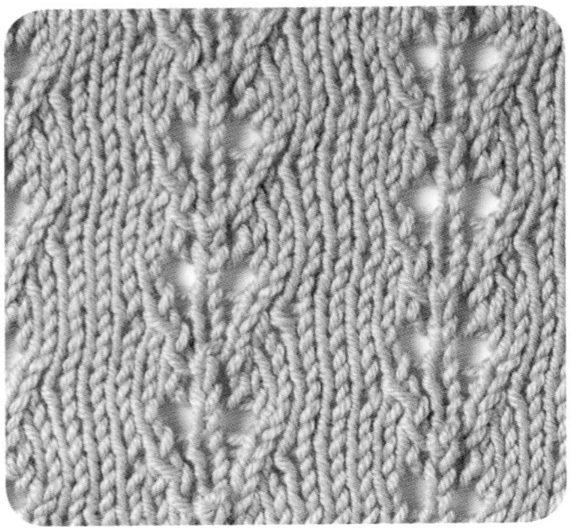

Climbing leaf pattern

Multiple of 16 + 1.

Row 1 (RS): K1, *yo, k5, k2tog, k1, k2tog tbl, k5, yo, k1; rep from * to end.

Row 2 and every alt row: Purl.

Row 3: As row 1.

Row 5: K1, *k2tog tbl, k5, yo, k1, yo, k5, k2tog, k1; rep from * to end.

Row 7: As row 5.

Row 8: Purl.

Rep these 8 rows.

Twin leaf lace panel

Worked over 23 sts on a background of st st.

Row 1 (RS): K8, k2tog, yo, k1, p1, k1, yo, skpo, k8.

Row 2: P7, p2tog tbl, p2, yo, k1, yo, p2, p2tog, p7.

Row 3: K6, k2tog, k1, yo, k2, p1, k2, yo, k1, skpo, k6.

Row 4: P5, p2tog tbl, p3, yo, p1, k1, p1, yo, p3, p2tog, p5.

Row 5: K4, k2tog, k2, yo, k3, p1, k3, yo, k2, skpo, k4.

Row 6: P3, p2tog tbl, p4, yo, p2, k1, p2, yo, p4, p2tog, p3.

Row 7: K2, k2tog, k3, yo, k4, p1, k4, yo, k3, skpo, k2.

Row 8: P1, p2tog tbl, p5, yo, p3, k1, p3, yo, p5, p2tog, p1.

Row 9: K2tog, k4, yo, k5, p1, k5, yo, k4, skpo.

Row 10: P11, k1, p11.

Row 11: K11, p1, k11.

Row 12: P11, k1, p11.

Rep these 12 rows.

Lacy diagonals

Multiple of 10 + 2.

Row 1 (RS): K1, *k6, skpo, yo, k2tog, yo; rep from * to last st, k1.

Row 2 and every alt row: Purl.

Row 3: *K6, skpo, yo, k2tog, yo; rep from * to last 2 sts, k2.

Row 5: K5, *skpo, yo, k2tog, yo, k6; rep from * to last 7 sts, skpo, yo, k2tog, yo, k3.

Row 7: K4, *skpo, yo, k2tog, yo, k6; rep from * to last 8 sts, skpo, yo, k2tog, yo, k4.

Row 9: K3, *skpo, yo, k2tog, yo, k6; rep from * to last 9 sts, skpo, yo, k2tog, yo, k5.

Row 11: K2, *skpo, yo, k2tog, yo, k6; rep from * to end.

Row 13: K1, *skpo, yo, k2tog, yo, k6; rep from * to last st, k1.

Row 15: *Skpo, yo, k2tog, yo, k6; rep from * to last 2 sts, k2.

Row 17: K1, k2tog, yo, *k6, skpo, yo, k2tog, yo; rep from * to last 9 sts, k6, skpo, yo, k1.

Row 19: K2tog, yo, *k6, skpo, yo, k2tog, yo; rep from * to last 10 sts, k6, skpo, yo, k2.

Row 20: Purl.

Rep these 20 rows.

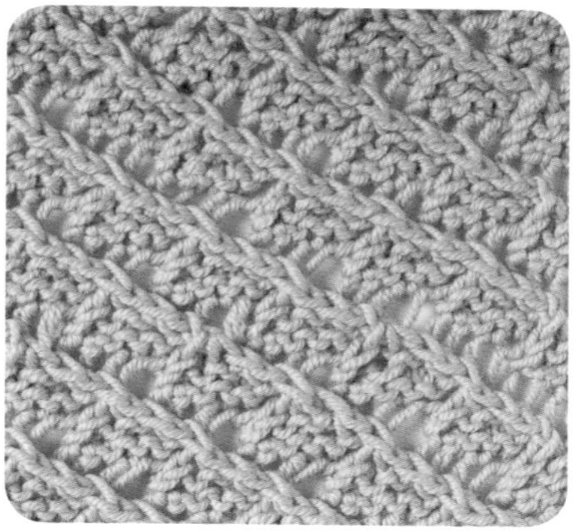

Diamond diagonal

Multiple of 8 + 2.

Row 1 (RS): K1, *yo, k2tog tbl, k6; rep from * to last st, k1.

Row 2: K1, *yo, p2tog, k3, p2tog tbl, yo, k1; rep from * to last st, k1.

Row 3: *K3, yo, k2tog tbl, k1, k2tog, yo; rep from * to last 2 sts, k2.

Row 4: K3, *yo, p3tog tbl, yo, k5; rep from * to last 7 sts, yo, p3tog tbl, yo, k4.

Row 5: K5, *yo, k2tog tbl, k6; rep from * to last 5 sts, yo, k2tog tbl, k3.

Row 6: K2, *p2tog tbl, yo, k1, yo, p2tog, k3; rep from * to end.

Row 7: K2, *k2tog, yo, k3, yo, k2tog tbl, k1; rep from * to end.

Row 8: P2tog tbl, *yo, k5, yo, p3tog tbl; rep from * to last 8 sts, yo, k5, yo, p2tog, k1.

Rep these 8 rows.

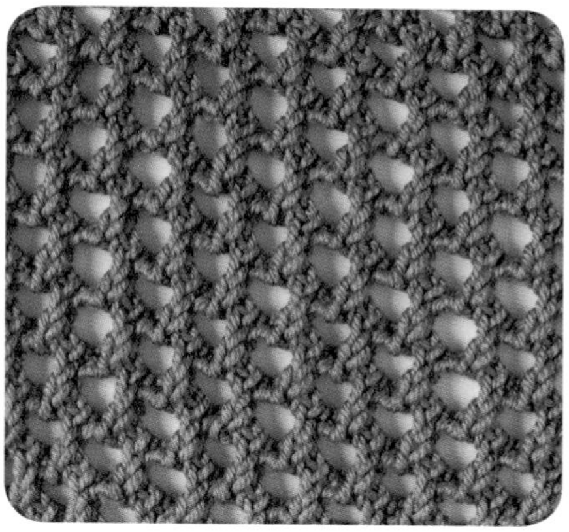

Fancy openwork

Multiple of 4.

Note: Stitches should only be counted after row 2 or 4.

Row 1 (RS): K2, *yo, k4; rep from * to last 2 sts, yo, k2.

Row 2: P2tog, *(k1, p1) into yo of previous row, [p2tog] twice; rep from * to last 3 sts, (k1, p1) into yo, p2tog.

Row 3: K4, *yo, k4; rep from * to end.

Row 4: P2, p2tog, *(k1, p1) into yo of previous row, [p2tog] twice; rep from * to last 5 sts, (k1, p1) into yo, p2tog, p2.

Rep these 4 rows.

Florette pattern

Multiple of 12 + 7.

Row 1 (RS): K1, *p2tog, yo, k1, yo, p2tog, k7; rep from * to last 6 sts, p2tog, yo, k1, yo, p2tog, k1.

Row 2 and every alt row: Purl.

Row 3: K1, *yo, p2tog, k1, p2tog, yo, k7; rep from * to last 6 sts, yo, p2tog, k1, p2tog, yo, k1.

Row 5: As row 3.

Row 7: As row 1.

Row 9: K7, *p2tog, yo, k1, yo, p2tog, k7; rep from * to end.

Row 11: K7, *yo, p2tog, k1, p2tog, yo, k7; rep from * to end.

Row 13: As row 11.

Row 15: As row 9.

Row 16: Purl.

Rep these 16 rows.

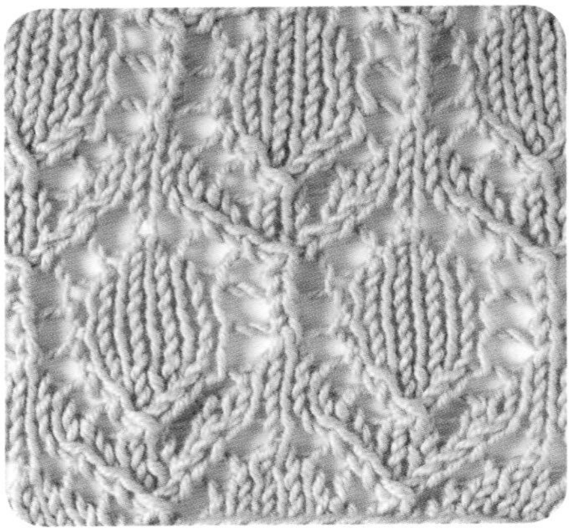

Cogwheel eyelets

Multiple of 8 + 1.

Row 1 (RS): K2, k2tog, yo, k1, yo, skpo, *k3, k2tog, yo, k1, yo, skpo; rep from * to last 2 sts, k2.

Row 2 and every alt row: Purl.

Row 3: K1, *k2tog, yo, k3, yo, skpo, k1; rep from * to end.

Row 5: K2tog, yo, k5, *yo, sk2po, yo, k5; rep from * to last 2 sts, yo, skpo.

Row 7: Skpo, yo, k5, *yo, sl 2tog knitwise, k1, p2sso, yo, k5; rep from * to last 2 sts, yo, k2tog.

Row 9: As row 7.

Row 11: K2, yo, skpo, k1, k2tog, yo, *k3, yo, skpo, k1, k2tog, yo; rep from * to last 2 sts, k2.

Row 13: K3, yo, sk2po, yo, *k5, yo, sk2po, yo; rep from * to last 3 sts, k3.

Row 15: K1, *yo, skpo, k3, k2tog, yo, k1; rep from * to end.

Row 17: As row 11.

Row 19: As row 13.

Row 21: K3, yo, sl 2tog knitwise, k1, p2sso, yo, *k5, yo, sl 2tog knitwise, k1, p2sso, yo; rep from * to last 3 sts, k3.

Row 23: As row 21.

Row 25: As row 3.

Row 27: As row 5.

Row 28: Purl.

Rep these 28 rows.

Bell lace

Multiple of 8 + 3.

Row 1 (RS): K1, p1, k1, *p1, yo, sk2po, yo, [p1, k1] twice; rep from * to end.

Row 2: P1, k1, p1, *k1, p3, [k1, p1] twice; rep from * to end.

Rep the last 2 rows twice more.

Row 7: K1, k2tog, *yo, [p1, k1] twice, p1, yo, sk2po; rep from * to last 8 sts, yo, [p1, k1] twice, p1, yo, skpo, k1.

Row 8: P3, *[k1, p1] twice, k1, p3; rep from * to end.

Rep the last 2 rows twice more.

Rep these 12 rows.

Inverted hearts

Multiple of 14 + 1.

Row 1 (RS): P2tog, yo, k11, *yo, p3tog, yo, k11; rep from * to last 2 sts, yo, p2tog.

Row 2: K1, *p13, k1; rep from * to end.

Row 3: P2, yo, skpo, k7, *k2tog, yo, p3, yo, skpo, k7; rep from * to last 4 sts, k2tog, yo, p2.

Row 4: K2, p11, *k3, p11; rep from * to last 2 sts, k2.

Row 5: P3, yo, skpo, k5, k2tog, yo, *p5, yo, skpo, k5, k2tog, yo; rep from * to last 3 sts, p3.

Row 6: K3, p9, *k5, p9; rep from * to last 3 sts, k3.

Row 7: P4, yo, skpo, k3, k2tog, yo, *p7, yo, skpo, k3, k2tog, yo; rep from * to last 4 sts, p4.

Row 8: K4, p7, *k7, p7; rep from * to last 4 sts, k4.

Row 9: P2, p2tog, yo, k1, yo, skpo, k1, k2tog, yo, k1, yo, p2tog, *p3, p2tog, yo, k1, yo, skpo, k1, k2tog, yo, k1, yo, p2tog; rep from * to last 2 sts, p2.

Row 10: As row 6.

Row 11: P1, *p2tog, yo, k3, yo, sk2po, yo, k3, yo, p2tog, p1; rep from * to end.

Row 12: As row 4.

Rep these 12 rows.

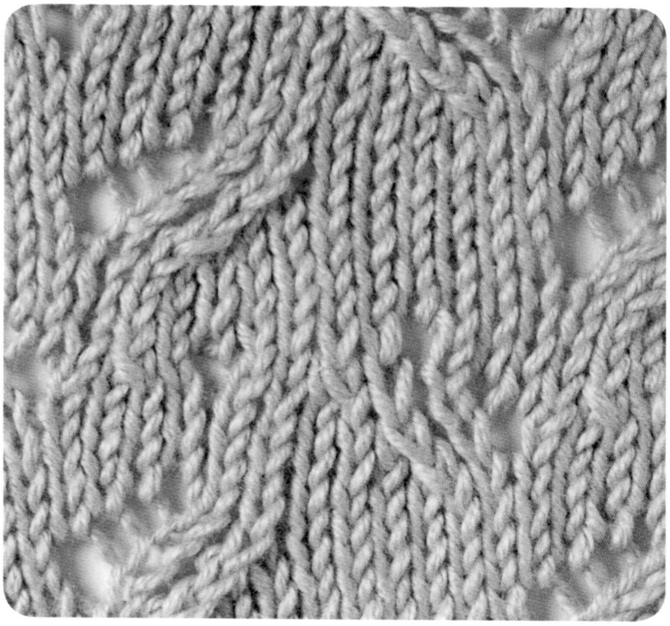

Ears of corn

Multiple of 12 + 2.

Row 1 (RS): Knit.

Row 2: Purl.

Row 3: K4, k2tog, k1, yo, *k9, k2tog, k1, yo; rep from * to last 7 sts, k7.

Row 4: P8, yo, p1, p2tog, *p9, yo, p1, p2tog; rep from * to last 3 sts, p3.

Row 5: K2, *k2tog, k1, yo, k9; rep from * to end.

Row 6: P10, yo, p1, p2tog, *p9, yo, p1, p2tog; rep from * to last st, p1.

Work 2 rows in st st, starting with knit.

Row 9: K7, yo, k1, skpo, *k9, yo, k1, skpo; rep from * to last 4 sts, k4.

Row 10: P3, p2tog tbl, p1, yo, *p9, p2tog tbl, p1, yo; rep from * to last 8 sts, p8.

Row 11: *K9, yo, k1, skpo; rep from * to last 2 sts, k2.

Row 12: P1, p2tog tbl, p1, yo, *p9, p2tog tbl, p1, yo; rep from * to last 10 sts, p10.

Rep these 12 rows.

Creeping vines

Multiple of 22 + 3.

Row 1 (RS): K4, k2tog, k3, [yo, k2tog] twice, *yo, k13, k2tog, k3, [yo, k2tog] twice; rep from * to last 12 sts, yo, k12.

Row 2 and every alt row: Purl.

Row 3: K3, *k2tog, k3, yo, k1, yo, [skpo, yo] twice, k3, skpo, k7; rep from * to end.

Row 5: K2, k2tog, [k3, yo] twice, [skpo, yo] twice, k3, skpo, *k5, k2tog, [k3, yo] twice, [skpo, yo] twice, k3, skpo; rep from * to last 6 sts, k6.

Row 7: K1, k2tog, k3, yo, k5, yo, [skpo, yo] twice, k3, skpo, *k3, k2tog, k3, yo, k5, yo, [skpo, yo] twice, k3, skpo; rep from * to last 5 sts, k5.

Row 9: K12, yo, [skpo, yo] twice, k3, skpo, *k13, yo, [skpo, yo] twice, k3, skpo; rep from * to last 4 sts, k4.

Row 11: *K7, k2tog, k3, [yo, k2tog] twice, yo, k1, yo, k3, skpo; rep from * to last 3 sts, k3.

Row 13: K6, k2tog, k3, [yo, k2tog] twice, [yo, k3] twice, skpo, *k5, k2tog, k3, [yo, k2tog] twice, [yo, k3] twice, skpo; rep from * to last 2 sts, k2.

Row 15: K5, k2tog, k3, [yo, k2tog] twice, yo, k5, yo, k3, skpo, *k3, k2tog, k3, [yo, k2tog] twice, yo, k5, yo, k3, skpo; rep from * to last st, k1.

Row 16: Purl.

Rep these 16 rows.

Snow shoe pattern

Multiple of 8 + 4.

Note: Stitches should only be counted after row 8, 9, 10, 18, 19, or 20.

Row 1 (RS): K2, M1, *k1, p2, k2, p2, k1, M1; rep from * to last 2 sts, k2.

Row 2: P4, k2, p2, k2, *p3, k2, p2, k2; rep from * to last 4 sts, p4.

Row 3: K4, p2, k2, p2, *k3, p2, k2, p2; rep from * to last 4 sts, k4.

Rep the last 2 rows twice more.

Row 8: P2, drop next st down 7 rows, *p1, k2, p2, k2, p1, drop next st down 7 rows; rep from * to last 2 sts, p2.

Row 9: K3, p2, *k2, p2; rep from * to last 3 sts, k3.

Row 10: P3, k2, *p2, k2; rep from * to last 3 sts, p3.

Row 11: K3, p2, k1, M1, k1, p2, *k2, p2, k1, M1, k1, p2; rep from * to last 3 sts, k3.

Row 12: P3, k2, p3, k2, *p2, k2, p3, k2; rep from * to last 3 sts, p3.

Row 13: K3, p2, k3, p2, *k2, p2, k3, p2; rep from * to last 3 sts, k3.

Rep the last 2 rows twice more.

Row 18: P3, k2, p1, drop next st down 7 rows, p1, k2, *p2, k2, p1, drop next st down 7 rows, p1, k2; rep from * to last 3 sts, p3.

Row 19: K3, p2, *k2, p2; rep from * to last 3 sts, k3.

Row 20: P3, k2, *p2, k2; rep from * to last 3 sts, p3.

Rep these 20 rows.

Chalice cup panel

Worked over 13 sts on a background of st st.

Note: Stitches should not be counted after row 7, 8, 15, or 16.

Row 1 (RS): P1, k3, k2tog, yo, k1, yo, skpo, k3, p1.

Row 2: K1, p11, k1.

Row 3: P1, k2, k2tog, yo, k3, yo, skpo, k2, p1.

Row 4: As row 2.

Row 5: P1, k1, k2tog, yo, k1, yo, sk2po, yo, k1, yo, skpo, k1, p1.

Row 6: As row 2.

Row 7: P1, k2tog, yo, k3, yo, k1, yo, k3, yo, skpo, p1.

Row 8: K1, p13, k1.

Row 9: P1, k2tog, yo, skpo, k5, k2tog, yo, skpo, p1.

Row 10: As row 2.

Row 11: P1, k2tog, yo, k1, yo, skpo, k1, k2tog, yo, k1, yo, skpo, p1.

Row 12: As row 2.

Rep the last 2 rows once more.

Row 15: P1, k1, yo, k3, yo, sk2po, yo, k3, yo, k1, p1.

Row 16: As row 8.

Row 17: P1, k3, k2tog, yo, sk2po, yo, skpo, k3, p1.

Row 18: As row 2.

Rep these 18 rows.

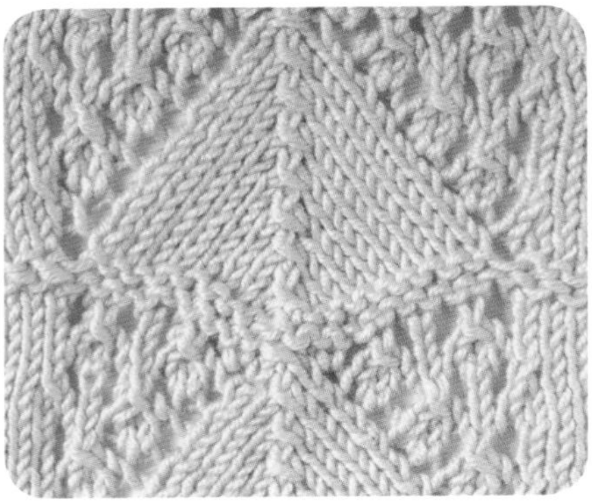

Pyramid lace panel

Worked over 25 sts on a background of st st.

Row 1 (RS): Purl.

Row 2: Knit.

Row 3: K3, yo, k8, sk2po, k8, yo, k3.

Row 4 and rem alt rows to 18: Purl.

Row 5: K4, yo, k7, sk2po, k7, yo, k4.

Row 7: K2, k2tog, yo, k1, yo, k6, sk2po, k6, yo, k1, yo, skpo, k2.

Row 9: K6, yo, k5, sk2po, k5, yo, k6.

Row 11: K3, yo, sk2po, yo, k1, yo, k4, sk2po, k4, yo, k1, yo, sk2po, yo, k3.

Row 13: K8, yo, k3, sk2po, k3, yo, k8.

Row 15: K2, k2tog, yo, k1, yo, sk2po, yo, k1, yo, k2, sk2po, k2, yo, k1, yo, sk2po, yo, k1, yo, skpo, k2.

Row 17: K10, yo, k1, sk2po, k1, yo, k10.

Row 19: K3, [yo, sk2po, yo, k1] 4 times, yo, sk2po, yo, k3.

Row 20: Knit.

Rep these 20 rows.

Staggered fern lace panel

Worked over 20 sts on a background of st st.

Row 1 (RS): P2, k9, yo, k1, yo, k3, sk2po, p2.

Row 2 and every alt row: Purl.

Row 3: P2, k10, yo, k1, yo, k2, sk2po, p2.

Row 5: P2, k3tog, k4, yo, k1, yo, k3, [yo, k1] twice, sk2po, p2.

Row 7: P2, k3tog, k3, yo, k1, yo, k9, p2.

Row 9: P2, k3tog, k2, yo, k1, yo, k10, p2.

Row 11: P2, k3tog, [k1, yo] twice, k3, yo, k1, yo, k4, sk2po, p2.

Row 12: Purl.

Rep these 12 rows.

Embossed rosebud panel

Worked over 9 sts on a background of rev st st.

Row 1 (WS): K3, p3, k3.

Row 2: P3, slip next st onto cable needle and hold at front of work, k1 from left-hand needle, (k1, yo, k1, yo, k1) into next st on left-hand needle, then knit st from cable needle, p3.

Row 3: K3, p1, [KB1] 5 times, p1, k3.

Row 4: P3, [k1, yo] 6 times, k1, p3.

Row 5: K3, p13, k3.

Row 6: P3, k13, p3.

Row 7: K3, p2tog, p9, p2tog tbl, k3.

Row 8: P3, skpo, k7, k2tog, p3.

Row 9: K3, p2tog, p5, p2tog tbl, k3.

Row 10: P3, skpo, k3, k2tog, p3.

Row 11: K3, p2tog, p1, p2tog tbl, k3.

Row 12: P3, k3, p3.

Rep these 12 rows.

Fish scale lace panel

Worked over 17 sts on a background of st st.

Row 1 (RS): K1, yo, k3, skpo, p5, k2tog, k3, yo, k1.

Row 2: P6, k5, p6.

Row 3: K2, yo, k3, skpo, p3, k2tog, k3, yo, k2.

Row 4: P7, k3, p7.

Row 5: K3, yo, k3, skpo, p1, k2tog, k3, yo, k3.

Row 6: P8, k1, p8.

Row 7: K4, yo, k3, sk2po, k3, yo, k4.

Row 8: Purl.

Rep these 8 rows.

Cascading leaves

Worked over 16 sts on a background of rev st st.

Row 1 (RS): P1, k3, k2tog, k1, yo, p2, yo, k1, skpo, k3, p1.

Row 2 and every alt row: K1, p6, k2, p6, k1.

Row 3: P1, k2, k2tog, k1, yo, k1, p2, k1, yo, k1, skpo, k2, p1.

Row 5: P1, k1, k2tog, k1, yo, k2, p2, k2, yo, k1, skpo, k1, p1.

Row 7: P1, k2tog, k1, yo, k3, p2, k3, yo, k1, skpo, p1.

Row 8: As row 2.

Rep these 8 rows.

Flower buds

Multiple of 8 + 5.

Row 1 (RS): K3, *yo, k2, p3tog, k2, yo, k1; rep from * to last 2 sts, k2.

Row 2: Purl.

Rep the last 2 rows twice more.

Row 7: K2, p2tog, *k2, yo, k1, yo, k2, p3tog; rep from * to last 9 sts, k2, yo, k1, yo, k2, p2tog, k2.

Row 8: Purl.

Rep the last 2 rows twice more.

Rep these 12 rows.

Puff stitch check

Multiple of 10 + 7.

Special abbreviation:

K5W = Knit next 5 sts winding yarn twice around needle for each st.

Row 1 (RS): P6, k5W, *p5, k5W; rep from * to last 6 sts, p6.

Row 2: K6, p5 dropping extra loops, *k5, p5 dropping extra loops; rep from * to last 6 sts, k6.

Rep the last 2 rows 3 times more.

Row 9: P1, k5W, *p5, k5W; rep from * to last st, p1.

Row 10: K1, p5 dropping extra loops, *k5, p5 dropping extra loops; rep from * to last st, k1.

Rep the last 2 rows 3 times more.

Rep these 16 rows.

Tip

If you are working a lace or eyelet design set against a plain knitted fabric (a lace panel on the front of an otherwise plain sweater, for example), then you will find stitch markers a useful aid. Count the stitches on your needles within each section of the pattern when you reach each marker. You can then check that you are on track and have not made any accidental extra yarnovers or decreases.

Lacy diamonds

Multiple of 6 + 1.

Row 1 (RS): *K1, k2tog, yo, k1, yo, k2tog tbl; rep from * to last st, k1.

Row 2 and every alt row: Purl.

Row 3: K2tog, *yo, k3, yo, [sl 1] twice, k1, p2sso; rep from * to last 5 sts, yo, k3, yo, k2tog tbl.

Row 5: *K1, yo, k2tog tbl, k1, k2tog, yo; rep from * to last st, k1.

Row 7: K2, *yo, [sl 1] twice, k1, p2sso, yo, k3; rep from * to last 5 sts, yo, [sl 1] twice, k1, p2sso, yo, k2.

Row 8: Purl.

Rep these 8 rows.

Eyelet ribs

Multiple of 11 + 4.

Row 1 (RS): K1, yo, p2tog, k1, *p1, k2, yo, skpo, k1, p1, k1, yo, p2tog, k1; rep from * to end.

Row 2 and every alt row: K1, yo, p2tog, *k2, p5, k2, yo, p2tog; rep from * to last st, k1.

Row 3: K1, yo, p2tog, k1, *p1, k1, yo, sk2po, yo, k1, p1, k1, yo, p2tog, k1; rep from * to end.

Row 5: As row 1.

Row 7: K1, yo, p2tog, k1, *p1, k5, p1, k1, yo, p2tog, k1; rep from * to end.

Row 8: As row 2.

Rep these 8 rows.

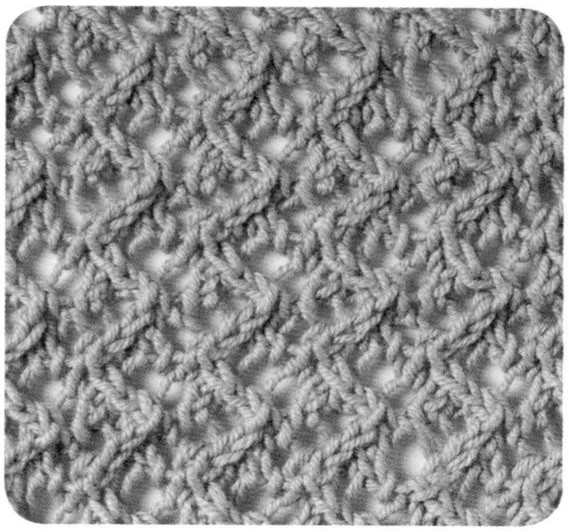

Zigzag lace

Multiple of 4 + 3.

Row 1 (RS): K4, *k2tog, yo, k2; rep from * to last 3 sts, k2tog, yo, k1.

Row 2: *P2, yo, p2tog; rep from * to last 3 sts, p3.

Row 3: *K2, k2tog, yo; rep from * to last 3 sts, k3.

Row 4: P4, *yo, p2tog, p2; rep from * to last 3 sts, yo, p2tog, p1.

Row 5: K1, *yo, skpo, k2; rep from * to last 2 sts, k2.

Row 6: P3, *p2tog tbl, yo, p2; rep from * to end.

Row 7: K3, *yo, skpo, k2; rep from * to end.

Row 8: P1, *p2tog tbl, yo, p2; rep from * to last 2 sts, p2.

Rep these 8 rows.

Little shell insertion

Worked over 7 sts on a background of st st.

Row 1 (RS): Knit.

Row 2: Purl.

Row 3: K1, yo, p1, p3tog, p1, yo, k1.

Row 4: Purl.

Rep these 4 rows.

Feather and fan

Multiple of 18 + 2.

Row 1 (RS): Knit.

Row 2: Purl.

Row 3: K1, *[k2tog] 3 times, [yo, k1] 6 times, [k2tog] 3 times; rep from * to last st, k1.

Row 4: Knit.

Rep these 4 rows.

Eyelet lattice insertion

Worked over 8 sts on a background of st st.

Row 1 (RS): K1, [k2tog, yo] 3 times, k1.

Row 2: Purl.

Row 3: K2, [k2tog, yo] twice, k2.

Row 4: Purl.

Rep these 4 rows.

Lacy openwork

Multiple of 4 + 1.

Row 1: K1, *yo, p3tog, yo, k1; rep from * to end.

Row 2: P2tog, yo, k1, yo, *p3tog, yo, k1, yo; rep from * to last 2 sts, p2tog.

Rep these 2 rows.

Double lace rib

Multiple of 6 + 2.

Row 1 (RS): K2, *p1, yo, k2tog tb1, p1, k2; rep from * to end.

Row 2: P2, *k1, p2; rep from * to end.

Row 3: K2, *p1, k2tog, yo, p1, k2; rep from * to end.

Row 4: As row 2.

Rep these 4 rows.

Gate and ladder pattern

Multiple of 9 + 3.

Foundation row (WS): Purl.

Row 1: K1, k2tog, k3, yo2, k3, *k3tog, k3, yo2, k3; rep from * to last 3 sts, k2tog, k1.

Row 2: P6, k1, *p8, k1; rep from * to last 5 sts, p5.

Rep the last 2 rows.

Diamond and bobble panel

Worked over 11 sts on a background of rev st st.

Special abbreviation:

MB (make bobble) = (K1, yo, k1, yo, k1) into next st, turn, p5, turn, k5, turn, p2tog, p1, p2tog tbl, turn, sk2po.

Row 1 (RS): P1, yo, skpo, p5, k2tog, yo, p1.

Row 2: K2, p1, k5, p1, k2.

Row 3: P2, yo, skpo, p3, k2tog, yo, p2.

Row 4: K3, [p1, k3] twice.

Row 5: P3, yo, skpo, p1, k2tog, yo, p3.

Row 6: K4, p1, k1, p1, k4.

Row 7: P4, yo, sk2po, yo, p4.

Row 8: K5, p1, k5.

Row 9: P3, k2tog, yo, p1, yo, skpo, p3.

Row 10: As row 4.

Row 11: P2, k2tog, yo, p3, yo, skpo, p2.

Row 12: As row 2.

Row 13: P1, k2tog, yo, p5, yo, skpo, p1.

Row 14: K1, p1, k7, p1, k1.

Row 15: K2tog, yo, p3, MB, p3, yo, skpo.

Row 16: K1, p1, k3, KB1, k3, p1, k1.

Rep these 16 rows.

Twist cable and ladder lace

Multiple of 7 + 6.

Row 1 (RS): K1, *k2tog, yo2, skpo, k3; rep from * to last 5 sts, k2tog, yo2, skpo, k1.

Row 2: K2, *(KB1, k1) into double yo, k1, p3, k1; rep from * to last 4 sts, (KB1, k1) into double yo, k2.

Row 3: K1, *k2tog, yo2, skpo, knit into 3rd st on left-hand needle, then knit into 2nd st, then knit into first st, slipping all 3 sts onto right-hand needle tog; rep from * to last 5 sts, k2tog, yo2, skpo, k1.

Row 4: As row 2.

Rep these 4 rows.

Eyelet twigs

Worked over 14 sts on a background of st st.

Row 1 (RS): K1, yo, k3tog, yo, k3, yo, sk2po, yo, k4.

Row 2 and every alt row: Purl.

Row 3: Yo, k3tog, yo, k5, yo, sk2po, yo, k3.

Row 5: K5, yo, k3tog, yo, k1, yo, sk2po, yo, k2.

Row 7: K4, yo, k3tog, yo, k3, yo, sk2po, yo, k1.

Row 9: K3, yo, k3tog, yo, k5, yo, sk2po, yo.

Row 11: K2, yo, k3tog, yo, k1, yo, sk2po, yo, k5.

Row 12: Purl.

Rep these 12 rows.

Large lattice lace

Multiple of 6 + 2.

Row 1 (RS): K1, p1, *yo, k2tog tbl, k2tog, yo, p2; rep from * to last 6 sts, yo, k2tog tbl, k2tog, yo, p1, k1.

Row 2: K2, *p4, k2; rep from * to end.

Row 3: K1, p1, *k2tog, yo2, k2tog tbl, p2; rep from * to last 6 sts, k2tog, yo2, k2tog tbl, p1, k1.

Row 4: K2, *p1, (k1, p1) into double yo, p1, k2; rep from * to end.

Row 5: K1, *k2tog, yo, p2, yo, k2tog tbl; rep from * to last st, k1.

Row 6: K1, p2, *k2, p4; rep from * to last 5 sts, k2, p2, k1.

Row 7: K1, yo, *k2tog tbl, p2, k2tog, yo2; rep from * to last 7 sts, k2tog tbl, p2, k2tog, yo, k1.

Row 8: K1, p2, k2, p1, *(k1, p1) into double yo, p1, k2, p1; rep from * to last 2 sts, p1, k1.

Rep these 8 rows.

Waterfall pattern

Multiple of 6 + 3.

Row 1 (RS): P3, *k3, yo, p3; rep from * to end.

Row 2: K3, *p4, k3; rep from * to end.

Row 3: P3, *k1, k2tog, yo, k1, p3; rep from * to end.

Row 4: K3, *p2, p2tog, k3; rep from * to end.

Row 5: P3, *k1, yo, k2tog, p3; rep from * to end.

Row 6: K3, *p3, k3; rep from * to end.

Rep these 6 rows.

Eyelet twigs and bobbles

Worked over 16 sts on a background of st st.

Row 1 (RS): K2, yo, k3tog, yo, k3, yo, sk2po, yo, k5.

Row 2 and every alt row: Purl.

Row 3: K1, yo, k3tog, yo, k5, yo, sk2po, yo, k4.

Row 5: MB, k5, yo, k3tog, yo, k1, yo, sk2po, yo, k3.

Row 7: K5, yo, k3tog, yo, k3, yo, sk2po, yo, k2.

Row 9: K4, yo, k3tog, yo, k5, yo, sk2po, yo, MB.

Row 11: K3, yo, k3tog, yo, k1, yo, sk2po, yo, k6.

Row 12: Purl.

Rep these 12 rows.

Diamond lace II

Multiple of 6 + 3.

Row 1 (RS): *K4, yo, skpo; rep from * to last 3 sts, k3.

Row 2 and every alt row: Purl.

Row 3: K2, *k2tog, yo, k1, yo, skpo, k1; rep from * to last st, k1.

Row 5: K1, k2tog, yo, *k3, yo, sk2po, yo; rep from * to last 6 sts, k3, yo, skpo, k1.

Row 7: K3, *yo, sk2po, yo, k3; rep from * to end.

Row 9: As row 1.

Row 11: K1, *yo, skpo, k4; rep from * to last 2 sts, yo, skpo.

Row 13: K2, *yo, skpo, k1, k2tog, yo, k1; rep from * to last st, k1.

Row 15: As row 7.

Row 17: As row 5.

Row 19: As row 11.

Row 20: Purl.

Rep these 20 rows.

Lacy chain

Worked over 16 sts on a background of st st.

Row 1 (RS): K5, yo, skpo, k2, yo, skpo, k5.

Row 2 and every alt row: Purl.

Row 3: K3, k2tog, yo, k1, yo, skpo, k2, yo, skpo, k4.

Row 5: K2, k2tog, yo, k3, yo, skpo, k2, yo, skpo, k3.

Row 7: K1, k2tog, yo, k2, k2tog, yo, k1, yo, skpo, k2, yo, skpo, k2.

Row 9: K2tog, yo, k2, k2tog, yo, k3, yo, skpo, k2, yo, skpo, k1.

Row 11: K2, yo, skpo, k2, yo, skpo, yo, k2tog, yo, k2, k2tog, yo, k2tog.

Row 13: K3, yo, skpo, k2, yo, sk2po, yo, k2, k2tog, yo, k2.

Row 15: K4, yo, skpo, k2, yo, skpo, k1, k2tog, yo, k3.

Row 16: Purl.

Rep these 16 rows.

Horseshoe print

Multiple of 10 + 1.

Row 1 (WS): Purl.

Row 2: K1, *yo, k3, sk2po, k3, yo, k1; rep from * to end.

Row 3: Purl.

Row 4: P1, *k1, yo, k2, sk2po, k2, yo, k1, p1; rep from * to end.

Row 5: K1, *p9, k1; rep from * to end.

Row 6: P1, *k2, yo, k1, sk2po, k1, yo, k2, p1; rep from * to end.

Row 7: As row 5.

Row 8: P1, *k3, yo, sk2po, yo, k3, p1; rep from * to end.

Rep these 8 rows.

Little dots (single)

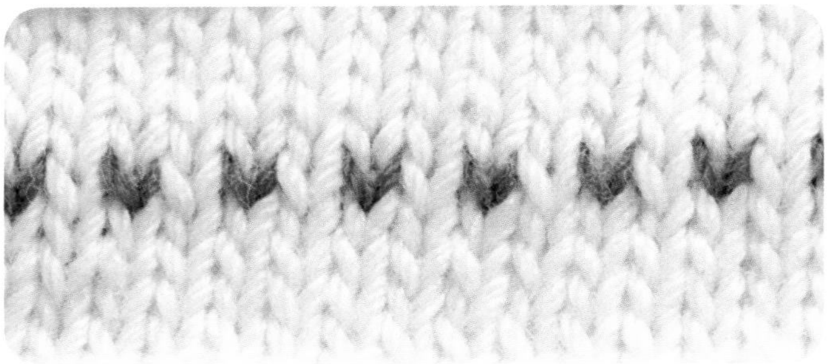

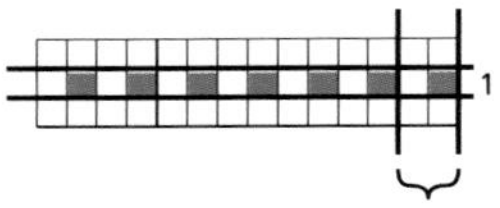

Rep 2 sts x 1 row

Little dots (double)

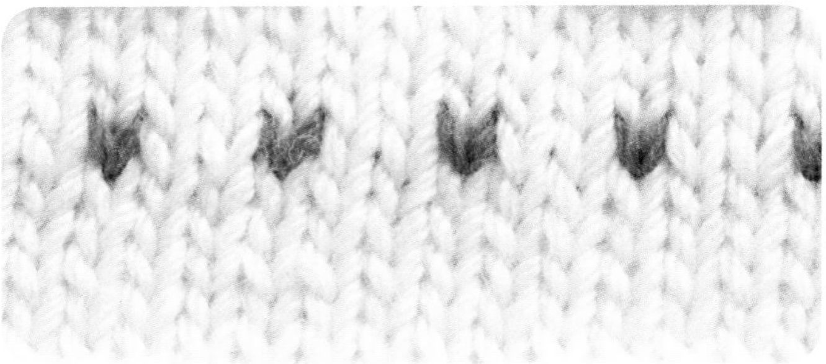

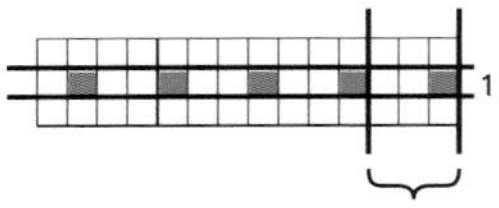

Rep 3 sts x 1 row

Short dash

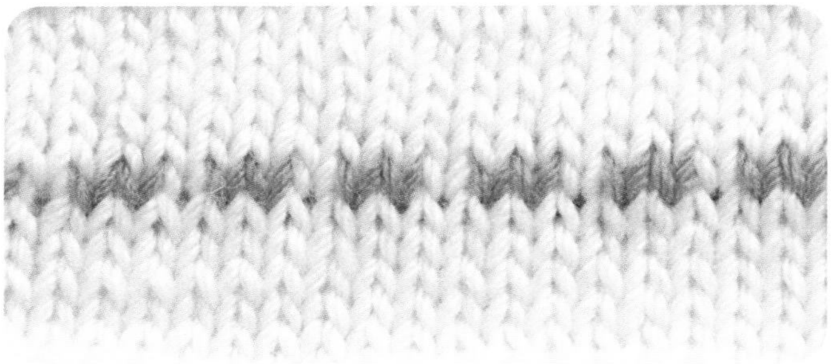

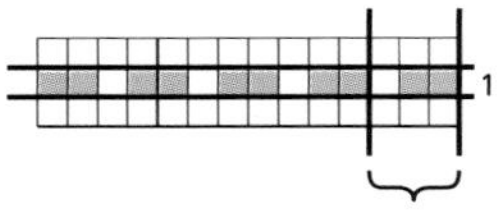

Rep 3 sts x 1 row

Dash

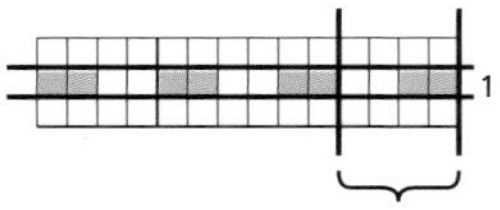

Rep 4 sts x 1 row

Dot and dash

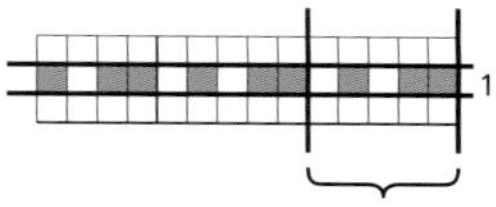

Rep 5 sts x 1 row

Long dash

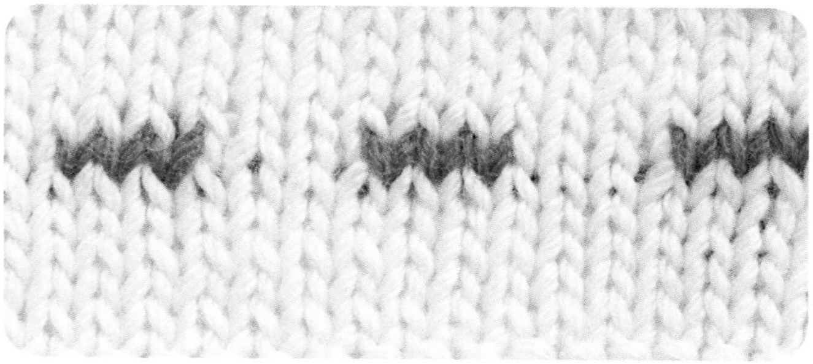

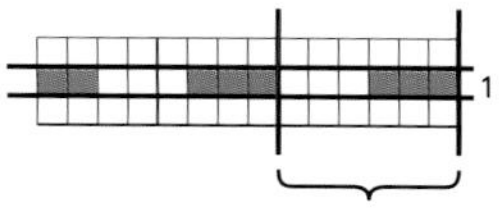

Rep 6 sts x 1 row

Dot and long dash

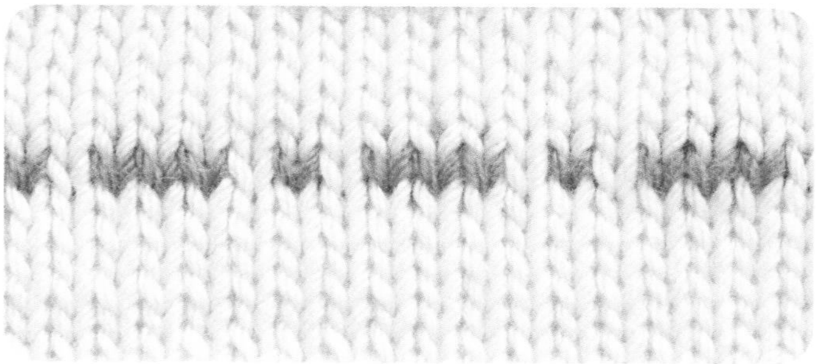

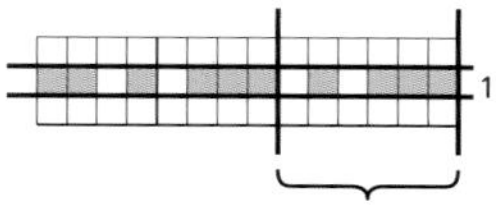

Rep 6 sts x 1 row

Small zigzag

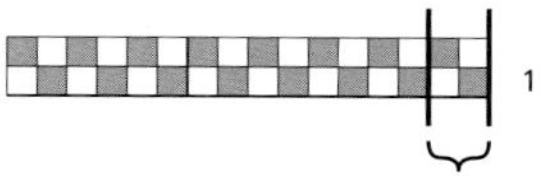

Rep 2 sts x 2 rows

Small wave

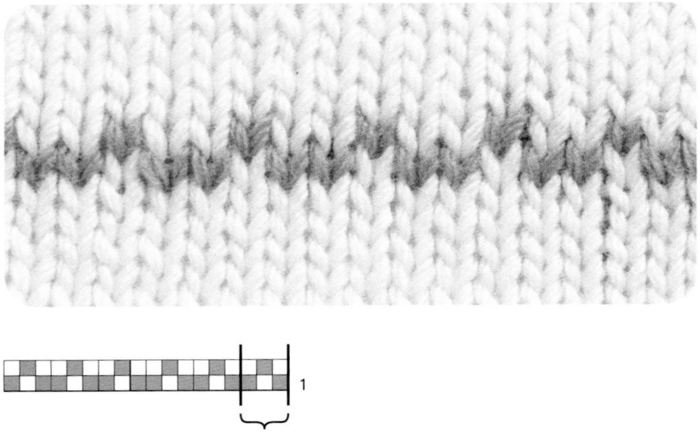

Rep 3 sts x 2 rows

Back stroke

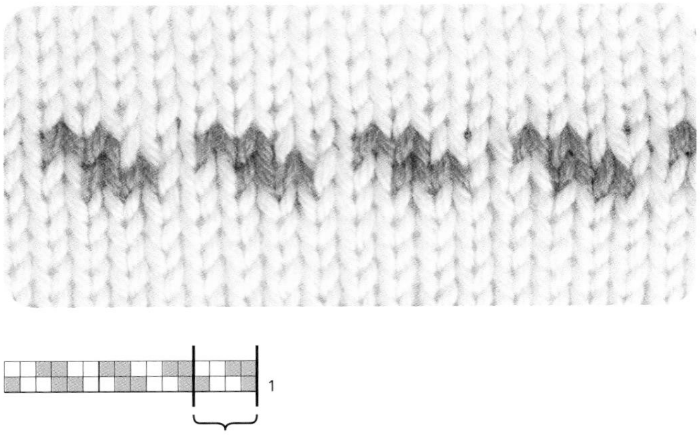

Rep 4 sts x 2 rows

Two wave

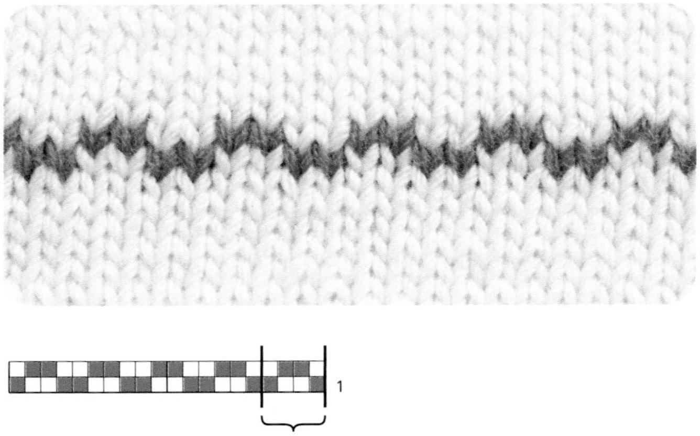

Rep 4 sts x 2 rows

Three wave

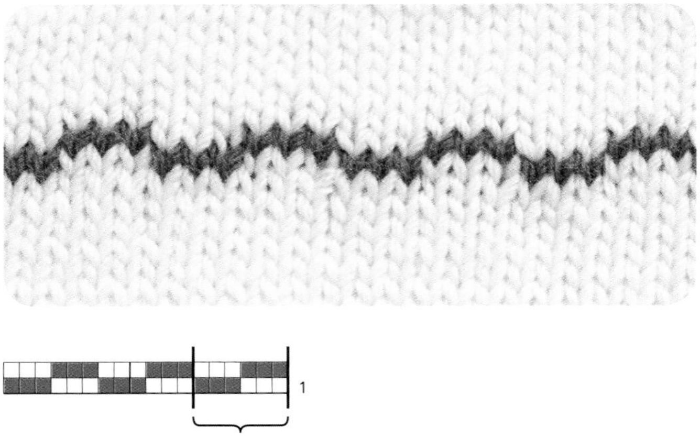

Rep 6 sts x 2 rows

Small arch

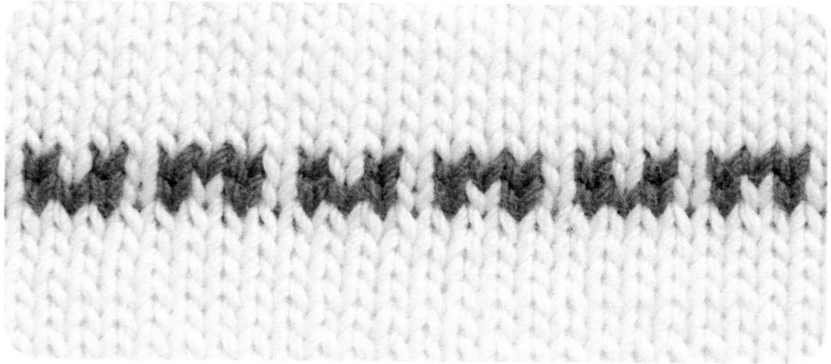

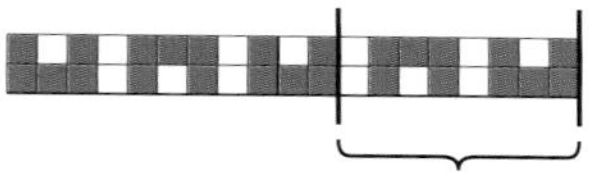

Rep 8 sts x 2 rows

Triangle wave I

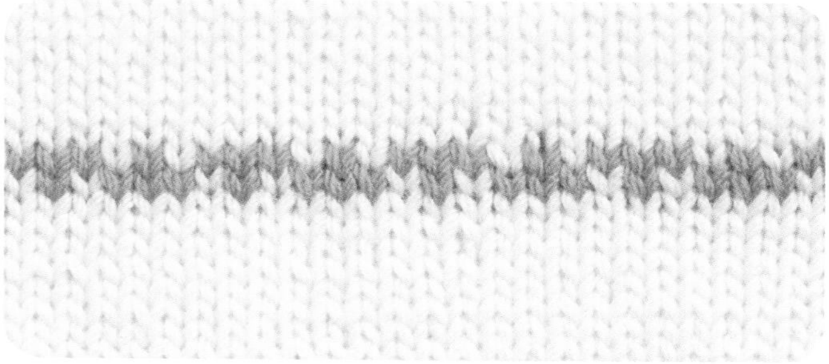

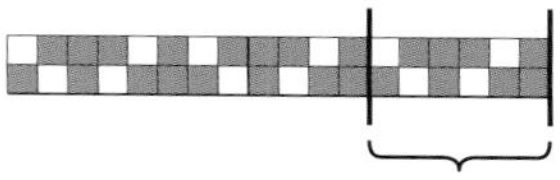

Rep 6 sts x 2 rows

Triangle and square I

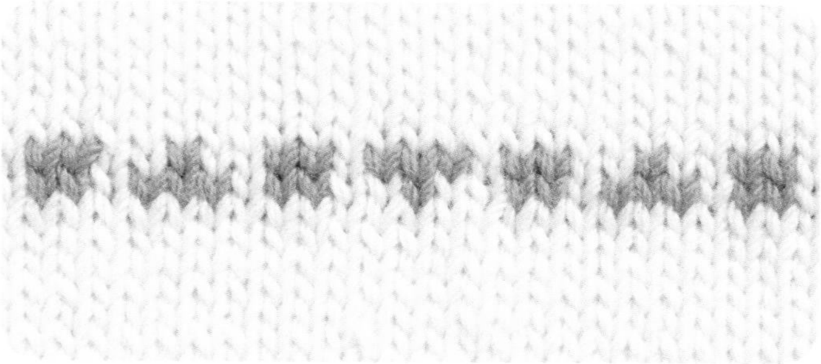

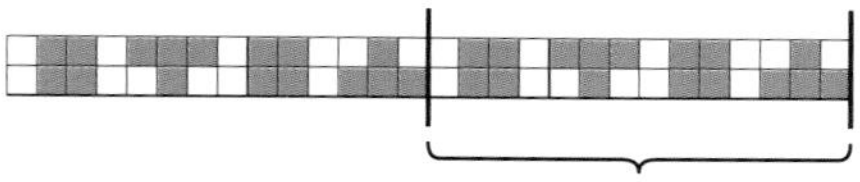

Rep 14 sts x 2 rows

Threaded squares

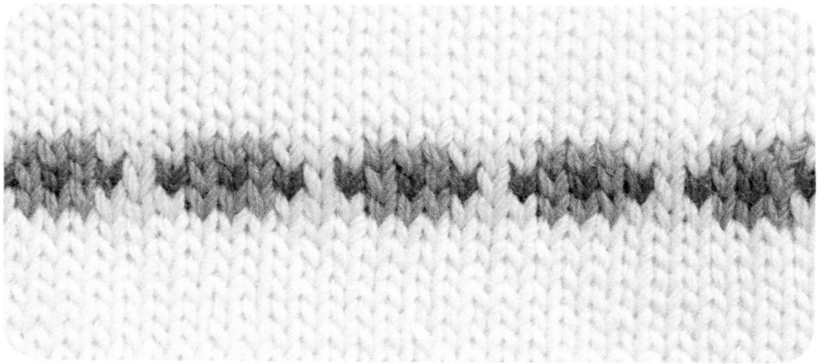

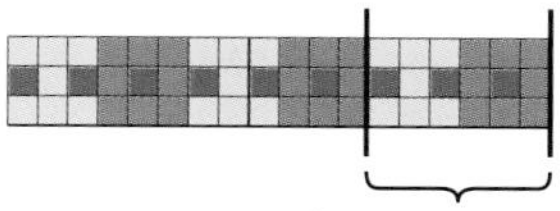

Rep 6 sts x 3 rows

Seeded vertical stripe

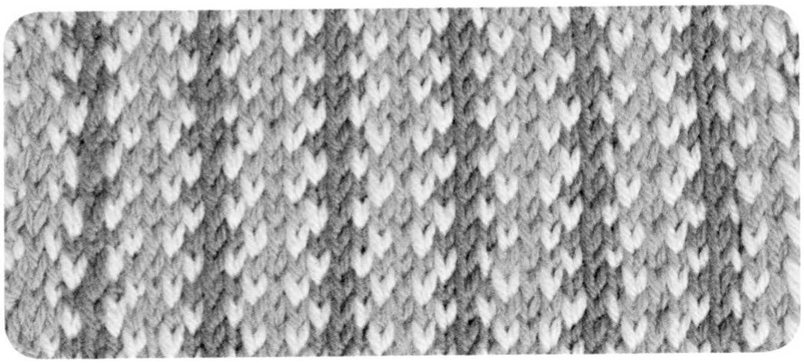

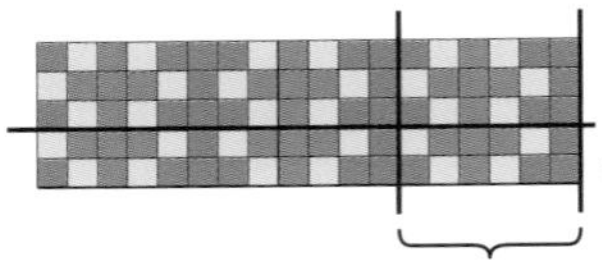

Rep 6 sts x 2 rows

Triangle and square II

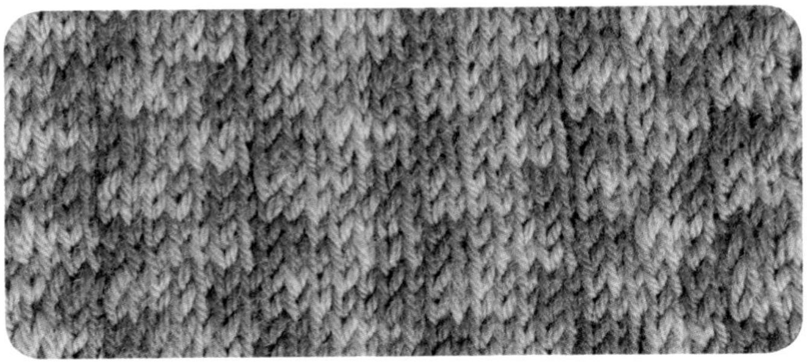

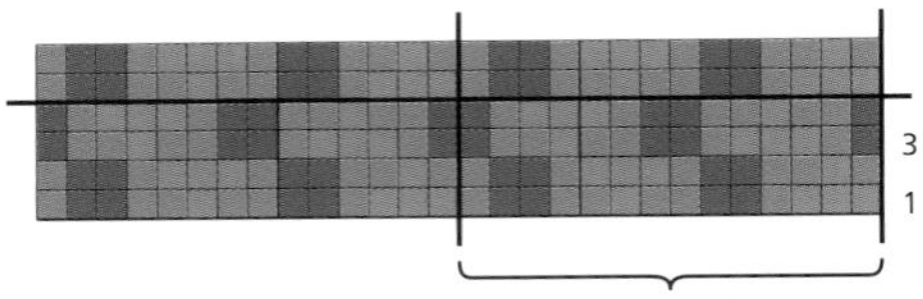

Rep 14 sts x 4 rows

Tall blocks

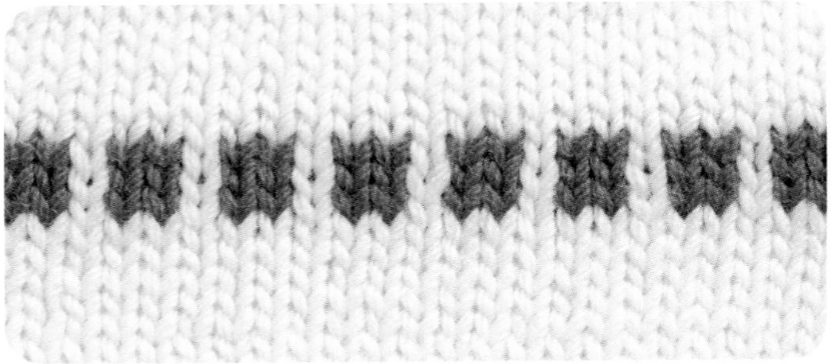

Rep 3 sts x 3 rows

Post and hook

Rep 3 sts x 3 rows

Broken fence

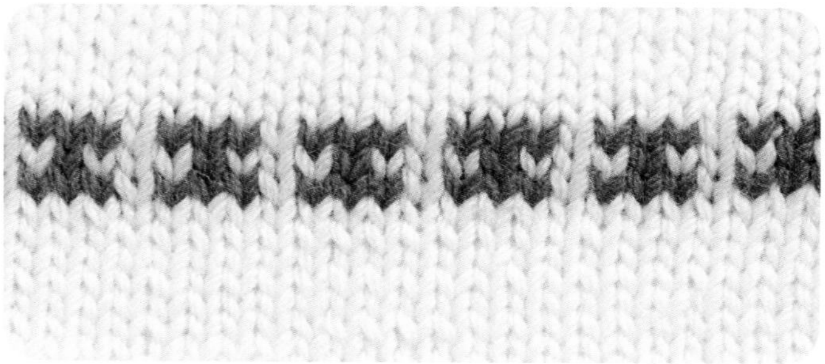

Rep 4 sts x 3 rows

Single fence

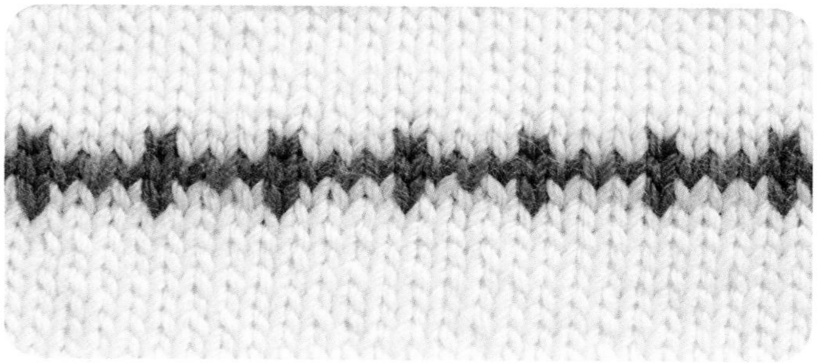

Rep 4 sts x 3 rows

Broken rows I

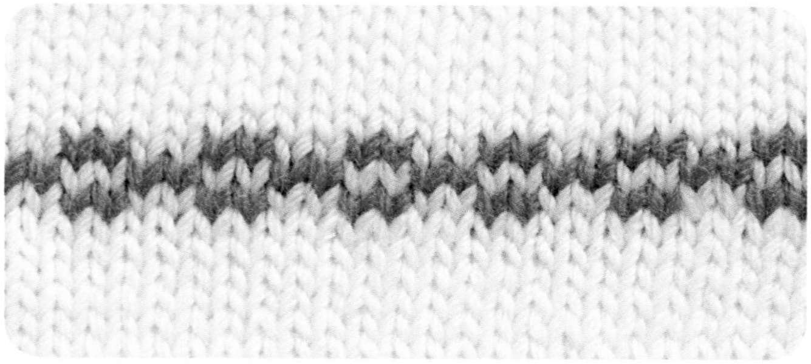

Rep 4 sts x 3 rows

Broken rows II

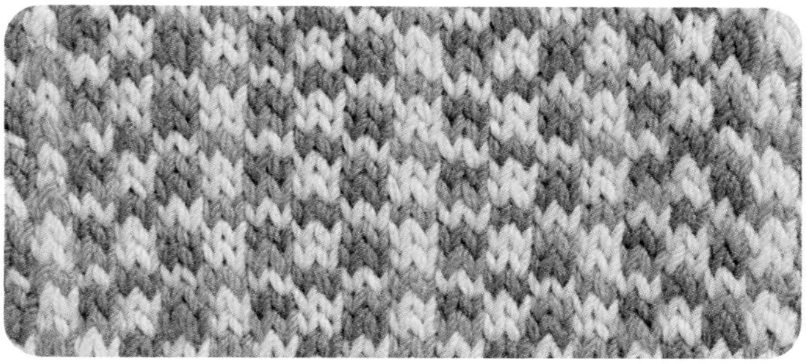

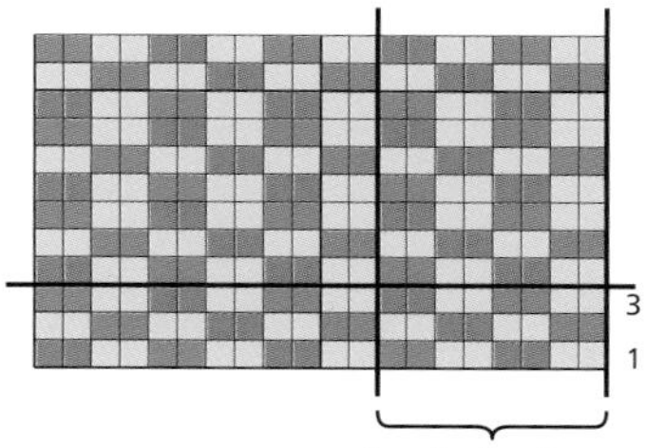

Rep 8 sts x 3 rows

Small arrowhead

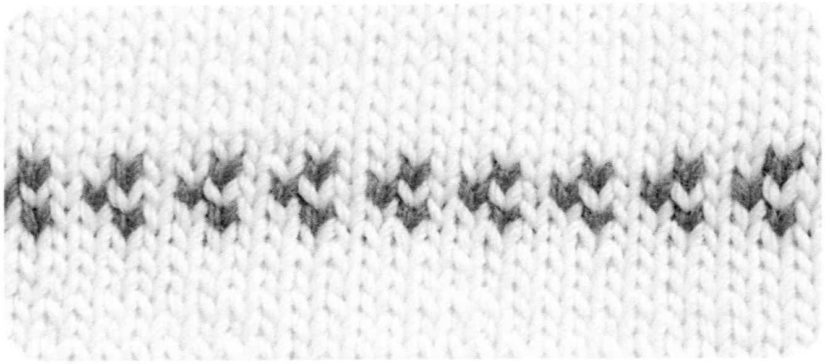

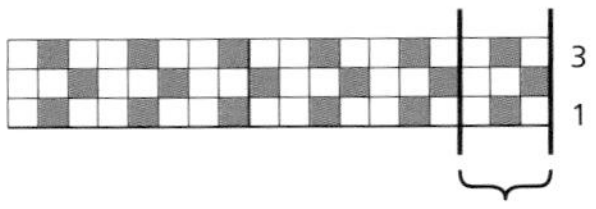

Rep 3 sts x 3 rows

Speckled fence

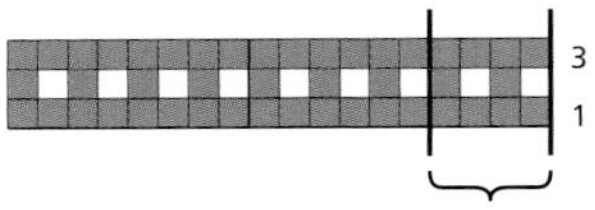

Rep 4 sts x 3 rows

High tide

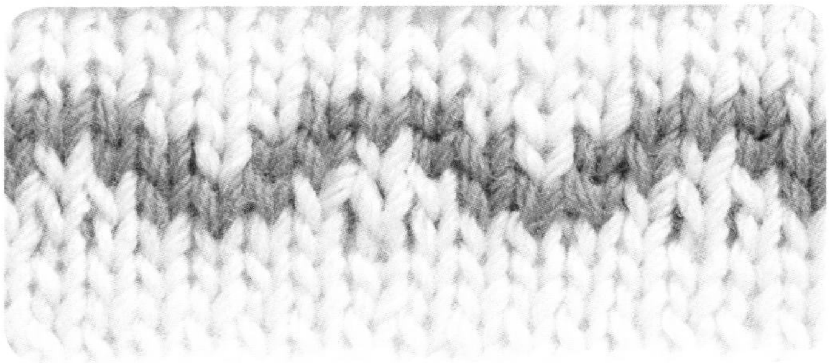

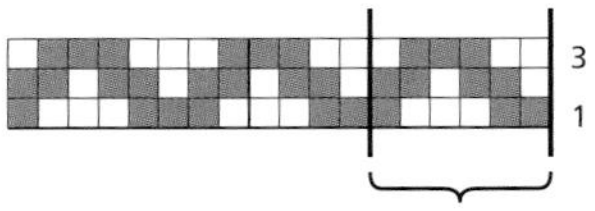

Rep 6 sts x 3 rows

Kirkwall border

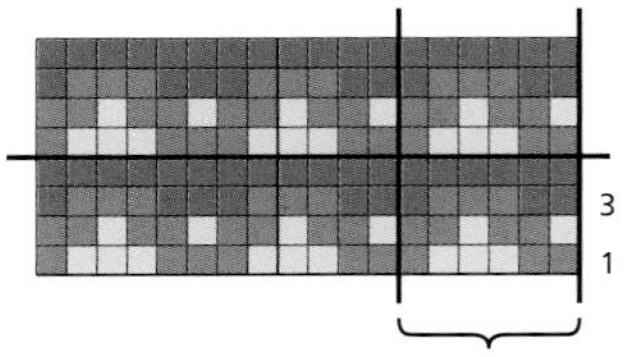

Rep 6 sts x 4 rows

Dancing bears

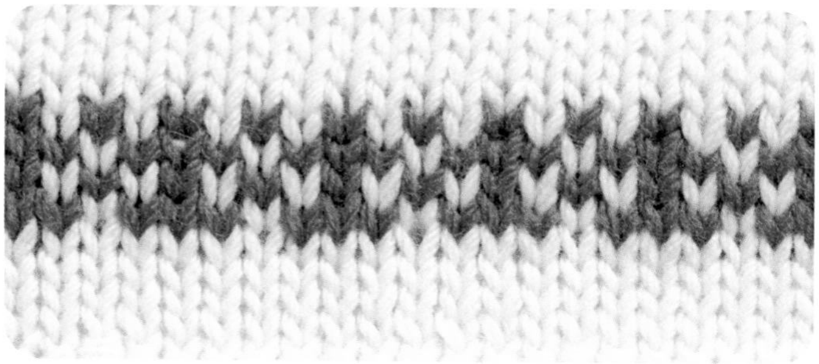

Rep 4 sts x 2 rows

Triangle stacks

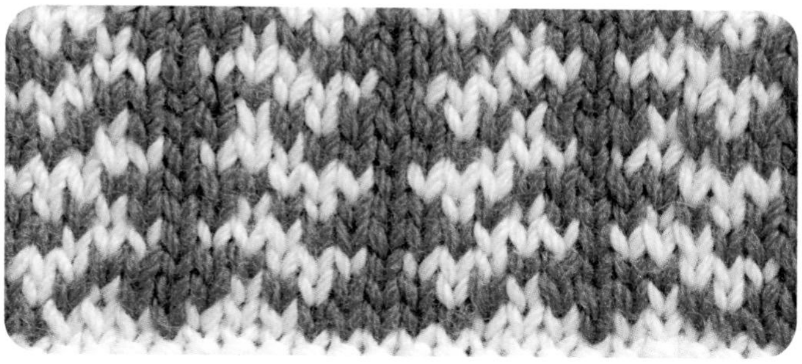

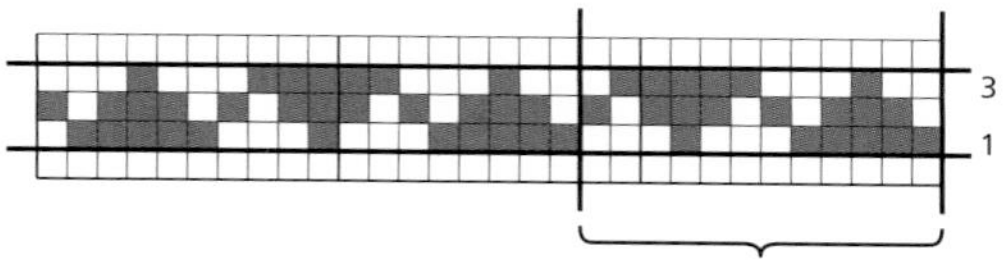

Rep 12 sts x 3 rows

Flotsam

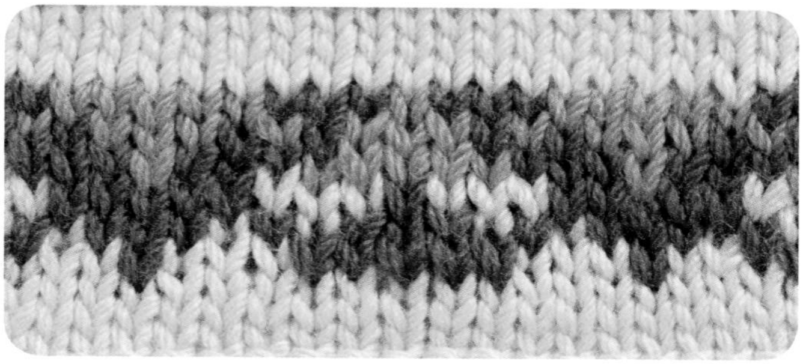

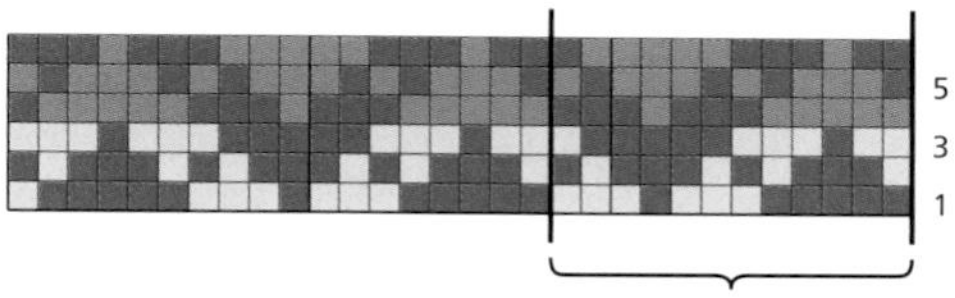

Rep 12 sts x 6 rows

Battlements (3-count)

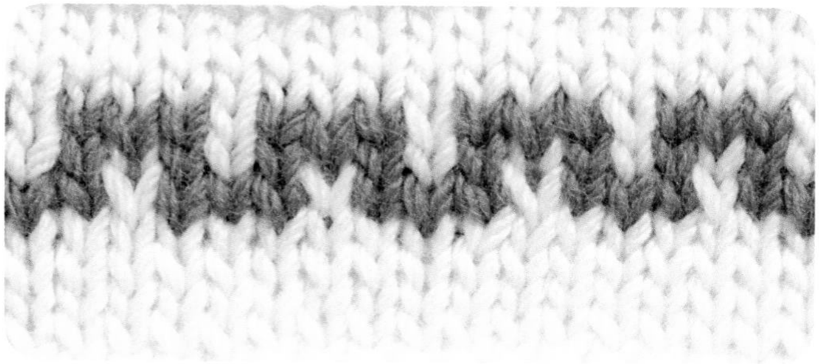

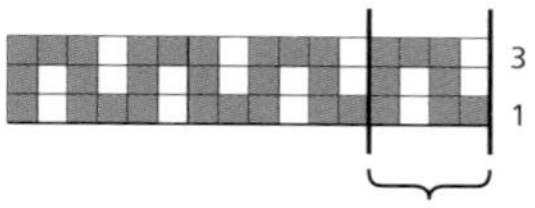

Rep 4 sts x 3 rows

Breakers

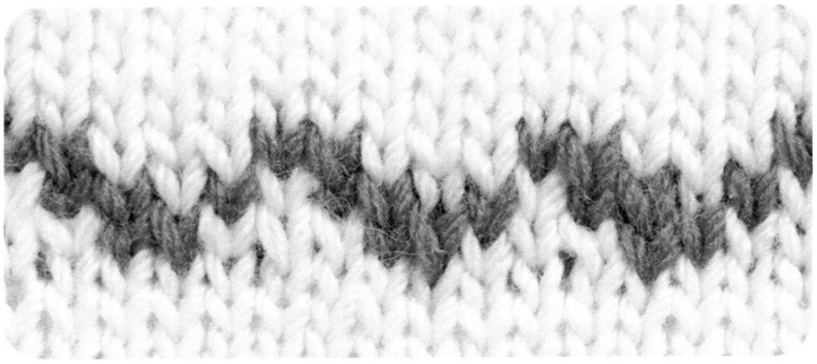

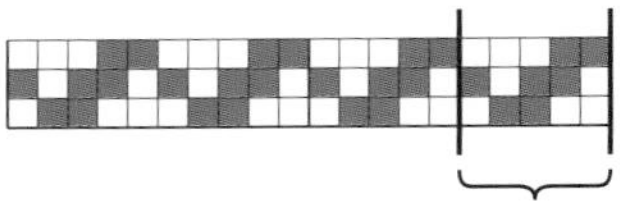

Rep 5 sts x 3 rows

Battlements (4-count) I

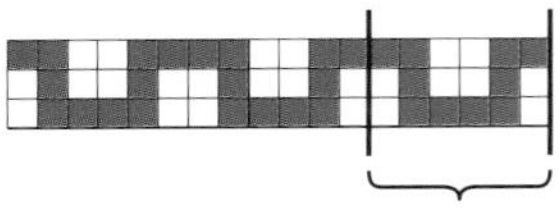

Rep 6 sts x 3 rows

Battlements (4-count) II

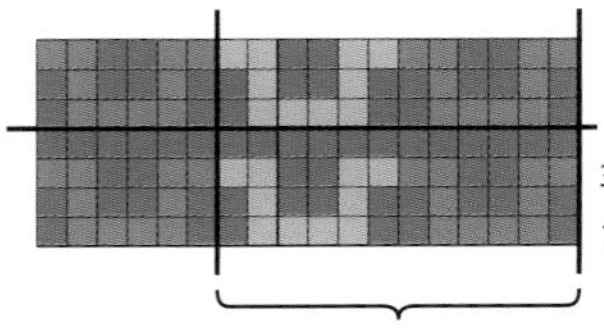

Rep 12 sts x 4 rows

Heather peerie

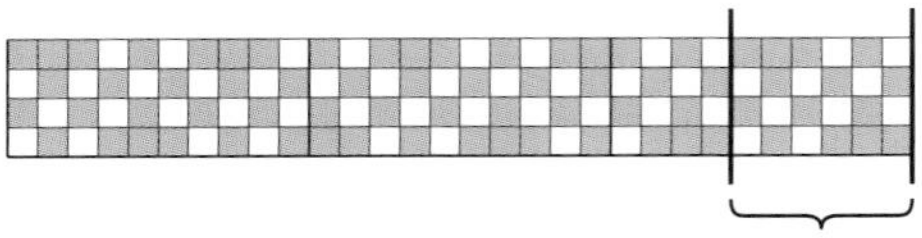

Rep 6 sts x 4 rows

Triangle and dot

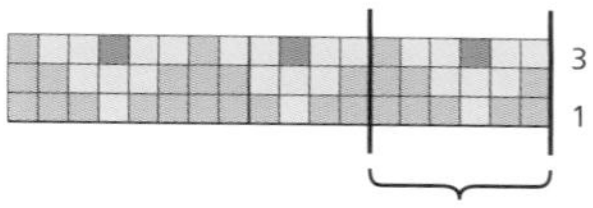

Rep 6 sts x 3 rows

Shoots and seeds

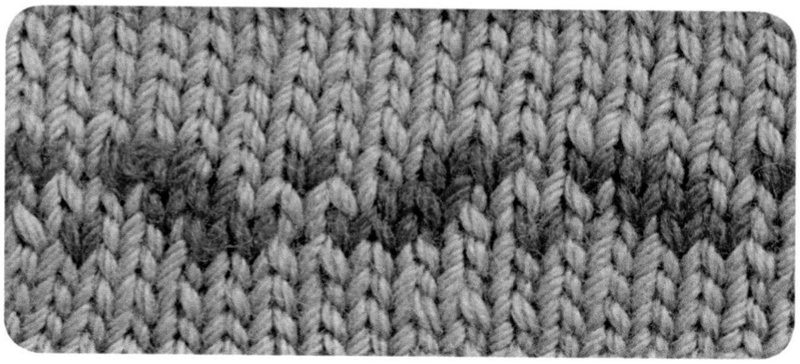

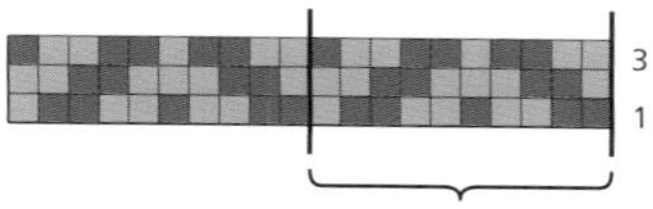

Rep 10 sts x 3 rows

Triangle wave II

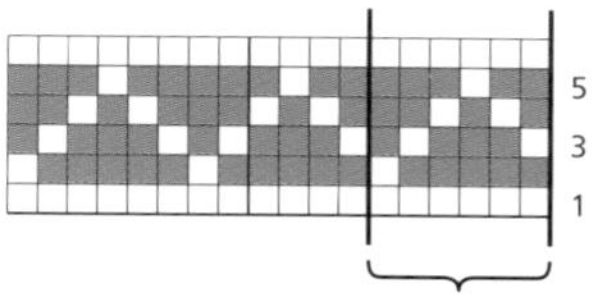

Rep 6 sts x 6 rows

Outline triangle

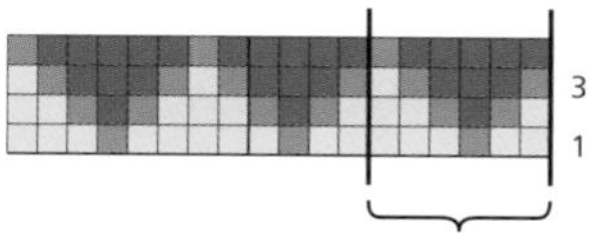

Rep 6 sts x 4 rows

Five and one

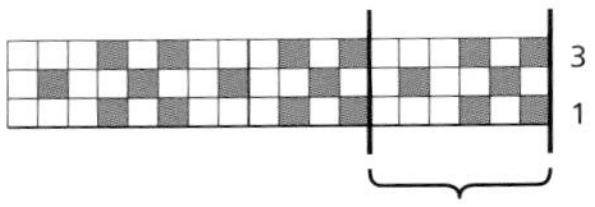

Rep 6 sts x 3 rows

Triangle wave III

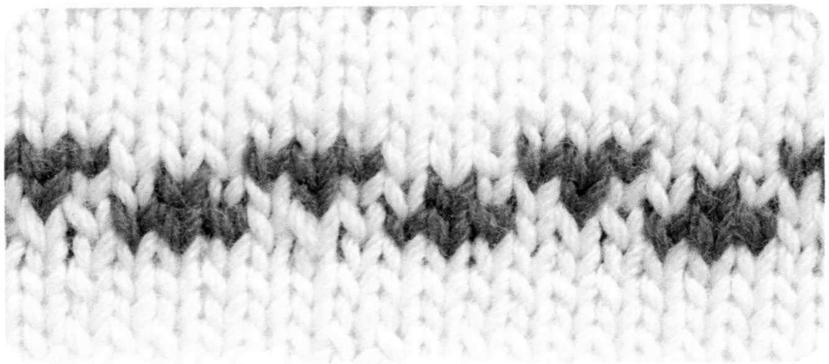

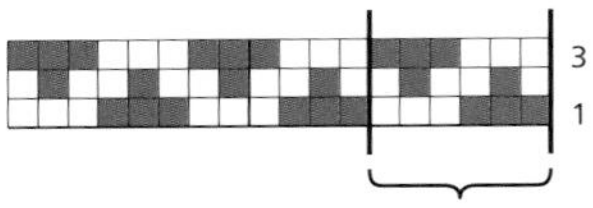

Rep 6 sts x 3 rows

Triangle wave border

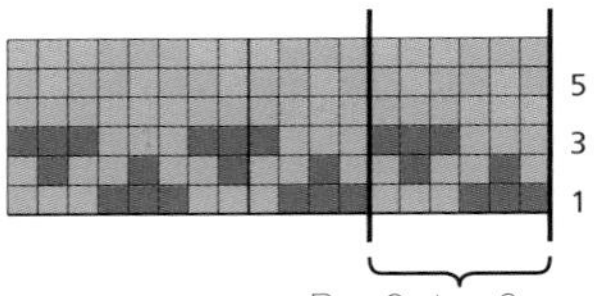

Rep 6 sts x 6 rows

H-border

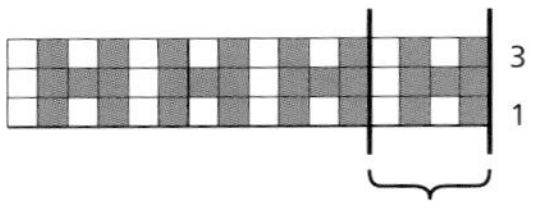

Rep 4 sts x 3 rows

Harvest furrows

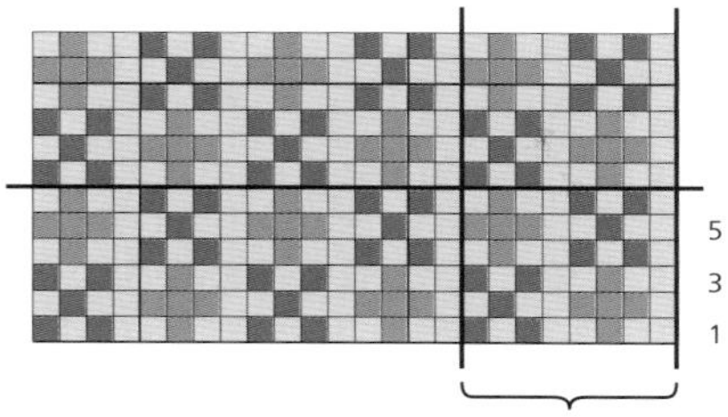

Rep 8 sts x 6 rows

Plowed furrows

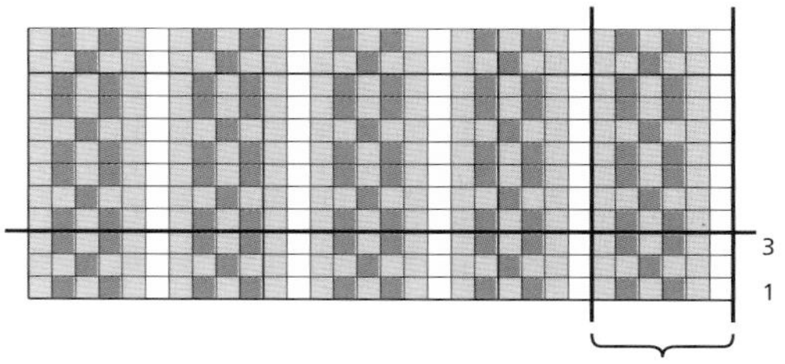

Rep 6 sts x 3 rows

Heraldic border

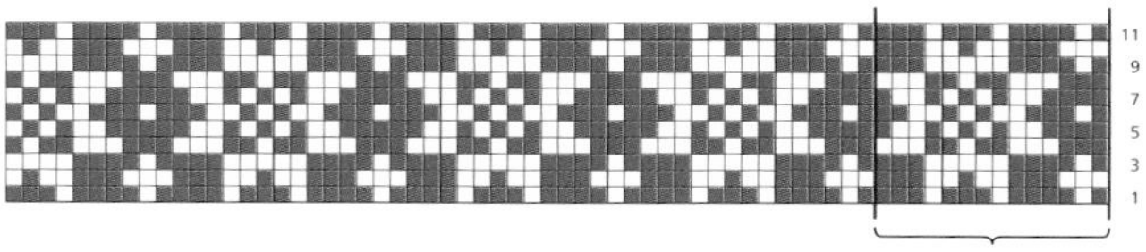

Rep 14 sts x 11 rows

Minerva

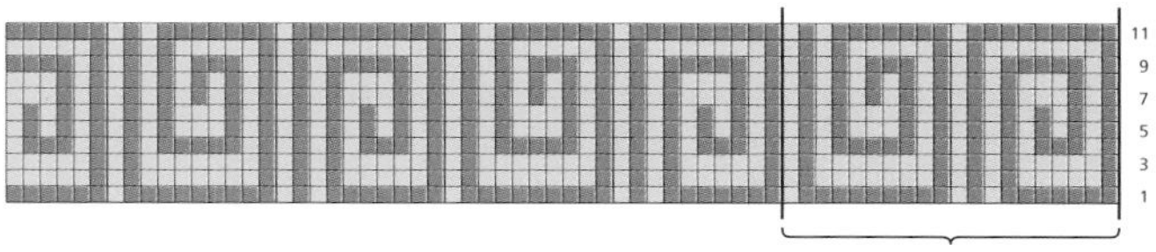

Rep 20 sts x 11 rows

Tree of life

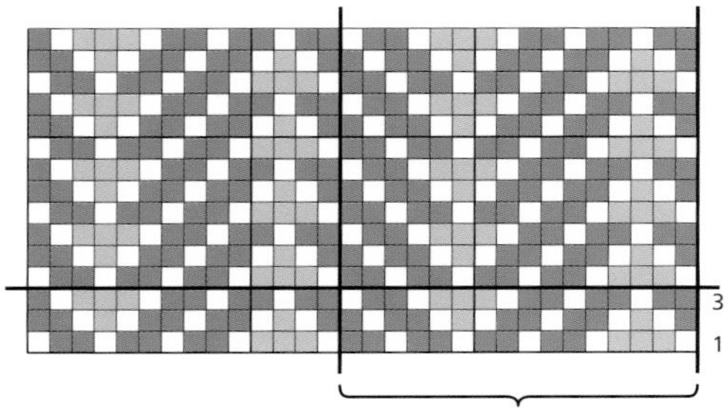

Rep 16 sts x 3 rows

Diagonal lattice

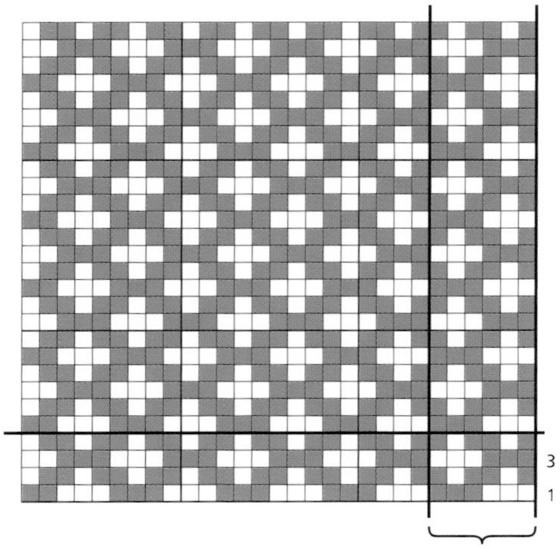

Rep 6 sts x 4 rows

Triangles and strokes

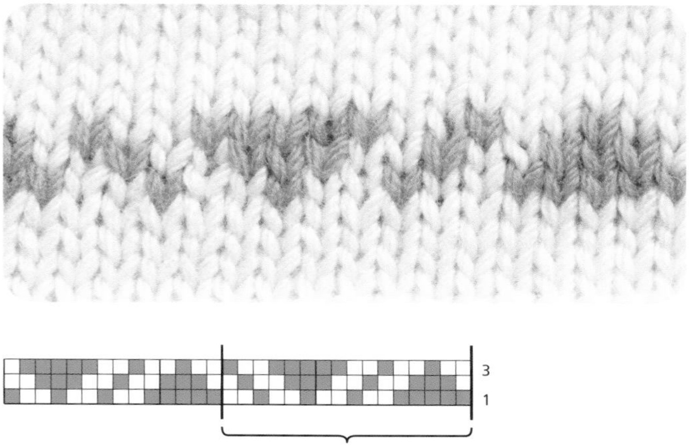

Rep 16 sts x 3 rows

Seeded back stroke

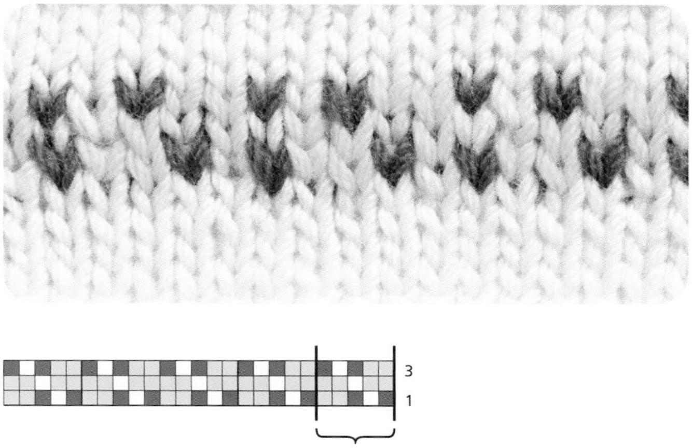

Rep 5 sts x 3 rows

Box and dot

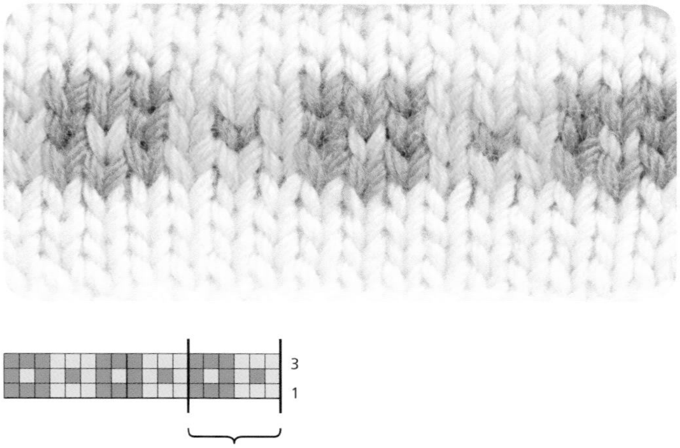

Rep 6 sts x 3 rows

Checkered dot border

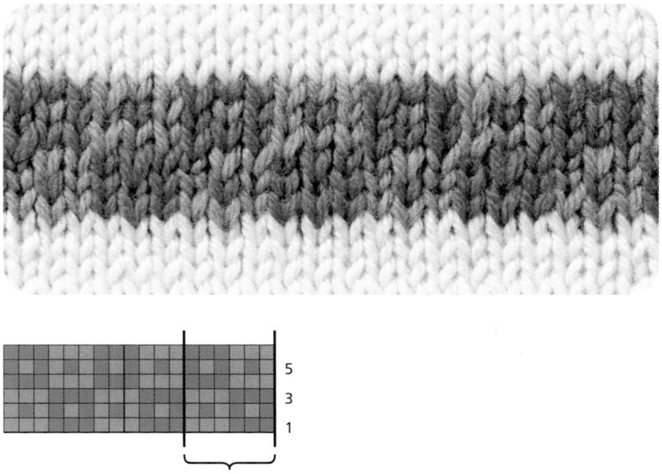

Rep 6 sts x 6 rows

Gull wings

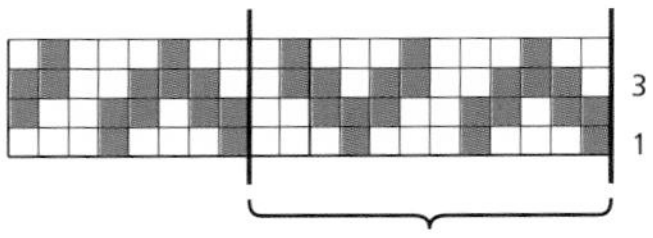

Rep 12 sts x 4 rows

Twinkling diamonds

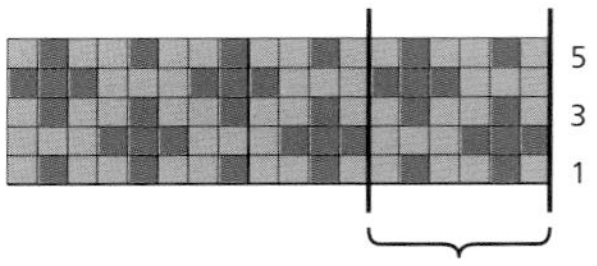

Rep 6 sts x 5 rows

Broken crests

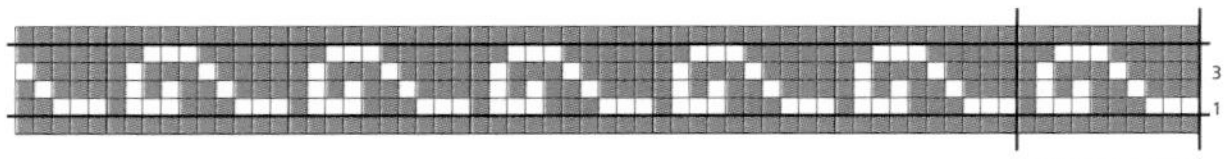

Rep 10 sts x 4 rows

Broken zigzags

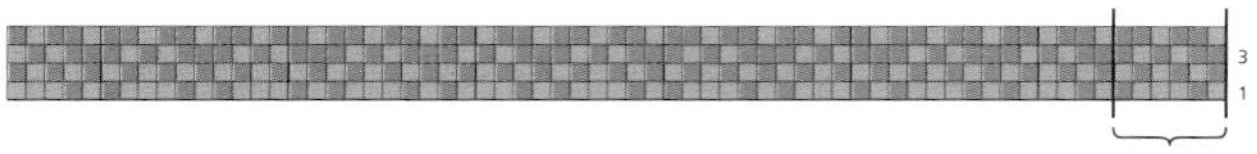

Rep 6 sts x 4 rows

Battlements (5-count)

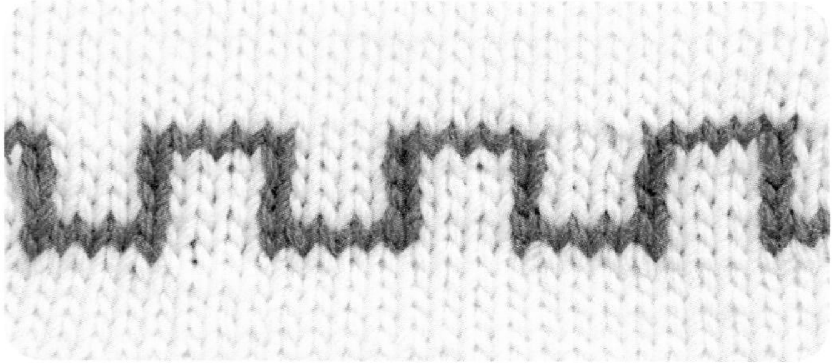

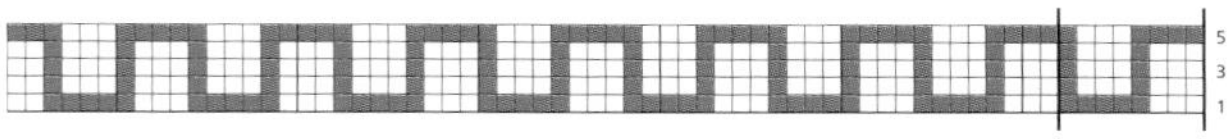

Rep 8 sts x 5 rows

Stormy sea

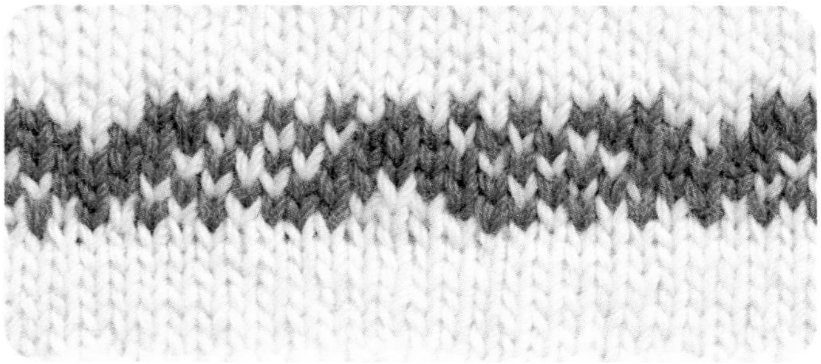

Rep 20 sts x 5 rows

Tulip wave

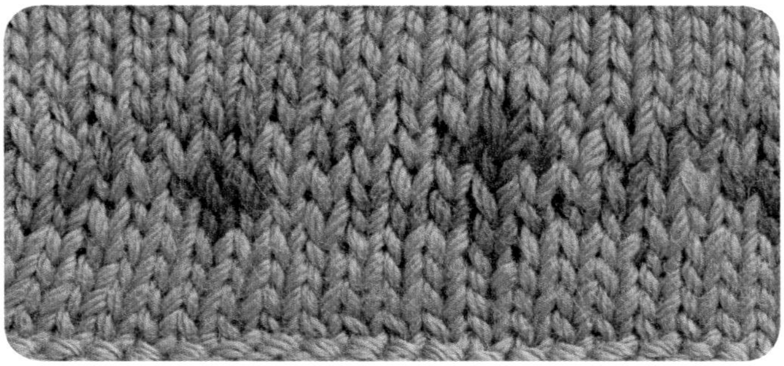

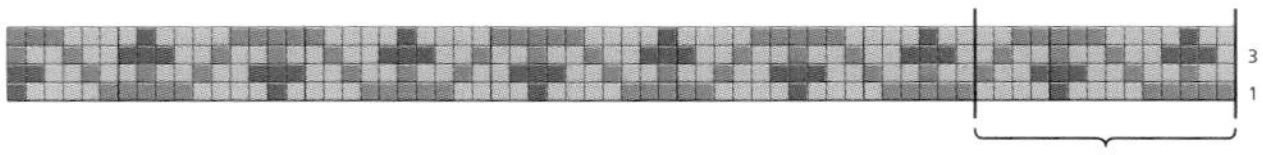

Rep 14 sts x 4 rows

Wave crest I

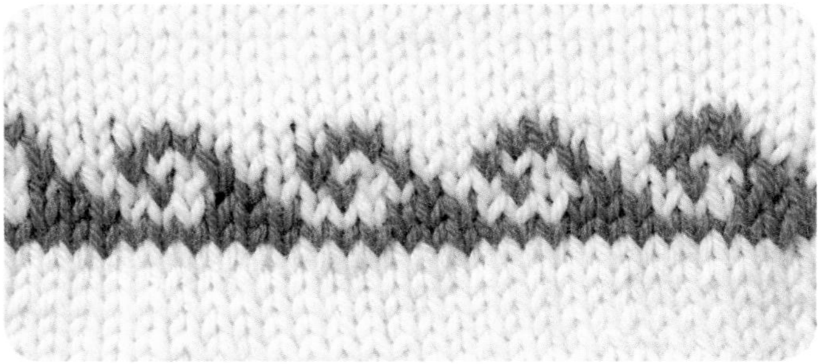

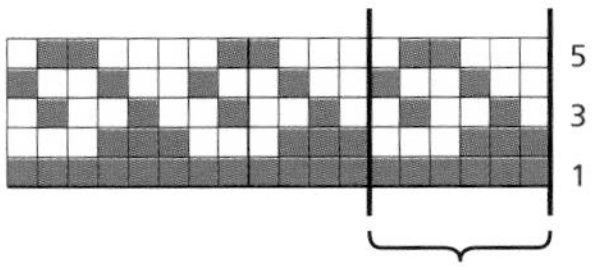

Rep 6 sts x 5 rows

Rocky shore

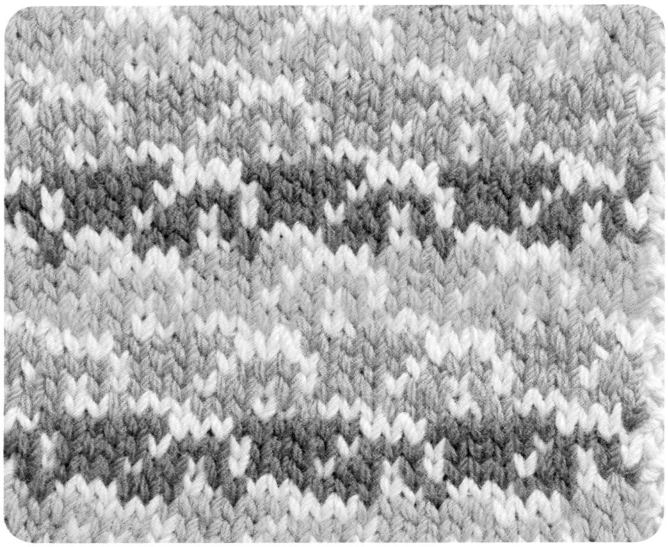

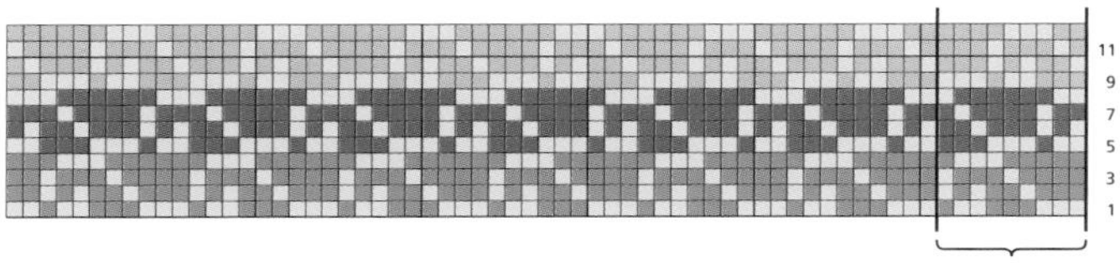

Rep 9 sts x 12 rows

Arrowhead tweed border

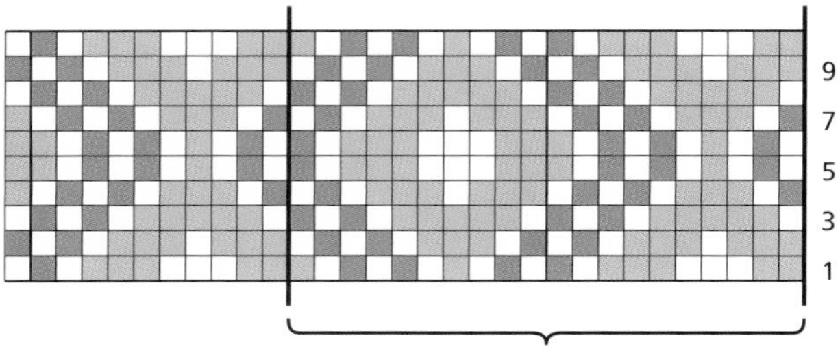

Rep 20 sts x 10 rows

Tip

If you are new to Fair Isle designs, tackling a simple banded pattern such as Pretty maids or Crossed battlements might be a good starting point. Try adapting a plain hat pattern and incorporating the colorwork to introduce one striking design element.

Flight

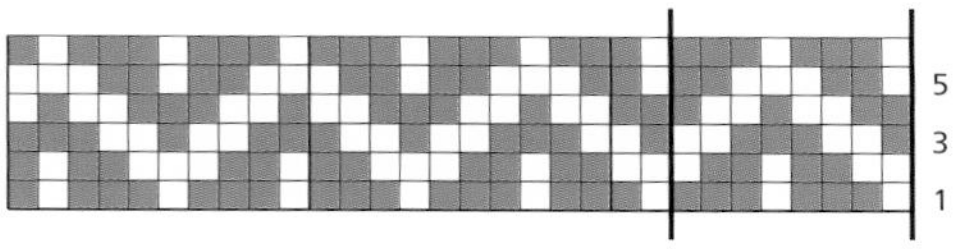

Rep 8 sts x 6 rows

Triangle zigzag

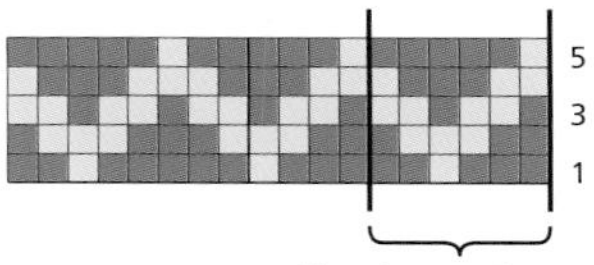

Rep 6 sts x 5 rows

Pretty maids

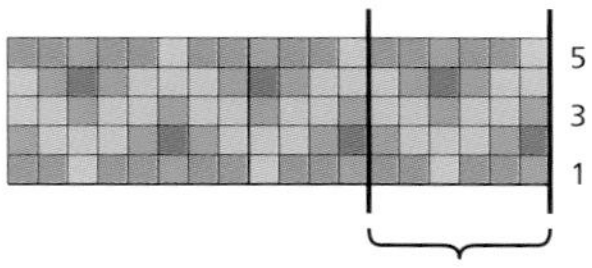

Rep 6 sts x 5 rows

Crossed battlements

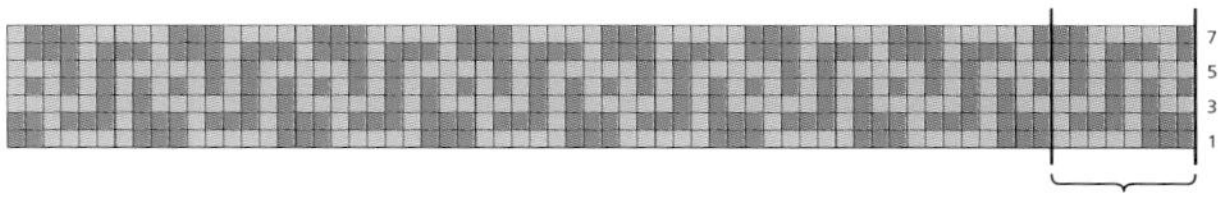

Rep 8 sts x 7 rows

Bannock trellis pattern

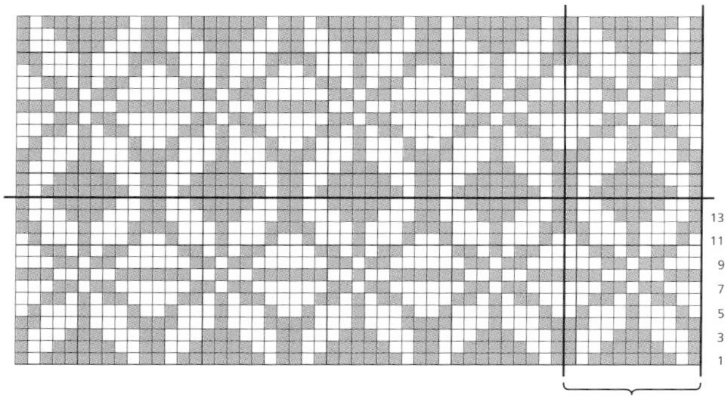

Rep 11 sts x 19 rows

Wave crest II

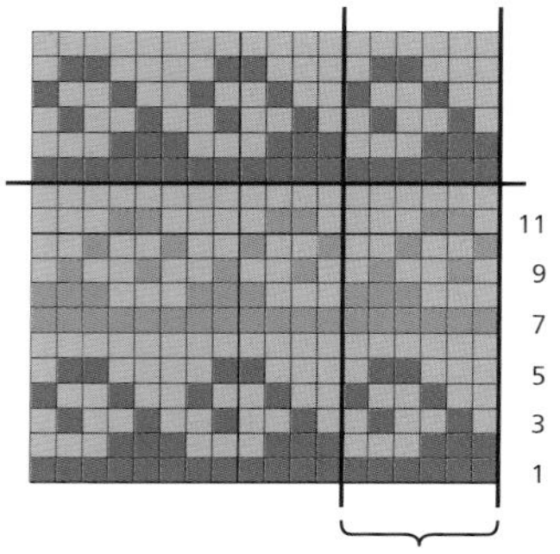

Rep 6 sts x 12 rows

Phlox

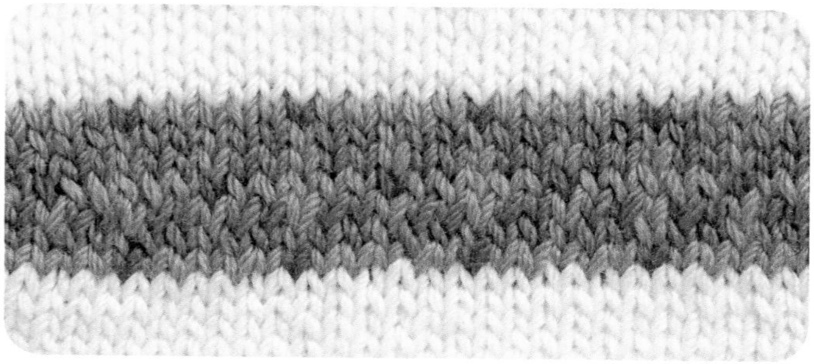

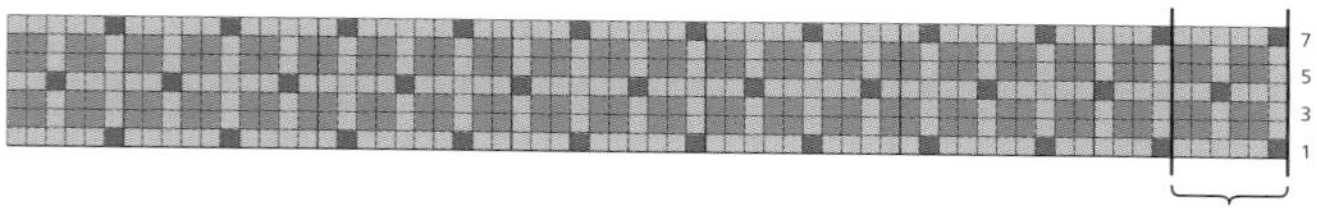

Rep 6 sts x 7 rows

Double-row diamond

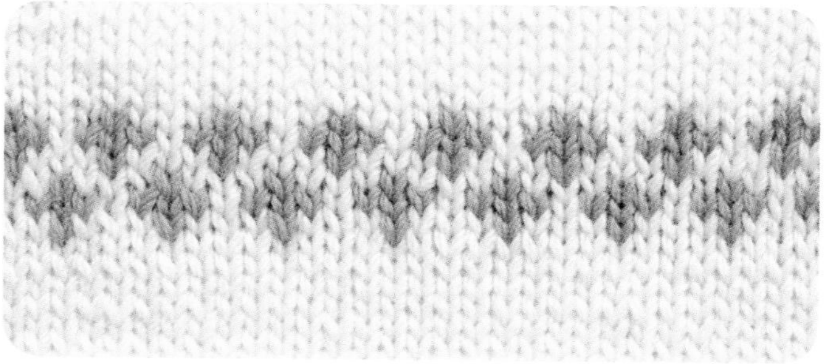

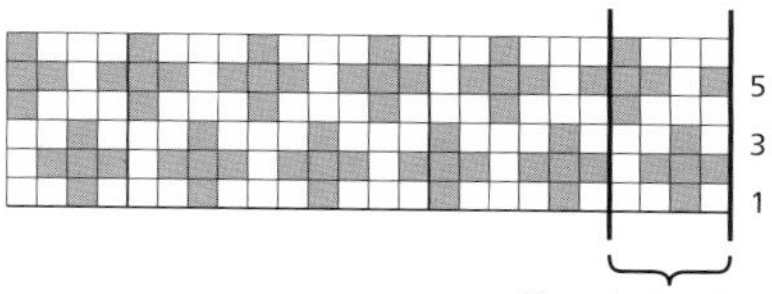

Rep 4 sts x 6 rows

Diamond footpath

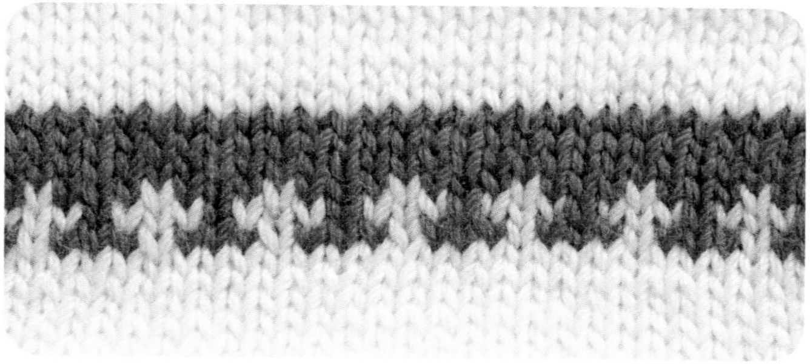

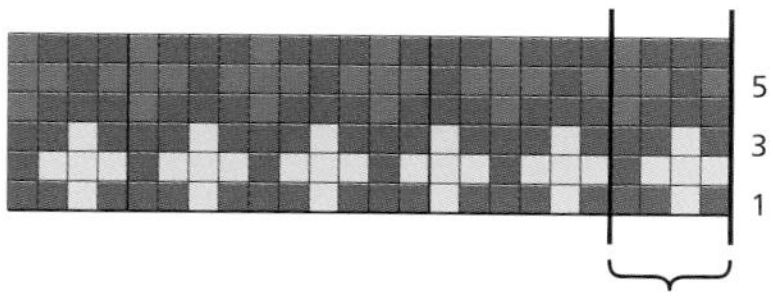

Rep 4 sts x 6 rows

Rose and thistle

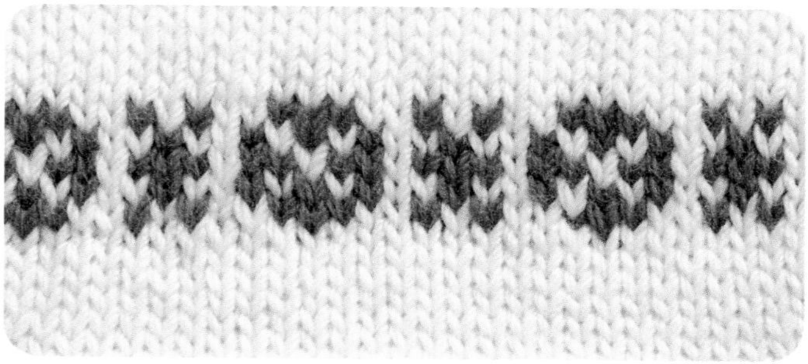

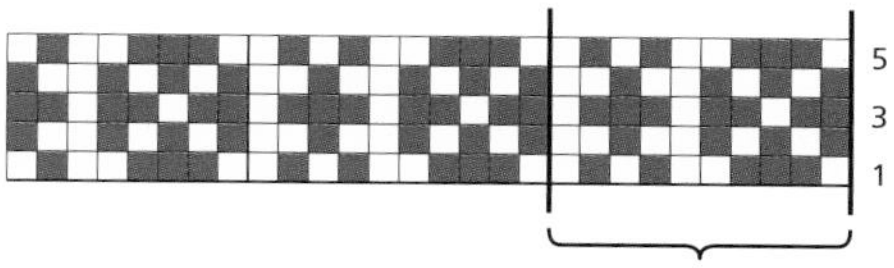

Rep 10 sts x 5 rows

Wave and diamond border

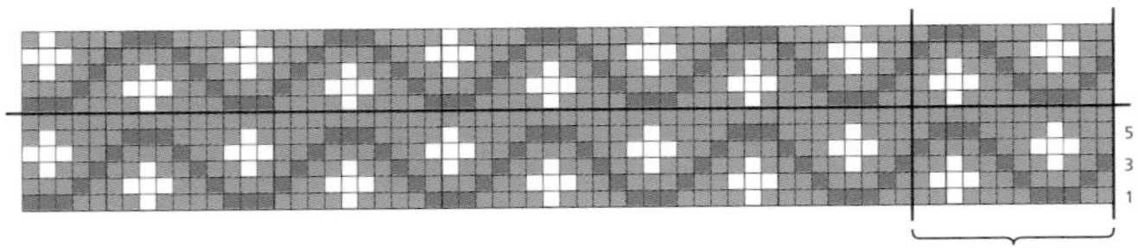

Rep 12 sts x 6 rows

Lattice window I

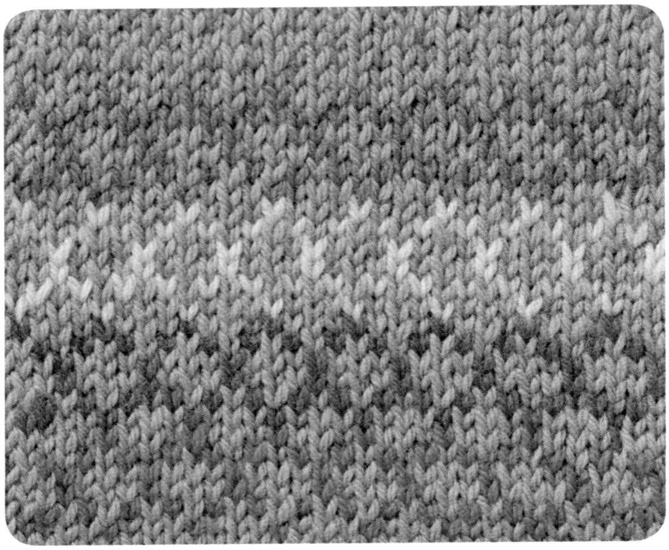

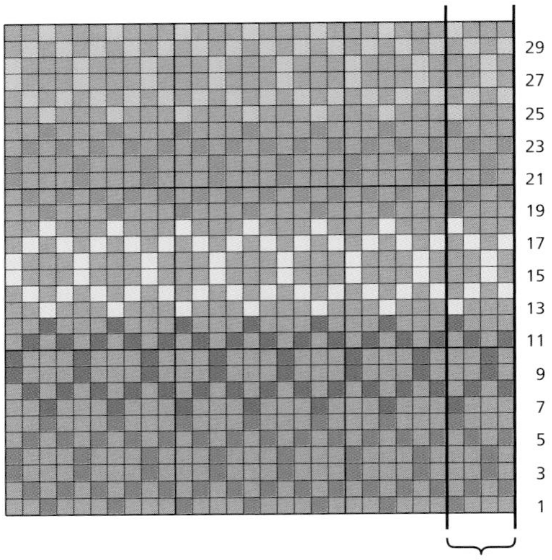

Rep 4 sts x 30 rows

Diamond tweed pattern

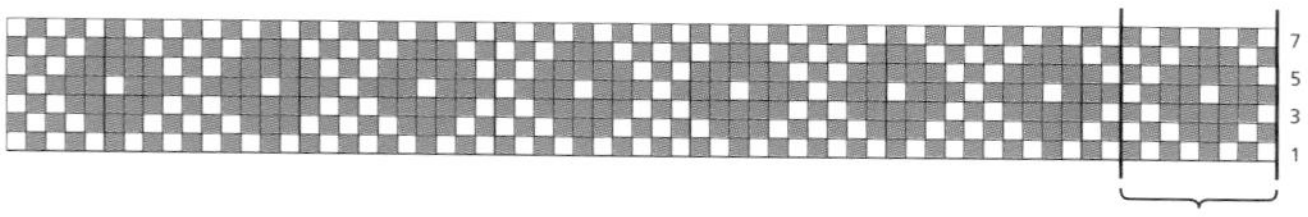

Rep 8 sts x 7 rows

Celtic rose

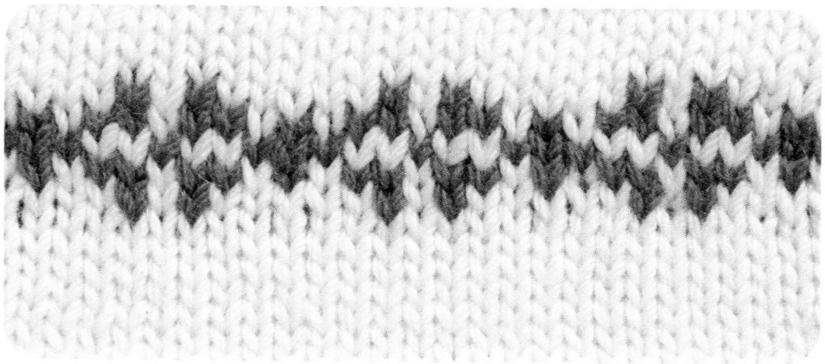

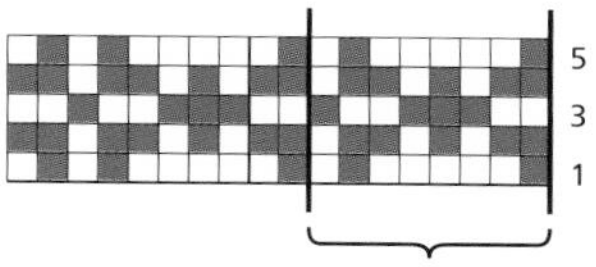

Rep 8 sts x 5 rows

Diamond link and dot

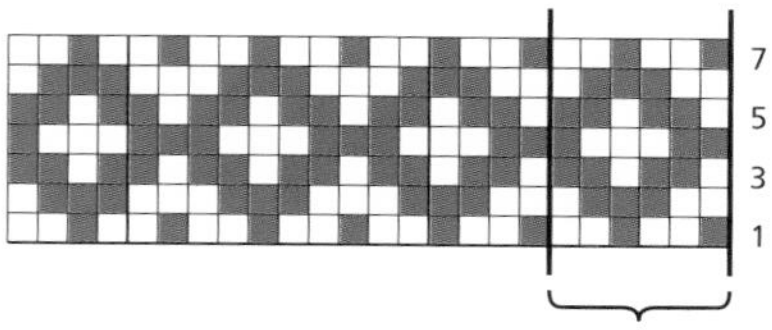

Rep 6 sts x 7 rows

Captive diamond border

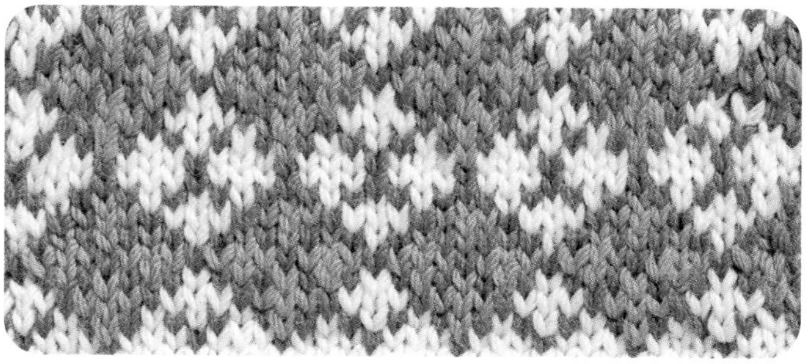

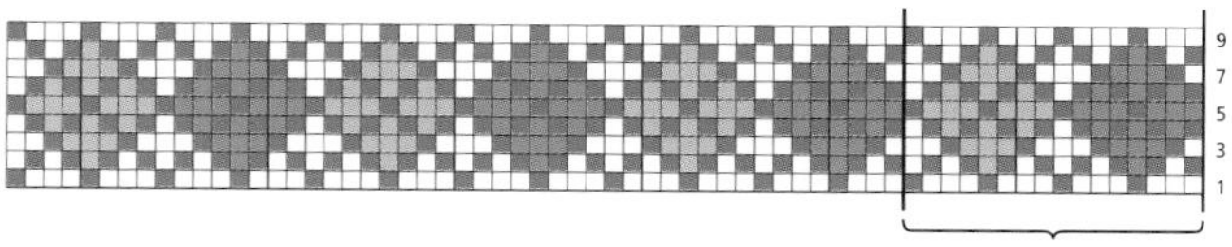

Rep 16 sts x 18 rows

Zigzag fence

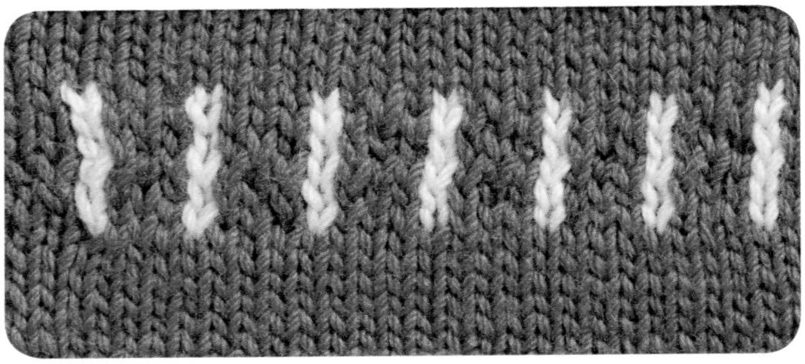

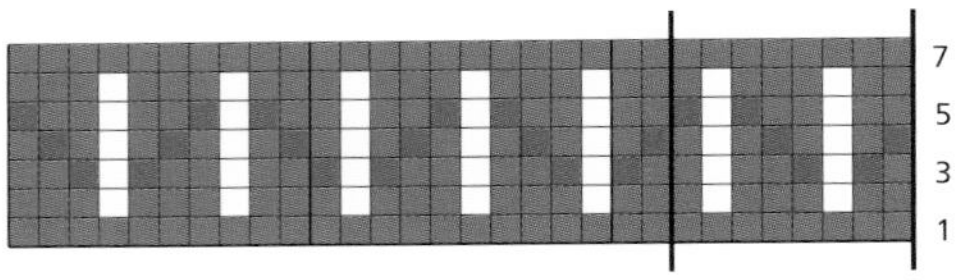

Rep 8 sts x 7 rows

Diamond filigree

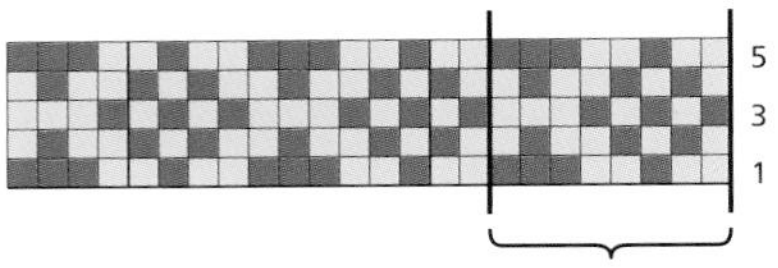

Rep 8 sts x 5 rows

Cabbages

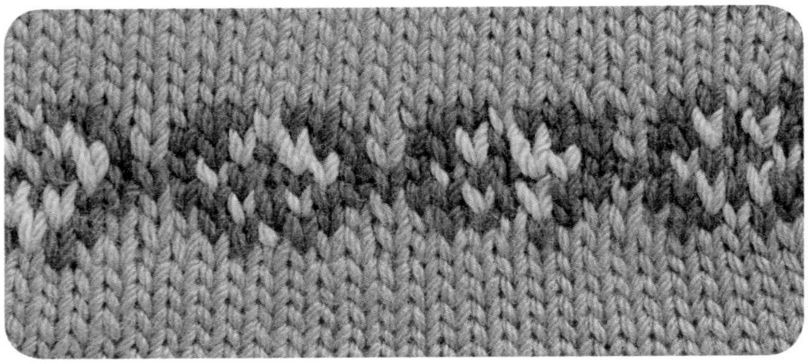

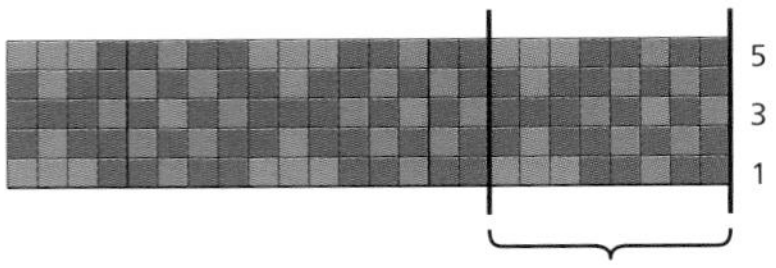

Rep 8 sts x 5 rows

Wandering zigzag

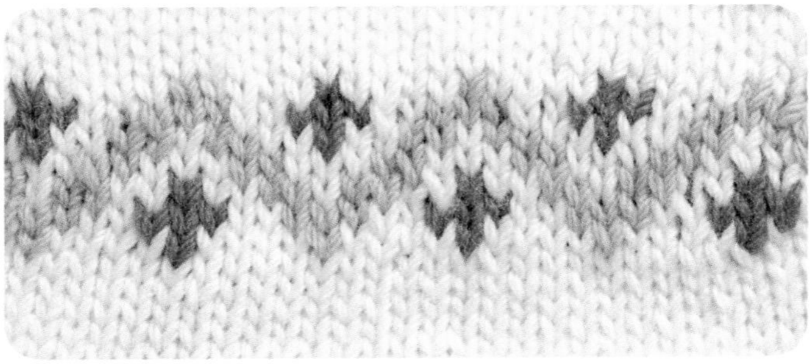

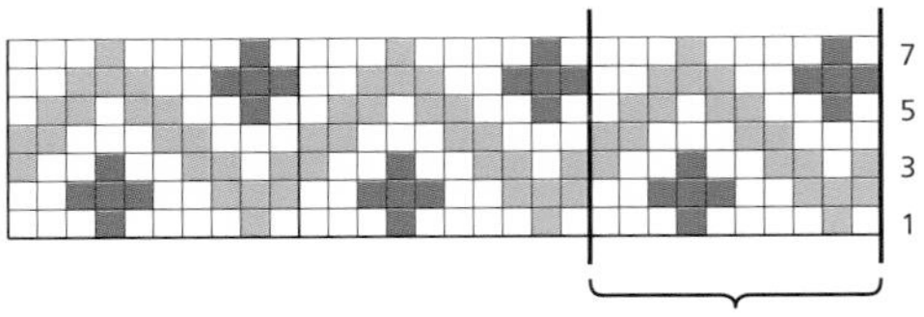

Rep 10 sts x 7 rows

Chain link I

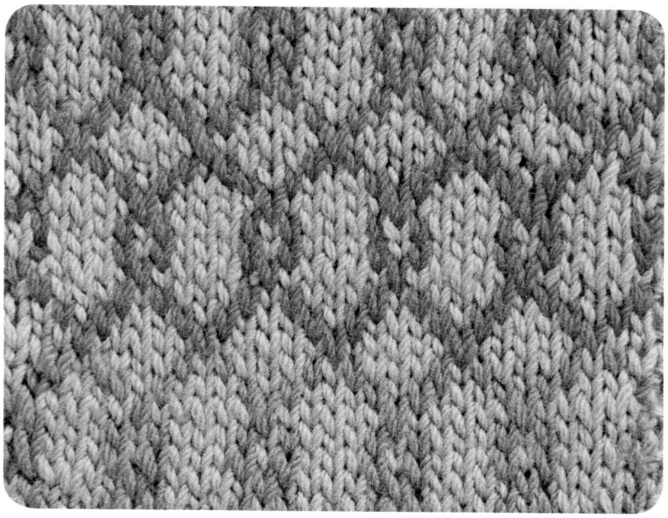

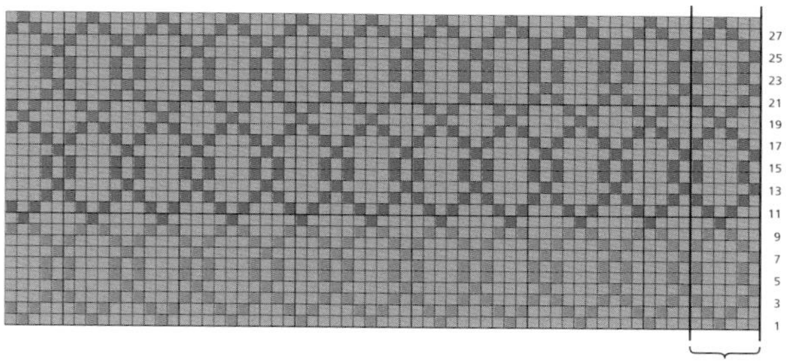

Rep 6 sts x 28 rows

Berwick

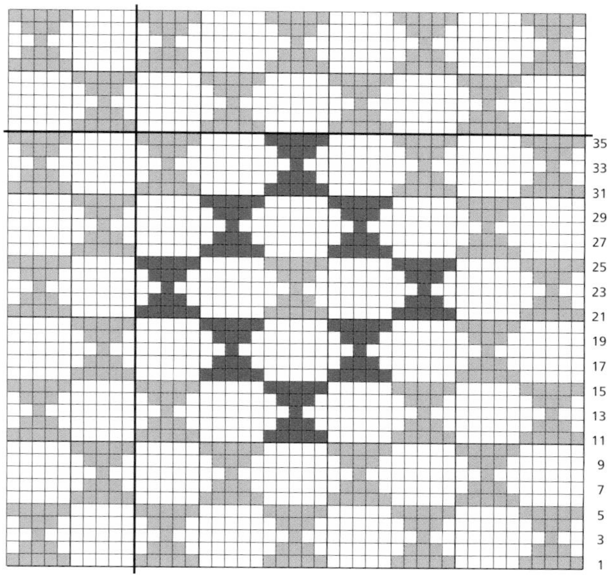

Rep 35 sts x 35 rows

Speckled trellis

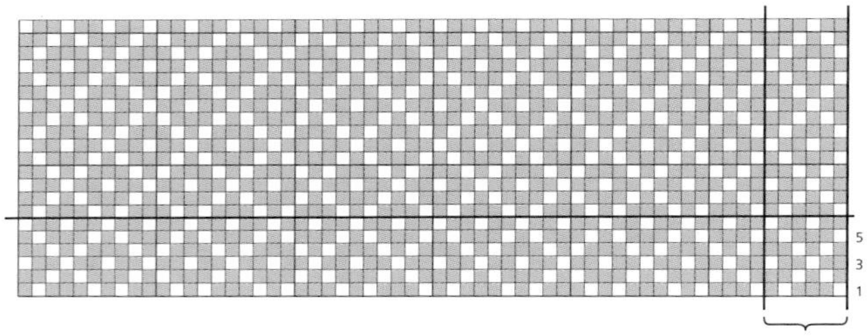

Rep 6 sts x 6 rows

Diamond box border

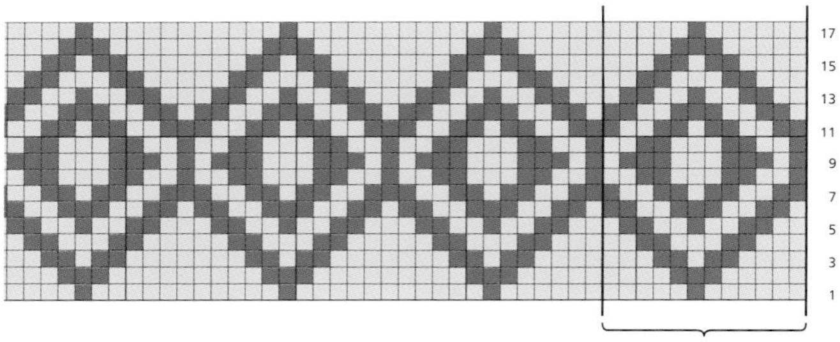

Rep 12 sts x 17 rows

Diamond and cross windowpane I

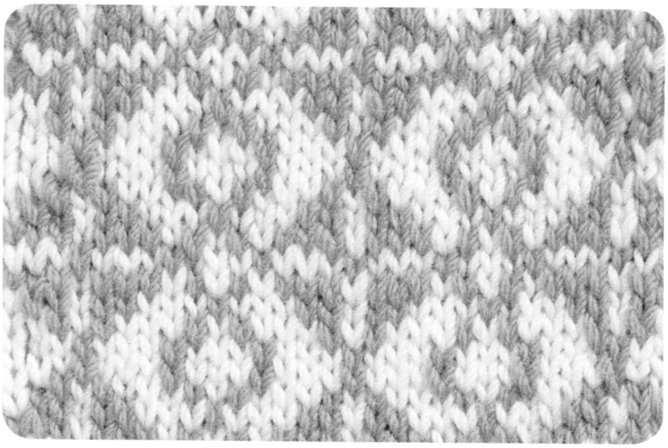

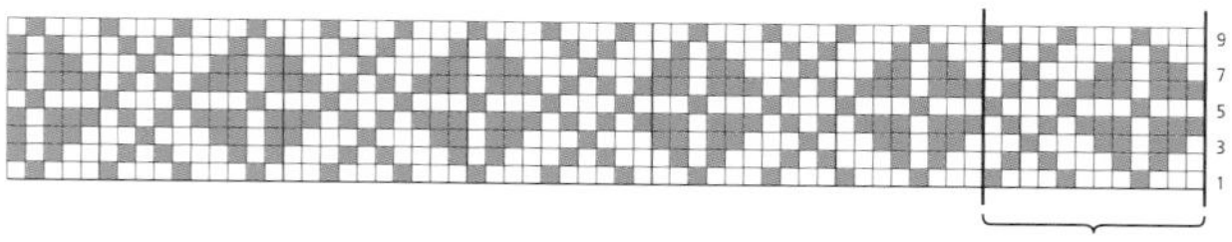

Rep 12 sts x 9 rows

Flower and chalice

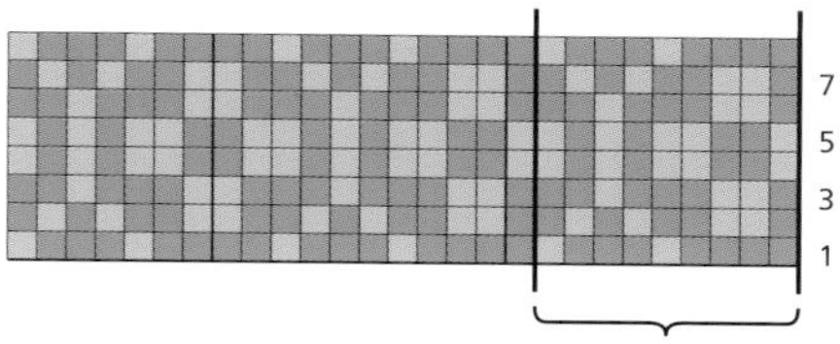

Rep 9 sts x 8 rows

Wall walk

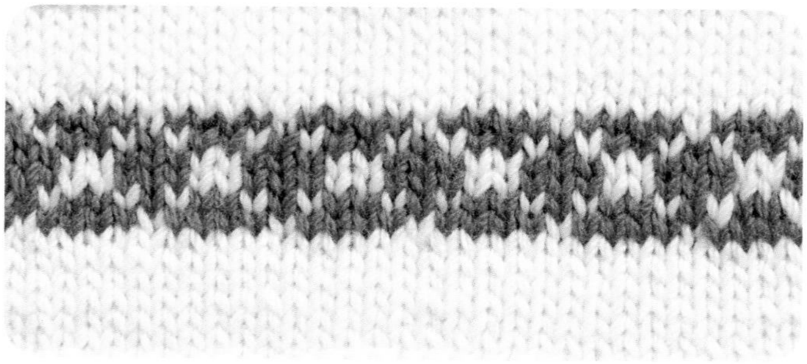

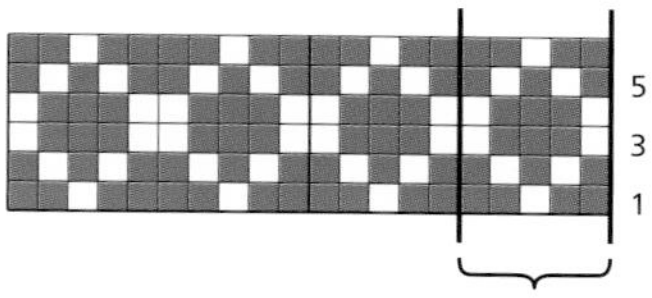

Rep 5 sts x 6 rows

Diamond and cross

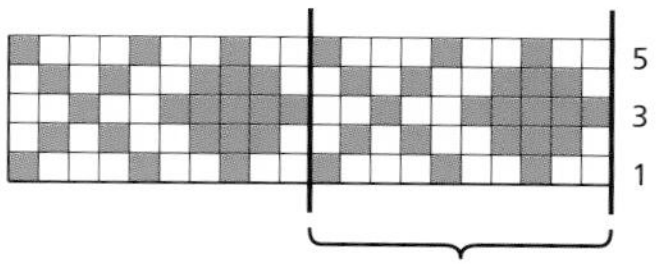

Rep 10 sts x 5 rows

Lattice window II

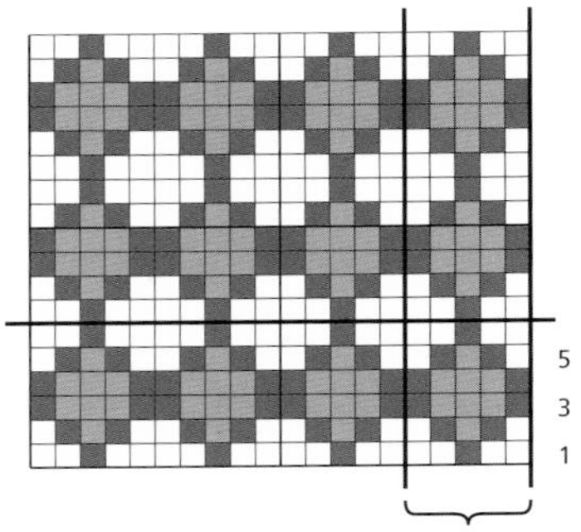

Rep 5 sts x 6 rows

Trellis with blocks

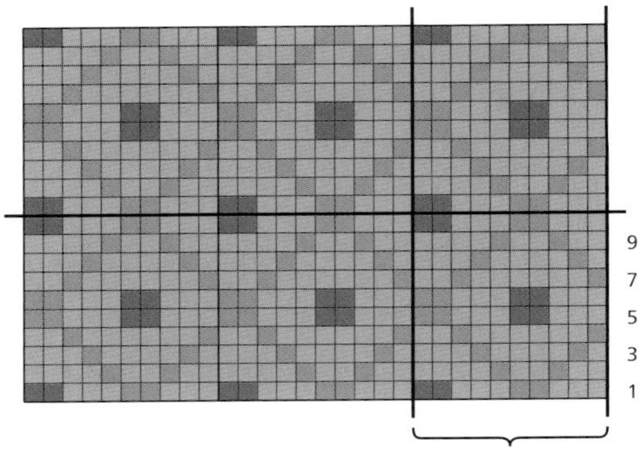

Rep 10 sts x 10 rows

Speckled zigzag

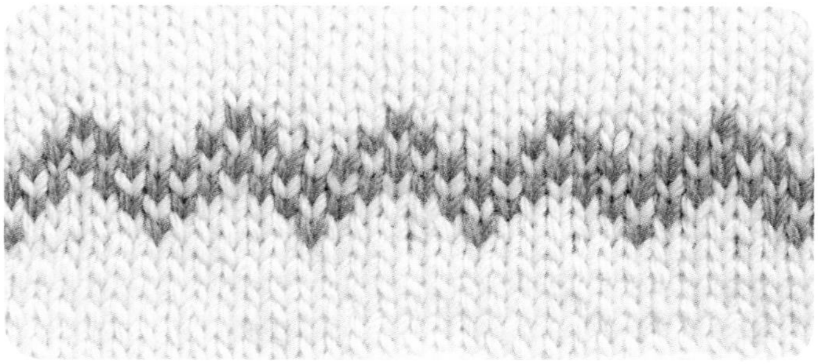

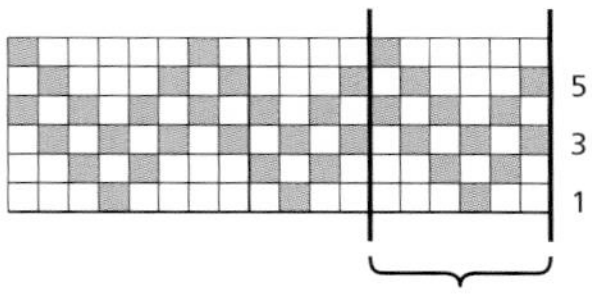

Rep 6 sts x 6 rows

Arrowhead zigzag

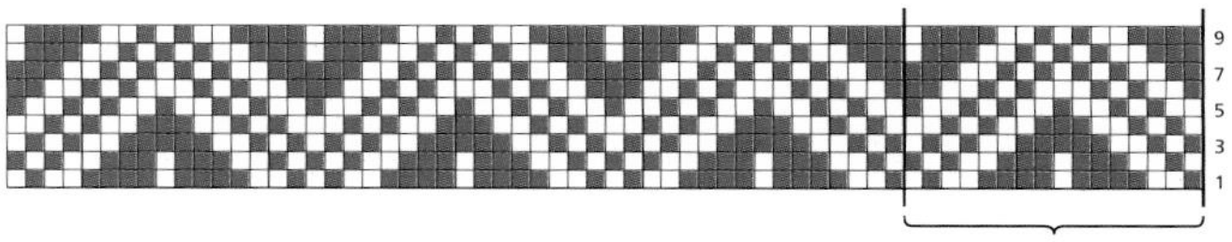

Rep 16 sts x 9 rows

Ripples border

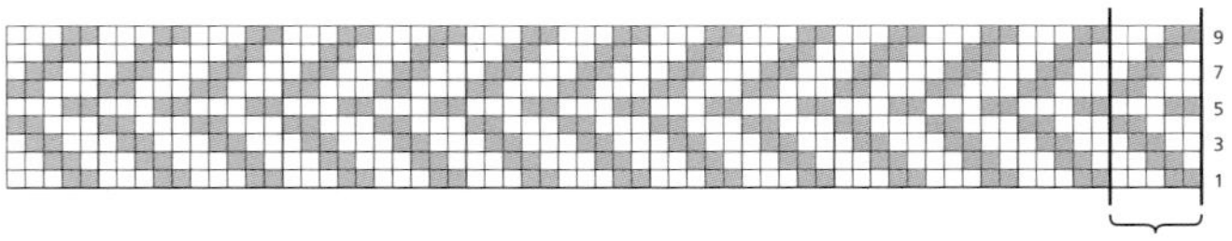

Rep 5 sts x 9 rows

Flora

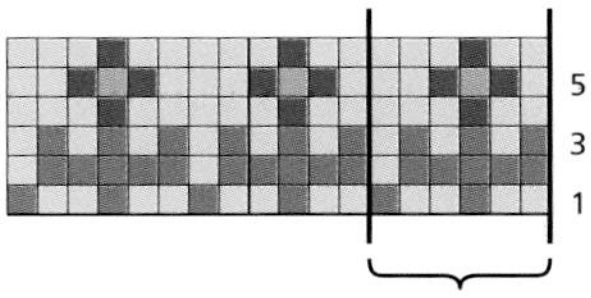

Rep 6 sts x 6 rows

Zigzag tweed

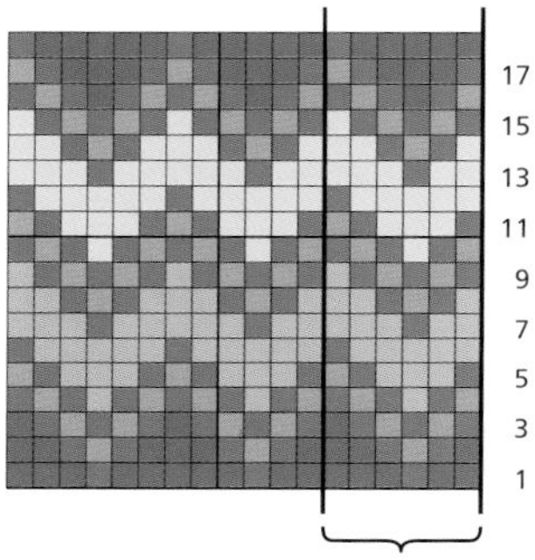

Rep 6 sts x 18 rows

Vertical basketweave lattice

Rep 30 sts x 8 rows

Aubrieta

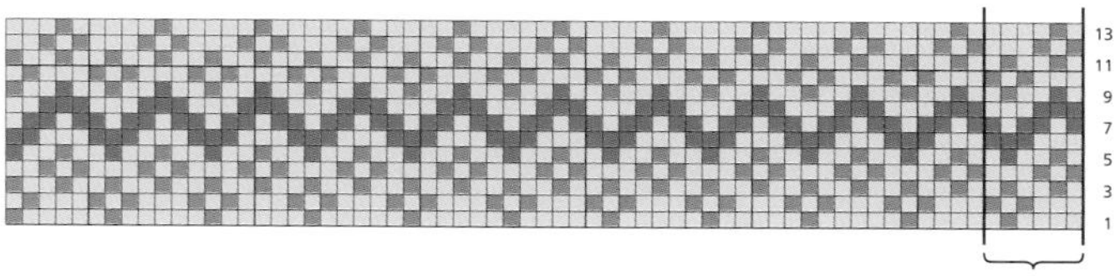

Rep 6 sts x 13 rows

Cosmea

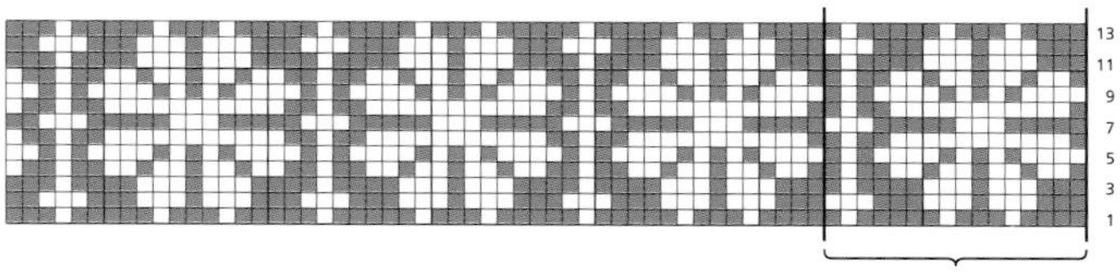

Rep 16 sts x 13 rows

Tip

Colorwork is nearly always worked in stockinette stitch fabric to provide a clean and simple canvas for the design. Otherwise complex and colorful patterns such as Aubrieta or Zigzag tweed could look overworked and fussy and lose their impact.

Diamond and cross windowpane II

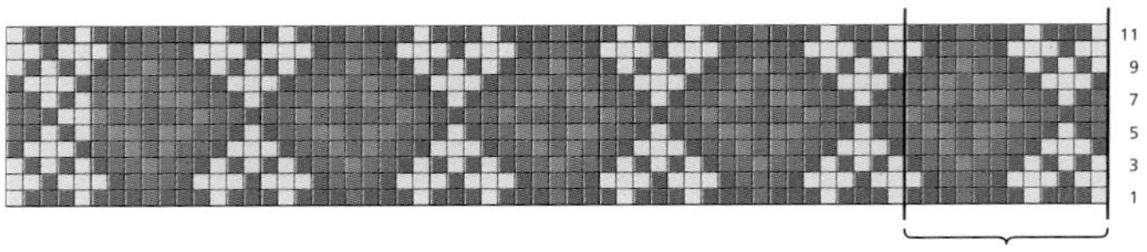

Rep 12 sts x 11 rows

Mosaic path

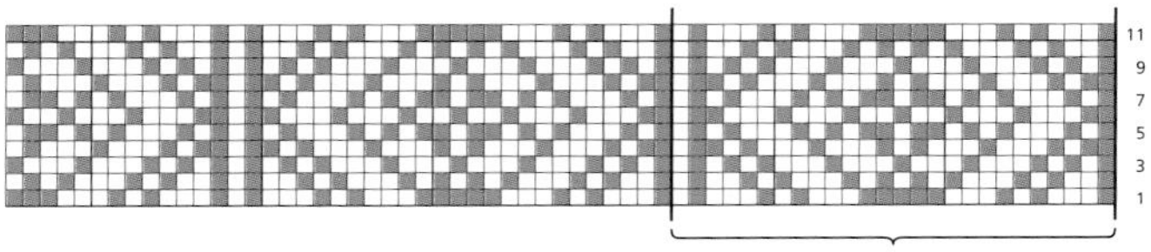

Rep 26 sts x 11 rows

Tip

Fair Isle patterns often include a vertical motif, as in the Castle window variations shown here. This means it is easy to adapt the design to fit all the way around a length of knitting, whether it forms the decorative element on a sweater or the brim of a hat.

Castle window I

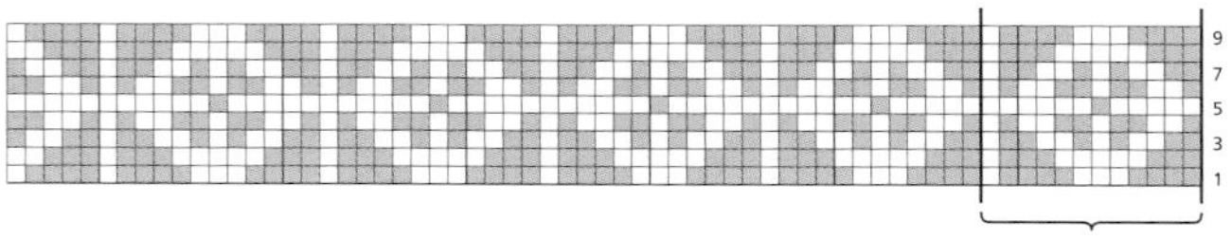

Rep 12 sts x 9 rows

Castle window II

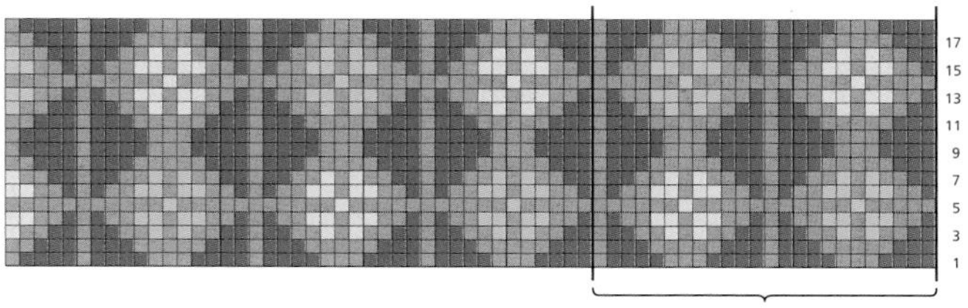

Rep 24 sts x 18 rows

Vertical stripes I

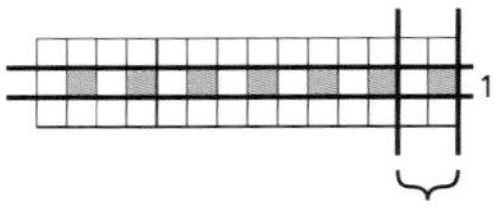

Rep 2 sts x 1 row

Line and dot

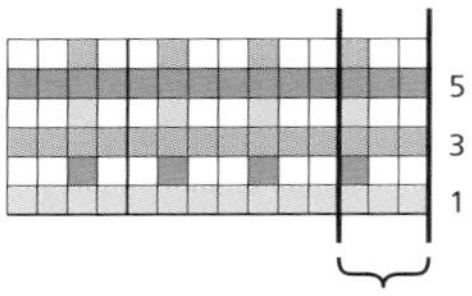

Rep 2 sts x 6 rows

Diamond links

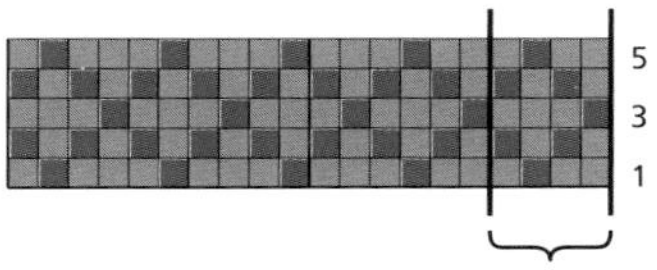

Rep 4 sts x 5 rows

Vertical stripes II

Rep 3 sts x 1 row

Country lanes

Rep 12 sts x 11 rows

Chain link II

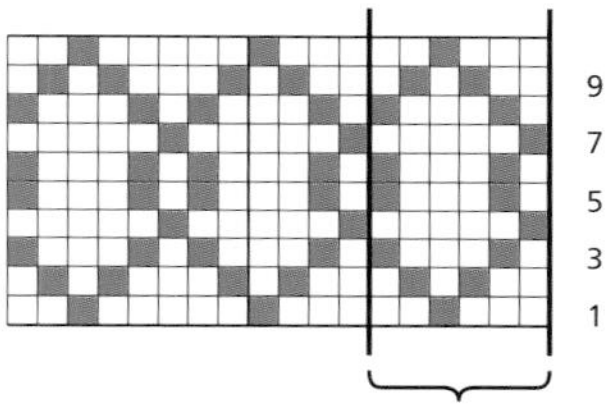

Rep 6 sts x 10 rows

Crossroads

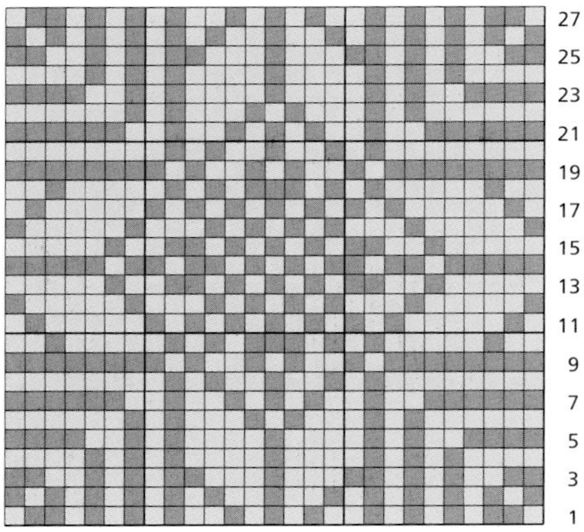

Rep 27 sts x 27 rows

Parterre

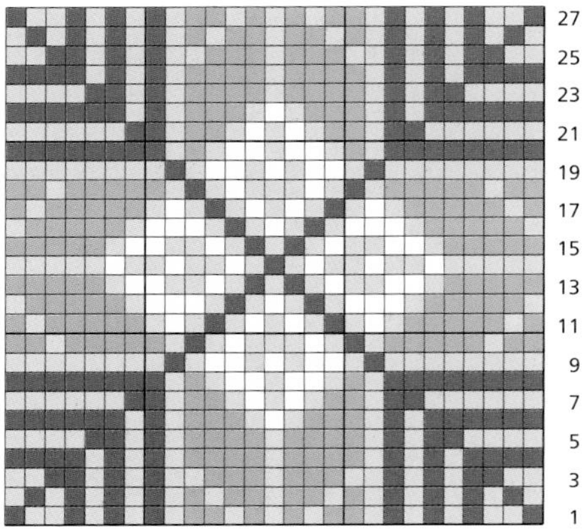

Rep 27 sts x 27 rows

Melissa

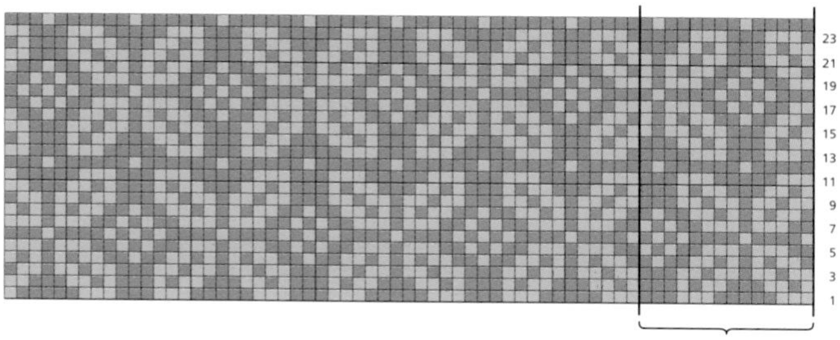

Rep 14 sts x 24 rows

Diamonds in the snow

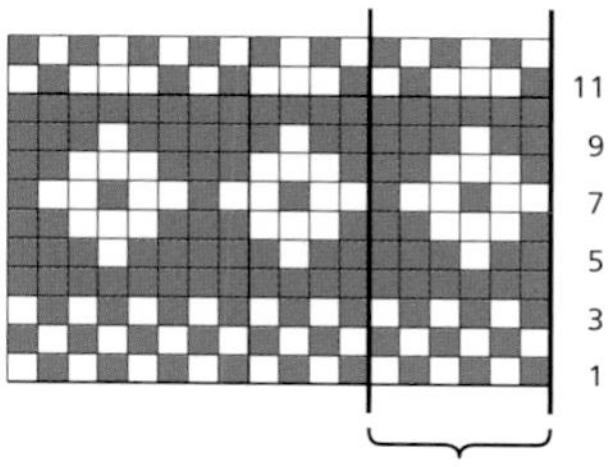

Rep 6 sts x 12 rows

Kirkwall

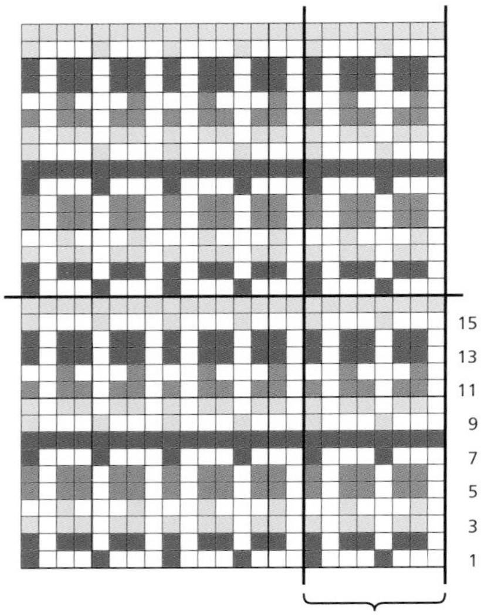

Rep 8 sts x 16 rows

Argyll check

Rep 32 sts x 28 rows

Diamond zigzag bands

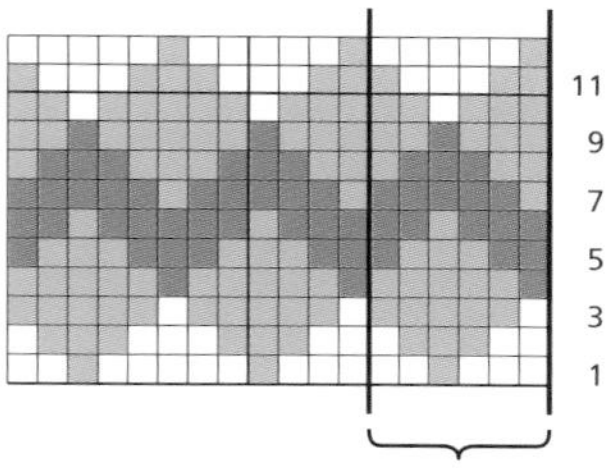

Rep 6 sts x 12 rows

Banded lattice and cross

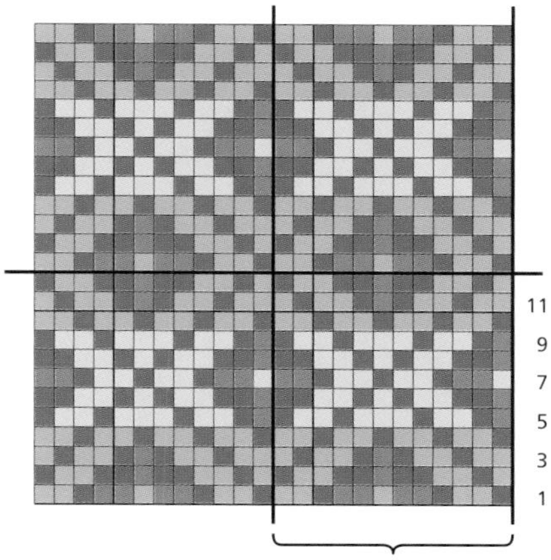

Rep 12 sts x 12 rows

Diamond flower border I

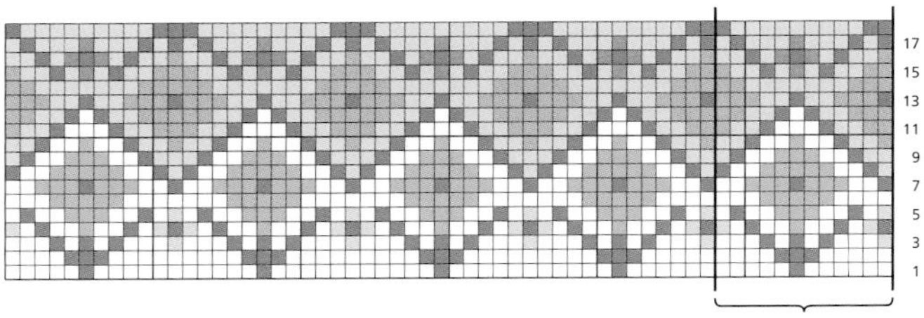

Rep 12 sts x 18 rows

Whirligig

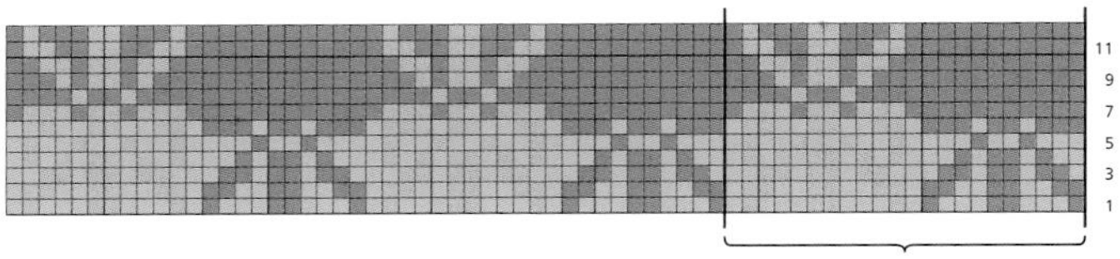

Rep 22 sts x 12 rows

Diamond and snowflake paths

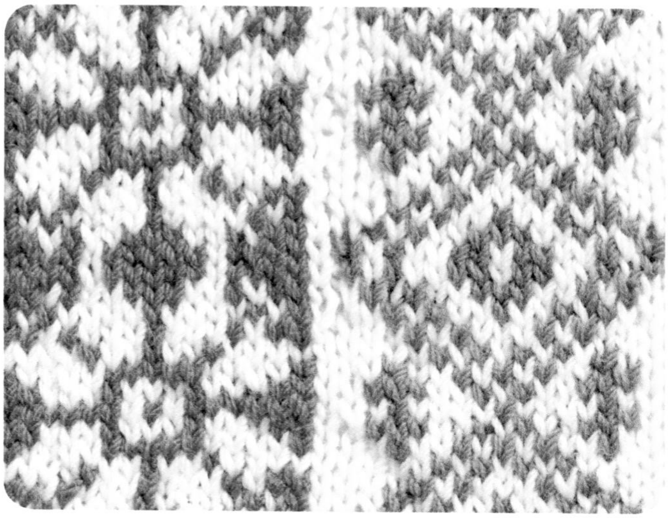

Rep 32 sts x 15 rows

Diamond flower border II

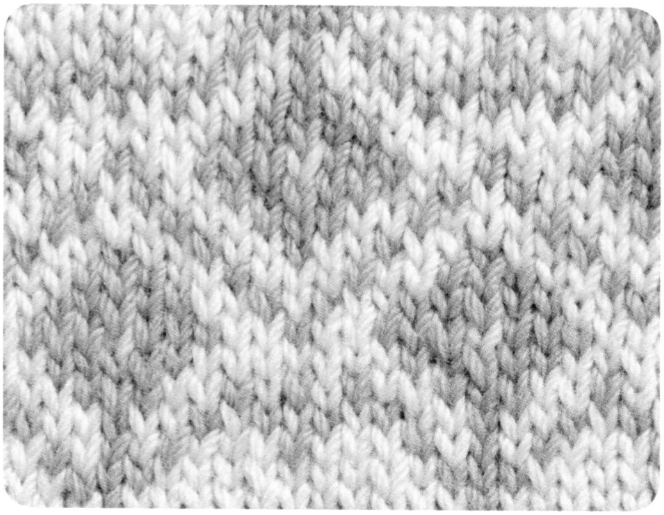

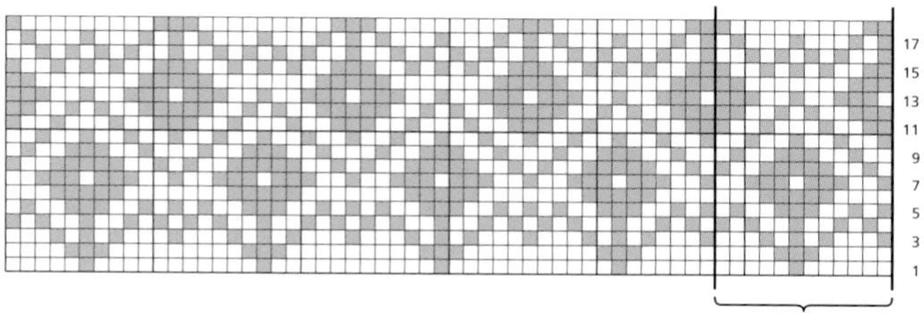

Rep 12 sts x 18 rows

Rose crest

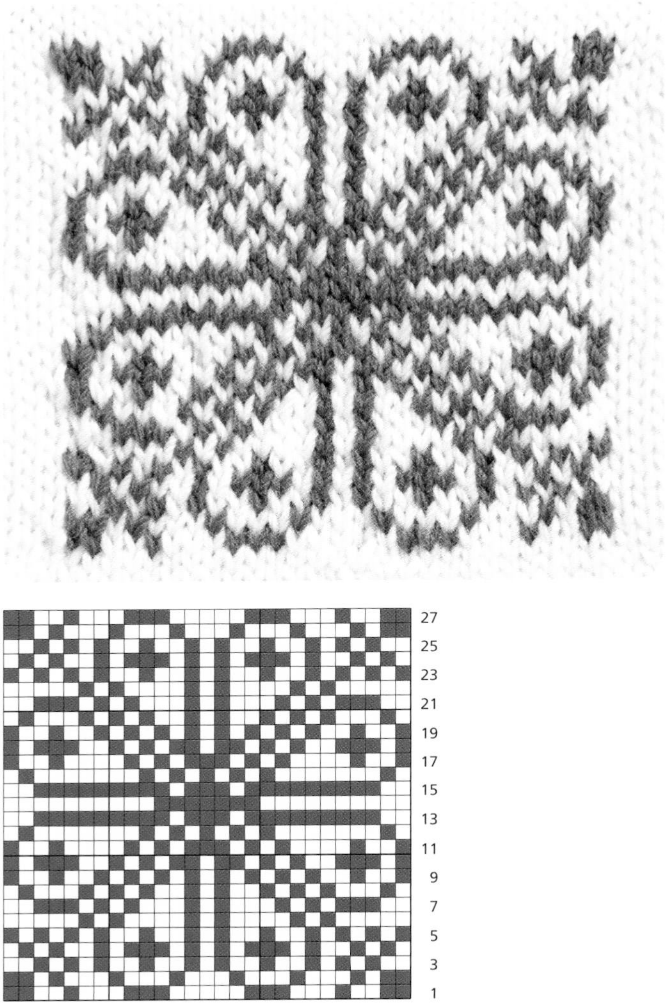

Rep 27 sts x 27 rows

Winter rose medallion

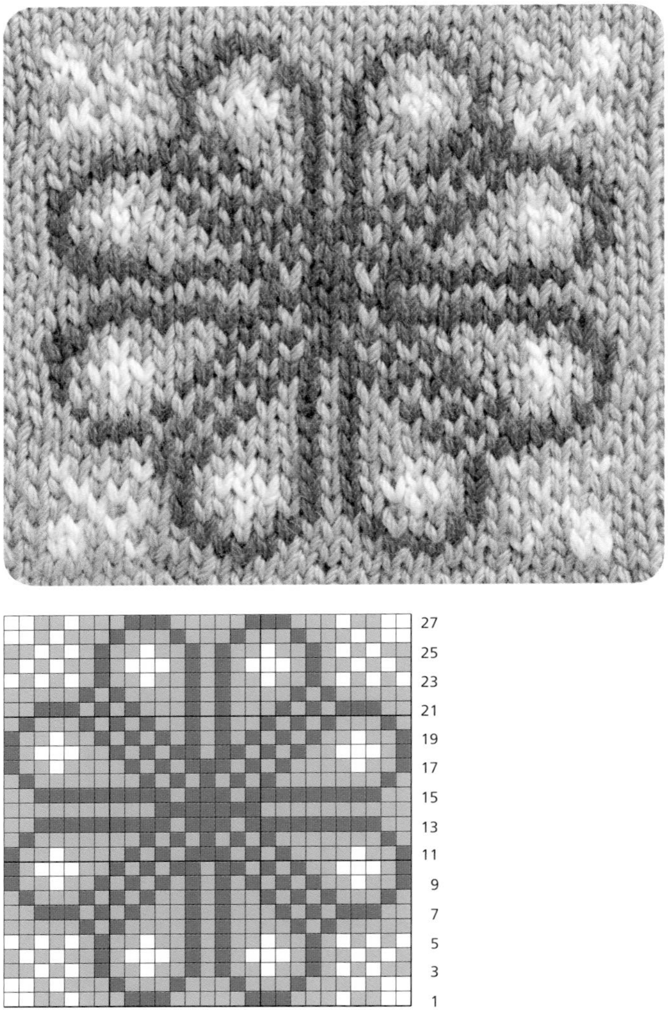

Rep 27 sts x 27 rows

Quatrefoil

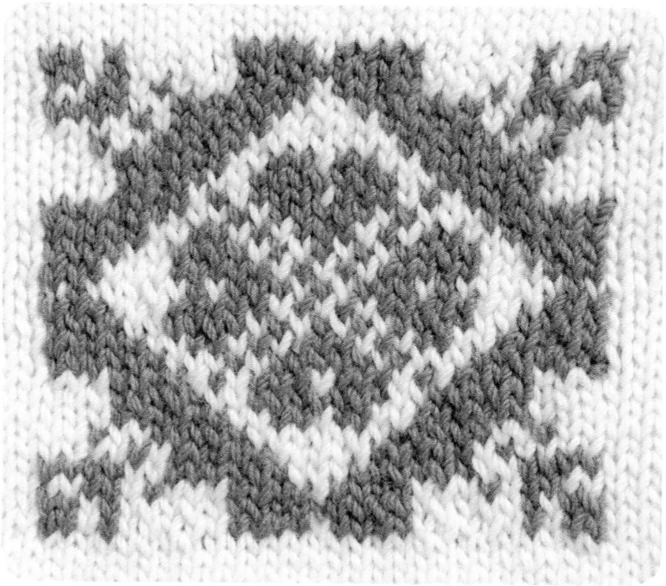

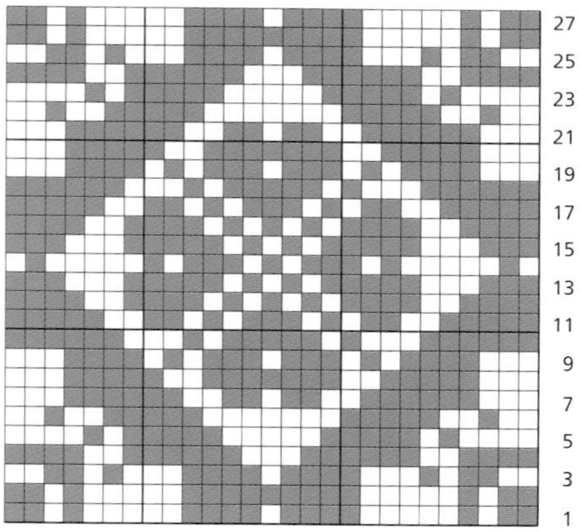

Rep 27 sts x 27 rows

Argyll diamond motif

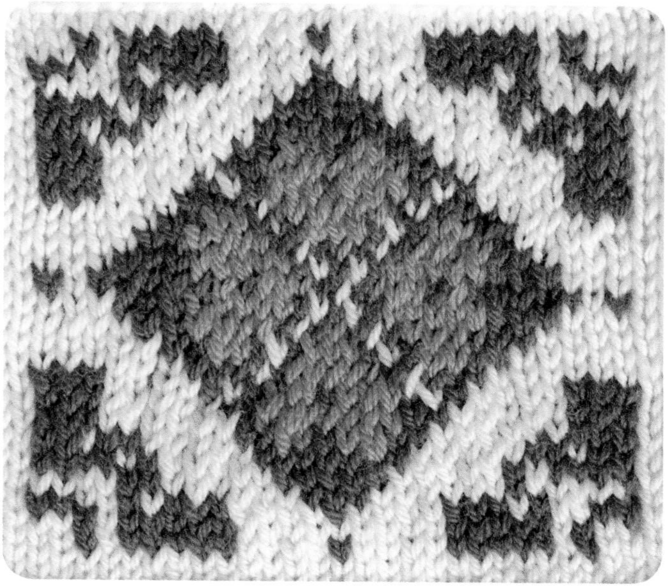

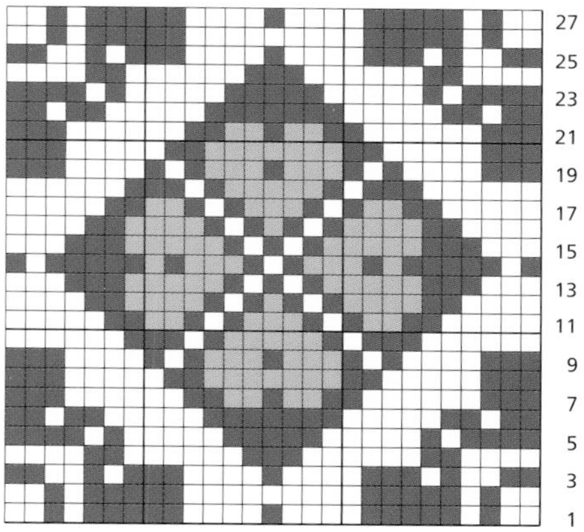

Rep 27 sts x 27 rows

Diamond and lozenge tweed border

Rep 10 sts x 27 rows

Diamond and lozenge banded border

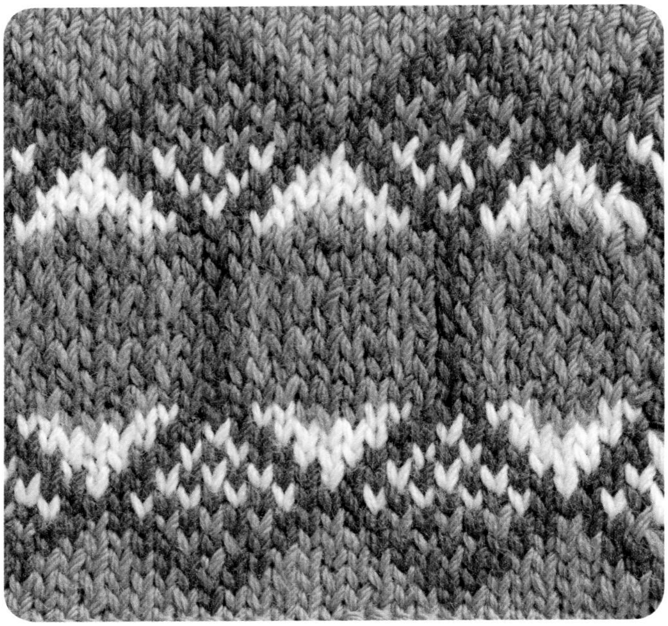

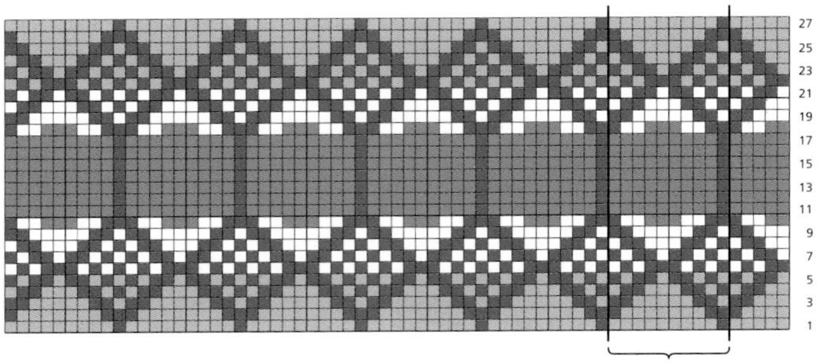

Rep 10 sts x 27 rows

Scottish thistles I

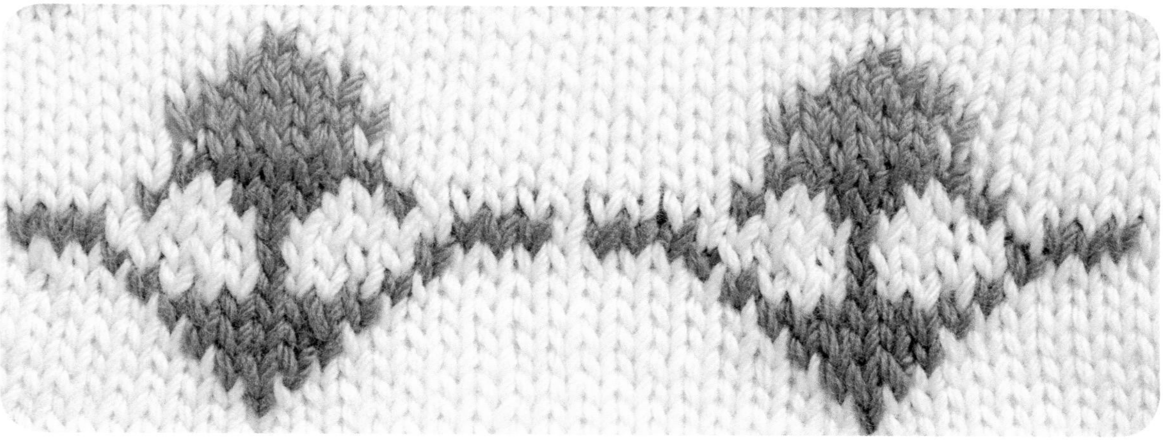

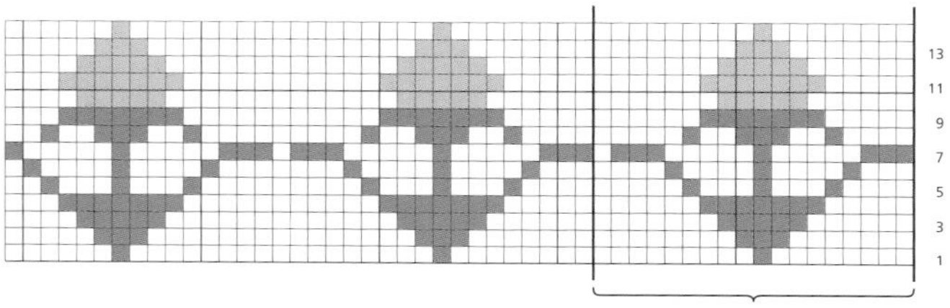

Rep 18 sts x 14 rows

Scottish thistles II

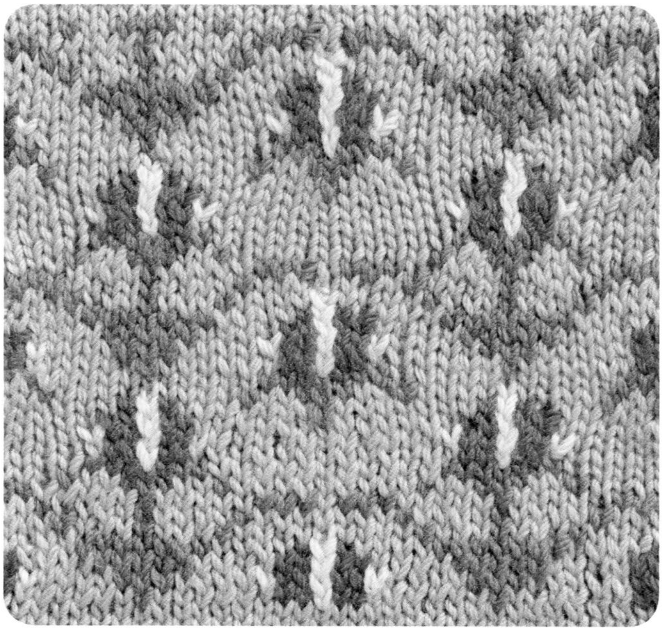

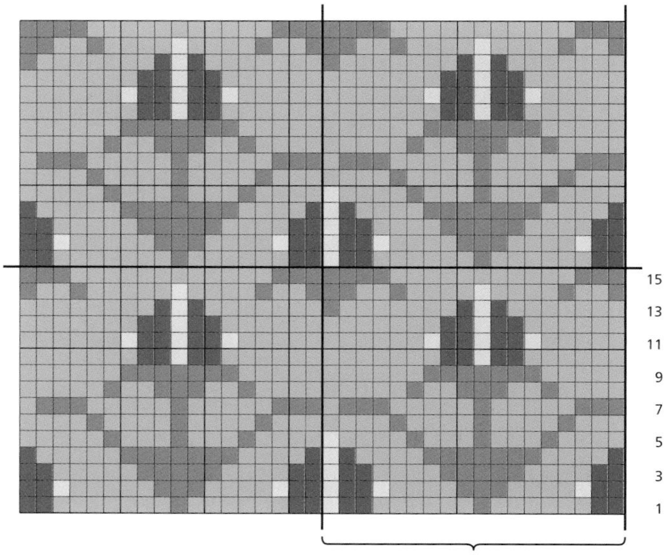

Rep 18 sts x 15 rows

Dancing diamonds

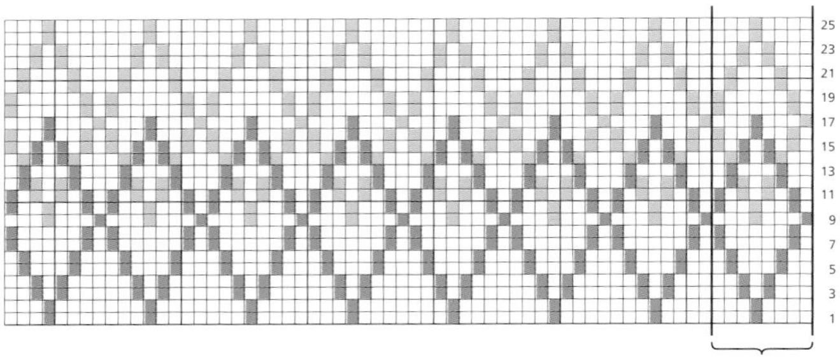

Rep 8 sts x 25 rows

Hellenic wave

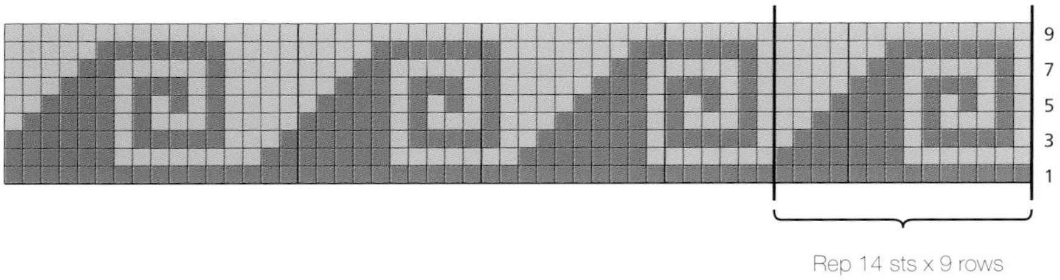

Rep 14 sts x 9 rows

Cairn

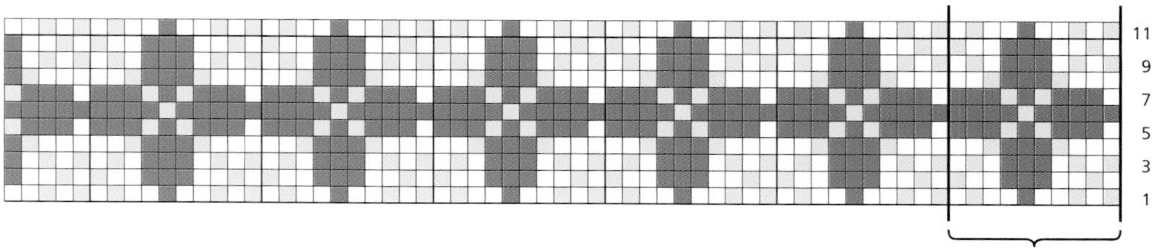

Rep 10 sts x 11 rows

Shield and cross

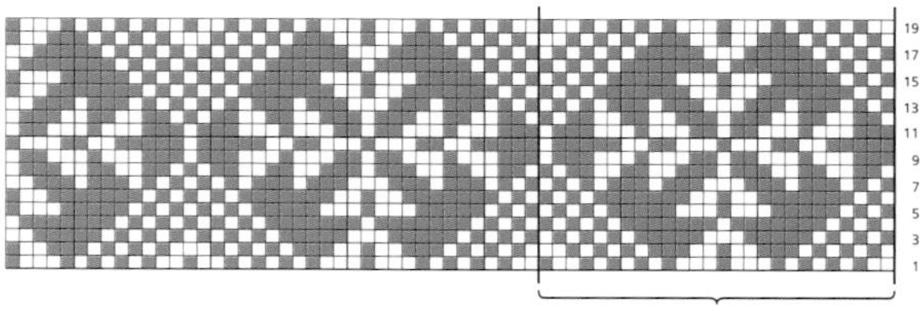

Rep 26 sts x 19 rows

Dianthus and pannier border

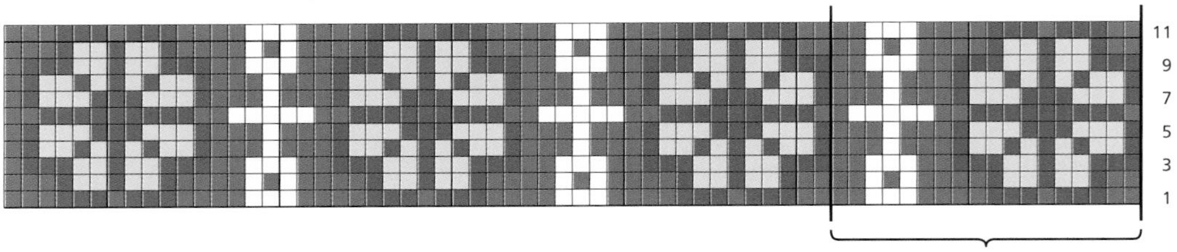

Rep 18 sts x 11 rows

Campion and pannier border

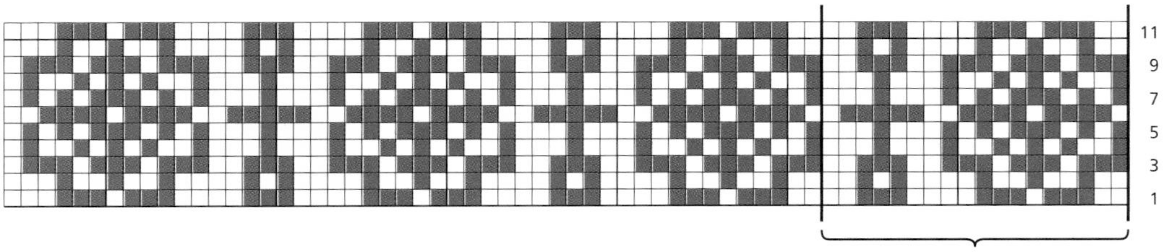

Rep 18 sts x 11 rows

Herbaceous border

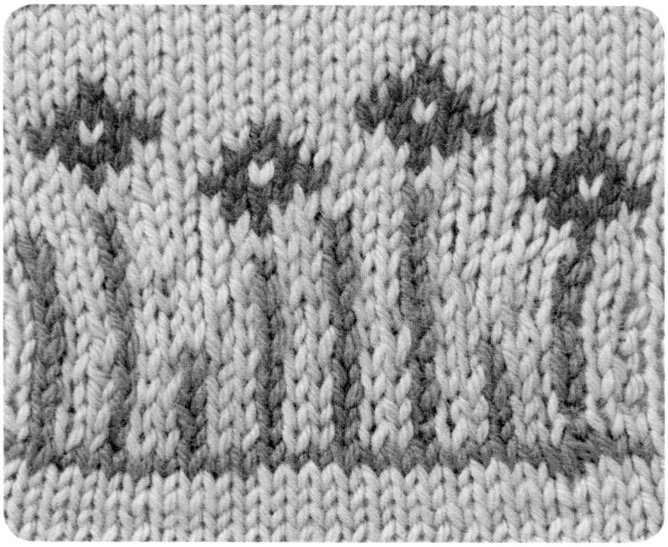

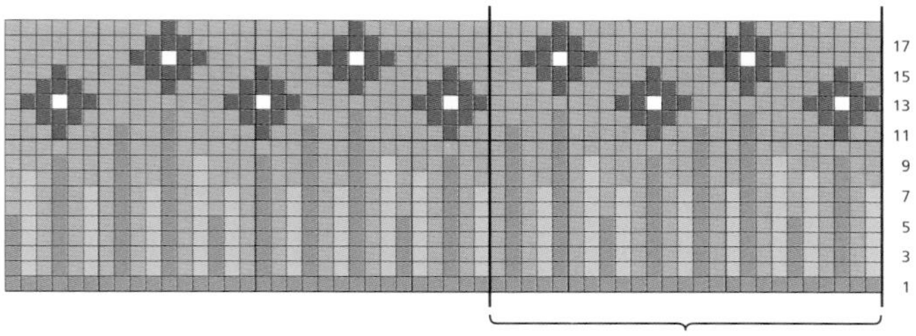

Rep 25 sts x 18 rows

Michaelmas

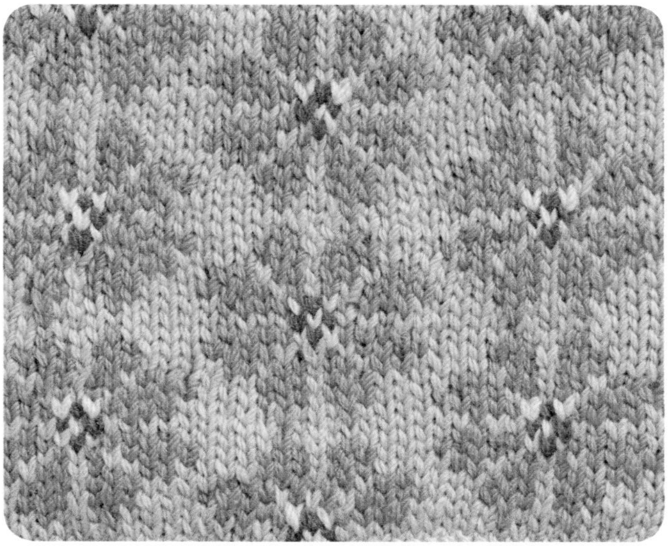

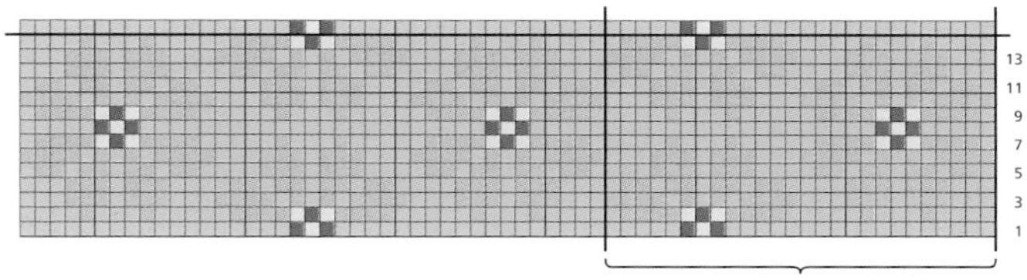

Rep 26 sts x 14 rows

Lads and lasses I

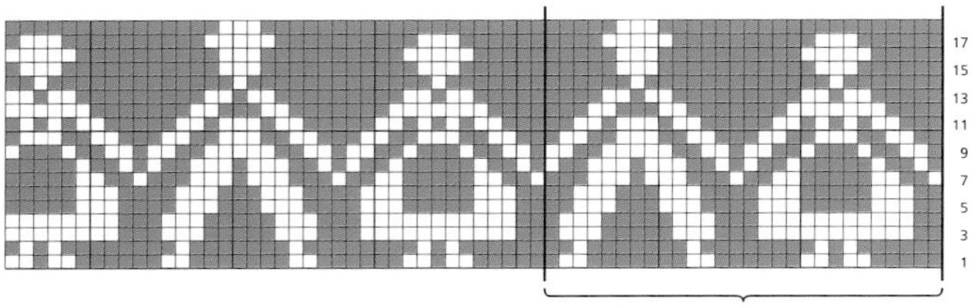

Rep 28 sts x 18 rows

Lads and lasses II

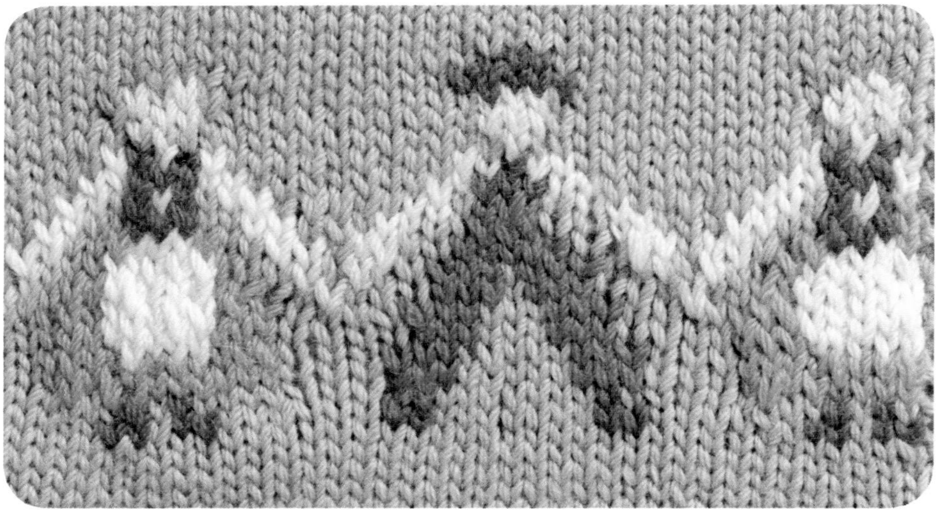

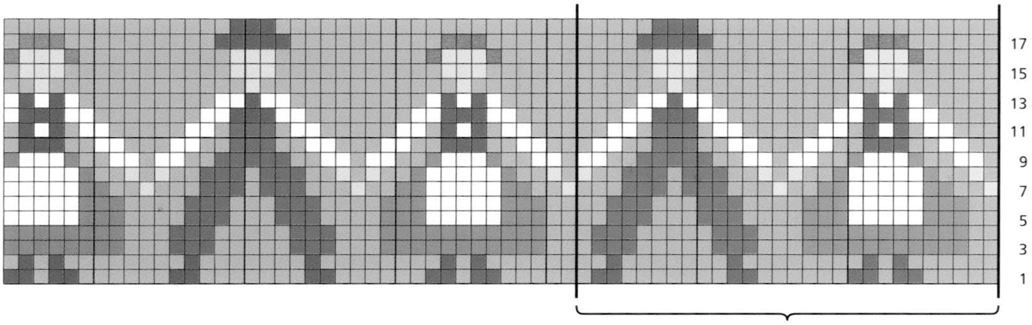

Rep 28 sts x 18 rows

Acrobats

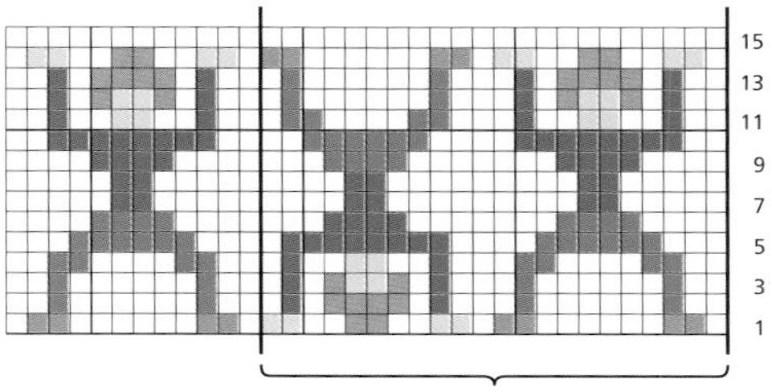

Rep 22 sts x 15 rows

Dancing ballerinas

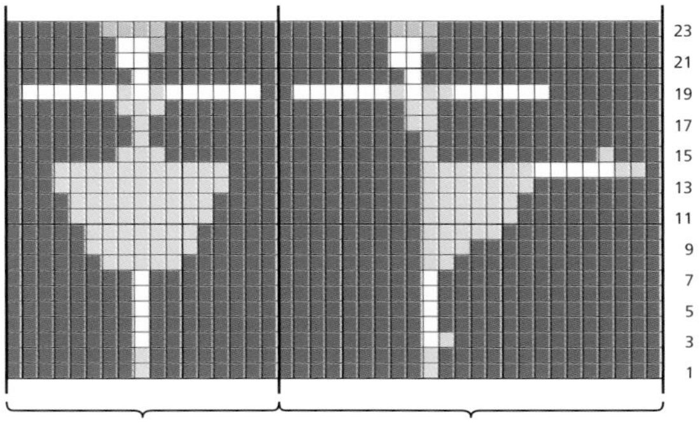

Rep 17 sts + 24 sts x 23 rows

Framed heart motif

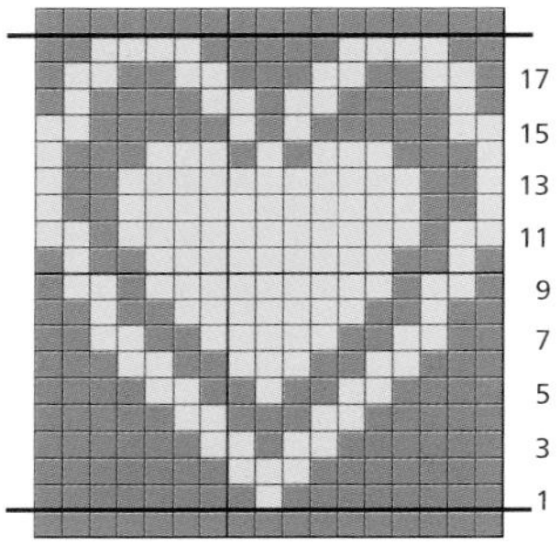

Rep 17 sts x 18 rows

Belladonna

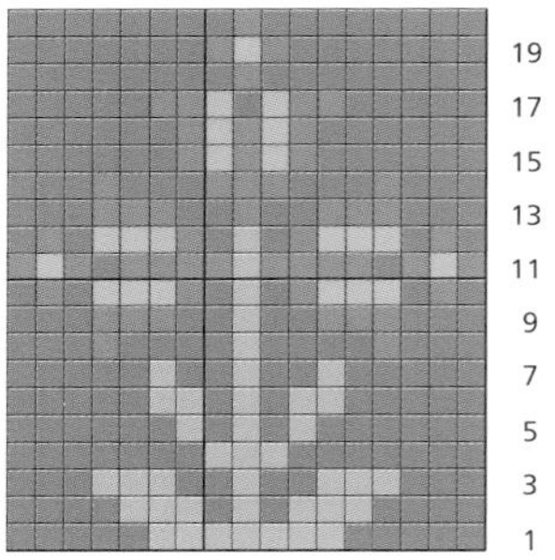

Rep 17 sts x 20 rows

Campion

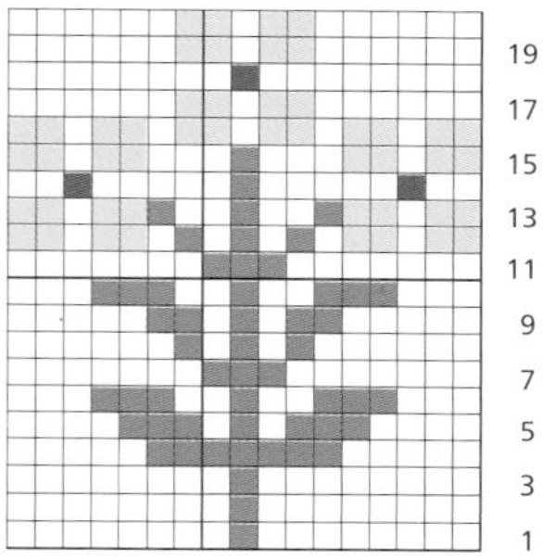

Rep 17 sts x 20 rows

Floret

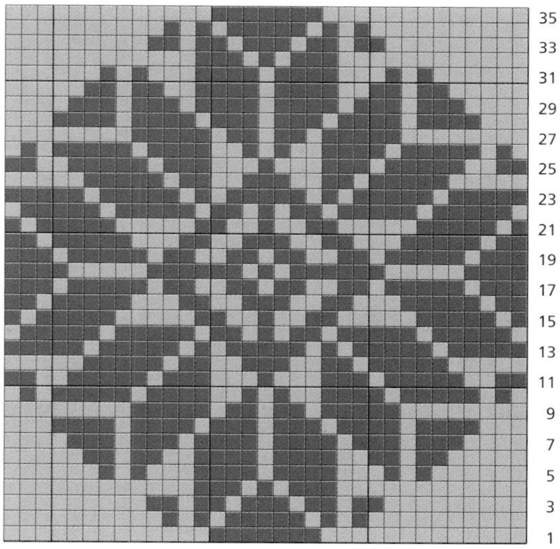

Rep 33 sts x 35 rows

Leaf edging

Worked lengthwise over 8 sts.

Note: Increases are worked purlwise.

Row 1 (RS): K5, yo, k1, yo, k2. (10 sts)

Row 2: P6, inc, k3. (11 sts)

Row 3: K4, p1, k2, yo, k1, yo, k3. (13 sts)

Row 4: P8, inc, k4. (14 sts)

Row 5: K4, p2, k3, yo, k1, yo, k4. (16 sts)

Row 6: P10, inc, k5. (17 sts)

Row 7: K4, p3, k4, yo, k1, yo, k5. (19 sts)

Row 8: P12, inc, k6. (20 sts)

Row 9: K4, p4, skpo, k7, k2tog, k1. (18 sts)

Row 10: P10, inc, k7. (19 sts)

Row 11: K4, p5, skpo, k5, k2tog, k1. (17 sts)

Row 12: P8, inc, k2, p1, k5. (18 sts)

Row 13: K4, p1, k1, p4, skpo, k3, k2tog, k1. (16 sts)

Row 14: P6, inc, k3, p1, k5. (17 sts)

Row 15: K4, p1, k1, p5, skpo, k1, k2tog, k1. (15 sts)

Row 16: P4, inc, k4, p1, k5. (16 sts)

Row 17: K4, p1, k1, p6, sk2po, k1. (14 sts)

Row 18: P2tog, bind off 5 sts purlwise using p2tog as first of these sts, k1, p1, k5. (8 sts)

Rep these 18 rows.

Beaded thumb cast-on

Worked from bottom edge upward.

Starts and ends with multiple of 2 + 1.

Note: Thread beads onto knitting yarn before casting on, 1 bead for each alt st, less 2, to give a selvage st at each end.

Leaving a tail of yarn long enough for the required number of sts to be cast on, make a slip knot in the yarn above the threaded beads and place this on the needle.

Cast on 1 st.

*Slide 1 bead up against the needle before looping the yarn around the thumb to cast on next st.

Cast on 1 st.

Rep from * until 1 less than required number of sts are on left-hand needle.

Cast on 1 st.

This forms the edging.

Cont as required. Usually row 1 will be a WS row to show the beads to best effect.

Layered rib

Worked from bottom edge upward.
Starts and ends with multiple of 2 + 1.
Note: Two colors of yarn are used, A and B. Cast on same number of sts for each layer using the thumb method and A.

Bottom layer

Row 1 (RS): K1, *p1, k1; rep from * to end.
Row 2: P1, *k1, p1; rep from * to end.
Row 3: As row 1.
Change to B.
Rep row 2 and then row 1, 4 times more.
Place sts on spare needle.

Top layer

Row 1 (RS): K1, *p1, k1; rep from * to end.
Change to B.
Row 2: P1, *k1, p1; rep from * to end.
Using B, rep the last 2 rows once more, then row 1 again.
WS facing, hold top layer in front of bottom layer. Using 3rd needle, work together 1 st from each needle across row working p1, *k1, p1; rep from * to end.
Rep the last 2 rows once more.
These rows form the edging.
Bind off or cont as required.

Box pleats

Worked from bottom edge upward.
Starts with multiple of 24.
Ends with multiple of 8.
Note: Cast on using the cable method. Slip all sts purlwise. Slipping the st wyif (with yarn in front) makes a back fold; slipping the st wyib (with yarn in back) makes a front fold.
Row 1 (RS): K4, *wyif sl 1, k3, wyib sl 1, k6, wyib sl 1, k3, wyif sl 1, k8; rep from *, ending k4.
Row 2: Purl.
Rep the last 2 rows 5 times more.
Row 13 (join pleats): *[Slip next 4 sts onto a double-pointed needle] twice, fold fabric on columns of slip sts so that left-hand needle and double-pointed needles are parallel and fold is at the back, [knit together 1 st from each needle] 4 times; rep from *, folding into box pleats.
Rows 14–15: Knit.
These 15 rows form the edging.
Bind off or cont as required.

Bind-off fringe

Worked lengthwise over 3 sts.

Note: Cast on using the cable method.

Rows 1–3: Sl 1, k2.

Row 4 (WS): Cast on 6 sts, bind off 6 sts, k2. (3 sts)

Rep these 4 rows, ending with row 3.

Twist edge

Worked from bottom edge upward.

Starts and ends with multiple of 6.

Note: Cast on using the thumb method.

Work 6 rows in st st, starting with knit.

Row 7 (RS): *K6, take the tip of the left-hand needle under the cast-on edge to the back of the work and around to the working position again; rep from *, ending k6.

These 7 rows form the edging.

Cont as required.

Seed stitch cord

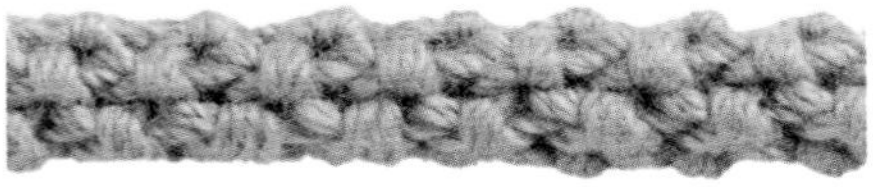

Worked lengthwise over 5 sts on double-pointed needles.

Row 1: K1, *p1, k1; rep from * to end, do not turn, slide sts to other end of needle.

Row 2: P1, *k1, p1; rep from * to end, do not turn, slide sts to other end of needle.

Rep these 2 rows.

Ridged eyelet edge

Worked from bottom edge upward.

Starts and ends with multiple of 2 + 1.

Note: Cast on using the thumb method.

Work 3 rows in garter st.

Row 4 (WS): *P2tog, yo; rep from * to last st, p1.

Work 3 rows in garter st.

These 7 rows form the edging.

Bind off or cont as required.

Picot braid

Worked lengthwise over 5 sts.

Foundation row: Knit.

Row 1 (RS): Cast on 2 sts, bind off 2 sts, k4.

Rep this row.

Trefoil bunting

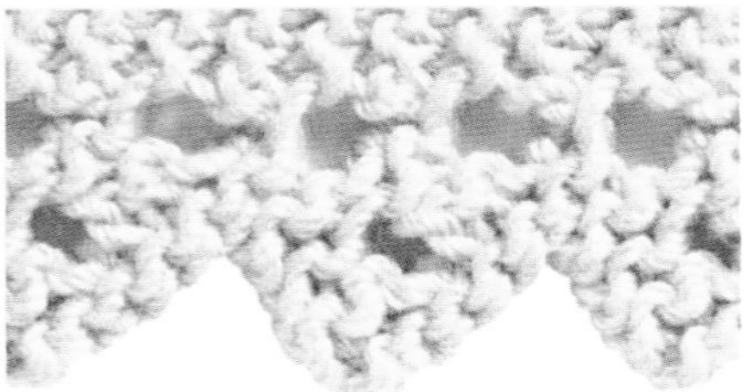

Worked lengthwise over 5 sts.

Row 1 (RS): K3, yo2, k2. (7 sts)

Row 2: K3, p1, k3.

Work 2 rows in garter st.

Row 5: K3, yo2, k2tog, yo2, k2. (10 sts)

Row 6: K3, p1, k2, p1, k3.

Row 7: Knit.

Row 8: Bind off 5 sts, k4. (5 sts)

Rep these 8 rows.

Ladder braid

Worked lengthwise over 11 sts.

Row 1 (RS): Sl 1, k10.

Row 2: Sl 1, k1, p7, k2.

Rep the last 2 rows once more.

Row 5: Sl 1, k1, p7, k2.

Row 6: As row 2.

Row 7: As row 1.

Rep the last 2 rows once more.

Row 10: Sl 1, k10.

Rep these 10 rows.

Butterfly edging

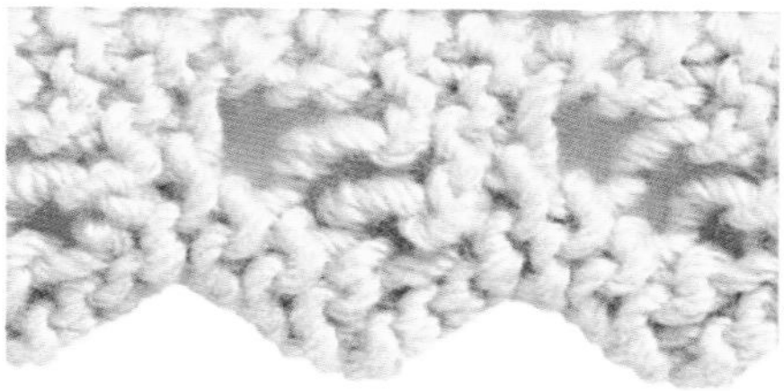

Worked lengthwise over 8 sts.

Row 1 (RS): Sl 1, k2, yo, k2tog yo2, k2tog, k1. (9 sts)

Row 2: K3, p1, k2, yo, k2tog, k1.

Row 3: Sl 1, k2, yo, k2tog, k1, yo2, k2tog, k1. (10 sts)

Row 4: K3, p1, k3, yo, k2tog, k1.

Row 5: Sl 1, k2, yo, k2tog, k2, yo2, k2tog, k1. (11 sts)

Row 6: K3, p1, k4, yo, k2tog, k1.

Row 7: Sl 1, k2, yo, k2tog, k6.

Row 8: Bind off 3 sts, k4, yo, k2tog, k1. (8 sts)

Rep these 8 rows.

Wavy border

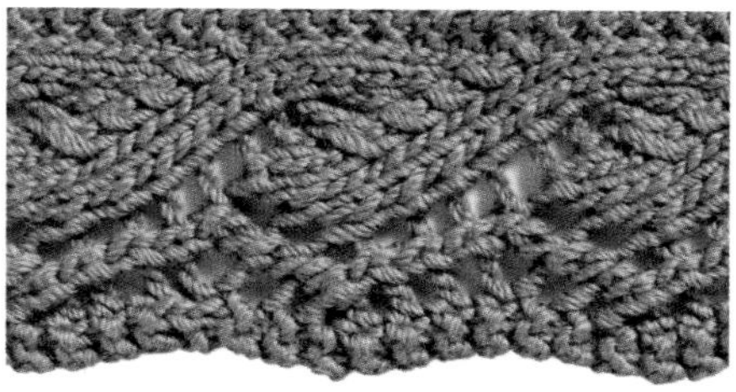

Worked lengthwise over 13 sts.

Row 1 (WS) and every alt row: K2, purl to last 2 sts, k2.

Row 2: K4, yo, k5, yo, k2tog, yo, k2. (15 sts)

Row 4: K5, sk2po, k2, [yo, k2tog] twice, k1. (13 sts)

Row 6: K4, skpo, k2, [yo, k2tog] twice, k1. (12 sts)

Row 8: K3, skpo, k2, [yo, k2tog] twice, k1. (11 sts)

Row 10: K2, skpo, k2, [yo, k2tog] twice, k1. (10 sts)

Row 12: K1, skpo, k2, yo, k1, yo, k2tog, yo, k2. (11 sts)

Row 14: K4, yo, k3, yo, k2tog, yo, k2. (13 sts)

Rep these 14 rows.

Arrow braid

Worked lengthwise over 9 sts.

Triangles

Put a slip knot on the needle.

Row 1 (RS): Inc. (2 sts)

Row 2: Inc, k1. (3 sts)

Row 3: Inc, k2. (4 sts)

Row 4: Inc, k3. (5 sts)

Row 5: Inc, k4. (6 sts)

Row 6: Inc, k5. (7 sts)

Row 7: Inc, k6. (8 sts)

Row 8: Inc, k7. (9 sts)

Cut yarn and leave sts on spare needle. Rep these 8 rows to make as many triangles as required.

Band

Cast on 9 sts.

Rows 1–6: Sl 1, k8.

Row 7 (RS): Slip 9 sts of one triangle onto cable needle, with RS facing hold cable needle in front of needle with band, then knit together 1 st from each needle across row.

Row 8: Sl 1, k8.

Rep these 8 rows, ending with row 6.

Seed and faggot stitch

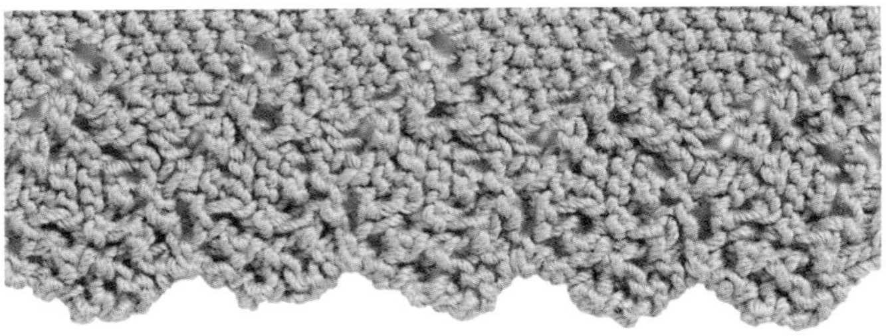

Worked lengthwise over 17 sts.

Row 1 (RS): K2, yo, k3, yo, k2tog, [p1, k1] 5 times. (18 sts)

Row 2: [K1, p1] 4 times, k1, k2tog, yo, k5, yo, k2. (19 sts)

Row 3: K2, yo, k1, k2tog, yo, k1, yo, k2tog, k1, yo, k2tog, [p1, k1] 4 times. (20 sts)

Row 4: [K1, p1] 3 times, k1, [k2tog, yo, k1] twice, k2, yo, k2tog, k1, yo, k2. (21 sts)

Row 5: K2, yo, k1, k2tog, yo, k5, yo, k2tog, k1, yo, k2tog, [p1, k1] 3 times. (22 sts)

Row 6: [K1, p1] twice, k1, [k2tog, yo, k1] twice, k6, yo, k2tog, k1, yo, k2. (23 sts)

Row 7: [K2tog, k1, yo] twice, k2tog, k3, [k2tog, yo, k1] twice, [p1, k1] 3 times. (22 sts)

Row 8: [K1, p1] 4 times, yo, k2tog, k1, yo, k2tog, [k1, k2tog, yo] twice, k1, k2tog. (21 sts)

Row 9: [K2tog, k1, yo] twice, k3tog, yo, k1, k2tog, yo, [k1, p1] 4 times, k1. (20 sts)

Row 10: [K1, p1] 5 times, yo, k2tog, k3, k2tog, yo, k1, k2tog. (19 sts)

Row 11: K2tog, k1, yo, k2tog, k1, k2tog, yo, [k1, p1] 5 times, k1. (18 sts)

Row 12: [K1, p1] 6 times, yo, k3tog, yo, k1, k2tog. (17 sts)

Rep these 12 rows.

Lace and bobble

Worked from bottom edge upward.

Starts and ends with multiple of 10 + 1.

Note: Cast on using the thumb method.

Special abbreviation:

MB (make bobble) = (P1, k1, p1) in next st, turn, k1, p1, k1, turn, p1, k1, p1, pass 2nd and 3rd sts over first st.

Row 1 (WS): *P5, MB, p4; rep from *, ending last rep p5.

Row 2: K1, *yo, k3, sk2po, k3, yo, k1; rep from * to end.

Row 3: Purl.

Row 4: P1, *k1, yo, k2, sk2po, k2, yo, k1, p1; rep from * to end.

Row 5: *K1, p9; rep from *, ending last rep k1.

Row 6: P1, *k2, yo, k1, sk2po, k1, yo, k2, p1; rep from * to end.

Row 7: As row 5.

Row 8: P1, *k3, yo, sk2po, yo, k3, p1; rep from * to end.

Row 9: Purl.

Row 10: K1, *k3, yo, sk2po, yo, k4; rep from * to end.

Row 11: Purl.

Rep the last 2 rows once more.

These 13 rows form the edging.

Bind off or cont as required.

Snail shell lace

Worked lengthwise over 19 sts.

Foundation row: Knit.

Row 1 (WS): K5, p1, yo, p2tog, k8, yo, k2tog, k1.

Row 2: K3, yo, k2tog, k5, k2tog, yo, k1, yo, ssk, k2, yo2, k2. (21 sts)

Row 3: K3, p1, k1, p2tog tbl, yo, p3, yo, p2tog, k6, yo, k2tog, k1.

Row 4: K3, yo, k2tog, k3, k2tog, yo, k2, k2tog, yo, k1, yo, ssk, k2, yo2, k2. (23 sts)

Row 5: K3, p1, k1, p2tog tbl, yo, p3, yo, p2tog, p2, yo, p2tog, k4, yo, k2tog, k1.

Row 6: K3, yo, k2tog, k1, [k2tog, yo, k2] twice, yo, ssk, k1, yo, ssk, k2, yo2, k2. (25 sts)

Row 7: K3, p1, k1, [p2tog tbl, yo, p1] twice, yo, p2tog, p1, yo, p2tog, p2, yo, p2tog, k2, yo, k2tog, k1.

Row 8: K3, yo, k3tog, yo, k2, k2tog, yo, k1, k2tog, yo, k3, yo, ssk, k1, yo, ssk, k2tog, yo2, k2tog.

Row 9: K2, p1, k1, p2, yo, p2tog, p1, yo, p3tog, yo, p1, p2tog tbl, yo, p2, p2tog tbl, yo, k3, yo, k2tog, k1.

Row 10: K3, yo, k2tog, [k2, yo, ssk] twice, k3, k2tog, yo, k2, sk2po, yo2, k2tog. (24 sts)

Row 11: K2, p5, yo, p2tog, p1, p2tog tbl, yo, p2, p2tog tbl, yo, k5, yo, k2tog, k1.

Row 12: K3, yo, k2tog, k4, yo, ssk, k2, yo, k3tog, yo, k2, k3tog, yo, k2tog, k1. (22 sts)

Row 13: K3, p1, k3, yo, p2tog, p1, p2tog tbl, yo, k7, yo, k2tog, k1.

Row 14: K3, yo, k2tog, k6, yo, k3tog, yo, k2, k3tog, yo, k3tog. (19 sts)

Rep rows 1–14.

Fern lace edging

Worked lengthwise over 14 sts.

Row 1 (RS): Sl 1, k2, [yo, k2tog] twice, k1, yo2, [k2tog] twice, yo, k2. (15 sts)

Row 2: K5, [k1, p1] twice in yo2, k8. (17 sts)

Row 3: Sl 1, k3, [yo, k2tog] twice, k5, k2tog, yo, k2.

Row 4 and rem alt rows: Knit.

Row 5: Sl 1, k4, [yo, k2tog] twice, k4, k2tog, yo, k2.

Row 7: Sl 1, k5, [yo, k2tog] twice, k3, k2tog, yo, k2.

Row 9: Sl 1, k6, [yo, k2tog] twice, k2, k2tog, yo, k2.

Row 11: Sl 1, k7, [yo, k2tog] twice, k1, k2tog, yo, k2.

Row 13: Sl 1, k8, [yo, k2tog] twice, k2tog, yo, k2.

Row 15: Sl 1, k9, [yo, k2tog] twice, k1, yo, k2. (18 sts)

Row 17: Sl 1, k10, yo, [k2tog] twice, slip last st back onto left-hand needle, lift next 3 sts one at a time over it, then return st to right-hand needle. (14 sts)

Row 18: Knit.

Rep these 18 rows, ending with row 17.

Accordion pleat

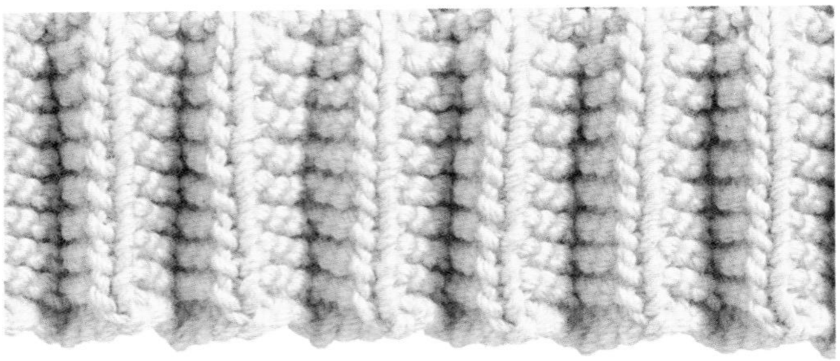

Worked from bottom edge upward.

Starts with twice the number of sts needed that is a multiple of 8.

Ends with multiple of 8.

Note: Cast on using the thumb method.

Row 1 (RS): *K7, p1; rep from * to end.

Row 2: K4, *p1, k7; rep from * to last 4 sts, p1, k3.

Rep the last 2 rows as required, ending with row 2.

Next row: [K2tog] to end.

These rows form the edging.

Bind off or cont as required.

Thick and thin rib

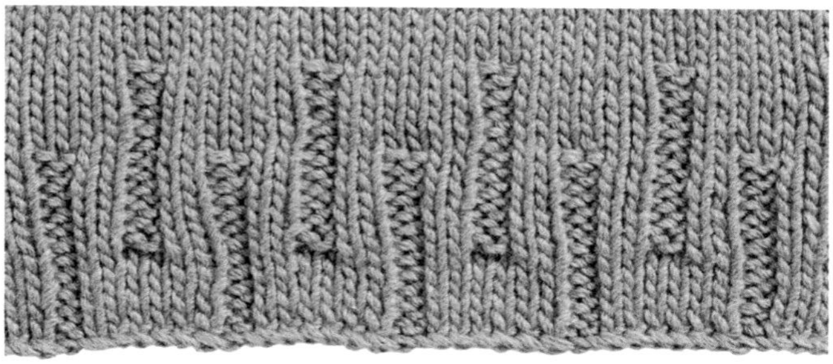

Worked from bottom edge upward.

Starts and ends with multiple of 8 + 6.

Note: Cast on using the thumb method.

Row 1 (RS): K6, *p2, k6; rep from * to end.

Row 2: P6, *k2, p6; rep from * to end.

Rep the last 2 rows twice more.

Row 7: K2, *p2, k2; rep from * to end.

Row 8: P2, *k2, p2; rep from * to end.

Rep the last 2 rows twice more.

Row 13: K2, p2, *k6, p2; rep from * to last 2 sts, k2.

Row 14: P2, k2, *p6, k2; rep from * to last 2 sts, p2.

Rep the last 2 rows twice more.

These 18 rows form the edging.

Bind off or cont as required.

Scallop lace edging

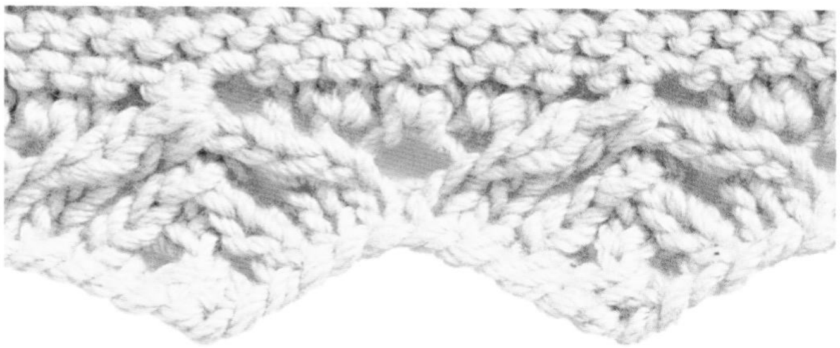

Worked from bottom edge upward.

Starts with multiple of 13 + 2.

Ends with multiple of 10 + 3.

Note: Cast on using the thumb method.

Row 1 (RS): K3, *skpo, sl 2, k3tog, p2sso, k2tog, k4; rep from * to last 12 sts, skpo, sl 2, k3tog, p2sso, k2tog, k3.

Row 2: P4, *yo, p1, yo, p6; rep from * to last 5 sts, yo, p1, yo, p4.

Row 3: K1, yo, *k2, skpo, k1, k2tog, k2, yo; rep from * to last st, k1.

Row 4: P2, *yo, p2, yo, p3, yo, p2, yo, p1; rep from * to last st, p1.

Row 5: K2, yo, k1, *yo, skpo, k1, sk2po, k1, k2tog, [yo, k1] 3 times; rep from * to last 12 sts, yo, skpo, k1, sk2po, k1, k2tog, yo, k1, yo, k2.

Row 6: Purl.

Row 7: K5, *yo, sl 2, k3tog, p2sso, yo, k7; rep from * to last 10 sts, yo, sl 2, k3tog, p2sso, yo, k5.

Work 4 rows in garter st.

These 11 rows form the edging.

Bind off or cont as required.

Loop flower appliqué

Note: Two colors of yarn are used, A and B.

With A, cast on 27 sts.

Row 1 (RS): ML in every st.

Row 2: K2tog to last st, k1. (14 sts)

Change to B.

Row 3: ML in first 5 sts, k2tog to last st, k1. (10 sts)

Row 4: [K2tog] twice, *pass first st over 2nd st, k2tog; rep from * twice more, pass first st over 2nd st, fasten off.

Coil up with B loops in center, loops facing inward.

Sew coil together around base.

Perforated rib

Worked from bottom edge upward.

Starts and ends with multiple of 4 + 1.

Note: Cast on using the thumb method.

Row 1 (RS): K1, *p3, k1; rep from * to end.

Row 2: P1, *k3, p1; rep from * to end.

Rep the last 2 rows once more.

Row 5: K1, *p2tog, yo, p1, k1; rep from * to end.

Row 6: As row 2.

Rep rows 1–6 once more, then rows 1–4 once more.

These 16 rows form the edging.

Bind off or cont as required.

Horizontal rib

Worked from bottom edge upward.

Worked over any odd number of sts for required depth of rib.

Note: 1 st can be picked up from each row end of the rib band for a fuller fabric. If a flatter fabric is required, skip every row 4 end when picking up. Stitch counts will need to be calculated accordingly.

Row 1 (RS): K1, *p1, k1; rep from * to end.

Row 2: P1, *k1, p1; rep from * to end.

Rep these 2 rows until rib band is required length and then bind off.

Pick up sts (see note above) along one side edge and cont as required.

Leaf and fringe

Worked lengthwise over 13 sts.

Foundation row: [K5, p1] twice, k1.

Row 1 (RS): P1, KB1, p2, ([k1, KB1, yo] twice, k1, KB1) in next st, p2, KB1, k5. (20 sts)

Row 2: K5, PB1, k2, p8, k2, PB1, k1.

Row 3: P1, KB1, p2, k6, k2tog, p2, KB1, k5. (19 sts)

Row 4: K5, PB1, k2, p7, k2, PB1, k1.

Row 5: P1, KB1, p2, k5, k2tog, p2, KB1, k5. (18 sts)

Row 6: K5, PB1, k2, p6, k2, PB1, k1.

Row 7: P1, KB1, p2, k4, k2tog, p2, KB1, k5. (17 sts)

Row 8: K5, PB1, k2, p5, k2, PB1, k1.

Row 9: P1, KB1, p2, k3, k2tog, p2, KB1, k5. (16 sts)

Row 10: K5, PB1, k2, p4, k2, PB1, k1.

Row 11: P1, KB1, p2, k2, k2tog, p2, KB1, k5. (15 sts)

Row 12: K5, PB1, k2, p3, k2, PB1, k1.

Row 13: P1, KB1, p2, k1, k2tog, p2, KB1, k5. (14 sts)

Row 14: K5, PB1, k2, p2, k2, PB1, k1.

Row 15: P1, KB1, p2, k2tog, p2, KB1, k5. (13 sts)

Row 16: K5, PB1, k2, p1, k2, PB1, k1.

Rep rows 1–16 as required, ending with row 16.

Next row: K5, bind off rem sts.

Slip 5 sts off needle and unravel across knitted fabric to create fringe. Loops can be cut to make strands.

Leafy trim

Worked lengthwise over 13 sts.

Row 1 (RS): Sl 1, k2, p2, [k1, yo] twice, k1, p2, k3. (15 sts)

Row 2: Sl 1, k4, p5, k5.

Row 3: Sl 1, k2, p2, k2, yo, k1, yo, k2, p2, k3. (17 sts)

Row 4: Sl 1, k4, p7, k5.

Row 5: Sl 1, k2, p2, k3, yo, k1, yo, k3, p2, k3. (19 sts)

Row 6: Sl 1, k4, p9, k5.

Row 7: Sl 1, k2, p2, k4, yo, k1, yo, k4, p2, k3. (21 sts)

Row 8: Sl 1, k4, p11, k5.

Row 9: Sl 1, k2, p2, k11, p2, k3.

Row 10: As row 8.

Row 11: Sl 1, k2, p2, skpo, k7, k2tog, p2, k3. (19 sts)

Row 12: As row 6.

Row 13: Sl 1, k2, p2, skpo, k5, k2tog, p2, k3. (17 sts)

Row 14: As row 4.

Row 15: Sl 1, k2, p2, skpo, k3, k2tog, p2, k3. (15 sts)

Row 16: As row 2.

Row 17: Sl 1, k2, p2, skpo, k1, k2tog, p2, k3. (13 sts)

Row 18: Sl 1, k4, p3, k5.

Row 19: Sl 1, k2, p2, M1P, sk2po, M1P, p2, k3.

Row 20: Sl 1, k5, p1, k6.

Rep these 20 rows.

Willow edging

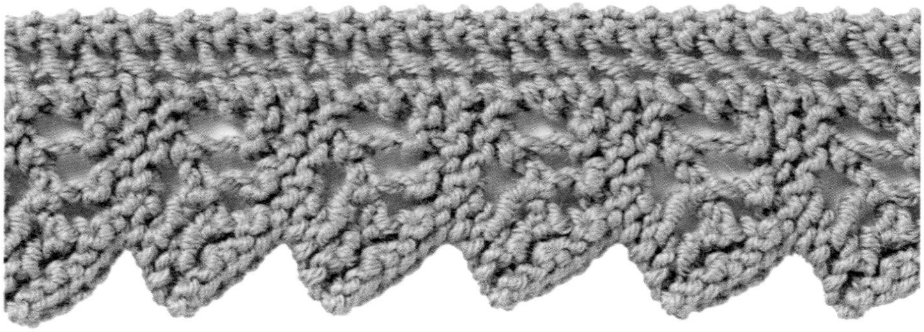

Worked lengthwise over 10 sts.

Row 1 (RS): Sl 1, k2, yo, k2tog, *yo2, k2tog; rep from * once more, k1. (12 sts)

Row 2: K3, [p1, k2] twice, yo, k2tog, k1.

Row 3: Sl 1, k2, yo, k2tog, k2, *yo2, k2tog; rep from * once more, k1. (14 sts)

Row 4: K3, p1, k2, p1, k4, yo, k2tog, k1.

Row 5: Sl 1, k2, yo, k2tog, k4, *yo2, k2tog; rep from * once more, k1. (16 sts)

Row 6: K3, p1, k2, p1, k6, yo, k2tog, k1.

Row 7: Sl 1, k2, yo, k2tog, k11.

Row 8: Bind off 6 sts, k6, yo, k2tog, k1. (10 sts)

Rep these 8 rows.

Scalloped ruffle

Worked from bottom edge upward.

Starts with multiple of 11 + 2.

Ends with multiple of 2.

Note: Cast on using the thumb method.

Row 1 (WS): Purl.

Row 2: K2, *k1, slip st back onto left-hand needle, with right-hand needle lift next 8 sts one at a time over this st and off needle, yo2, knit first st again, k2; rep from * to end.

Row 3: K1, *p2tog, drop first loop of yo2, [k1, p1] twice in second loop, p1; rep from *, ending k1.

Row 4: *K4, yo, k2tog; rep from * to last 2 sts, k2.

Row 5: Purl.

Rep the last 2 rows twice more.

Row 10: K2, *k2tog, k1; rep from * to end.

Work 3 rows in garter st.

These 13 rows form the edging.

Bind off or cont as required.

Buttoned tags

Worked from bottom edge upward.

Starts and ends with multiple of 7.

Note: Cast on using the thumb method. Each tag is worked separately and then joined on one row. Tags can be same length or, as here, different lengths.

Cast on 7 sts.

Row 1 (RS): K1, [p1, k1] three times.

Rep the last row 6 times more.

Row 8: K1, p1, k1, yo, k2tog, p1, k1.

Rep row 1 as required, ending with WS row. These rows form one tag. Cut yarn and leave finished tag on needle. On the same needle, cast on 7 sts and work 2nd tag.

Cont in this way until there are as many tags as required.

Join tags

Do not cut yarn after completing the last tag.

Next row (RS): K1, [p1, k1] three times, *cast on 3 sts, k1, [p1, k1] three times across next tag; rep from * until all tags are joined.

Next row: K1, *p1, k1; rep from * to end.

Rep the last row 5 times more.

These rows form the edging.

Bind off or cont as required.

Sew buttons to fabric above tags and slip eyelets over buttons.

Lace cable

Worked from bottom edge upward.

Starts and ends with multiple of 11 + 7.

Note: Cast on using the thumb method.

Row 1 (WS) and every alt row: Purl.

Row 2: K1, *yo, ssk, k1, k2tog, yo, k6; rep from *, ending last rep k1.

Row 4: K2, *yo, sk2po, yo, k1, C6B, k1; rep from *, ending yo, sk2po, yo, k2.

Row 6: As row 2.

Row 8: K2, *yo, sk2po, yo, k8; rep from *, ending last rep k2.

Rep the last 8 rows once more.

Row 17: Purl.

These 17 rows form the edging.

Bind off or cont as required.

Smocked rib

Worked from bottom edge upward.

Starts and ends with multiple of 6 + 3.

Special abbreviation:

S3 (smock 3) = Yb, slip next 3 sts purlwise, yf, slip same 3 sts back onto left-hand needle, yb, slip same 3 sts back onto right-hand needle.

Note: Cast on using the thumb method.

Rows 1 (RS) and 3: P3, *k3, p3; rep from * to end.

Rows 2 and 4: K3, *p3, k3; rep from * to end.

Row 5: P3, *S3, p3; rep from * to end.

Row 6: K3, *p3, k3; rep from * to end.

Rep the last 6 rows once more.

These 12 rows form the edging.

Bind off or cont as required.

Double diamond edging

Worked lengthwise over 9 sts.

Row 1 (RS) and every alt row: Knit.

Row 2: K3, k2tog, yo, k2tog, [yo, k1] twice. (10 sts)

Row 4: K2, [k2tog, yo] twice, k3, yo, k1. (11 sts)

Row 6: K1, [k2tog, yo] twice, k5, yo, k1. (12 sts)

Row 8: K3, [yo, k2tog] twice, k1, k2tog, yo, k2tog. (11 sts)

Row 10: K4, yo, k2tog, yo, k3tog, yo, k2tog. (10 sts)

Row 12: K5, yo, k3tog, yo, k2tog. (9 sts)

Rep these 12 rows.

Hunter's rib

Worked from bottom edge upward.

Starts and ends with multiple of 11 + 4.

Note: Cast on using the thumb method.

Row 1 (RS): P4, *[KB1, p1] 3 times, KB1, p4; rep from * to end.

Row 2: K4, *p1, [KB1, p1] 3 times, k4; rep from * to end.

Rep the last 2 rows 4 times more.

These 10 rows form the edging.

Bind off or cont as required.

Tip

You can use a knitted edging or trim as a means to experiment with color in a design. Keep in mind that your edging does not need to be the same color as the main knitted piece—you could use a contrasting or a complementary color. Other decorative elements, such as beads and tassels, can also be added in either contrasting or complementary colors. Also remember that knitted trims can be added to other types of fabric, such as woven material. Attach the knitted trim with a sharp sewing needle and matching sewing thread.

Points and bobbles

Worked lengthwise over 6 sts.
Special abbreviation:
MB (make bobble) = (K1, p1, k1, p1, k1) in next st, [turn, sl 1, k4] 4 times, turn, lift 2nd, 3rd, 4th, and 5th sts one at a time over first st.
Row 1 (RS): K3, yo, k3. (7 sts)
Row 2 and every alt row to 10: Knit.
Row 3: K3, yo, k4. (8 sts)
Row 5: K3, yo, k5. (9 sts)
Row 7: K3, yo, k6. (10 sts)
Row 9: K3, yo, k7. (11 sts)
Row 11: K3, yo, k7, MB. (12 sts)
Row 12: Bind off 6 sts, knit to end. (6 sts)
Rep these 12 rows.

Tassel fringe

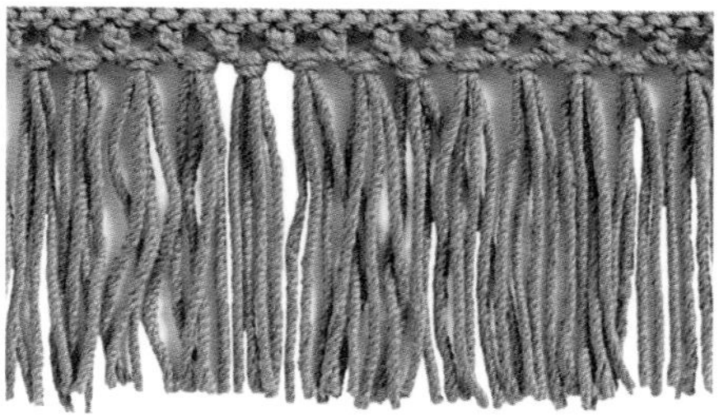

Worked lengthwise over any odd number of sts.
Row 1 (RS): *K2tog, yo; rep from * to last st, k1.
Work 2 rows in garter st.
Bind off or cont as required.

Tassels

Cut two 4 in. (10 cm) lengths of yarn for each eyelet. Fold two strands in half together. WS facing, put a crochet hook through an eyelet and pull the folded loop of the strands through. Slip the cut ends through the loop and pull taut. When all the tassels have been added, trim the ends of the strands.

Scalloped eyelet edging

Worked lengthwise over 11 sts.
Row 1 (RS): Sl 1, k2, yo, p2tog, yo, skpo, [yo, skpo] twice.
Row 2: Yo, *p1, (k1, p1) in next st; rep from * twice more, p2, yo, p2tog, KB1. (15 sts)
Row 3: Sl 1, k2, yo, p2tog, k10.
Row 4: Sl 1, p11, yo, p2tog, KB1.
Row 5: Sl 1, k2, yo, p2tog, k10.
Row 6: Bind off 4 sts purlwise, p7, yo, p2tog, KB1. (11 sts)
Rep these 6 rows.

Diagonal rib and scallop

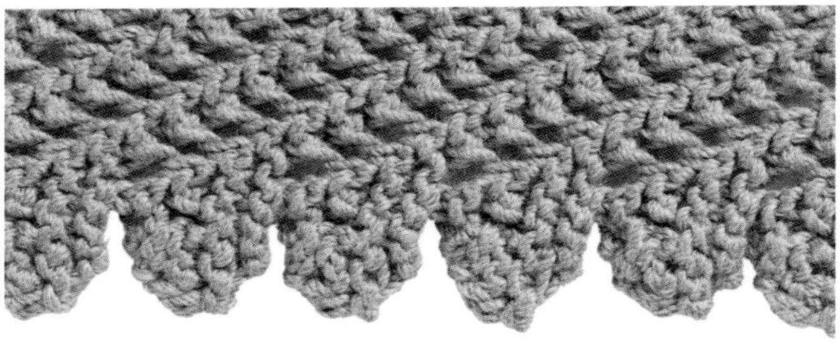

Worked lengthwise over 8 sts.

Foundation row 1 (RS): K6, inc, wyif sl 1 purlwise. (9 sts)

Foundation row 2: KB1, k1, [yo, skpo, k1] twice, wyif sl 1 purlwise. (9 sts)

Row 1: KB1, knit to last st, inc, turn and cast on 2 sts. (12 sts)

Row 2: K1, inc, k2, [yo, skpo, k1] twice, yo, k1, wyif sl 1 purlwise. (14 sts)

Row 3: KB1, knit to last 2 sts, inc, wyif sl 1 purlwise. (15 sts)

Row 4: KB1, inc, k2, [yo, skpo, k1] 3 times, k1, wyif sl 1 purlwise. (16 sts)

Row 5: KB1, knit to last 2 sts, k2tog. (15 sts)

Row 6: Sl 1 purlwise, k1, psso, skpo, k4, [yo, skpo, k1] twice, wyif sl 1 purlwise. (13 sts)

Row 7: KB1, knit to last 2 sts, k2tog. (12 sts)

Row 8: Bind off 3 sts, k2, yo, skpo, k1, yo, skpo, wyif sl 1 purlwise. (9 sts)

Rep these 8 rows.

Ribbed tags

Worked from bottom edge upward.

Starts and ends with multiple of 9.

Note: Cast on using the thumb method. Each tag is worked separately and then joined on one row.

Cast on 9 sts.

Row 1 (RS): Knit.

Row 2: K1, purl to last st, k1.

Rep row 2 twice more.

Rows 5–6: Knit.

Rep rows 1–5 once more.

Rows 1–11 form one tag. Cut yarn and leave finished tag on needle. On the free needle, cast on 9 sts and work 2nd tag. Cont in this way until there are as many tags as required.

Join tags

Do not cut yarn after completing the last tag, but turn and knit across all tags on needle.

Rep rows 1– 6 once more.

These 18 rows form the edging.

Bind off or cont as required.

Lace ruffle

Worked from bottom edge upward.
Starts with twice the number of sts needed that is a multiple of 4 + 2.
Ends with multiple of 2 + 1.
Note: Cast on using the thumb method.
Row 1 (WS): Knit.
Row 2: K1, *skpo, yo2, k2tog; rep from *, ending k1.
Row 3: P1, *p1, (p1, k1) in yo2, p1; rep from *, ending p1.
Rep the last 2 rows 6 times more.
Row 10: [K2tog] to end.
Row 11: Purl.
Row 12: K1, *yo, k2tog; rep from * to end.
Work 3 rows in st st.
These 15 rows form the edging.
Bind off or cont as required.

Big lace check

Worked from bottom edge upward.
Starts and ends with multiple of 18 + 9.
Note: Cast on using the thumb method.
Rows 1 (WS) and 3: Purl.
Row 2: K1, *[yo, k2tog] 4 times, k10; rep from * to last 8 sts, [yo, k2tog] 4 times.
Row 4: *[Skpo, yo] 4 times, k10; rep from * to last 9 sts, [skpo, yo] 4 times, k1.
Rep the last 4 rows twice more.
Rows 13 and 15: Purl.
Row 14: *K10, [yo, k2tog] 4 times; rep from * to last 9 sts, k9.
Row 16: K9 *[skpo, yo] 4 times, k10; rep from * to end.
Rep the last 4 rows twice more.
These 24 rows form the edging.
Bind off or cont as required.

Heart appliqué

Cast on 2 sts.

Row 1 (RS): Inc, k1. (3 sts)

Row 2 and every alt row to 16: Purl.

Row 3: K1, [M1, k1] twice. (5 sts)

Row 5: K2, M1, k1, M1, k2. (7 sts)

Row 7: K3, M1, k1, M1, k3. (9 sts)

Row 9: K4, M1, k1, M1, k4. (11 sts)

Row 11: K5, M1, k1, M1, k5. (13 sts)

Row 13: K 6, knit in back loop of st one row below next st, then knit in next st, k6. (14 sts)

Row 15: Ssk, k3, k2tog, turn.

Cont on these 5 sts only and leave rem sts on a stitch holder.

Row 17: Ssk, k1, k2tog. (3 sts)

Row 18: P3tog tbl.

Fasten off.

Next row (RS): Rejoin yarn to inner end of rem sts, ssk, k3, k2tog. (5 sts)

Next row: Purl.

Next row: Ssk, k1, k2tog. (3 sts)

Next row: P3tog.

Fasten off.

Eyelet rib

Worked from bottom edge upward.

Starts and ends with multiple of 8 + 2.

Note: Cast on using the thumb method.

Row 1: *P2, k2; rep from *, ending p2.

Row 2: K2, p2, *yo, k2tog, p2; rep from *, ending k2.

Rep the last 2 rows 3 times more.

Row 9: P2, *k6, p2; rep from * to end.

Row 10: K2, p6, *yo, k2tog, p6; rep from *, ending k2.

Rep the last 2 rows once more, then row 9 again.

These 13 rows form the edging.

Bind off or cont as required.

Tiny bobble braid

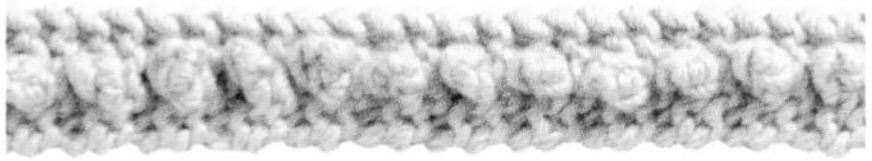

Worked lengthwise over 5 sts.

Special abbreviation:

MB (make bobble) = (K1, p1, k1, p1, k1) in next st, lift 2nd, 3rd, 4th, and 5th sts one at a time over first st.

Rows 1–2: Sl 1, k4.

Row 3 (RS): Sl 1, k1, MB, k2.

Row 4: Sl 1, k4.

Rep these 4 rows, ending with row 2.

Casing and drawstring

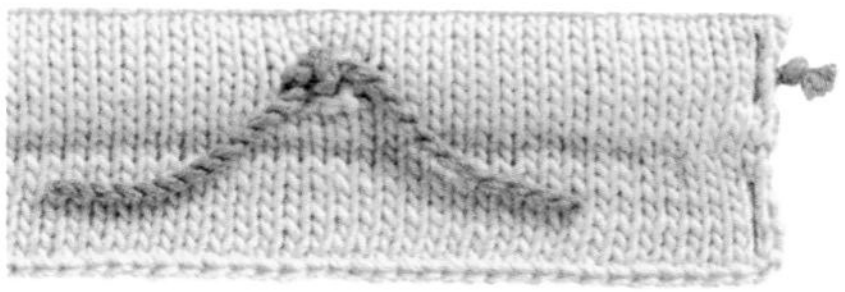

Worked from bottom edge upward or top edge downward.
Starts and ends with multiple of 2 + 1.
Work 7 rows in st st, starting with knit.
Row 8 (WS): Knit.
Work 3 rows in st st, starting with knit.
Row 12 (drawstring opening): Purl to center 3 sts, bind off 3 sts, purl to end.
Row 13: Knit to bound off sts, cast on 3 sts, knit to end.
Work 3 rows in st st, starting with purl.
Fold hem over at ridge row (row 8).
Row 17: *Slip horizontal strand from first cast-on st onto left-hand needle, then knit this strand tog with first st on needle; rep from * to end.
Cont as required.

Cord

Make a twisted cord, a braided cord, or a three-stitch I-cord of required length.
Thread cord through casing.

Double pintuck

Worked from bottom edge upward.
Starts and ends with multiple of 2 + 1.
Note: Two colors of yarn are used, A and B, but the pintuck can be worked in one color if preferred.
Using A, work 12 rows in st st, starting with knit.
Row 13 (RS): *Lift horizontal strand from cast-on edge below st on needle and place on left-hand needle, then knit this strand tog with st on needle; rep from * to end.
Work 7 rows in st st, starting with purl.
Change to B and work 12 rows in st st, starting with knit.
Row 33 (RS): *Lift stitch loop from 12 rows below st on needle and place on left-hand needle, then knit this loop tog with st on needle; rep from * to end.
These 33 rows form the edging.
Bind off or cont as required.

Tic-tac-toe trim

Worked lengthwise over 16 sts.
Row 1 (RS): Sl 1, k15.
Row 2: Sl 1, k1, p12, k2.
Rep the last 2 rows once more.
Row 5: Sl 1, k1, C6B, C6F, k2.
Row 6: Sl 1, k1, p12, k2.
Rep the last 6 rows once more.
Row 13: Sl 1, k15.
Row 14: Sl 1, k1, p12, k2.
Rep the last 2 rows once more.
Row 17: Sl 1, k1, C6F, C6B, k2.
Row 18: Sl 1, k1, p12, k2.
Rep the last 6 rows once more.
Rep these 24 rows.

Lace picot

Worked from bottom edge upward.

Starts and ends with multiple of 8 + 1.

Note: Cast on using the thumb method.

Work 3 rows in st st, starting with knit.

Row 4 (WS): P1, *yo, p2tog; rep from * to end.

Work 4 rows in st st.

Row 9: K2 *yo, k2tog; rep from *, ending k1.

Work 3 rows in st st.

Row 13: K1, *yo, ssk, k3, k2tog, yo, k1; rep from * to end.

Row 14: P2, yo, p2tog, k1, p2tog tbl, yo, *p3, yo, p2tog, p1, p2tog tbl, yo; rep from *, ending p2.

Row 15: K2, *k1, yo, k3tog, yo, k4; rep from *, ending last rep k3.

Row 16: P2, p2tog tbl, yo, p1, yo, p2tog, *p3, p2tog tbl, yo, p1, yo, p2tog; rep from *, ending p2.

Row 17: K1, k2tog, *yo, k3, yo, ssk, k1, k2tog; rep from *, ending last rep yo, k3, yo, ssk, k1.

Row 18: P2tog tbl, yo, p5, *yo, p3tog, yo, p5; rep from *, ending yo, p2tog.

Work 2 rows in st st.

Row 21: As row 9.

Work 3 rows in st st.

Fold hem to back along row 4 and slip stitch in place.

These 24 rows form the edging.

Bind off or cont as required.

Fern and bobble edging

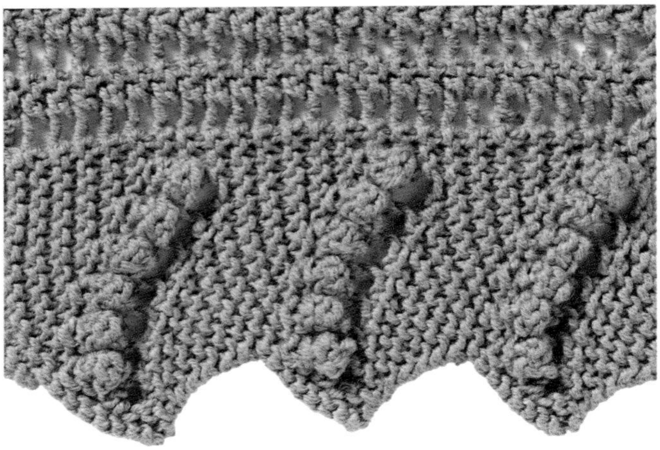

Worked lengthwise over 21 sts.

Special abbreviation:

MB (make bobble) = (K1, KB1, k1) in next st, turn, k3, turn, p3, turn, k3, sk2po.

Row 1 (RS): K2, k2tog, yo2, [k2tog] twice, yo2, k2tog, k2, yo2, k2tog, k7. (22 sts)

Row 2: K9, p1, k4, [p1, k3] twice.

Row 3: K2, k2tog, yo2, [k2tog] twice, yo2, k2tog, k1, MB, k2, yo2, k2tog, k6. (23 sts)

Row 4: K8, p1, k6, [p1, k3] twice.

Row 5: K2, k2tog, yo2, [k2tog] twice, yo2, k2tog, k3, MB, k2, yo2, k2tog, k5. (24 sts)

Row 6: K7, p1, k8, [p1, k3] twice.

Row 7: K2, k2tog, yo2, [k2tog] twice, yo2, k2tog, k5, MB, k2, yo2, k2tog, k4. (25 sts)

Row 8: K6, p1, k10, [p1, k3] twice.

Row 9: K2, k2tog, yo2, [k2tog] twice, yo2, k2tog, k7, MB, k2, yo2, k2tog, k3. (26 sts)

Row 10: K5, p1, k12, [p1, k3] twice.

Row 11: K2, k2tog, yo2, [k2tog] twice, yo2, k2tog, k9, MB, k2, yo2, k2tog, k2. (27 sts)

Row 12: K4, p1, k14, [p1, k3] twice.

Row 13: K2, k2tog, yo2, [k2tog] twice, yo2, k2tog, k11, MB, k2, yo2, k2tog, k1. (28 sts)

Row 14: K3, p1, k16, [p1, k3] twice.

Row 15: K2, k2tog, yo2, [k2tog] twice, yo2, k2tog, k18. (28 sts)

Row 16: Bind off 7 sts, knit until there are 13 sts on right-hand needle, [p1, k3] twice. (21 sts)

Rep these 16 rows.

Garter stitch points

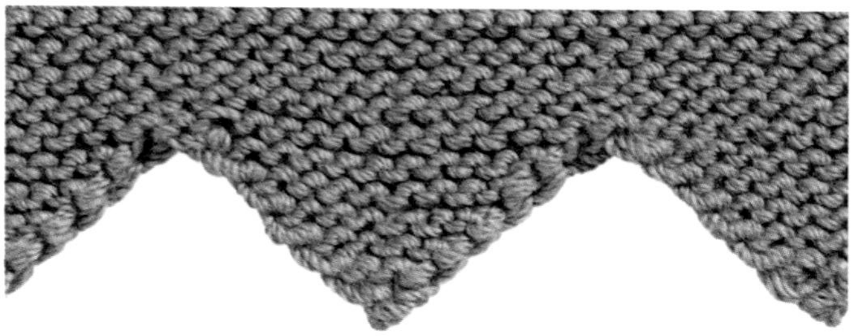

Worked from bottom edge upward.
Ends with multiple of 13.
Note: Each point is worked separately and then joined on one row.
Cast on 2 sts.
Row 1: K2.
Row 2: Yo, k2. (3 sts)
Row 3: Yo, k3. (4 sts)
Row 4: Yo, k4. (5 sts)
Row 5: Yo, k5. (6 sts)
Row 6: Yo, k6. (7 sts)
Row 7: Yo, k7. (8 sts)
Row 8: Yo, k8. (9 sts)
Row 9: Yo, k9. (10 sts)
Row 10: Yo, k10. (11 sts)
Row 11: Yo, k11. (12 sts)
Row 12: Yo, k12. (13 sts)
Rows 1–12 form one point.
Cut yarn and leave finished point on needle.
On the same needle, cast on 2 sts and work 2nd point.
Cont in this way until there are as many points as required.
Do not cut yarn after completing the last point, but turn and knit across all points on needle.
Work 9 rows in garter st.
These 21 rows form the edging.
Bind off or cont as required.

Seed stitch diamonds edging

Worked from bottom edge upward.
Starts and ends with multiple of 10 + 9.
Note: Cast on using the thumb method.
Row 1 (RS): P1, *k1, p1; rep from * to end.
Row 2: As row 1.
Row 3: K4, *p1, k9; rep from * to last 5 sts, p1, k4.
Row 4: P3, *k1, p1, k1, p7; rep from * to last 6 sts, k1, p1, k1, p3.
Row 5: K2, *[p1, k1] twice, p1, k5; rep from * to last 7 sts, [p1, k1] twice, p1, k2.
Row 6: [P1, k1] 4 times, *p3, [k1, p1] 3 times, k1; rep from * to last st, p1.
Row 7: P1, *k1, p1; rep from * to end.
Row 8: As row 6.
Row 9: As row 5.
Row 10: As row 4.
Row 11: As row 3.
Row 12: As row 2.
Row 13: As row 1.
These 13 rows form the edging.
Bind off or cont as required.

Leaf appliqué

Cast on 3 sts.
Row 1 (RS): KB1, yo, k1, yo, KB1. (5 sts)
Rows 2, 4, and 6: PB1, purl to last st, PB1.
Row 3: KB1, k1, [yo, k1] twice, KB1. (7 sts)
Row 5: KB1, k2, yo, k1, yo, k2, KB1. (9 sts)
Row 7: KB1, k3, yo, k1, yo, k3, KB1. (11 sts)
Row 8 and rem alt rows: Purl.
Row 9: Ssk, k7, k2tog. (9 sts)
Row 11: Ssk, k5, k2tog. (7 sts)
Row 13: Ssk, k3, k2tog. (5 sts)
Row 15: Ssk, k1, k2tog. (3 sts)
Row 17: Sk2po. (1 st)
Fasten off.

Daisy appliqué

Cast on 6 sts.
Row 1 (RS): Knit.
Row 2: (K1, p1, k1, p1, k1) in first st, turn, k5, turn, p5, turn, k5, turn, [p2tog] twice, p1, wyib lift 2nd and 3rd sts one at a time over first st*, p3, turn, sl 1, k3.
Row 3: Purl.
Rep the last 3 rows 6 times more, then row 1 again and row 2 to *.
Bind off purlwise.
Join cast on and bound off edges.
Press.
Sew button to center of flower.

Cable rib

Worked from bottom edge upward.
Starts and ends with multiple of 10 + 6.
Note: Cast on using the thumb method.
Row 1 (RS): *P2, k2, p2, k4; rep from *, ending p2, k2, p2.
Row 2: *K2, p2, k2, p4; rep from *, ending k2, p2, k2.
Rep the last 2 rows once more.
Row 5: *P2, k2, p2, C4B; rep from *, ending p2, k2, p2.
Row 6: As row 2.
Rep the last 6 rows once more.
These 12 rows form the edging.
Bind off or cont as required.

Zigzag seed stitch edging

Worked from bottom edge upward.
Starts and ends with multiple of 6 + 1.
Note: Cast on using the thumb method.
Row 1 (RS): K1, *p1, k1; rep from * to end.
Row 2: As row 1.
Row 3: Knit.
Row 4: Purl.
Row 5: P1, *k5, p1; rep from * to end.
Row 6: P1, *k1, p3, k1, p1; rep from * to end.
Row 7: P1, *k1, p1; rep from * to end.
Row 8: As row 7.
Row 9: K2, p1, k1, p1, *k3, p1, k1, p1; rep from * to last 2 sts, k2.
Row 10: P3, k1, *p5, k1; rep from * to last 3 sts, p3.
Row 11: Knit.
Row 12: Purl.
These 12 rows form the edging.
Bind off or cont as required.

Daisy braid

Worked lengthwise over 12 sts.
Row 1 (RS): Sl 1, k11.
Rows 2 and 4: Sl 1, k1, p8, k2.
Row 3: Sl 1, k11.
Row 5: Sl 1, k3, k2tog, yo2, skpo, k4.
Row 6: Sl 1, k1, p3, k1, p4, k2.
Row 7: Sl 1, k1, [k2tog, yo2, skpo] twice, k2.
Row 8: Sl 1, k1, p1, k1, p3, k1, p2, k2.
Row 9: As row 5.
Row 10: As row 6.
Row 11: As row 7.
Row 12: As row 8.
Row 13: As row 5.
Row 14: As row 6.
Rep these 14 rows, ending with row 3.

Castle edging

Worked lengthwise over 7 sts.
Note: Cast on using the cable method.
Work 3 rows in garter st.
Row 4 (WS): Cast on 3 sts, knit all sts. (10 sts)
Work 3 rows in garter st.
Row 8: Cast on 3 sts, knit all sts. (13 sts)
Row 9: K1, *p1, k1; rep from * to end.
Row 10: P1, *k1, p1; rep from * to end.
Rep the last 2 rows twice more, then row 9 again.
Row 16: Bind off 3 sts knitwise, knit to end. (10 sts)
Work 3 rows in garter st.
Row 20: Bind off 3 sts knitwise, knit to end. (7 sts)
Rep these 20 rows.

Lace bunting

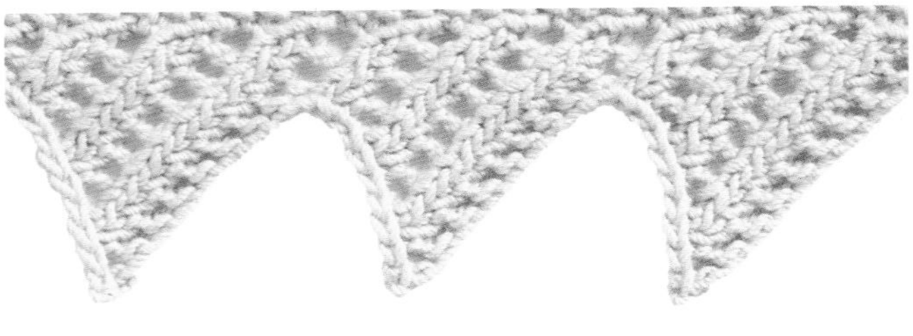

Worked lengthwise over 4 sts.

Foundation row: K1, yo, k1, p1, k1. (5 sts)

Row 1 (WS) and every alt row: K2, purl to end.

Row 2: K1, yo, k2, p1, k1. (6 sts)

Row 4: K1, yo, k1, k2tog, yo, p1, k1. (7 sts)

Row 6: K1, yo, k1, k2tog, yo, k1, p1, k1. (8 sts)

Row 8: K1, yo, k1, k2tog, yo, k2, p1, k1. (9 sts)

Row 10: K1, yo, [k1, k2tog, yo] twice, p1, k1. (10 sts)

Row 12: K1, yo, [k1, k2tog, yo] twice, k1, p1, k1. (11 sts)

Row 14: K1, yo, [k1, k2tog, yo] twice, k2, p1, k1. (12 sts)

Row 16: K1, yo, [k1, k2tog, yo] 3 times, p1, k1. (13 sts)

Row 18: Loosely bind off 9 sts, yo, k1, p1, k1. (5 sts)

Rep rows 1–18.

Fir cone and twig lace

Worked from bottom edge upward.

Starts and ends with multiple of 10 + 1.

Note: Cast on using the thumb method.

Row 1 (WS): Purl.

Row 2: K1, *yo, k3, sk2po, k3, yo, k1; rep from * to end.

Rep the last 2 rows 3 times more.

Row 9: Purl.

Row 10: K2tog, *k3, yo, k1, yo, k3, sk2po; rep from * to last 9 sts, k3, yo, k1, yo, k3, skpo.

Rep the last 2 rows 3 times more.

These 16 rows form the edging.

Bind off or cont as required.

Bell edging I

Worked from bottom edge upward.
Starts with multiple of 12 + 3.
Ends with multiple of 4 + 3.
Note: Cast on using the cable method.
Row 1 (RS): P3, *k9, p3; rep from* to end.
Row 2: K3, *p9, k3; rep from * to end.
Row 3: P3, *skpo, k5, k2tog, p3; rep from * to end.
Row 4: K3, *p7, k3; rep from * to end.
Row 5: P3, *skpo, k3, k2tog, p3; rep from * to end.
Row 6: K3, *p5, k3; rep from * to end.
Row 7: P3, *skpo, k1, k2tog, p3; rep from * to end.
Row 8: K3, *p3, k3; rep from * to end.
Row 9: P3, *sk2po, p3; rep from * to end.
Row 10: K3, *p1, k3; rep from * to end.
Row 11: P3, *k1, p3; rep from * to end.
Row 12: As row 10.
These 12 rows form the edging.
Bind off or cont as required.

Arches lace

Worked from bottom edge upward.
Starts and ends with multiple of 11.
Note: Cast on using the thumb method.
Row 1 (RS): *Ssk, [KB1] 3 times, yo, k1, yo, [KB1] 3 times, k2tog; rep from * to end.
Row 2, 4, 6, and 8: Purl.
Row 3: *Ssk, [KB1] twice, yo, k1, yo, ssk, yo, [KB1] twice, k2tog; rep from * to end.
Row 5: *Ssk, KB1, yo, k1, [yo, ssk] twice, yo, KB1, k2tog; rep from * to end.
Row 7: *Ssk, yo, k1, [yo, ssk] 3 times, yo, k2tog; rep from * to end.
Row 9: *K1, p1, k7, p1, k1; rep from * to end.
Row 10: *P1, k1, p7, k1, p1; rep from * to end.
Rep the last 2 rows once more.
These 12 rows form the edging.
Bind off or cont as required.

Oyster shells lace

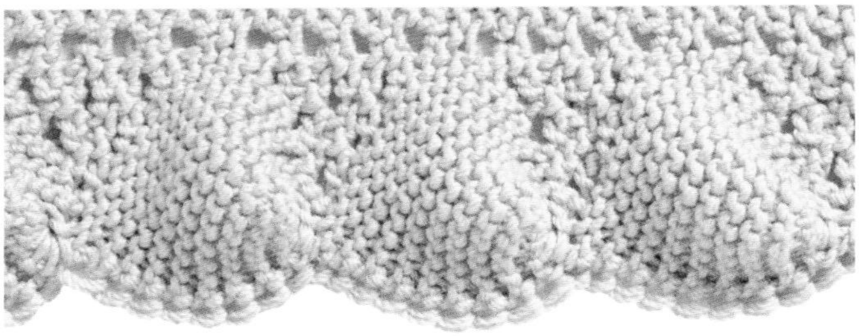

Worked lengthwise over 16 sts.

Row 1 (RS): Sl 1, k2, yo2, k13. (18 sts)
Row 2: Yo, k2tog, k12, p1, k3.
Row 3: Sl 1, knit to end.
Row 4: Yo, k2tog, k16.
Row 5: Sl 1, k2, yo2, k2tog, yo2, k13. (21 sts)
Row 6: Yo, k2tog, k12, p1, k2, p1, k3.
Row 7: As row 3.
Row 8: Yo, k2tog, k19.
Row 9: Sl 1, k2, [yo2, k2tog] 3 times, k12. (24 sts)
Row 10: Yo, k2tog, k12, p1, [k2, p1] twice, k3.
Row 11: As row 3.
Row 12: Yo, k2tog, k22.
Row 13: Sl 1, k2, [yo2, k2tog] 4 times, k13. (28 sts)
Row 14: Yo, k2tog, k13, p1, [k2, p1] 3 times, k3.
Row 15: As row 3.
Row 16: Yo, k2tog, k26.
Row 17: Sl 1, k13, sl 1, then lift 10 sts one at a time over first 2 sts on left-hand needle, knit these 2 sts tog, pass slipped st over, k1. (16 sts)
Row 18: Yo, k2tog, k14.

Rep these 18 rows, ending with row 17.

Hearts braid

Worked from bottom edge upward.

Starts and ends with multiple of 12 + 9.

Note: Cast on using the thumb method.

Work 2 rows in garter st.

Row 3 (RS): P4, k1, *p11, k1; rep from *, ending p4.
Row 4: K3, p3, *k9, p3; rep from *, ending k3.
Row 5: P3, k3, *p9, k3; rep from *, ending p3.
Row 6: K2, p5, *k7, p5; rep from *, ending k2.
Row 7: P1, k7, *p5, k7; rep from *, ending p1.
Row 8: P9, *k3, p9; rep from * to end.
Row 9: K9, *p3, k9; rep from * to end.
Row 10: As row 8.
Row 11: K4, p1, *k4, p3, k4, p1; rep from *, ending k4.
Row 12: K1, p2, k3, p2, *k5, p2, k3, p2; rep from *, ending k1.
Row 13: Purl.

Work 2 rows in garter st.

Row 16: Purl.

These 16 rows form the edging.

Bind off or cont as required.

Loop trim

Worked from bottom edge upward.
Ends with multiple of 12 for an odd number of strips.
Ends with multiple of 12 + 6 for an even number of strips.
Note: Each strip is worked separately and then joined to make loops on one row. Loops can be longer if required.
Cast on 6 sts.
Row 1 (RS): Sl 1, k5.
Row 2: Sl 1, p5.
Rep the last 2 rows 12 times more.
Rows 1–26 form one strip. Cut yarn and leave strip on needle.
On the same needle, cast on 6 sts and work second strip.
Cont in this way until there are as many strips as required.

Join strips and make loops

Do not cut yarn after completing last strip.
*K6 of first strip, with RS facing position cast-on edge of first strip behind second strip, *slip horizontal strand from first cast-on st onto left-hand needle, then knit this strand tog with first st of second strip; rep from * for each st.
Cont in this way across strips, ending with k6 from cast-on edge of last strip.
Purl 1 row.
These rows form the edging.
Bind off or cont as required.

Scallops trim

Worked from bottom edge upward.
Starts with multiple of 12.
Ends with multiple of 8.
Note: Cast on using the thumb method.
Row 1 (RS): Knit.
Row 2: Purl.
Row 3: *[K2tog] twice, [M1, k1] 4 times, [skpo] twice; rep from * to end.
Row 4: Purl.
Row 5: *[K2tog] twice, k4, [skpo] twice; rep from * to end.
Work 2 rows in garter st.
These 7 rows form the edging.
Bind off or cont as required.

Striped slip stitch edging

Worked from bottom edge upward.
Starts and ends with multiple of 2 + 1.
Note: Three colors of yarn are used, A, B, and C. Strand colors not in use up side of work. Cast on using the cable method and A.
Row 1 (RS): With A, knit.
Row 2: With A, purl.
Row 3: With B, k1, *sl 1 purlwise, k1; rep from * to end.
Row 4: With B, k1, *yf, sl 1 purlwise, yb, k1; rep from * to end.
Row 5: With C, knit.
Row 6: With C, purl.
Row 7: With A, k1, *sl 1 purlwise, k1; rep from * to end.
Row 8: With A, k1, * yf, sl 1 purlwise, yb, k1; rep from * to end.
Row 9: With B, knit.
Row 10: With B, purl.
Row 11: With C, k1, *sl 1 purlwise, k1; rep from * to end.
Row 12: With C, k1, * yf, sl 1 purlwise, yb, k1; rep from * to end.
Row 13: With A, knit.
Row 14: With A, purl.
These 14 rows form the edging.
Bind off or cont as required.

Lace stripes

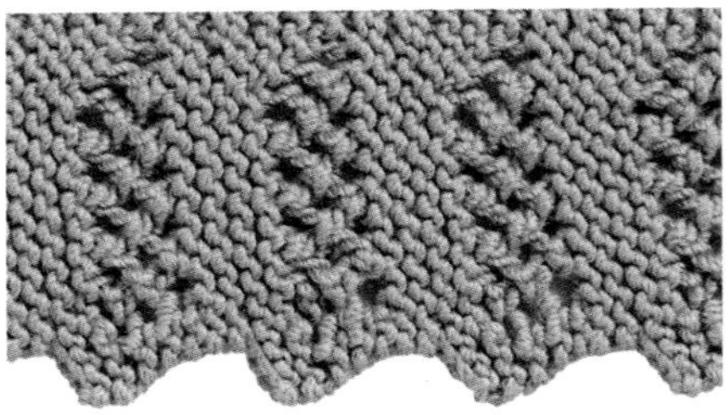

Worked lengthwise over 15 sts.
Note: To prevent holes from forming when turning, wrap the yarn around the next stitch in this way: turn leaving the yarn at the front, slip the first st from the right-hand needle onto the left-hand needle, take the yarn to the back, slip the st back onto the right-hand needle, then cont.
Row 1 (WS): Knit.
Row 2: K12, turn, knit to end.
Row 3: Knit.
Row 4: K4, [yo, k2tog] 4 times, yo2, k2tog, k1. (16 sts)
Row 5: K3, p1, k12.
Row 6: K5, [yo, k2tog] 4 times, yo2, k2tog, k1. (17 sts)
Row 7: K3, p1, k13.
Row 8: K6, [yo, k2tog] 4 times, yo2, k2tog, k1. (18 sts)
Row 9: K3, p1, k14.
Row 10: Knit.
Row 11: K15, turn, knit to end.
Row 12: Bind off 3 sts, k14. (15 sts)
Rep these 12 rows.

Star braid

Worked lengthwise over 17 sts.
Row 1 (WS): Sl 1, k1, p13, k2.
Row 2: Sl 1, k16.
Row 3: Sl 1, k1, p6, k1, p6, k2.
Row 4: Sl 1, k16.
Row 5: Sl 1, k2, [p5, k1] twice, k2.
Row 6: Sl 1, k2, p1, k9, p1, k3.
Row 7: Sl 1, k1, p2, [k1, p3] twice, k1, p2, k2.
Row 8: Sl 1, k4, p1, k5, p1, k5.
Row 9: Sl 1, k1, p4, [k1, p1] twice, k1, p4, k2.
Row 10: Sl 1, k6, p1, k1, p1, k7.
Rep row 10 twice more.
Row 13: Sl 1, k1, p4, [k1, p1] twice, k1, p4, k2.
Row 14: Sl 1, k4, p1, k5, p1, k5.
Row 15: Sl 1, k1, p2, [k1, p3] twice, k1, p2, k2.
Row 16: Sl 1, k2, p1, k9, p1, k3.
Row 17: Sl 1, k2, [p5, k1] twice, k2.
Row 18: Sl 1, k16.
Row 19: Sl 1, k1, p6, k1, p6, k2.
Row 20: Sl 1, k16.
Rep rows 3–20.

Openwork points

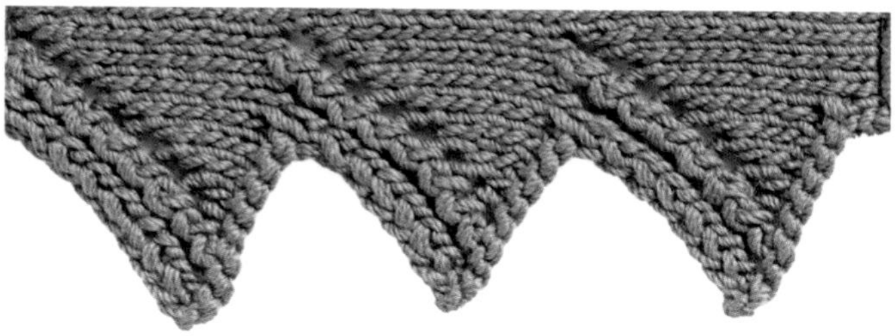

Worked lengthwise over 7 sts.
Row 1 (RS): K3, yo, skpo, yo, k2. (8 sts)
Row 2 and every alt row to 14: Sl 1, purl to last 2 sts, k2.
Row 3: K4, yo, skpo, yo, k2. (9 sts)
Row 5: K5, yo skpo, yo, k2. (10 sts)
Row 7: K6, yo, skpo, yo, k2. (11 sts)
Row 9: K7, yo, skpo, yo, k2. (12 sts)
Row 11: K8, yo, skpo, yo, k2. (13 sts)
Row 13: K9, yo, skpo, yo, k2. (14 sts)
Row 15: K10, yo, skpo, yo, k2. (15 sts)
Row 16: Bind off 8 sts knitwise, p4, k2. (7 sts)
Rep these 16 rows.

Long loop fur

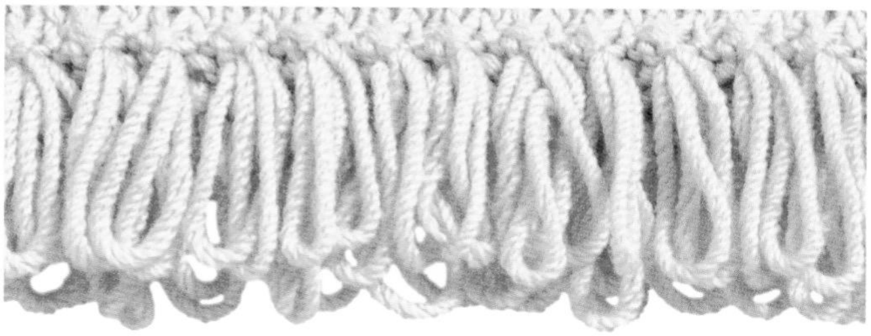

Worked from bottom edge upward.
Starts and ends with multiple of 2 + 1.
Special abbreviation:
ML2 (make double loop) = Insert right-hand needle knitwise into next st, [wind yarn over right-hand needle and around first and second fingers of left hand] twice, then over right-hand needle point once more, draw all 3 loops through st and slip onto left-hand needle, insert right-hand needle through back of these 3 loops and original st and knit them tog tbl.
Note: Cast on using the cable method. Loops appear on RS rows but are made on WS rows.
Work 3 rows in garter st.
Row 4 (WS): K1, *ML2, k1; rep from * to end.
Work 3 rows in garter st.
Row 8: K1, *k1, ML2; rep from * to last 2 sts, k2.
Rep these 8 rows.

Unraveled fringe

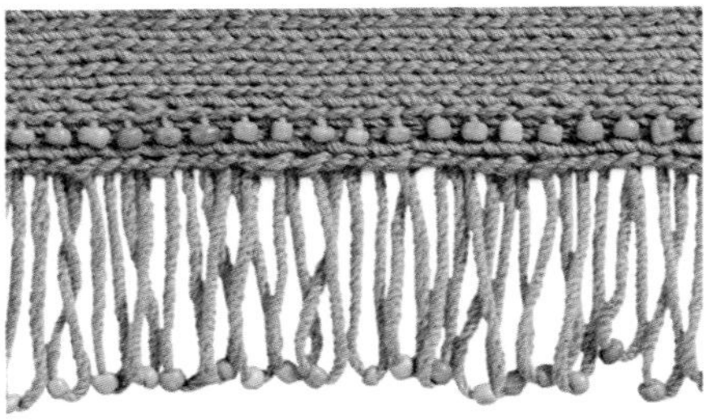

Worked lengthwise over any number of sts.

Note: Thread beads onto knitting yarn before casting on, 2 beads for each alt row. The first bead is not knitted in.

Row 1 (RS): K2, slide bead up to back of work, k2, PB, knit to end.

Row 2: Purl.

Rep the last 2 rows as required, ending with row 2.

Next row: K3, bind off rem sts.

Slip 3 sts off needle and unravel across knitted fabric to create fringe. Slide 1 bead down to sit at the bottom of each loop.

Antique edging

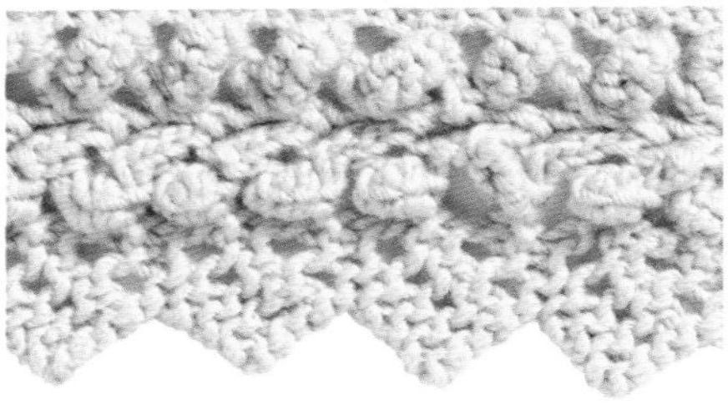

Worked lengthwise over 13 sts.

Note: Bind off knitwise throughout.

Row 1 (RS): K2, yo, skpo, yo, k1, yo, sk2po, yo, k3, yo, k2. (15 sts)

Row 2: K4, [k1, p1] 3 times into next st, p2, k1, p3, k4. (20 sts)

Row 3: K2, yo, skpo, [k1, p1] 3 times into next st, skpo, p1, k2tog, bind off next 5 sts, knit to last 2 sts, yo, k2. (19 sts)

Row 4: K5, yo, [k1, p1] twice, bind off next 5 sts, knit to end. (15 sts)

Row 5: K2, yo, skpo, yo, k1, yo, sk2po, yo, k3, yo, k2tog, yo, k2. (17 sts)

Row 6: K6, [k1, p1] 3 times into next st, p2, k1, p3, k4. (22 sts)

Row 7: K2, yo, skpo, [k1, p1] 3 times into next st, skpo, p1, k2tog, bind off next 5 sts, knit to last 4 sts, yo, k2tog, yo, k2. (21 sts)

Row 8: Bind off 4 sts, k2, yo, p2, k1, p1, bind off next 5 sts, knit to end. (13 sts)

Rep these 8 rows.

Bell edging II

Worked from upper edge downward.

Starts with multiple of 8 + 7.

Ends with multiple of 20 + 7.

Row 1 (RS): P7, *k1, p7; rep from * to end.

Row 2: K7, *p1, k7; rep from * to end.

Row 3: P7, *yo, k1, yo, p7; rep from * to end.

Row 4: K7, *PB1, p1, PB1, k7; rep from * to end.

Row 5: P7, *yo, k3, yo, p7; rep from * to end.

Row 6: K7, *PB1, p3, PB1, k7; rep from * to end.

Row 7: P7, *yo, k5, yo, p7; rep from * to end.

Row 8: K7, *PB1, p5, PB1, k7; rep from * to end.

Row 9: P7, *yo, k7, yo, p7; rep from * to end.

Row 10: K7, *PB1, p7, PB1, k7; rep from * to end.

Row 11: P7, *yo, k9, yo, p7; rep from * to end.

Row 12: K7, *PB1, p9, PB1, k7; rep from * to end.

Row 13: P7, *yo, k11, yo, p7; rep from * to end.

Row 14: K7, *PB1, p11, PB1, k7; rep from * to end.

Bind off.

These 14 rows form the edging.

Beaded frill

Worked from bottom edge upward.
Starts with twice the number of sts required + 1.
Note: Thread beads onto knitting yarn before casting on, 1 bead for each alt st. Cast on using Beaded thumb cast-on (see page 234), omitting the selvage sts.
Row 1 (WS): Purl.
Row 2: [K2tog] to last st, k1.
These 2 rows form the edging.
Cont as required.

Maypole lace

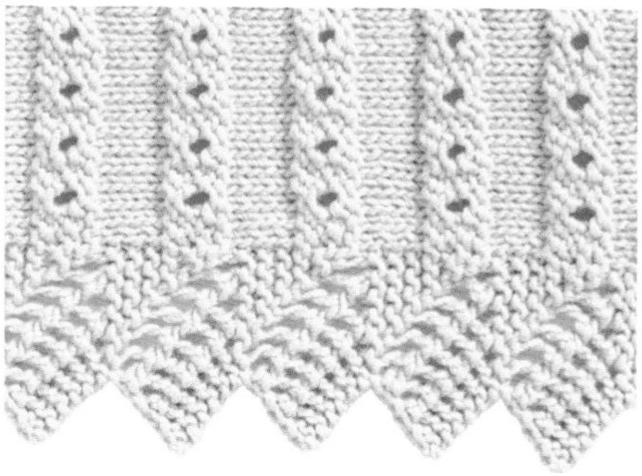

Worked lengthwise over 26 sts.
Foundation row: Knit.
Row 1: Sl 1, k19, [yo, k2tog] twice, yo, k2. (27 sts)
Row 2: K8, p14, k5.
Row 3: Sl 1, k6, [yo, k2tog, k1] 4 times, k2, [yo, k2tog] twice, yo, k2. (28 sts)
Row 4: K9, p14, k5.
Row 5: Sl 1, k21, [yo, k2tog] twice, yo, k2. (29 sts)
Row 6: Knit.
Row 7: Sl 1, k4, p14, k4, [yo, k2tog] twice, yo, k2. (30 sts)
Row 8: Knit.
Row 9: Sl 1, k4, p14, k5, [yo, k2tog] twice, yo, k2. (31 sts)
Row 10: Knit.
Row 11: Sl 1, k4, p14, k6, [yo, k2tog] twice, yo, k2. (32 sts)
Row 12: Bind off 6 sts, k25. (26 sts)
Rep rows 1–12.

Spiral rib edging

Worked from bottom edge upward.
Starts and ends with multiple of 7.
Note: Cast on using the thumb method.
Row 1 (RS): P2, k4, *p3, k4; rep from * to last st, p1.
Row 2: K1, p3, *k4, p3; rep from * to last 3 sts, k3.
Row 3: P1, k1, p2, *k2, p2, k1, p2; rep from * to last 3 sts, k2, p1.
Row 4: K1, p1, k2, p2, *k2, p1, k2, p2; rep from * to last st, k1.
Row 5: P1, k3, *p4, k3; rep from * to last 3 sts, p3.
Row 6: K2, p4, *k3, p4; rep from * to last st, k1.
Row 7: P1, k5, *p2, k5; rep from * to last st, p1.
Row 8: K1, p5, *k2, p5; rep from * to last st, k1.
Rep the last 8 rows once more.
These 16 rows form the edging.
Bind off or cont as required.

Bobble rib edging

Worked from bottom edge upward.
Starts and ends with multiple of 4 + 3.

Special abbreviation:

MB (make bobble) = (K1, KB1, k1, KB1) in next st, turn, p4, turn, k4, turn, p4, turn, ssk, k2tog, slip 2nd st over first st.

Note: Cast on using the thumb method.

Row 1 (RS): P1, *k1, p1; rep from * to end.

Rows 2 and 4: K1, *p1, k1; rep from * to end.

Row 3: P1, k1, p1, *MB, p1, k1, p1; rep from * to end.

Row 5: As row 1.

These 5 rows form the edging.
Bind off or cont as required.

Beaded bind-off

Note: Before binding off, measure out a length of yarn 4 times the width of the knitted fabric. Cut yarn. Thread on beads, 1 bead for every alt st.

Bind off 1 st.

*Slide 1 bead up to sit behind next st, insert right-hand needle knitwise into st and draw loop through, drawing bead through with it, then lift first st on right-hand needle over 2nd st and off needle.

Bind off 1 st.

Rep from *, fastening off last st.

Ruched edging

Worked from bottom edge upward.
Starts and ends with multiple of 3.

Note: Cast on using the thumb method.

Row 1 (RS): K2, *sl 1 purlwise, k2; rep from * to last st, k1.

Row 2: P3, *sl 1 purlwise, p2; rep from * to end.

Row 3: K2, *C3F; rep from * to last st, k1.

Rows 4 and 6: Purl.

Row 5: K2, *yo, k2tog, k1; rep from * to last st, k1.

Row 7: K4, *sl 1 purlwise, k2; rep from * to last 2 sts, sl 1 purlwise, k1.

Row 8: P1, *sl 1 purlwise, p2; rep from * to last 2 sts, p2.

Row 9: K2, *C3B; rep from * to last st, k1.

These 9 rows form the edging.
Bind off or cont as required.

Scallop shell lace

Worked from bottom edge upward.
Starts with multiple of 5 + 2.
Ends with multiple of 4 + 5.

Note: Cast on using the thumb method.

Row 1 (RS): K1, yo, *k5, lift 2nd, 3rd, 4th, and 5th sts just worked one at a time over first st and off needle, yo; rep from * to last st, k1.

Row 2: P1, *(p1, yo, KB1) into next st, p1; rep from * to end.

Row 3: K2, KB1, *k3, KB1; rep from * to last 2 sts, k2.

Work 3 rows in garter st.

These 6 rows form the edging.

Bind off or cont as required.

Short loop fur

Worked from bottom edge upward.
Starts and ends with multiple of 2 + 1.

Note: Cast on using the cable method. Loops are made and appear on RS rows.

Row 1 (RS): Knit.

Row 2 and every alt row: Purl.

Row 3: *K1, ML; rep from * to last st, k1.

Row 5: Knit.

Row 7: K1, *k1, ML; rep from * to last 2 sts, k2.

Row 8: Purl.

Rep these 8 rows.

Parasol lace

Worked lengthwise over 23 sts.

Row 1: Sl 1, k2, yo, k1, [p3, k1] 4 times, yo, k3. (25 sts)

Row 2 and every alt row: Sl 1, k1, purl to last 2 sts, k2.

Row 3: Sl 1, k3, yo, k1, [p3, k1] 4 times, yo, k4. (27 sts)

Row 5: Sl 1, k4, yo, k1, [p3, k1] 4 times, yo, k5. (29 sts)

Row 7: Sl 1, k5, yo, k1, [p2tog, p1, k1] 4 times, yo, k6. (27 sts)

Row 9: Sl 1, k6, yo, k1, [p2tog, k1] 4 times, yo, k7. (25 sts)

Row 11: Sl 1, k7, yo, k1, [k3tog, k1] twice, yo, k8. (23 sts)

Row 12: As row 2.

Rep these 12 rows.

Lace bells

Worked from bottom edge upward.

Starts with multiple of 14 + 3.

Ends with multiple of 4 + 3.

Note: Cast on using the thumb method.

Work 2 rows in garter st.

Row 3 (RS): P3, *k11, p3; rep from * to end.

Row 4: K3, *p11, k3; rep from * to end.

Row 5: P3, *skpo, k2, yo, sk2po, yo, k2, k2tog, p3; rep from * to end.

Row 6: K3, *p9, k3; rep from * to end.

Row 7: P3, *skpo, k1, yo, sk2po, yo, k1, k2tog, p3; rep from * to end.

Row 8: K3, *p7, k3; rep from * to end.

Row 9: P3, *skpo, yo, sk2po, yo, k2tog, p3; rep from * to end.

Row 10: K3, *p5, k3; rep from * to end.

Row 11: P3, *skpo, k1, k2tog, p3; rep from * to end.

Row 12: K3, *p3, k3; rep from * to end.

Row 13: P3, *sk2po, p3; rep from * to end.

Row 14: K3, *p1, k3; rep from * to end.

Row 15: P3, *k1, p3; rep from * to end.

Row 16: As row 14.

These 16 rows form the edging.

Bind off or cont as required.

Laburnum edging

Worked lengthwise over 13 sts.

Row 1 (RS): K2, yo, p2tog, k1, [yo, skpo] 3 times, yo2, k2tog. (14 sts)

Row 2: P1, k1, p9, yo, p2tog, k1.

Row 3: K2, yo, p2tog, k2, [yo, skpo] 3 times, yo2, k2tog. (15 sts)

Row 4: P1, k1, p10, yo, p2tog, k1.

Row 5: K2, yo, p2tog, k3, [yo, skpo] 3 times, yo2, k2tog. (16 sts)

Row 6: P1, k1, p11, yo, p2tog, k1.

Row 7: K2, yo, p2tog, k4, [yo, skpo] 3 times, yo2, k2tog. (17 sts)

Row 8: P1, k1, p12, yo, p2tog, k1.

Row 9: K2, yo, p2tog, k5, [yo, skpo] 3 times, yo2, k2tog. (18 sts)

Row 10: P1, k1, p13, yo, p2tog, k1.

Row 11: K2, yo, p2tog, k6, [yo, skpo] 3 times, yo2, k2tog. (19 sts)

Row 12: P1, k1, p14, yo, p2tog, k1.

Row 13: K2, yo, p2tog, k7, [yo, skpo] 3 times, yo2, k2tog. (20 sts)

Row 14: P1, k1, p15, yo, p2tog, k1.

Row 15: K2, yo, p2tog, k8, yo, k1, slip last st worked back onto left-hand needle, then lift next 7 sts one at a time over this st and off needle, then slip st back onto right-hand needle. (14 sts)

Row 16: P2tog, p9, yo, p2tog, k1. (13 sts)

Rep these 16 rows.

Layered tags

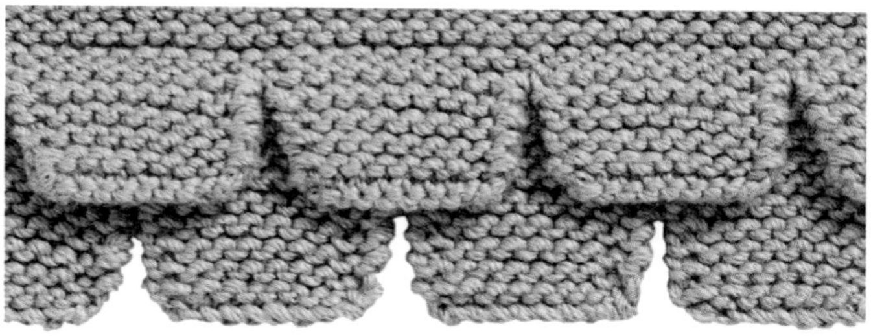

Worked from bottom edge upward.
Starts and ends with multiple of 10.
Note: Cast on using the thumb method. Each tag is worked separately and then joined on one row.

Bottom layer

Cast on 10 sts.
Rows 1–10: Sl 1, k9.
Rows 1–10 form one tag. Cut yarn and leave finished tag on needle. On the same needle, cast on 10 sts and work 2nd tag. Cont in this way until there are as many tags as required.

Join tags

Do not cut yarn after completing the last tag, but turn and knit across all tags on needle.
Work 7 rows in garter st.
Leave sts on spare needle.

Top layer

Cast on 5 sts to make a half-width tag.
Rows 1–10: Sl1, k4.
Cut yarn and leave sts on needle.
Make full-width tags as for bottom layer, making one less tag, and end with another half-width tag.

Join layers

RS facing, hold top layer in front of bottom layer. Using 3rd needle, knit together 1 st from each needle across row.
These rows form the edging.
Bind off or cont as required.

Lace diamonds

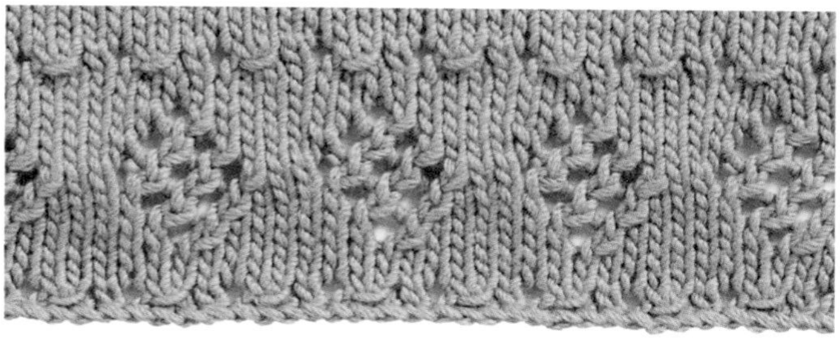

Worked from bottom edge upward.
Starts and ends with multiple of 8.
Note: Cast on using the thumb method.
Row 1 (WS) and every alt row: Purl.
Row 2: *K1, yo, k3, pass 3rd st on right-hand needle over first 2 sts; rep from * to end.
Row 4: Knit.
Row 6: K3, *yo, skpo, k6; rep from * to last 5 sts, yo, skpo, k3.
Row 8: K2, *[yo, skpo] twice, k4; rep from * to last 6 sts, [yo, skpo] twice, k2.
Row 10: K1, *[yo, skpo] 3 times, k2; rep from * to last 7 sts, [yo, skpo] 3 times, k1.
Row 12: As row 8.
Row 14: As row 6.
Row 16: Knit.
Row 18: As row 2.
Row 19: Purl.
These 19 rows form the edging.
Bind off or cont as required.

Two-color fringe

Worked lengthwise over 12 sts using 1 strand each of A and B held together.

Row 1: K2, yo, k2tog, k1, yo, k2tog, k5.

Row 2: P4, k2, [yo, k2tog, k1] twice.

Rep the last 2 rows as required, ending with row 2.

Next row: Bind off 8 sts and fasten off 9th st.

Slip rem 3 sts off needle and unravel across knitted fabric to make fringe. Loops can be cut to make single strands.

Little lace

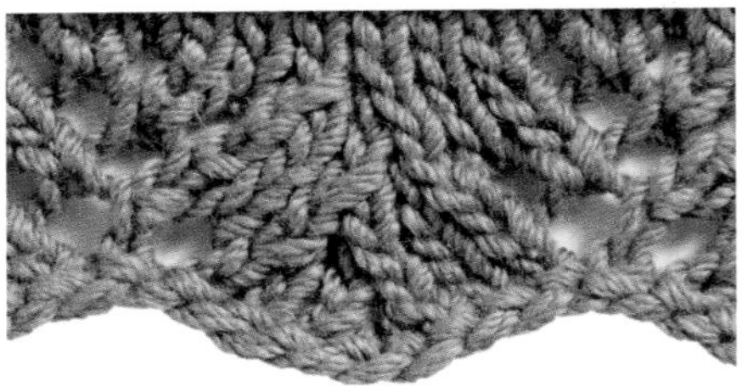

Worked from bottom edge upward.

Starts and ends with multiple of 9 + 4.

Note: Cast on using the thumb method.

Rows 1 (WS) and 3: Purl.

Row 2: K3, *yo, k2, ssk, k2tog, k2, yo, k1; rep from *, ending last rep k2.

Row 4: K2, *yo, k2, ssk, k2tog, k2, yo, k1; rep from *, ending last rep k3.

Rep the last 4 rows once more.

Row 9: Knit.

These 9 rows form the edging.

Bind off or cont as required.

Sugar scallops

Worked from bottom edge upward.

Starts with multiple of 11 + 2.

Ends with multiple of 6 + 2.

Note: Cast on using the thumb method.

Row 1 (RS): Purl.

Row 2: K2, *k1, slip this st back onto left-hand needle, lift the next 8 sts on left-hand needle one at a time over this st and off needle, yo2, knit the first st again, k2; rep from * to end.

Row 3: K1, *p2tog, drop first yo, [k1, p1] twice in 2nd yo, p1; rep from * to last st, k1.

Work 5 rows in garter st.

These 8 rows form the edging.

Bind off or cont as required.

Holly leaf appliqué

Cast on 3 sts.

Row 1 (RS): KB1, yo, k1, yo, KB1. (5 sts)

Row 2 and foll 3 alt rows: PB1, purl to last st, PB1.

Row 3: KB1, M1, k1, [yo, k1] twice, M1, KB1. (9 sts)

Row 5: KB1, k3, yo, k1, yo, k3, KB1. (11 sts)

Row 7: KB1, k4, yo, k1, yo, k4, KB1. (13 sts)

Row 9: Bind off 3 sts, k2, yo, k1, yo, k5, KB1. (12 sts)

Row 10: Bind off 3 sts, p7, PB1. (9 sts)

Row 11: As row 5. (11 sts)

Rows 12 and 14: PB1, purl to last st, PB1.

Row 13: As row 7. (13 sts)

Row 15: Bind off 3 sts, k8, KB1. (10 sts)

Row 16: Bind off 3 sts, p5, PB1. (7 sts)

Row 17: Ssk, k3, k2tog. (5 sts)

Rows 18 and 20: PB1, purl to last st, PB1.

Row 19: Ssk, k1, k2tog. (3 sts)

Row 21: Sk2po. (1 st)

Fasten off.

Knots or bobbles can be worked for berries.

Star lace

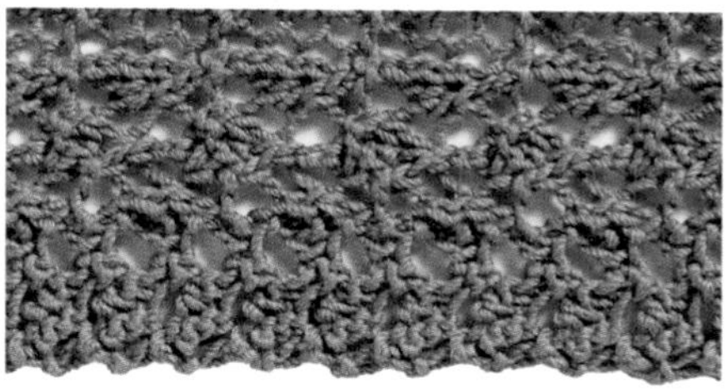

Worked lengthwise over 15 sts.

Foundation row: Knit.

Row 1 (RS): K3, yo, k3tog, yo, k3, yo, k2tog, [yo2, k2tog] twice. (17 sts)

Row 2: Yo, [k2, p1] twice, k2, yo, k2tog, k7. (18 sts)

Row 3: K3, [yo, k2tog] twice, p1, k2tog, yo, k8.

Row 4: K1, bind off 3 sts, k3, p6, k1, yo, k2tog, k1. (15 sts)

Row 5: K3, yo, k2tog, k1, yo, k3tog, yo, k2, [yo2, k2tog] twice. (17 sts)

Row 6: Yo, [k2, p1] twice, k1, p6, k1, yo, k2tog, k1. (18 sts)

Row 7: K3, yo, [k2tog] twice, yo, k1, yo, k2tog, k8.

Row 8: K1, bind off 3 sts, k3, p6, k1, yo, k2tog, k1. (15 sts)

Rep rows 1–8.

Cable and eyelet rib

Worked from bottom edge upward.

Starts and ends with multiple of 7 + 3.

Note: Cast on using the thumb method.

Row 1 (RS): P3, *k4, p3; rep from * to end.

Row 2: K1, yo, k2tog, *p4, k1, yo, k2tog; rep from * to end.

Row 3: P3, *C4B, p3; rep from * to end.

Row 4: As row 2.

Row 5: As row 1.

Row 6: As row 2.

Rep the last 6 rows once more.

These 12 rows form the edging.

Bind off or cont as required.

Double knot edge

Worked lengthwise over 8 sts.

Row 1 (RS): Sl 1, k1, *yo, p2tog, (k1, p1, k1) in next st; rep from * once more. (12 sts)

Row 2: [K3, yo, p2tog] twice, k2.

Row 3: Sl 1, k1, [yo, p2tog, k3] twice.

Row 4: Bind off 2 sts knitwise, yo, p2tog, bind off next 2 sts knitwise (4 sts on right-hand needle), yo, p2tog, k2. (8 sts)

Rep these 4 rows.

Cable rope

Worked lengthwise over 10 sts.

Row 1 (WS): K2, p6, k2.

Row 2: P2, k6, p2.

Row 3: As row 1.

Row 4: P2, C6B, p2.

Row 5: As row 1.

Row 6: P1, T4BR, T4FL, p1.

Row 7: K1, p3, k2, p3, k1.

Row 8: P1, k3, p2, k3, p1.

Rep the last 2 rows 5 times more, then row 7 again.

Row 20: P1, T4FL, T4BR, p1.

Rep rows 1–4 once more, then rows 1–2 once more.

Rep these 26 rows.

Layered picots

Worked from bottom edge upward.

Multiple of 3.

Note: Two colors of yarn are used, A and B. Use cable cast-on throughout. Cast on same number of sts for each layer.

Bottom layer

*Using A, cast on 6 sts, bind off 3 sts, slip st from right-hand needle onto left-hand needle; rep from * until required number of stitches are on the left-hand needle.

Row 1 (RS): Knit.

Row 2: Purl.

Rep the last 2 rows once more.

Put sts on spare needle.

Top layer

*Using B, cast on 6 sts, bind off 3 sts, slip st form right-hand needle onto left-hand needle; rep from * until required number of stitches are on the left-hand needle.

Row 1 (WS): Purl.

RS facing, hold top layer in front of bottom layer. Using 3rd needle, knit together 1 st from each needle across row.

These rows form the edging.

Bind off or cont as required.

Beaded fringe

Worked lengthwise over 5 sts.

Note: Thread beads onto knitting yarn before casting on, 1 bead for each loop.

Special abbreviation:

MBL (make bead loop) = K1 but do not slip st off left-hand needle, bring yarn between needles to the front, slide bead up to sit below needles, wrap yarn under and over your left thumb, take yarn back between needles to the WS, knit st on left-hand needle again making sure bead remains on loop, then slip 2nd st on right-hand needle over first st.

Row 1 (RS): Sl 1, k1, MBL, k2.

Row 2: Sl 1, k4.

Rep row 2 twice more.

Rep these 4 rows.

Layered ruffle

Worked from bottom edge upward.

Starts with twice the number of sts needed that is an even number. Cast on same number of sts for each layer.

Note: Cast on using the thumb method.

Bottom layer

Work 5 rows in garter st.

Work 9 rows in st st, starting with purl.

Row 15 (RS): [K2tog] to end.

Row 16: Purl.

Row 17: Knit.

Place sts on spare needle.

Top layer

Work 3 rows in garter st.

Work 5 rows in st st, starting with purl.

Row 9 (RS): [K2tog] to end.

Join layers

RS facing, hold top layer in front of bottom layer. Using 3rd needle, knit together 1 st from each needle across row.

Work 4 rows in garter st.

These rows form the edging.

Bind off or cont as required.

Layered leaves braid

Worked lengthwise over 18 sts.

Row 1 (RS): K3, k2tog, yo, k5, yo, k3, skpo, k3.

Row 2 and every alt row: K3, p12, k3.

Row 3: K3, k2tog, k5, yo, k1, yo, k2, skpo, k3.

Row 5: K3, k2tog, k4, yo, k3, yo, k1, skpo, k3.

Row 7: K3, k2tog, k3, yo, k5, yo, skpo, k3.

Row 9: K3, k2tog, k2, yo, k1, yo, k5, skpo, k3.

Row 11: K3, k2tog, k1, yo, k3, yo, k4, skpo, k3.

Row 12: As row 2.

Rep these 12 rows.

Cockleshells trim

Worked lengthwise over 23 sts.

Work 2 rows in garter st.

Row 3 (RS): K3, yo2, p2tog tbl, k13, p2tog, yo2, k3. (25 sts)

Row 4: K4, p1, k15, p1, k4.

Work 2 rows in garter st.

Row 7: K3, yo2, p2tog tbl, yo2, p2tog tbl, k11, p2tog, yo2, p2tog, yo2, k3. (29 sts)

Row 8: K4, p1, k2, p1, k13, p1, k2, p1, k4.

Row 9: Knit.

Row 10: K7, k15 wrapping yarn 3 times around needle for each st, k7.

Row 11: K3, yo2, p2tog tbl, yo2, p2tog tbl, yo2, slip next 15 sts onto right-hand needle dropping extra loops, slip same 15 sts back onto left-hand needle and purl together all 15 sts, yo2, p2tog, yo2, p2tog, yo2, k3. (23 sts)

Row 12: K3, p1, [k2, p1] twice, k3, [p1, k2] twice, p1, k3.

Rep these 12 rows.

Rickrack

Worked from bottom edge upward.
Starts with multiple of 10 + 1.
Ends with multiple of 8 + 1 before binding off.
Note: Cast on using the thumb method.
Row 1 (RS): K4, *sk2po, k7; rep from *, ending sk2po, k4.
Row 2 and every alt row: Knit.
Row 3: K1, *M1, k2, sk2po, k2, M1, k1; rep from * to end.
Row 5: As row 3.
Row 6: Knit.
Bind off, working k1, *M1, k7, M1, k1; rep from * across row.
These 6 rows form the edging.

Scallop edging

Worked from top edge downward.
Starts and ends with multiple of 13 + 2.
Note: Cast on using the thumb method.
Row 1 (RS): K1, *skpo, k9, k2tog; rep from * to last st, k1.
Rows 2 and 4: Purl.
Row 3: K1, *skpo, k7, k2tog; rep from * to last st, k1.
Row 5: K1, *skpo, yo, [k1, yo] 5 times, k2tog; rep from * to last st, k1.
Row 6: Knit.
These 6 rows form the edging.

Beaded cable cast-on

Worked from bottom edge upward.
Starts and ends with multiple of 2 + 1.
Note: Thread beads onto knitting yarn before casting on, 1 bead for every alt st, less 2, to give a selvage st at each end.
Place a slip knot on the needle.
Cast on 1 st.
*Slide 1 bead up to sit behind the st, insert right-hand needle knitwise into st and draw loop through, drawing bead through with it. Slip loop onto left-hand needle and make sure that bead is sitting at base of st.
Cast on 1 st.
Rep from * until 1 less than required number of sts are on left-hand needle.
Cast on 1 st.
This forms the edging.
Cont as required. Usually row 1 will be a RS row to show the beads to best effect.

Catherine wheels braid

Worked lengthwise over 19 sts.

Special abbreviation:

Work 5tog (work 5 sts together) = Skpo, k3tog, pass the st resulting from skpo over the st resulting from k3tog.

Row 1 (WS) and every alt row: Sl 1, k2, purl to last 3 sts, k3.

Row 2: Sl 1, k7, sl 3, yf, pass 3 slipped sts back onto left-hand needle, yb, knit 3 slipped sts, k8.

Row 4: Sl 1, k5, k3tog, yo, inc 2, yo, k3tog tbl, k6.

Row 6: Sl 1, k3, k3tog, yo, k2tog, yo, inc 2, yo, skpo, yo, k3tog tbl, k4.

Row 8: Sl 1, k2, [k2tog, yo] 3 times, KB1, [yo, skpo] 3 times, k3.

Row 10: Sl 1, k3, [yo, k2tog] twice, yo, sk2po, [yo, skpo] twice, yo, k4.

Row 12: Sl 1, k2, [skpo, yo] 3 times, KB1, [yo, k2tog] 3 times, k3.

Row 14: Sl 1, k3, inc, yo, skpo, yo, work 5tog, yo, k2tog, yo, inc, k4.

Row 16: Sl 1, k5, inc, yo, work 5tog, yo, inc, k6.

Rep these 16 rows.

Cherry basket

Worked from bottom edge upward.

Starts and ends with multiple of 11 + 2.

Note: Cast on using the thumb method.

Special abbreviation:

MB (make bobble) = (K1, p1, k1, p1, k1) in next st, turn, p5, turn, lift 2nd, 3rd, 4th, and 5th sts one at a time over first st. (Knit next st tbl).

Work 3 rows in garter st.

Row 4 (WS) and every foll alt row: Purl.

Row 5: *K5, k2tog, yo, k4; rep from *, ending k2.

Row 7: *K4, k2tog, yo, k1, yo, ssk, k2; rep from *, ending k2.

Row 9: *K3, [k2tog, yo] twice, k1, yo, ssk, k1; rep from *, ending k2.

Row 11: *K2, [k2tog, yo] twice, k1, [yo, ssk] twice; rep from *, ending k2.

Row 13: *K3, k2tog, yo, k1, MB, k1, yo, ssk, k1; rep from *, ending k2.

Row 15: *K4, MB, k3, MB, k2; rep from *, ending k2.

Row 17: *K6, MB, k4; rep from *, ending k2.

Row 19: Knit.

Row 20: Purl.

Work 4 rows in garter st.

These 24 rows form the edging.

Bind off or cont as required.

Wheatsheaf cable rib

Worked from bottom edge upward.

Starts and ends with multiple of 16 + 8.

Note: Cast on using the thumb method.

Rows 1 (RS), 3, and 5: P1, k6, *p4, k2, p4, k6; rep from *, ending p1.

Rows 2 and 4: K11, p2, *k14, p2; rep from *, ending k11.

Row 6: K1, p6, *k4, p2, k4, p6; rep from *, ending k1.

Row 7: P3, k2, *T4F, p2, k2, p2, T4B, k2; rep from *, ending p3.

Row 8: K3, p2, *k2, p2; rep from *, ending k3.

Row 9: P3, k2, *p2, T4F, k2, T4B, p2, k2; rep from *, ending p3.

Row 10: K3, p2, *k4, p6, k4, p2; rep from *, ending k3.

Rows 11, 13, and 15: P3, k2, *p4, k6, p4, k2; rep from *, ending p3.

Rows 12 and 14: K3, p2, *k14, p2; rep from *, ending k3.

Rows 16 and 18: As row 10.

Row 17: P3, k2, *p4, C6B, p4, k2; rep from *, ending p3.

Rows 19, 21, and 23: As row 11.

Rows 20 and 22: As row 12.

Row 24: As row 10.

Row 25: P3, k2, *p2, T4B, k2, T4F, p2, k2; rep from *, ending p3.

Row 26: As row 8.

Row 27: P3, k2, *T4B, p2, k2, p2, T4F, k2; rep from *, ending p3.

Row 28: As row 6.

Row 29: As row 1.

Row 30: As row 2.

These 30 rows form the edging.

Bind off or cont as required.

Leaf braid

Worked lengthwise over 17 sts.

Row 1 (RS): Sl 1, k3, [k2tog, yo] twice, k1, [yo, skpo] twice, k4.

Row 2: Sl 1, k5, p5, k6.

Row 3: Sl 1, k2, k2tog, yo, k2tog, k1, [yo, k1] twice, skpo, yo, skpo, k3.

Row 4: Sl 1, k4, p7, k5.

Row 5: Sl 1, k1, k2tog, yo, k2tog, k2, yo, k1, yo, k2, skpo, yo, skpo, k2.

Row 6: Sl 1, k3, p9, k4.

Row 7: Sl 1, k2tog, yo, k2tog, k3, yo, k1, yo, k3, skpo, yo, skpo, k1.

Row 8: Sl 1, k2, p11, k3.

Row 9: Sl 1, k2, yo, skpo, k7, k2tog, yo, k3.

Row 10: Sl 1, k3, p9, k4.

Row 11: Sl 1, k3, yo, skpo, k5, k2tog, yo, k4.

Row 12: Sl 1, k4, p7, k5.

Row 13: Sl 1, k4, yo, skpo, k3, k2tog, yo, k5.

Row 14: Sl 1, k5, p5, k6.

Row 15: Sl 1, k5, yo, skpo, k1, k2tog, yo, k6.

Row 16: Sl 1, k6, p3, k7.

Row 17: Sl 1, k6, yo, sk2po, yo, k7.

Row 18: Sl 1, k7, p1, k8.

Rep these 18 rows.

Openwork picot

Worked lengthwise over 3 sts.
Cast on 3 sts.
*Bind off 2 sts. (1 st)
Slip this st onto left-hand needle.
Cast on 2 sts. (3 sts)
Rep from * for required length.
Bind off 2 sts. (1 st)
Without turning, work along straight edge of picot: **yo, put tip of left-hand needle under bar across top of picot and knit into this bar; rep from ** to end.
Work 2 rows in garter st.
This cast-on and 2 rows form the edging.
Bind off or cont as required.

Little bobble rib

Worked from bottom edge upward.
Starts and ends with multiple of 8 + 3.
Special abbreviation:
MB (make bobble) = (P1, k1, p1, k1) in next st, then lift 2nd, 3rd, and 4th sts one at a time over first st.
Note: Cast on using the thumb method.
Row 1 (RS): K3, *p2, MB, p2, k3; rep from * to end.
Row 2: P3, *k5, p3; rep from * to end.
Row 3: K3, *p5, k3; rep from * to end.
Row 4: As row 2.
Rep the last 4 rows once more, then row 1 again.
These 9 rows form the edging.
Bind off or cont as required.

Diamond edge

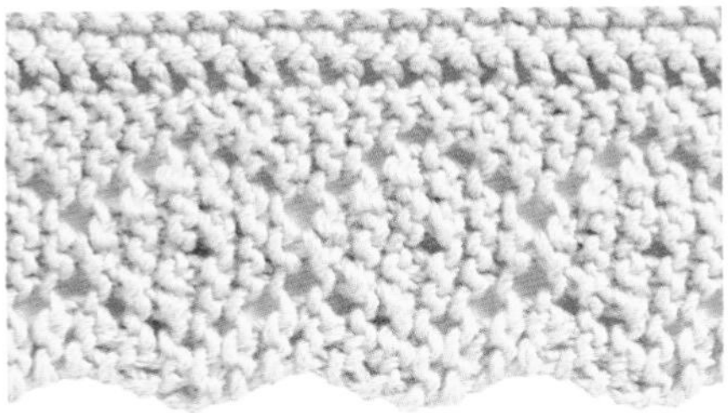

Worked lengthwise over 12 sts.
Row 1 (RS) and every alt row: K1, yo, p2tog, knit to end.
Row 2: K2, yo, k3, yo, skpo, k2, yo, p2tog, k1. (13 sts)
Row 4: K2, yo, k5, yo, skpo, k1, yo, p2tog, k1. (14 sts)
Row 6: K2, yo, k3, yo, skpo, k2, yo, skpo, yo, p2tog, k1. (15 sts)
Row 8: K1, k2tog, yo, skpo, k3, k2tog, yo, k2, yo, p2tog, k1. (14 sts)
Row 10: K1, k2tog, yo, skpo, k1, k2tog, yo, k3, yo, p2tog, k1. (13 sts)
Row 12: K1, k2tog, yo, sk2po, yo, k4, yo, p2tog, k1. (12 sts)
Rep these 12 rows.

Twisted fringe

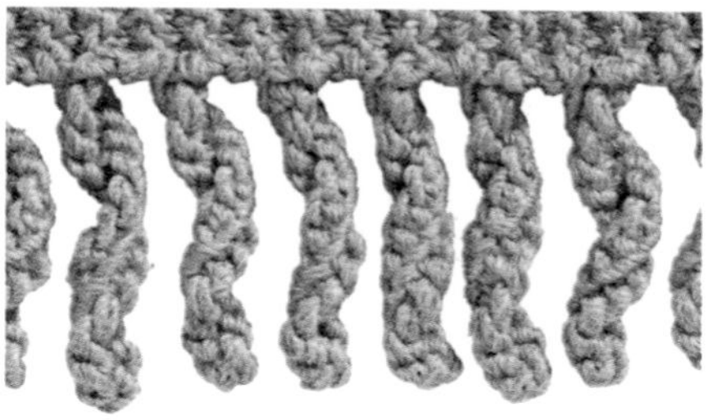

Worked lengthwise over 3 sts.
Work 3 rows in garter st.
Row 4 (WS): Cast on 10 sts, inc in each of these 10 sts, binding off 1 st as each st is made, k2. (3 sts)
Rep these 4 rows, ending with row 2.

Beaded garter edge

Worked lengthwise over 4 sts.
Note: Thread beads onto knitting yarn before casting on, 1 bead for each row 3.
Row 1 (RS): Sl 1, k3.
Row 2: As row 1.
Row 3: Slide 1 bead up to needle, yo, k2tog tbl, k2.
Row 4: Sl 1, k3.
Rep these 4 rows.

Beaded cord

Worked lengthwise over 5 sts on double-pointed needles.
Note: Thread beads onto knitting yarn before casting on, 1 bead for every row 3.
Rows 1–2: Knit, do not turn, slide sts to other end of needle.
Row 3: K2, PB, k2, do not turn, slide sts to other end of needle.
Rep these 3 rows.

Bird's eye edging

Worked lengthwise over 7 sts.
Row 1 (RS): K1, k2tog, yo2, k2tog, yo2, k2. (9 sts)
Row 2: K3, [p1, k2] twice.
Row 3: K1, k2tog, yo2, k2tog, k4.
Row 4: Bind off 2 sts, k3, p1, k2. (7 sts)
Rep these 4 rows.

Picot point bind-off

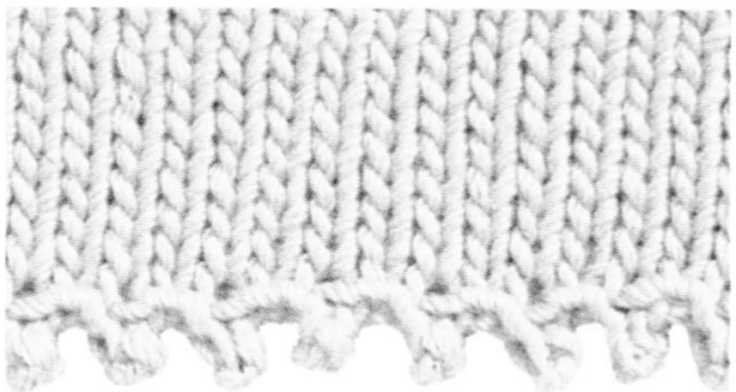

Worked from upper edge downward.
Multiple of 3 + 2.
Note: Cast on using the cable method.
Bind off 2 sts, *slip rem st from right-hand needle onto left-hand needle, cast on 2 sts, bind off 4 sts; rep from * to end and fasten off rem st.

Ribbed rib

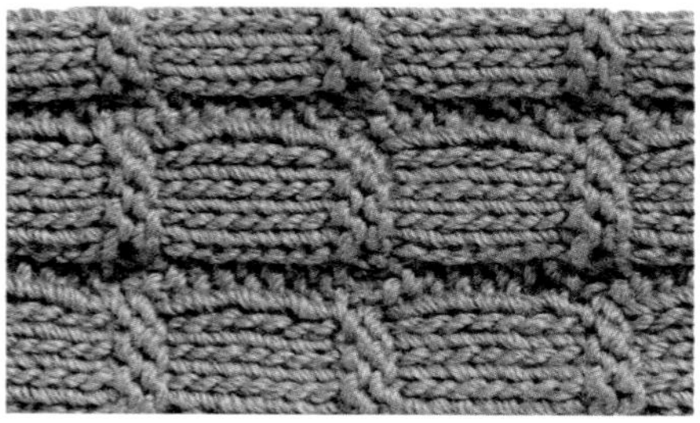

Worked lengthwise over 17 sts.
Rows 1 (RS), 3, and 5: K5, [p2, k4] twice.
Rows 2, 4, and 6: [P4, k2] twice, p5.
Row 7: K1, [p4, k2] twice, p4.
Row 8: [K4, p2] twice, k4, p1.
Rows 9–10: As rows 1–2.
Rep these 10 rows, ending with row 4.

Beaded loop rib

Worked from bottom edge upward.
Starts and ends with multiple of 2 + 1.
Note: Thread beads onto knitting yarn before casting on, 5 beads for each loop.
Row 1 (RS): [K1, p1] to last st, k1.
Row 2 and every alt row: [P1, k1] to last st, p1.
Row 3: K1, p1, *k1, yf, slide 5 beads up to right-hand needle, PB1, k1, p1; rep from * to last st, k1.
Row 5: *K1, yf, slide 5 beads up to right-hand needle, PB1, k1, p1; rep from * to last st, k1.
Row 6: As row 2.
These 6 rows form the edging.
Bind off or cont as required.

Unraveled fringe with eyelets

Worked lengthwise over any number of sts.
Row 1 (RS): K5, k2tog, yo, knit to end.
Row 2: Purl.
Rep the last 2 rows as required, ending with row 2.
Next row: K5, bind off rem sts.
Slip 5 sts off needle and unravel across knitted fabric to create fringe.

Cabled fringe

Worked lengthwise over 14 sts.
Note: Two colors of yarn are used, A and B, but the edging can be worked in one color if preferred.
Using cable method, cast on 9 sts with A and 5 sts with B.
Rows 1 and 5 (RS): K5 B, k9 A.
Row 2 and every alt row: P9 A, p5 B.
Row 3: K5 B, with A, C6F, k3.
Row 7: K5 B, with A, k3, C6B.
Row 8: As row 2.
Rep rows 1–8 as required, ending with row 2.
Next row: K4 B, bind off rem sts.
Slip 4 sts off needle and unravel across knitted fabric to create fringe. Loops can be cut to make strands.

Fancy leaf edging

Worked lengthwise over 17 sts.

Row 1 (RS): K3, yo, p2tog, yo, p2tog, yo, KB1, k2tog, p1, skpo, KB1, yo, k3.

Row 2: K3, p3, k1, p3, k2, yo, p2tog, yo, p2tog, k1.

Rep the last 2 rows once more.

Row 5: K3, yo, p2tog, yo, p2tog, yo, KB1, yo, k2tog, p1, skpo, yo, k4. (18 sts)

Row 6: K4, p2, k1, p4, k2, yo, p2tog, yo, p2tog, k1.

Row 7: K3, yo, p2tog, yo, p2tog, yo, KB1, k1, KB1, yo, sk2po, yo, k5. (19 sts)

Row 8: K5, p7, k2, yo, p2tog, yo, p2tog, k1.

Row 9: K3, yo, p2tog, yo, p2tog, yo, KB1, k3, KB1, yo, k7. (21 sts)

Row 10: Bind off 4 sts knitwise, k2, p7, k2, yo, p2tog, yo, p2tog, k1. (17 sts)

Rep these 10 rows.

Lacy arrow edging

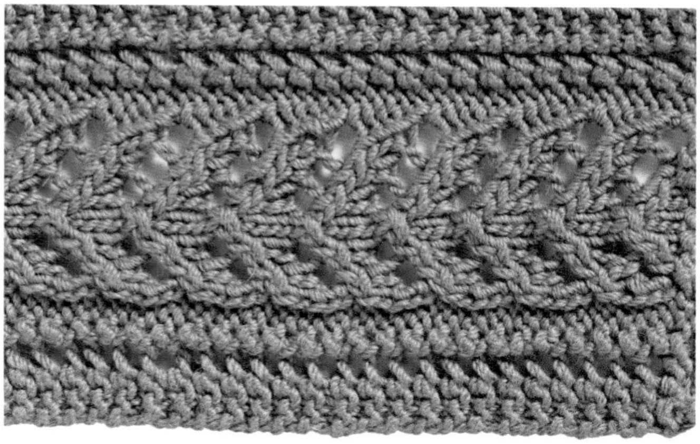

Worked lengthwise over 21 sts.

Row 1 (RS): K3, yo, k2tog, p2, yo, skpo, k3, k2tog, yo, p2, k1, yo, k2tog, k2.

Row 2 and every alt row: K3, yo, k2tog tbl, k2, p7, k3, yo, k2tog tbl, k2.

Row 3: K3, yo, k2tog, p2, k1, yo, skpo, k1, k2tog, yo, k1, p2, k1, yo, k2tog, k2.

Row 5: K3, yo, k2tog, p2, k2, yo, sk2po, yo, k2, p2, k1, yo, k2tog, k2.

Row 6: As row 2.

Rep these 6 rows.

Double picots and eyelets

Worked from bottom edge upward.
Worked over any odd number of sts.
Note: Use cable cast-on throughout.
Cast on 6 sts, bind off 4 sts, slip st from right-hand needle onto left-hand needle, cast on 4 sts, bind off 4 sts, slip st from right-hand needle onto left-hand needle, *cast on 5 sts, bind off 4 sts, slip st from right-hand needle onto left-hand needle, cast on 4 sts, bind off 4 sts, slip st from right-hand needle onto left-hand needle; rep from * until 1 picot less than the required number of sts has been made.
Row 1 (RS): *K1, yo; rep from * to last st, k1.
This cast-on and row form the edging.
Bind off or cont as required.

Garter bunting

Worked lengthwise over 8 sts.
Row 1 (RS): Sl 1, k7.
Row 2: Ssk, k6. (7 sts)
Row 3: Sl 1, k6.
Row 4: Ssk, k5. (6 sts)
Row 5: Sl 1, k5.
Row 6: Ssk, k4. (5 sts)
Row 7: Sl 1, k4.
Row 8: Ssk, k3. (4 sts)
Row 9: Sl 1, k3.
Row 10: Cast on 4 sts, knit all 8 sts.
Rep these 10 rows, ending with row 9.

Puff ball cluster edging

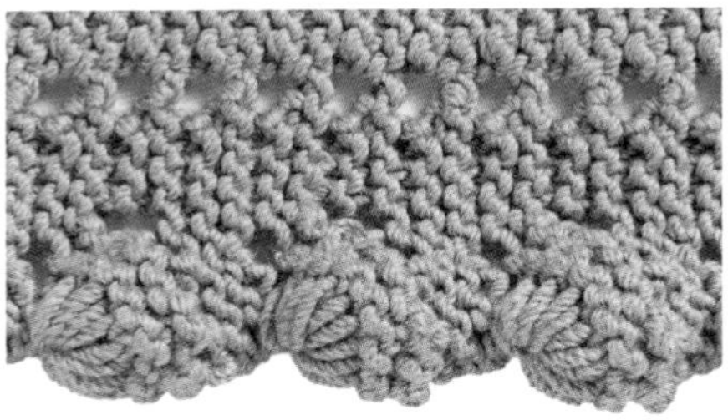

Worked lengthwise over 13 sts.
Row 1 (WS): K2, k2tog, yo2, k2tog, k7.
Row 2: K9, p1, k3.
Work 2 rows in garter st.
Row 5: K2, k2tog, yo2, k2tog, k2, [yo2, k1] 3 times, yo2, k2. (21 sts)
Row 6: K3, [p1, k2] 3 times, p1, k4, p1, k3.
Work 2 rows in garter st.
Row 9: K2, k2tog, yo2, k2tog, k15.
Row 10: K12 winding yarn twice around needle for each st, yo2, k5, p1, k3. (23 sts)
Row 11: K10, (p1, k1) in next st, slip next 12 sts onto right-hand needle dropping extra loops, return sts to left-hand needle and k12tog. (13 sts)
Row 12: Knit.
Rep these 12 rows.

Square filet edging

Worked lengthwise over 15 sts.

Foundation row: Knit.

Row 1 (RS): K1, k2tog, yo2, k2tog, k1, yo2, k7, yo2, k2. (19 sts)

Row 2: K3, p1, k8, p1, k3, p1, k2.

Row 3: K1, k2tog, yo2, k2tog, k1, [yo2, k2tog] twice, k3, k2tog, yo2, k4. (22 sts)

Row 4: K5, p1, k6, p1, k2, p1, k3, p1, k2.

Row 5: K1, k2tog, yo2, k2tog, k1, yo2, [k2tog, k1, k2tog, yo2] twice, k6. (24 sts)

Row 6: K7, [p1, k4] twice, p1, k3, p1, k2.

Row 7: K1, k2tog, yo2, k2tog, k1, yo2, k2tog, k3, k2tog, yo2, k3tog, yo2, k8. (26 sts)

Row 8: K9, p1, k2, p1, k6, p1, k3, p1, k2.

Row 9: K1, k2tog, yo2, k2tog, k21.

Row 10: Bind off 10 sts, k8, k2tog, k2, p1, k2. (15 sts)

Rep rows 1–10.

Flower bud trim

Worked lengthwise over 7 sts.

Row 1 (RS): KB1, [p2, KB1] twice.

Row 2: P1, [k2, PB1] twice.

Row 3: KB1, p2, (k1, p1, k1, p1, k1) in next st, p2, KB1. (11 sts)

Row 4: P1, k2, p5, k2, PB1.

Row 5: KB1, p2, k5, p2, KB1.

Row 6: As row 4.

Row 7: KB1, p2, skpo, k1, k2tog, p2, KB1. (9 sts)

Row 8: P1, k2, p3, k2, PB1.

Row 9: KB1, p2, sk2po, p2, KB1. (7 sts)

Row 10: As row 2.

Rep these 10 rows, ending with row 1.

Picot point chain

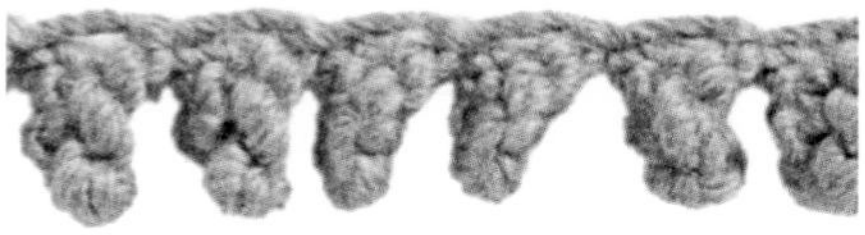

Worked lengthwise over 5 sts.

Note: Cast on using the cable method.

*Bind off 4 sts, slip st from right-hand needle onto left-hand needle, cast on 4 sts; rep from * until chain is required length.

Garter scallops

Worked lengthwise over 7 sts.
Foundation row: Knit.
Row 1: K4, inc, k2. (8 sts)
Row 2: K1, inc, k6. (9 sts)
Row 3: K6, inc, k2. (10 sts)
Row 4: K1, inc, k8. (11 sts)
Row 5: K8, inc, k2. (12 sts)
Row 6: K1, inc, k10. (13 sts)
Row 7: K10, inc, k2. (14 sts)
Row 8: K1, inc, k12. (15 sts)
Row 9: K12, k2tog, k1. (14 sts)
Row 10: K1, k2tog tbl, k11. (13 sts)
Row 11: K10, k2tog, k1. (12 sts)
Row 12: K1, k2tog tbl, k9. (11 sts)
Row 13: K8, k2tog, k1. (10 sts)
Row 14: K1, k2tog tbl, k7. (9 sts)
Row 15: K6, k2tog, k1. (8 sts)
Row 16: K1, k2tog tbl, k5. (7 sts)
Rep rows 1–16.

Simple ruffle

Worked from bottom edge upward.
Starts with twice the number of sts needed.
Note: Cast on using the thumb method. If an odd number of sts is required, deduct 1 st from the final count, cast on double that number of sts + 1 st, and on the decrease row, end k1.
Row 1: Knit.
Row 2: Purl.
Rep the last 2 rows as required, ending with row 2.
Next row: [K2tog] to end.
These rows form the edging.
Bind off or cont as required.

Star flower appliqué

Put a slip knot on the needle.
Row 1 (RS): (K1, KB1, k1) in st. (3 sts)
Row 2 and every alt row: Purl.
Row 3: K1, [M1, k1] twice. (5 sts)
Row 5: K1, M1, k3, M1, k1. (7 sts)
Row 7: K1, M1, k5, M1, k1. (9 sts)
Row 9: K1, M1, k7, M1, k1. (11 sts)
Row 11: KB1, k2tog, k5, ssk, k1. (9 sts)
Row 13: KB1, k2tog, k3, ssk, k1. (7 sts)
Row 15: KB1, k2tog, k1, ssk, k1. (5 sts)
Row 17: KB1, sk2po, k1. (3 sts)
Row 19: Sk2po. (1 st)
Fasten off.
Make 4 more petals.
Press.
With slip knots in the center and taking 1 st from each edge into seam, join the five petals from row 1 to row 10.

Crown edging

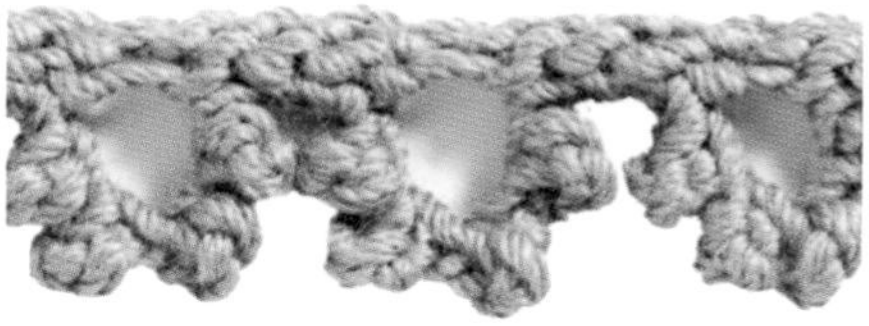

Worked from upper edge downward.
Multiple of 5.
Note: If working this as a separate edging to be sewn on, cast on using the cable method.
Row 1 (WS): Knit.
Row 2: Bind off 2 sts, *slip st from right-hand needle onto left-hand needle, [cast on 2 sts, bind off 2 sts, slip st onto left-hand needle] 3 times, cast on 2 sts, bind off 6 sts; rep from * to end and fasten off rem st.
These 2 rows form the edging.

Tassel rib

Worked from bottom edge upward.
Starts and ends with multiple of 6 + 1.
Note: Cast on using the thumb method.
Row 1 (RS): *K4, p2; rep from *, ending k1.
Row 2: P1, *k2, p4; rep from * to end.
Rep the last 2 rows 3 times more.
Row 9: *Place right-hand needle between 4th and 5th sts from tip of left-hand needle and draw through a loop, knit together this loop with next st, p2, k3; rep from *, ending k1.
These 9 rows form the edging.
Bind off or cont as required.

Tip

Appliqué shapes, such as the Star flower shown here, the Loop flower on page 242, the Heart on page 250, and the Leaf and Daisy on page 254, can be sewn on as embellishments to a knitted piece. They can also be used individually—for example, as pins or brooches.

Index

Acknowledgments

Thanks to Kate Haxell, Susie Johns, and Erika Knight for selecting and compiling the stitches.

Thanks to Nicola Hodgson for putting together this volume.

Knitters: Rosalind Campbell, Carole Downie, Sarah Hazell, Melina Kalatzi, Cathy MacDonald, Jenny McHardy, Annette Travers

Photography: Geoff Dann, Holly Jolliffe, Michael Wicks

Chart illustrator: Lotte Oldfield

Technical editor: Luise Roberts

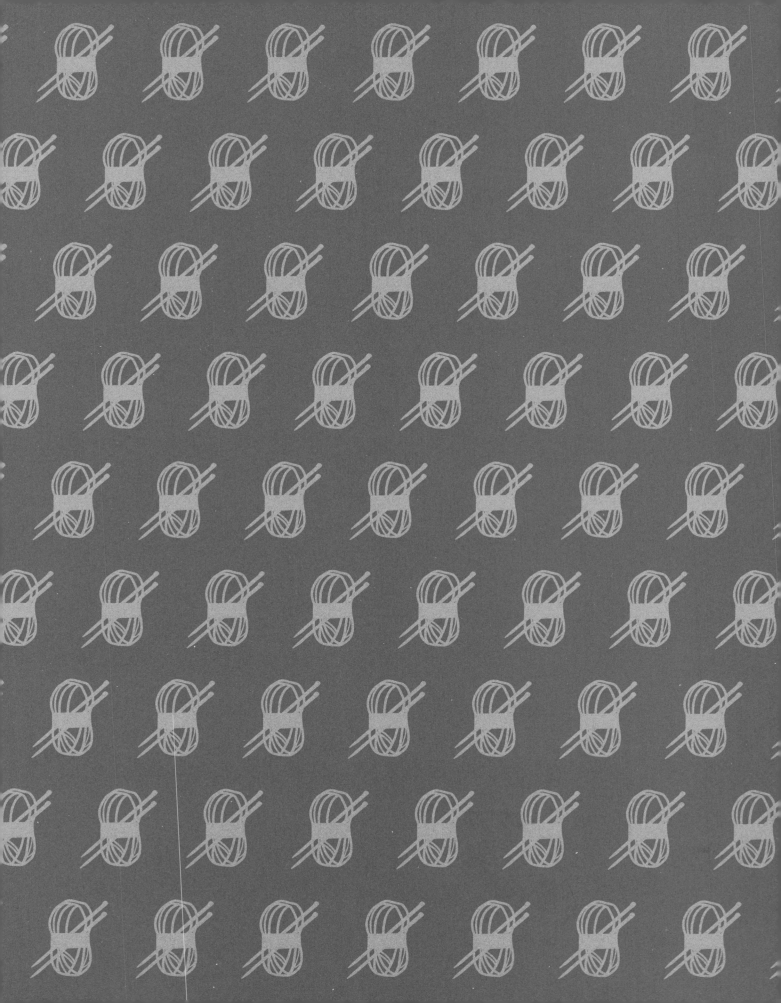